66 speakers' spotlight 99

800.333.4453
speakers.ca

D1263104

THE DOLPHIN'S TOOTH

BRUCE KIRKBY

THE
DOLPHIN'S

TOOTH

A DECADE IN SEARCH OF ADVENTURE

Copyright © 2005 by Bruce Kirkby

All rights reserved. The use of any part of this publication reproduced, transmitted in any form or by any means, electronic, mechanical, photocopying, recording, or otherwise, or stored in a retrieval system, without the prior written consent of the publisher – or, in case of photocopying or other reprographic copying, a licence from the Canadian Copyright Licensing Agency – is an infringement of the copyright law.

Library and Archives Canada Cataloguing in Publication

Kirkby, Bruce, 1968-
 The dolphin's tooth : a decade in search of adventure / Bruce Kirkby.

ISBN 0-7710-9566-X

1. Kirkby, Bruce, 1968-   -Travel. 2. Adventure travel. 3. Adventure and adventurers-
Canada – Biography. I. Title.

G465.K57 2005   910.4   C2005-902304-X

We acknowledge the financial support of the Government of Canada through the Book Publishing Industry Development Program and that of the Government of Ontario through the Ontario Media Development Corporation's Ontario Book Initiative. We further acknowledge the support of the Canada Council for the Arts and the Ontario Arts Council for our publishing program.

Typeset in Minion by M&S, Toronto

Printed and bound in Canada

This book is printed on acid-free paper that is 100% recycled, ancient-forest friendly (100% post-consumer recycled).

McClelland & Stewart Ltd.
The Canadian Publishers
75 Sherbourne Street
Toronto, Ontario
M5A 2P9
www.mcclelland.com

1 2 3 4 5   09 08 07 06 05

page i: *Casting for bonefish in the inner lagoon, Glovers Reef Atoll, Belize.*
page ii, iii: *Near the remote outpost of Tura, western China, where the
    Tibetan plateau soars straight up from the Taklamakan Desert.*
above: *Sunset over Vatnajökull Icecap, Iceland. This image was taken on
    the rim of Grímsvötn volcano, which erupted in 2004, one year after our visit.*
opposite: *Tai Long Wan Bay, Hong Kong; 27 km from 7 million people.*
frontispiece: *Beach sauna on shore of Alsek Lake, Tatshenshini River, Alaska.*
dedication: *Puja ceremony in Taktsang Monastery, Bhutan.*

TABLE OF CONTENTS

Pakistan
Ottawa
West Coast
Rockies
Swiss Alps
Tatshenshini
Belize
Nepal
Arabia
Ethiopia
Tibet
British Columbia
Myanmar
Arctic

Albert Camus, the great philosopher and author, once commented:
"I believe in justice, but I will defend my mother before justice."
Although he was referring to Algeria, this expression of devotion comes as
close as words can to capturing the love of a child for its parents.

Both of my parents dedicated their lives to the well-being of their children.
My first book, *Sand Dance*, was for Dad. Now, with great pride and much love,

THIS BOOK IS FOR MUM

Steady as a rock,
Gentle as the willow.

Without her foundation,
and unflagging support, none of these trips
would have been possible.

THE
DOLPHIN'S TOOTH

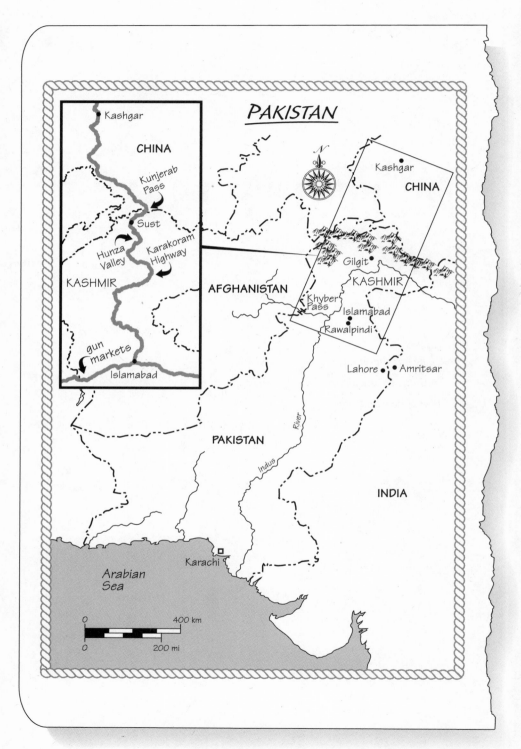

one

Awakenings

The Karakoram Highway

The fact that many a man who goes his own way ends up in ruin means nothing. He must obey his own law, as if it were a daemon whispering to him of new and wonderful paths.

C.G. Jung, Collected Works

Pakistan,
1990

SEPTEMBER 19, 1990. Dawn sweeps across the Islamic Republic of Pakistan. A blood-red sun floats up from the Arabian Sea and 120 million people drop to their knees, bowing their heads in submission. Dust storms race over the barren plains of Baluchistan. In the Karakoram's deep valleys, frost lingers on yellowing leaves. Punjabi thermometers are already climbing skywards.

Benazir Bhutto, sacked as prime minister a month earlier on charges of incompetence, is in Islamabad fiercely campaigning for re-election. The narrow streets of Rawalpindi and Lahore are clogged with rallies. Groups of bearded men have gathered, raising fists and placards in the air, forcing traffic to a standstill.

Meanwhile, New Zealand's cricket team is arriving at Karachi's National Stadium and a crowd has gathered to watch them practise. In the weeks to come the Kiwis will be drubbed by the home side. Alcohol is outlawed in the stands, and vendors instead sell heaping portions of rice and curry chicken for the equivalent of a quarter.

Along the isolated northwestern frontier, lawlessness reigns, as it has for centuries. Bricks of hash and replica AK-47s fill markets near the Afghani border. For ten dollars, young Western backpackers can take their turn launching grenades into the fields of mustard. Violence is escalating in nearby Kashmir, where kidnappings have unsettled the populace and refugees are swamping the border. Eventually, a Norwegian tourist will be beheaded.

As far as nations go, Pakistan is young, an infant really. Just forty-three years old, the country is not even double my age this September day. During its short existence, Pakistan has already suffered the slaughters of partition and the humiliation of losing its other half, Bangladesh, in a battle with hated India. Now the fledgling republic brandishes nuclear weapons, staring across an arbitrary line of control at a temperamental neighbour. In two weeks the U.S. will embargo seventy-one F-16 fighter aircraft, bought and paid for by the Pakistan army. Distrust is being planted. Mr. Bin Laden's appearance is still a decade away.

Peering from the window of a crowded jumbo jet passing into Pakistani airspace, I am aware of none of this. I am a product of white-collar Canadian suburbia; a mall-shopping, Much Music–listening, pickup-truck-driving, backward-ball-cap-wearing, mullet-adorned recent engineering graduate. Posters featuring bikini-clad models and beer still clutter my bedroom walls. I know nothing about Pakistan.

Well, that's not entirely true. A bunch of "Pakis" did move into the apartments at the end of my street when I was in the fifth grade. Friends complained they smelled. "Curry-ina-hurry!" we yelled as we passed beneath their window. My parents threatened to wash my mouth out with soap if they ever heard the "P-word" again. Of course it was still whispered on the playground, the worst insult imaginable, although no one really knew what it meant.

"Punjabi-Afghani-Kashmiri-Indus"–stan; a country named by acronym. The land of the Paks, the spiritually pure and clean; an Islamic patchwork risen from the ashes of British meddling in the subcontinent. Until my discovery that a lot of really, really big mountains were tucked in its northern hinterlands, I couldn't even point to Pakistan on a map of the world.

The jumbo jet flares and lands with a thud. Plains of baked gravel and scrub brush stretch beyond the wing tips. Brakes whine, engines roar, and clouds of dust obliterate my view. Gradually, the giant framework of aluminum slows, and 550 tired passengers breathe a collective sigh of relief. Lumbering to the end of the runway, the jetliner parks alone, far from any buildings.

Soldiers quickly flank the plane. Feet shoulder-width apart, rifles clutched across chests, they stare unflinchingly outward, braced against turbulent gusts of wind. Plumes of shimmering heat rise from gravel flats, and beyond, an armada of minarets floats upon a wavering horizon.

Workers with long, stringy beards and loose robes soon appear, pushing a skittering set of stairs ahead of them. As the forward bulkhead cracks open, fingers of warm air rush in and snake through the cabin. Joining a slow parade down the centre aisle, I pause at the aircraft door, taking a deep breath, letting dry heat fill my lungs, and committing to memory my first vision of this foreign land. Then, as impatient passengers pile up behind me, I sling my new backpack and camera over one shoulder, climb down the aluminum stairs, and step into Pakistan.

Half an hour later, just beyond Immigration, the world dissolves into mayhem.

"Mee-ster! Mee-ster! Hello, Mee-ster!"

Frenzied porters surround the exit, pressing forward, blocking my way. A sea of hands grab at my shirt, my backpack, my cart.

"Taxi? Taxi? Rupees? Change money?"

I am tugged in every direction. Cardboard signs are pressed to my face, bearing the names of tourists sought by hotel shuttle drivers.

"Hotel? Mee-ster! Hello! Hotel?" Whistles and shouts vie for my attention.

"Please sir, your bag. Your bag. Give me your bag!"

I lower my head and push forward like a battering ram, parting the pandemonium with a tattered bicycle box balanced atop my cart. Eventually the men give up and turn their attention elsewhere. The hubbub fades behind. Tired, hungry, confused, and overwhelmed, I pull a guidebook from my backpack, looking for directions to the domestic terminal. This proves to be a major blunder. Lingering porters sense my indecision and descend like vultures.

"Sir, where you go? Domestic Terminal?" A tall, thin porter with a wispy beard and two gold front teeth elbows me away from the cart's handle. "You don't need book. Put book away. I show way. Please, my friend, allow me."

"Thank you," I force myself to smile back, leaning into Goldtooth, pushing him away, "but I am only going to the Domestic Terminal. I can handle the cart myself."

"As you wish, sir, as you wish," he nods, but as he does, an accomplice grabs the other side of the cart handle, and succeeds in squeezing me out of the way. Now they begin to serenade me in unison. "Please, sir, you are a visitor to our country, and our guest. By good fortune we happen to be going to the Domestic Terminal ourselves. By the grace of God, let us help you. Come, come."

"But I can't pay," I plead. "I have no rupees."

"As you wish," Goldtooth repeats, and then steps closers, lowering his voice. "What is your country? The U.S.A.?" The crowd of porters that has been watching draws closer, and I find their dark eyes and expressionless stares unsettling.

"Canada," I announce, proudly pointing to a flag sewn on my backpack, a sure sign of a young Canadian on their first trip abroad, or someone impersonating one.

"Christian?" Goldtooth asks, raising one eyebrow, head tilted.

The question takes me by surprise. Before arriving in Pakistan, I had naively decided I would avoid the subject of religion. My guidebook warned that the absence of faith was both incomprehensible and abhorrent to most Pakistanis, devout Muslims themselves. Better to assume the mantle of Christianity than delve into discussions of atheism and agnosticism, it counselled. Although I was raised an Anglican, and attended Sunday school as a youth, it feels farcical to now proclaim myself Christian. I haven't been to church in years. I am a young engineer who still perceives everything as black and white. I believe in what I can see and prove. How could two fish and five loaves feed five thousand? The truthful answer to Goldtooth's question is "No."

"Yes . . ." I stammer after much consideration, "Christian." The men nod indifferently. My answer hardly seems to matter.

We cover the short distance to the Domestic Terminal in two minutes. The men return the cart, and I thank them profusely, but Goldtooth and his henchman do not leave. Instead they stand directly in front of me, hands outstretched.

"Five hundred rupees," Goldtooth smiles. "EACH."

What? A part of me had innocently clung to the hope this had been a gesture of kindness. *Five hundred rupees?* I do a quick currency conversion in my head. *Twenty-five U.S. dollars! This can't be right?* I have no experience with the floating prices and great games of barter that characterize nearly every monetary transaction in non-Western culture, but the demand is completely ridiculous, and I balk.

"Please, sir, this was a two-man push," Goldtooth explains firmly. "A two-man push is much better, and muuuch more expensive than a one-man push." The second *muuuch* rolls slowly and luxuriantly from his lips, and as it does I struggle to understand why anyone would voluntarily opt for a "two-man push," but grasping fingers bring me back to the dilemma at hand. The conversation grows steadily more insistent and threatening.

A group of porters squatting nearby appears aghast. How dare I dispute the charge? What a rude visitor! Suddenly energetic, they gather around and begin voicing opinions. "Mr. Canada, you must understand, five hundred rupees is a special price. Not for everybody. Just for you." I clutch nervously at the money belt hidden around my waist, trying to decide what to do.

For shit's sake. I didn't want help in the first place. I told them I was fine, but they wouldn't listen. It is their fault if they don't get paid. Slowly my resolve weakens. Looking at the men, with tattered clothes and betel-stained teeth, it is clear that I am financially better off. *Am I being needlessly frugal? Have I already become the caricature of the insensitive, ignorant Western tourist? Or is this a pivotal moment? Do I need to draw a line in the sand right here and now?* If I don't learn to stand up for myself, I suspect I will be ripped off at every turn in the trip to come.

After a long and heated discussion I reluctantly agree to pay each man one hundred rupees. Escorted to a money-changer by the crowd, the men press close and oversee the transaction. There is a murmur of approval as I pull a wad of U.S. currency from my belt. Several porters reach out and examine the bills. There is much haggling and argument over the exchange rate, even by those uninvolved in the transaction.

Business, it appears, is a communal affair. Commissions are paid. Goldtooth and his henchman disappear.

Inside the air-conditioned terminal I flop down on a hard bench, relieved. The mayhem is behind me. Leafing through my guidebook, I discover that in Karachi, an average taxi ride costs four rupees, a dinner ten rupees, and a hotel room thirty rupees. The book suggests one or two rupees as a fair and common tip for baggage handlers. I have been royally ripped off.

My connecting flight to Islamabad departs long after an inky darkness has descended. There are only a handful of passengers aboard the aging Pakistan International Airways 747, and a tired flight attendant distributes water in foil-sealed cups, handing out slices of Wonder Bread from a bag. Despite the late hour another throng of porters and taxi drivers await our arrival. The sight of my bike sends them into affectations of horror, followed by exorbitant demands and another round of negotiations. Too tired to care, I load my bike onto the roof of the nearest car and point on a city map to the Shaw Taj, a guest house recommended by the guidebook as "cheap and clean." We speed off into the night, bumping down dark roads, past barricaded storefronts and occasional donkeys.

The Shaw Taj is locked tight when we arrive. Motioning me back into the cab, the taxi driver stops around the corner, in front of a dingy guest house identified by a peeling sign as "The Cantt View Hotel." Its grumpy proprietor stumbles out, wrapped only in a loose sheet. As I pull my bicycle from the roof, the taxi driver demands an additional one hundred rupees. "Extra distance," he explains. I refuse. The fifty rupees I have already paid is far too much.

The driver and hotel owner stand before me, arms crossed. "Hotel full," the owner announces, and walks back inside. There is no way I am going to give in. Not again. The taxi driver starts his car, preparing to leave me standing all alone, in a dark alley, somewhere in Rawalpindi, at one in the morning. Fear washes away resolve. I rap on the taxi window and pay the driver. He toots his horn. The owner reappears, suddenly remembering that there is a room available after all.

A narrow, winding flight of stairs leads to the uppermost floor of the guest house. As I fumble with the padlock on my door, an unintelligible tirade of screams erupts from the neighbouring room. Muffled thuds shake the walls. Pushing the bike box, I stumble into darkness and bolt the entrance behind me. Blindly rummaging through my pack, I manage to find a headlamp. The narrow beam of light reveals a barren cement room. In one corner stands a metal bed frame with no mattress. Cool air drifts through a barred window. I peer out, but can see nothing. A round of gunfire echoes somewhere in the distance. I search through my guidebook to find its appraisal of the Cantt View Hotel. "Cockroach ridden, the worst of the lot," it declares.

After fifty-six hours of flights, five airports, eight airplane meals, three cab rides, and one crushed bike box, I have arrived in Pakistan. Apart from family visits to England, I have never been abroad before. I am shattered.

Pictures of idyllic surf beaches, sun-drenched mountain peaks, and thundering whitewater rivers litter the walls of my small cubicle in Ontario Hydro's Research Division in Toronto. I am supposed to be constructing a computer model that will simulate the head-on collision of a freight train with a container of spent nuclear fuel, but I am bored and distracted. Careful not to make a sound, I climb up onto my desk, and peer over the walls. An unending sea of beige surrounds me, a honeycomb of cubicles that stretches into the distance. The tappity-tap of keyboards and the unremitting drone of fluorescent lights fills the air. Somewhere in each dim cave sits a listless worker. Entombed. No one is at the coffee machine. No one walks the aisles. Everyone is quiet.

Growing bolder, I wave my arms overhead. *Hello! Is anyone out there? Anyone alive?*

No one glances up. On an air-conditioned office afternoon, as numbers are crunched and beans are counted, not a single soul notices that their co-worker is standing atop his desk, waving both arms in the air like a monkey. Enter the realm of daytime hibernation.

Slumping back into my chair, I glance at the clock. *Two and a half hours. An eternity.* Two and a half more hours until I can tear off my tie and pressed shirt, change into shorts, and dash out into the sunshine. I usually spend the precious daylight hours after work on my new mountain bike, traversing city ravines and abandoned construction sites, following trails trampled by dog-walkers, joggers, and the homeless.

I am planning a long bike ride again tonight, that is, unless afternoon thunderstorms develop. If heavy rains come, the creek running through our neighbourhood golf course will flood, and if that happens I am going to blow up an air mattress and jump in. My younger brother and I have been waiting all summer for the right day. Mom has agreed to drop us off with the car, and pick us up downstream a few hours later, although she remains upset by a sign on the bank that reads "Creek extremely dangerous when flooding. Parents, keep children away." There are no shortage of things to do on evenings and weekends, and my office job is becoming a serious impediment to the business of having fun. Another clock check. *Two hours and twenty-five minutes.*

Glossy adventure magazines lie hidden between reports and papers on my desk. I spend the afternoon daydreaming, gazing at images of far-off places. With a shuffle and a cough I feign work whenever my supervisor walks by. Apart from family trips to England, I have never travelled abroad. I have never sat in a kayak, climbed a rock face, or stood atop a mountain. The images I have torn from the magazines and plastered across my cubicle walls were chosen because they speak to me. Far beyond the specific activities, they invoke a feeling, a memory of childhood wonderment, a state of being which seems real, yet ever more elusive.

Why not quit? Leave this cubicle and this boring job behind? I have been hearing that voice a lot lately.

Twenty-two years of social conditioning speak back, the combined voices of friends' parents and parents' friends: Are you crazy? You just graduated! You need to focus, build a career. If you work hard, in five years you might be a supervisor, and in ten, a manager. This unsettled feeling is just a stage. You'll get over it. Best for you to hunker down now, and start working toward a pension.

Something inside screams back, *Hunker down till I get a pension? You've got to be joking! That is a lifetime away. What if I don't enjoy what I am doing right now? At this very moment. Isn't life too precious to waste a single second?*

Come on, Bruce. You need to get serious, grow up. Think of the future. You'll need to buy a house soon, and pay the mortgage. There will be children, and education funds. And don't forget retirement savings. Don't worry. You'll get used to the grind.

That's what I am afraid of! Hello, I'm twenty-two!

Slouching down, I glance at the clock. One hour and fifty-five minutes of my "good job" left for today. I don't know what the right thing is to do.

My interest in adventure and foreign travel first surfaced during university. Sitting in the back of a sweaty passenger van as a storm raged in the darkness outside, our cross-country ski team was returning from a race in Northern Ontario. The van swerved, buffeted by winds, but I hardly noticed. Huddled with the others under a yellow, flickering interior light, I watched in wonderment as three senior teammates passed around photographs from a biking journey through South America they had undertaken the summer before.

The images of snowy peaks and penguin-speckled beaches were staggering, but what really impressed me was that my friends, my regular-ordinary-sitting-right-in-front-of-me friends had been on such an adventure. They had actually seen the soaring Andes, ridden dusty paths, crossed the *altiplano*, dodged llamas, and drunk *cervesas* with dark-eyed *señoritas*. Previously I imagined that only a select few – *National Geographic* photographers perhaps – went to such exotic and remote locations. I was awed, and deeply jealous.

Many months later, as discontent with my mind-numbing job at Ontario Hydro continued to grow, I stumbled across an article describing the recently inaugurated Karakoram Highway. This rugged track cuts through a bristling knot of peaks in northern Pakistan, where the Himalaya, Hindu Kush, Pamir, and Karakoram ranges swirl together. It connects the plateaus of western China with the sweltering plains of the Punjab. One photo of the highway in particular piqued my interest, showing nothing more than a notch carved into sheer granite, tracing a perilous path thousands of feet above the valley floor.

Further investigation unearthed a newly published guidebook to the region, which promised savage terrain, inhospitable weather, and "the most mind-bending mountain scenery anywhere." The author ended his description of the road with an obscure note: "The Karakoram Highway looks like a harrowing, but spectacular trip for the superfit cyclist." That was all the prompting I needed. Reminded of my teammates' journey in South America, I decided to bike the route.

Hidden in my cubicle, I secretly began planning a voyage of my own: I researched the gear needed, sent away for visa applications, and scavenged the library for information. Mysterious and intriguing names floated from maps of the region: *Kashgar, Kashmir, Gilgit, Rakaposhi, Nanga Parbat.* At the same time, my physical training was blessed with a renewed sense of vigour and purpose; I biked religiously for two hours before work each morning, swimming at lunch, and lifting weights in the evenings.

Johan Kruss was one of the skiing teammates whose journey had inspired my plans, and when I called him, he quickly agreed to join me on the adventure. We decided to leave in the autumn, at the end of Johan's tree-planting season. After pedalling the Karakoram Highway, we would keep going, by bus, bike, and train, through India to Nepal, and on toward Thailand, Malaysia, Australia, and New Zealand. We envisaged six months on the road at the very least, probably a year.

Although I had committed to the journey in my mind, I kept my travel plans a secret at work. A small part of me worried that I was being impulsive and irresponsible. *Will I be able to find another job when I return? Am I creating a black smudge on my resume that will haunt me in the future? Perhaps it would be smarter to wait a few years? Get more experience under my belt.*

The decision to quit was made for me by a senior manager who stopped outside my cubicle one morning. After staring in for a moment (I suspect he found my long hair, sandals, and rope bracelets disconcerting), the stiff man abruptly barked, "Kirkby, don't you think it is time to get a haircut?"

Without thinking I jumped to my feet and announced I would rather go to Pakistan. My bewildered boss looked like he had just coughed up a furball, simultaneously pleased to be rid of my subversive influence but concerned over my flagrant disregard for a career.

Preparations now shifted into high gear. I needed a mass of new equipment. A visit to the local outfitting store left me confused. There were endless comparisons of weight, durability, breathability, versatility, and compactability. Each choice felt monumental, when in fact it really didn't matter. I would do fine with whatever I took, but it would be years before I learned that.

Giddy from my expensive pilgrimage, I dashed to the back garden and eagerly set up a new lightweight tent. My mom took photos as I jumped into a three-season sleeping bag and cinched the drawstring of the mummy bag tight around my face. Affixing low-riding panniers to my bike, I stuffed them with gear, put on new hiking boots, and rode in circles around the lawn. Under the plum tree, Dad and I struggled to light a finicky mountaineering stove. The specially crafted "international model" claimed it could burn almost any fuel on the planet, but even with highly flammable white gas it only sputtered and fizzled. We kept pumping, priming, and striking matches, leaning closer and closer. Suddenly the contraption burst to life with the intensity of a jet engine, leaving our eyebrows singed and faces blackened.

The phone woke me late one night, only weeks before the planned departure. I stumbled from bed. It was Johan, calling from a phone booth in northern British Columbia. The instant I heard his voice I knew he wasn't coming. "I've fallen in love," he told me. "I'm engaged."

Congratulating Johan with all the heartfelt emotion I could muster, I promised to call soon and slowly lowered the phone to its cradle, an emptiness spreading through me. *Was the trip was over?* Staring out the dark window, I wondered if I could ever find another partner on such short notice.

In the days that followed I half-heartedly tried posting messages in local travel stores, seeking a biking companion, but no one replied. It seemed my options were dwindling when I abruptly realized I did not need anyone else.

"You're going alone?" The universal reaction was one of shock. "You'll be a natural target for thieves: tall, long-haired, and blond. Can you eat spicy food? No, I didn't think so. You know that everything over there is dirty, don't you? You're bound to get sick. And what about traffic? It will be insanity; you will be hit within minutes. There are no hospitals. At least no clean ones. Are you aware of the recent uprising in western China? I heard on the news that prisons are full to overflowing, and police are being forced to break inmates' ankles to stop them from running away! Why not go somewhere nice. Somewhere safe. We'll lend you our condo in Florida."

My parents thankfully chose to say nothing. In the face of bountiful and unsolicited advice to the contrary, I decided to bike the Karakoram Highway alone.

The sun rouses me gently. Cool air pours in the open window, and a cacophony of horns, barking dogs, roosters, and shouts is building outside. Stiffly crawling from my sleeping bag, I rub the bed-spring creases from my face, and lean out through the bars to survey a wakening sea of humanity. Throngs of men, packed into narrow alleyways below, flow seamlessly in all directions. Donkeys haul wooden carts laden with bricks and vendors push wagons of fruit. A lone car crawls past, slowly parting the crowds. A tangled warren of flat cement buildings stretches before me, every roof clogged with hand-washed clothes that flutter from makeshift lines. The morning breeze carries the sweet smell of jasmine. Night has wiped away the heat, humidity, dust, and squalor, blessing Rawalpindi with a sense of renewal.

My stomach gurgles ominously. *It can't be diarrhea? I haven't even eaten in Pakistan yet!* I carefully packed purifying tablets and a water filter, but this upset ironically started on the flight from Canada. Shuffling groggily toward the bathroom door, I stop dead in my tracks.

The small cinderblock room is barren. No sink, no toilet, no shower. There are just two porcelain foot-pads, straddling a hole the size of a mug in the centre of the floor. A rusty faucet in one corner slowly drips into a cracked red bucket. The cement by my feet is damp, and the odour of urine overpowering.

I look at the hole. That's it? I question the accuracy of my aim, but there is no other choice. I simply cannot wait. Tentatively placing my feet on the cool pads, I lower my pyjama bottoms and squat. The position is awkward, and just as I start to pee, I notice the seat of my pants resting on the damp floor. Trying to pluck them up, I lose my balance and am forced to slap a hand down in a puddle. *Damn!*

Wriggling my feet apart, I manage to keep the pyjamas taut between my shins. This holds them off the floor, but directly over the hole. Hopping my feet forward and leaning my buttocks back clears the pathway, but soon my thighs are screaming in protest. Before long, I have both hands on the damp ground behind me, and I am perched over the hole like an upside-down spider. Relieving myself proves to be an exhausting process.

As I dress, the screaming and banging from the previous night returns. Stepping into the hall, I find the ruckus has brought the hotel manager.

"Iranian," he mutters, pointing to the locked door of my neighbour. "Drugged in market. Robbed of everything. Except his underpants. No passport, no papers. Police tell me to lock him in room. They are checking his story. Maybe smuggler?"

Muffled cries rise from behind the door, followed by vigorous banging. Then silence.

"You must be carefully on the streets," the manager turns and warns me. "Especially at night. In the market, men will kill you with a knife . . . pistol . . . even their fist," he says, giving a low, stabbing motion at my belly. "Just for your wallet." I assure the manager that I will be cautious, and then wander toward the stairs. "Be carefully," I hear him call after me.

Stepping through the hotel's front door, I am swallowed by crowds, swept away like a piece of driftwood. Paper-thin men jostle past, hidden under massive loads of wheat and flour. Veiled women balance earthenware jugs atop their heads. I watch a young boy drag an immense, groaning camel by a frayed rope that runs through a nose ring. In a parched riverbed, barefoot children chase rusty bicycle rims.

Street vendors whistle and wave for attention, standing behind carts piled with golden sheaves of fresh baked nan bread. The smell of mutton curry wafts from bubbling pots. I pause at a stand where stalks of sugar cane are being crushed in a rusty hand-cranked press. Sweet, translucent juice pours out. Mixed with lemons and crushed ice, it is sold by the cupful. I am tempted to try some, but decide not to. The guidebook warns never to trust ice, as it is likely made from unpurified water.

Traffic on busier thoroughfares is a deafening combination of brakes, horns, and engines. Towering lorries chug past, trailing billowing clouds of purple exhaust. Taxis honk incessantly and bicycles weave through all lanes, pedalled by serene gentlemen who sit bolt upright, apparently oblivious to the chaos. Policemen languish at roundabouts, chatting amongst themselves, occasionally directing traffic with stiff wooden canes and sharp blasts of their whistles.

Motorized scooters obey no rules, bouncing over sidewalks, through ditches, and racing straight at oncoming vehicles. I notice one carrying an entire family. The father is driving, while a young son perched on the gas tank grips the handlebars. Behind is a woman seated sidesaddle, with an infant on each knee. "Be careful!" I almost yell as they swerve to miss a turning car. Unused to the ways of Asia, I am horrified that not one of them is wearing a helmet.

For hours I wander the streets, engrossed by the mundane details of daily life. It is midday before I glance at my watch. I have not changed the time since leaving Canada and it is now midnight in Toronto. My mind rushes home; Mom and Dad are probably sleeping; my friends will be at the campus bar, surrounded by pitchers of draft and plates of nachos; my girlfriend's last exam is tomorrow. I can picture her, curled on her couch, wearing fluffy slippers, studying chemistry. I miss her dark eyes, and the way she pushes her glasses up her rounded nose. Waves of homesickness roll over me, and as they do, I grow furious with myself for being so weak. After dreaming about this trip for months, it seems ridiculous that I feel so miserable after only one day. I struggle in vain to banish thoughts of home from my mind.

Providence, or perhaps serendipity, leads me to the doorstep of Rawalpindi's "Burger Express," the sole Western food diner in town, a quiet, air-conditioned vacuum, removed from the bustle of the streets. The restaurant is deserted, and I take a seat, and look over a handwritten menu. A short, rotund man appears outside the window, his forehead beaded with sweat. Glancing nervously around, he slips through the front door and sits down opposite me.

"Desmond Hope," the man whispers, holding out a hand. "What is your country?"

"Canada."

"How long have you been in Pakistan?"

"One day."

I am beginning to wonder where this is leading when Desmond leans over and gets to the point. "What is your religion?"

"Christian?" I reply, almost asking if it is the correct answer.

Desmond sits back and smiles, yellow teeth flashing. He relaxes. "I too am a Christian," he whispers, and with a flourish, pulls open his shirt, revealing a simple golden cross. "I cannot tell anyone here, so I must look for tourists to share this secret with."

You picked the wrong dude, I think. Luckily we have something else in common, for Desmond's sister lives in Toronto. He has not seen her since she emigrated, ten years earlier. I show him photographs from home, and "Des," as he asks me to call him, peppers me with endless questions about life in Canada.

"You can marry anyone you want? Your parents don't choose a bride for you?" I nod. "Incredible, that is incredible!" Des gets excited. "You are very lucky. How old are you?"

"Twenty-two."

"What!" Desmond slaps a hand against his expansive forehead. "And you are not married? Can you not find anyone you like?"

I feel momentarily self-conscious, ungrateful for freedoms I never considered before, but Des has already moved on. With great care he inscribes his address in my journal, and I promise to write to him upon returning home. A meagre burger arrives, tasting gamey. My stomach churns and boils after the first bite, but I wolf it down anyways. Neither nausea nor gamey tastes have ever stopped me from eating. Des watches.

When it is time to go, Des tags along, ambling beside me, warning of one danger after another. Never go out after dark (too dangerous); never pay the first price asked (I'll get ripped off); don't eat from street vendors (Canadian stomachs are weak); and, above all, he implores me to abandon my biking plans. "The northerners are an unruly lot. And they don't like Christians. This crazy plan of yours will surely lead to suffering and disaster."

I grow tired of the disheartening talk. The achy hollow of loneliness has returned. I want to go back to the hotel, bury myself in my sleeping bag, and cry. Desmond insists I come to his house instead, and nothing I say can dissuade him. He glances up and down a dusty alley behind the market before unlocking a narrow door, herding me through, and locking it after us.

Drawing the blinds, he roots about underneath his bed, eventually emerging with an ancient gramophone player wrapped in blankets. His pride is clear. We listen to Frank Sinatra in silence while I watch time crawl past on a clock. Outside a donkey brays and Desmond begins to dance alone, languorously, holding himself in a tight hug, swaying to the rhythm. Maybe he is just trying to cheer me up, but I feel strangely anxious. It is time to go.

Despite Des's objections, I leave to wander the streets alone, feeling more homesick than ever. I am painfully aware that even if I were to pull a thousand dollars from my money belt and buy a ticket home this minute, it would still be three days before I got there. The separation seems unbearable.

Looking at my watch I realize it is morning in Canada. Perhaps I can call home. Before leaving on the journey, I told my mother no news was good news. Funds would be tight. "It won't be long till I'm back," I promised when she dropped me at the airport, "and I'll write lots."

Once the idea of calling home has entered my head, I can't banish it. It haunts me at every street corner, with every burble of my stomach, with every wave of loneliness. Before long I am standing before Rawalpindi's main telephone exchange. An attendant explains it will be an hour before there is any space on the international trunk lines. I reserve a three-minute call, entering the details of my passport, hotel, and occupation into a dog-eared tome, and then sit down to wait in the courtyard.

An hour later the attendant bangs on his window, directing me toward one of six small booths on the outside of the brick building. I pull back the heavy black drapes and settle on a rickety stool. The receiver rings and I pick it up hastily. I can hear the operator's breath, the heavy click of a rotary dial, and then, after a long delay, a far-off ringing. Once, twice . . .

"Hello?" my mother answers, the familiarity of her distant voice instantaneously uncorking a jumbled avalanche of loneliness and heartache. Speaking is impossible; I can only muster a garbled, teary croak of a reply. It feels as if a bird's nest of emotions has lodged in my throat.

"Peter, it's Bruce!" I can hear her yelling to my father, before returning to the receiver. "Oh Bruce, how are you? Where are you for goodness' sakes?" I can hear her warmth, affection, and worry as if she were beside me. I want to tell her that I am fine, that I am enjoying Pakistan, but only funny-sounding sobs come out. I can see our precious time ticking away on a small clock beside the phone. I compose myself and try again. My mother waits and listens patiently. "I'm fine," I finally manage to spit out. "Heading north to Gilgit tomorrow. I'll begin biking there." The counter is almost down to zero. "I'll send a letter to tell you more, and I will call again as soon as I can." The counter goes blank. "I love you," I squeak out as the call ends, unceremoniously cut off.

I cry all the way back to the hotel and collapse into a deep catatonic sleep, never to feel so catastrophically homesick again. My mother, on the other hand, later confesses that she did not feel at ease for months.

~

The first rays of sun are stretching across Pir Wadhai as I arrive, bathing Rawalpindi's long-distance bus terminal in golden light. A boisterous crowd has already gathered in the brick-walled compound, swarming ticket sellers. Coaches jockey for position in a tangled knot, inching forward even as boxes and trunks are hoisted to their roofs. Hundreds of musical horns blare out a symphony of welcome.

Pakistan has developed a near obsession with the decoration of buses and trucks. The vehicles littering the courtyard could be aptly described as art galleries on wheels. Each has been painstakingly adorned, and no two are alike. Flowing, hand-painted images of flowers, swastikas, jet fighters, tigers, swords, and warriors cover every available inch. A buttress of vaulted panelling rises above each cab like the prow of a ship, decorated with gaudy reflectors, shiny trim, and flags. Verses of poetry, odes to country, and passages from the Koran have been splashed across dented bumpers. Chrome sequins hang from mudguards, ribbons adorn rearview mirrors.

There are several buses bound for Gilgit, and since there appears to be no set schedule, I pick one, gambling it will be the first to leave. After hoisting my bike to the roof and lashing it between sacks of grain, I duck inside. Small barred windows offer insignificant amounts of light, and as my eyes adjust, I see that every seat is taken. An impenetrable wall of bodies fills the aisle, and the tang of sweat is heavy in the air. Every head turns my way, expressionless eyes watching as the conductor yells back, evicting a man from his seat in the last row and motioning for me to take it instead.

"It's OK," I protest, "I'm happy to stand."

I don't want special treatment, and I especially don't want any of the locals to think I expect it, but the conductor shakes his head. He will hear nothing of it. As I squeeze awkwardly down the crowded aisle, several chickens burst out from under a seat. Squawks and feathers erupt as I stumble to my knees.

Two elderly gentlemen are seated on the last bench, grim-looking characters with stringy, henna-bleached beards, who could have walked straight in from another century. Standing, they curtly wave me toward the window. Even as I collapse into the far seat, I realize there is a problem. I cannot fit. The benches are mercilessly close together, and my legs are simply too long to jam in. The only solution is to rest my knees against the seatback ahead, which leaves my feet dangling several centimetres off the floor.

Then we wait. And wait. And wait. Eventually the sagging bus begins to creep forward, and as it does, a surge of hope passes amongst the passengers, but the driver turns back and makes another slow round of the compound, searching for more fares. Swinging from the door, the noisy conductor harangues stragglers. "Hut, hut! Gilgit. *Giiiiiilgit!*" Only when the vehicle is packed tighter than a hay bale do we pass through the wide gates and into the confusion of traffic beyond.

Hindi pop music soon blares from speakers over my head, the nasal wails distorted beyond all recognition. No one else seems to notice. Instead conversations escalate to yelling matches. Coupled with the fumes and dust pouring in, my head quickly throbs. I wonder what my two elderly neighbours think, but they stare blankly ahead, either deaf or immune to the assault.

In the seat in front, a mysterious-looking man grasps two young girls on his lap, both of whom bawl and struggle to get away. The man ignores their outbursts, gripping the girls tightly. Tears stream down their cheeks and I wonder if they are being abducted, destined for child labour camps where they will spend their days tanning hides, under-nourished, living on scraps of food, confined to sleep in a cave. Most likely they just miss their mother, or perhaps they have never been on a bus before. This particular bus would make any sane person cry.

Sensing an opportunity, I rummage through my pack and hold up a handful of boiled candies. The screams abate. Two hands reach back over their oblivious father's shoulder and pluck the sweets from my palm. We share a smile of understanding. The girls quietly suck on their treats, and I turn to the open window, closing my eyes, enjoying the breeze against my cheek.

Moments later both girls simultaneously puke straight out their window. At least I think that is what happens, because a spray of half-digested food and bile whistles in my window, covering my face. The mystery man looks back and shrugs his shoulders. I wipe myself clean with toilet paper.

The bus races across the parched fields of Pakistan's Punjab, endless rows checkered with brick kilns, gravel quarries, and stone-crushing factories. Soaring eucalyptus line the roadside, and men sit idly in their shade, resting on their haunches, some in conversation, others reading folded newspapers, most simply watching the traffic roar past. On barren stretches of road, far from any settlement, I continue to spot men squatting along the roadside and in the middle of empty fields, gazing expressionlessly into the distance. It seems strange, and I can't figure out what they are doing.

By midafternoon, gentle pine-covered hills begin to rise ahead, and the road cuts steadily upward, through switchbacks of rich brick-red soil. Men are squatting here too. Eventually I realize this versatile position, a sort of bum-on-the-heels, arms-around-the-knees squat, is employed not only for relaxation, but also for the performance of bodily functions. The design of Pakistan's ubiquitous *shalwar khamis* shirt, with its baggy drapes of cloth hanging fore and aft, proves extremely practical for this purpose, allowing complete modesty while doing one's business in public.

Foothills give way to snow-capped mountains, and we enter a tangled network of bleak valleys. The road follows the Indus River northward, clinging to steep canyon walls and growing ever more harrowing.

At last our bus driver comes to life! The engine roars. Blind corners are taken squarely in the middle. Braking is unthinkable. A berserk combination of speed and nonchalance appear to be the enlivened man's only goals. Whenever head-on collisions appear imminent (and they often do), our driver uses the bus's size to force oncoming vehicles into the ditch, passing them with a blast of his musical horn. When there is no ditch, just a rock wall on one side and a yawning chasm on the other, vehicles still manage to race past each other without slowing, although side mirrors do occasionally clang together.

At one such "near-miss" I glance downward, and am horrified to see nothing but air beneath my window. Somehow a few centimetres of the rear tire manage to stay on the tarmac, and we continue onward at breakneck speed. I spot the charred remains of vehicles, strewn across fields of granite boulders far below. At the next tea break I corner the driver and ask (as casually as possible) if buses ever tumble from the road.

"Oh yes!" the short man with bloodshot eyes replies, nodding and smiling enthusiastically. My face must have turned white, for he quickly reverts to a tone of gravity. "But please, sir, do not worry. You have the good fortune to be travelling with NATCO, the very best bussing company in Pakistan. We have lost only one motor coach all year."

What an immense relief.

Night comes suddenly, a blanket of darkness thrown across the land. I can see nothing, no reflections from the river below, no stars or moon above, no lights ahead or behind. Just impenetrable black.

The driver leans forward, peering into the narrow cone of his headlights, and the bus accelerates at ever more terrifying speeds. Without scenery to distract me, misery takes over. I can feel my hip bones grating against the gentleman beside me. I glance over, wishing he had a little more meat on his body. He glances back, no doubt wishing he had not suffered the misfortune and indignity of sitting beside such a fleshy foreigner. My knees, still wedged up against the seatback and supporting the full weight of my dangling feet, ache mercilessly. Every bump is torture. My stomach gurgles, I battle to hold my bowels. I can smell kerosene leaking from a bottle in my backpack mingling with the little girls' vomit from hours earlier.

Just before midnight we stop at a police checkpoint. From here on we must travel in convoy. Border skirmishes with India coupled with rising tensions prior to the national elections have placed the Northern Areas in a heightened state of alert. A soldier boards our bus, wandering the aisle, occasionally stooping to stare out into the dark night. As we pitch down the bumpy road, I cannot take my eyes from his worn gun, which swings back and forth over the sleeping passengers. Growing up in Canada, Hollywood has been my only exposure to firearms. I try to remember if I have ever seen a real gun before. The guard's finger rests against the trigger guard, shaking with each jolt. Praying the safety catch is on, I silently duck and dodge the muzzle, unable to rest.

At two in the morning the bus stops. We've arrived. There has been no indication of entering Gilgit, absolute darkness continues to envelop everything. The bus empties before my eyes, like sand pouring from a fist. Packages are snatched from the roof, and those with whom

I suffered, side by side for eighteen hours, disappear without a word. I drag my bike into the compound of a nearby guest house, find the dorm room, and collapse into my sleeping bag, crammed between two snoring bodies.

Tucked deep in the remote valleys of the Karakoram, the lonesome outpost of Gilgit lies at the crossroads of ancient trading routes. Buddhist monks, Arab soldiers, Silk Route traders, Mongolian bandits, and Afghani chieftains all passed this way. More recently, British and Russian agents criss-crossed the region, disguised as scholars and holy men, part of the imperial hide-and-seek known as the Great Game. The diverse local ethnicity that can be found today is a testament to centuries of interlopers who mingled with the indigenous Shin people.

The town's religious roots are also convoluted. Hinduism, Buddhism, and to a lesser extent, Christianity, all thrived here once, but were swept aside by the explosive spread of Islam. Today Gilgit marks the intersection of three Islamic sects. Shia and Sunni are present – the primary branches of Islam which populate the southern country – as well as the rare Ismaili sect, which flourishes to the north. Existing only in isolated pockets around the world, including northern Pakistan, India, East Africa, Syria, and Iran, Ismailis are ruled by the Aga Khan, their "living infallible leader." Ismailism represents a gentler, more esoteric doctrine of Islam. Prayer is a personal matter and meeting halls have replaced mosques in most communities. Women are far less isolated.

Casting the guest-house drapes aside, I find jagged peaks rising before me. I have to strain my neck to look up toward their summits, which are grey and devoid of vegetation. The crowds filling the streets here are markedly different from those in the south. Gone are the fezzes and turbans. Every man wears a *topi*, an upside-down pie crust of scratchy wool characteristic of northern Pakistan. Women are conspicuous simply by their presence, wandering through the market stalls in unveiled groups.

My stomach is still giving me problems, having churned incessantly since arriving in Pakistan. After a breakfast of fresh yogourt mixed with local fruits and nuts, I move to the highly recommended "Tourist Cottages" on the outskirts of town, to recuperate for a few days before beginning my cycle journey northward. I spend the afternoon in a smelly cement room, struggling to maintain the upside-down spider position over a black hole in the floor. I am cursing my luck when a loud knock at the door startles me.

"Hello? HELLO?"

"Just a second!" I yell from the dark bathroom.

"My good friend, many apologies for this intrusion," the unseen visitor speaks through the closed door, his voice laced with an almost farcical mix of Pakistani and British accents. "We have not yet had the pleasure of acquaintance, but please allow me to introduce myself. I am Afrazullah Beg, the owner of these Tourist Cottages, here to offer welcome and cheer to a sick friend. Having spent more than twenty good years as an officer in the Pakistani Army, I am well acquainted with foreigners. When Mr. Ali [the receptionist] told me of your deteriorating condition, I felt the compulsion to visit you in person."

Pulling on pants and scrubbing my hands, I rush to the door. Before me stands an impeccably dressed Pakistani version of Peter Sellers. The retired Army colonel wears a collared shirt, plaid vest, and pleated pants. A thin, well-groomed moustache traces his upper lip. Greying hair is oiled straight back. We shake hands, and I feel an instant liking for the man. He carries a nasty-looking black concoction, a glass of dark medicinal syrup, which he insists I drink in a single gulp. I cannot get a word in edgewise, and eventually submit, gagging on the foul taste.

"Bedrest for you now. That's all there is to it. Don't show your head until dinner or I'll chase you back to your room with a cane."

I spend the next three days in the sanctuary of Mr. Beg's cottages, resting and preparing. The friendly eccentric passes each afternoon in his garden, reading, and I often join him; we sip black tea from English china and exchange views. Mr. Beg has a passionate interest in foreign affairs, and talks at length about issues I hardly understand. He is angry at the United States for what he feels are unfair sanctions. "Do they not think we are capable of taking care of our own business? They are provoking a nest of hornets, and should be careful." He is equally worried about the situation at home. "Who controls the nuclear arms in this country? The government? The army? No one knows!"

I value these conversations. For the first time in my life I am hearing the views of someone born and raised outside my frame of reference, someone who once trained with English officers, experienced the turmoil of Partition, and then spent ten years fighting a border war in Kashmir. Mr. Beg wonders about the growing number of tourists visiting his remote valley. "They are all very nice people, and may God bless them, but they are always in a rush. In the old days, people were happy to stop and talk. Some would stay a week, some would stay a month. One Swede came for a night, and stayed for two years. Now my guests are just taking photos, photos, photos . . . click, click, click . . . and rushing on. Maybe if they spent more time they wouldn't need the camera to remember?"

As days pass I grow increasingly anxious to begin my journey northward. When energy permits, I wander into town to buy supplies. Soon my bicycle is tuned and oiled. Gear and food are packed, the panniers loaded. On the fourth morning, despite no noticeable improvement in my health, I decide to bid farewell to Mr. Beg.

As the first calls of the muezzin float across the frost-filled valley, I wheel my bike from the guest house and quietly close the gate behind me. The morning air is cool. Long tendrils of mist weave through riverside forests. In the distance a rooster crows. I climb onto the saddle and slip away, soaring noiselessly downhill, passing through the sleepy town without seeing a soul. The din of horns, engines, and shouts will soon echo from the valley walls, but in the silence of early morning I hear nothing but air whistling through my spokes. Rows of aspens rush past, yellow sentinels lining the roadside. The landscape, so austere and harsh in the glare of the daytime sun, now shows a gentle face. I feel completely at ease, and for the first time since arriving, sense the essence of the land seeping into me.

An airy suspension bridge connects Gilgit with the Karakoram Highway. I ride slowly over the swaying deck, peering at the blue waters rushing underneath just as the first rays of sun break over a distant ridge. I want to remember this moment, the beginning of a long-dreamed-about journey, but the photography of bridges is strictly prohibited in Pakistan due to their military and strategic importance. Glancing around to confirm my absolute solitude, I decide to risk it. With my camera set atop a boulder, I activate the self-timer and pose stiffly beside my bike. Then I pack it all away, stand up on my pedals, and begin slowly grinding uphill.

In the days that follow I pedal northward, through desiccated moonscapes of rock and gravel. Only occasional ravens break the isolation. The road weaves up and down, and hours pass without any sign of vegetation or habitation. Lorries and buses chug past intermittently, the drivers staring in disbelief. Loaded with thirty-two kilograms (70 pounds) of gear, my bike handles like a tank. Blisters form on my feet and my knees grow sore. I camp in flats by roadside streams, and use my finicky mountaineering stove to cook noodles. *Eid Milad-un-Nabi* arrives, the national holiday celebrating Mohammed's birthday, and for twenty-four hours the road is completely deserted. I feel alone but not lonely.

Occasional oases exist in the desolation, small farms and irrigated terraces that have sprung up wherever the valley floor widens. Fields of golden maize stand ready for harvest, and there are orchards at the bigger settlements, where mulberries, apples, walnuts, and peaches have been placed to dry on wicker baskets. Children cower behind bushes, watching me pass, their stark eyes rimmed with *kohl*. This derivative of powdered antimony has been used for millennia to protect Arab and Persian eyes from the sun's glare, as well as for cosmetic effect. Despite a near complete conversion to Islam, many old, shamanistic beliefs still endure in these northern mountains. Here the dark powder is thought to guard the wearer against the mercurial spirits of the high peaks, which can enter the body through unprotected eyes.

Strings of new shops have appeared along the recently opened high-way, catering to the growing long-distance truck traffic. These roadside stalls sell everything from chewing tobacco to toothpaste and cassette tapes. Crowds of children often loiter outside. More capricious than their country cousins, they hurl stones as I pass, running beside my bike and screaming in unison, "Bye-bye, Mister. Where are you going, Mister?" Some try to poke twigs through my spokes, others sprint behind, desperately trying to whack me with sticks. One time I make the mistake of reaching out to shake a sea of waving hands. Several boys latch on to my arm and refuse to let go. I swerve, fighting to control the bike with one hand, until they finally release their grip.

Another young boy gives chase, the soft pat-pat of his bare feet trailing behind me. Whenever I begin to suspect that the child has dropped off, a glance back reveals he is still in wholehearted pursuit. Worried about dragging the boy too far from home, I slow and try to wave him off, but this only redoubles his enthusiasm and I can hear tiny giggles mixed with heaving breaths. Eventually I stop, and quickly he catches up, winded. We shake hands, and he strokes the frame of my bicycle as if it were a pet, a smile spreading from ear to ear. After he is done inspecting my panniers, pump, and water bottles, I show him pictures from my guidebook and offer some water, which he gulps down thirstily.

"Bye-bye," I wave and prepare to leave.

"Bye-bye" he waves back. I begin to pedal away, and once again he takes up the chase. There is nothing to do but keep biking. It is several minutes before the sound of his little feet fades behind me.

A few kilometres later I stop to fill my water bottles at a rushing creek. The innocent interaction has left me unexpectedly overwhelmed. While the young boy's physical exertion was humbling, running barefoot on sharp rocks to catch me, it is his spirit that made the deepest imprint. Dressed in rags, long tails of yellow snot snaking from both nostrils, hands dirtier than a mechanic's, he was unabashedly joyous. I left home with the naive impression that living with less meant a corresponding lack of happiness and satisfaction. Since arriving in Gilgit I have travelled amongst a people more outwardly challenged by the uncertainties of daily survival than anything I know at home yet there appears to be a quiet acceptance of life and fate. There are no self-help books here, no weekend seminars about finding the warrior within, no "Come Alive!" retreats. People get on with the business of living. I see only a snapshot of their lives, but for the first time I find myself questioning whether Western society represents the pinnacle of achievement that I complacently believed.

After ten days on the road, Rakaposhi rears up before me, a fortress of ice and snow soaring to 7,700 metres (25,500 feet). I have entered the fabled Hunza Valley, a lost Shangri-La, a land renowned for its natural beauty and exalted for the longevity of its residents. The hillsides above me are awash with colour, a quilt of ripening orchards and golden corn, and the guidebook explains this abundance is hard-won. Long before the existence of iron tools, the local Hunzakuts carved a web of irrigation channels through the rocky hillsides by hand. Carrying glacial melt from the high slopes, it is these burbling canals that bring the parched land to life.

Beyond Hunza, the valley narrows again, and swings northward toward the Chinese border. The scale of the land is immense. Razor-edged summits rise on both sides of the highway, their barren walls impossibly steep. Sporadic fans of alluvium spread across the floor, emanating from dark canyons. Land and mud slides obliterate long sections of highway. Most have been cleared away but, at some, the road has simply been rerouted over twenty-metre- (60-foot-) thick piles of hardened muck. Every centimetre of the road's tarmac surface is pitted and scarred by rockfall. Some of the boulders that come crashing down are too massive to move, even with bulldozers, forming an obstacle course that traffic must weave through. Maintenance of the route is a never-ending job, and I pass several roadwork camps, the yards jammed with bulldozers, loaders, and graders.

Strong afternoon winds become my nemesis. Plumes of dust roar down the valley toward me, stalling my progress and occasionally forcing me to get off my bike and walk. I change my regime, and begin rising before dawn, hoping to cover distance before the gales rise. The predawn hours are frigid. Feathers of frost greet me outside the tent, and within minutes of mounting the bike, my fingers grow white and numb, too stiff to operate the brakes. The sky lightens, but I bike for hours in shadow.

The instant the high-altitude sun crests the peaks, it chases away every memory of chill. Sweat pours from my brow. I want to tear off my shirt and ride in only shorts, but exposed skin, even on men, is frowned upon. Instead I wear long pants and a long-sleeved shirt, soaked in perspiration.

White clouds tumble across clear, blue skies, casting shadows on the mountains that endlessly morph and change. I apply thick gobs of sunscreen, but the backs of my hands and neck still burn. The mountain air is arid, and the four water bottles I carry don't last long, forcing me to replenish often at clear streams. I catch my first glimpse of the region's immense glaciers, the Passu and Batura, blue and white highways of ice slowly oozing down from high summits, pushing piles of gravel and rock before them.

A peculiar flatness overtakes me as I approach the border post of Sust. I have been on the road seventeen days, and for the first time, my enthusiasm for the spectacular surroundings is beginning to fade. Struggling into town, I collapse into the first guest house I find, where fifteen rupees (seventy-five cents) gets me a barren room with a rope bed.

Within hours a fever breaks. I have been sick since arriving in Asia, and simply assumed that diarrhea was par for the course. Now I worry something bigger is at play. There is an acute ache below my rib cage that throbs with every heartbeat and breath. I dread my frequent pilgrimages to the outhouse, for the short walk is exhausting, and in my nauseated state, the smell of the pit is unbearable. The day crawls past excruciatingly slowly.

Lying alone in darkness that night, I try to sleep but can't. I dig through my pack, pulling out a candle and matches. In the flickering light I begin a self-examination at the hands of the Lonely Planet Travel Guide. It seems every ailment listed in the "Health" section matches my symptoms, and unfortunately the prognosis gets progressively worse. At first I suspect simple traveller's diarrhea, but reading on I find a digestive tract infection sounds right as well, as do heat exhaustion, acute mountain sickness, amoebic dysentery, bacillary dysentery, giardia, Hepatitis A, and malaria. Worry grips my tired mind. *Where is the pain exactly? Which side is my liver on? Could it be my appendix? Is my urine dark?* I don't know. It is hard to judge while peeing into a black hole in the ground.

When morning arrives I decide to take a sponge bath. The manager lends me something that resembles a curling-iron, which I suspect is meant to heat a bucket of water. Instead it gives me a violent shock, causing me to jerk about on the concrete floor like a dying fish before finally yanking my hand free. There is a certain dignity to dying in a remote land from a rare foreign illness that being found electrocuted, naked, on a wet concrete floor does not share. I give up and retreat to my sleeping bag, defeated, spending the day reading in my own oily, sweaty stew.

Only eighty-five kilometres (53 miles) remain to the border with China, the planned end of my travels northward. I am loath to consider retreat, but after two torturous days without sign of improvement, I decide to return to Gilgit. I need to see a doctor. Dragging my gear to the roadside, I raise my thumb and join eleven others crushed into the back of a Land Cruiser. What took seventeen days to ride passes in a blur. My sole memory is of a farmer's rifle that slips and comes to rest with the muzzle against my testicles, evoking a catlike jump backward, despite my compromised state.

In Gilgit I go directly to the district hospital, a grey stone building that was once either a jail or barracks. I can find no reception or waiting room. Wandering the halls, I chance upon a caretaker who leads me to a darkened office. A distracted doctor pries himself from his reading, has me lie out across a wooden table, quickly prods my abdomen, jots an illegible prescription, and directs me toward the door.

"Bad stomach," he notes, scrunching his nose in either sympathy or aversion.

The dispensary lies in the outer courtyard where several men wait patiently before a small window. Eventually the pharmacist waves for my attention. I pass him the pink prescription, and minutes later a mixed handful of pills are shoved across the cement sill toward me. No bottle. No label. No instructions. I stare at the array of capsules and tablets. I have no idea what they are, or how many I should be taking.

Pushing the pills back, I indicate my confusion. The pharmacist ducks below the counter, tears a couple of pages from a medical text-book, divides the pills into groups, and hands them back to me in crumpled packets of paper. I scribble hasty annotations on each package as he uses sign language to convey the suggested regime.

At the Tourist Cottages, a clearly agitated Mr. Beg races out to simultaneously embrace and scold me. Immediately, he sends Mr. Ali for dinner supplies and more medicine.

"Is your wristwatch still showing Toronto time?" Mr. Beg asks as he puts on a kettle for tea.

I nod with embarrassment. I have been away from Canada for almost a month and my watch has become a last, stubborn tie to the world I left behind. Mr. Beg found this habit strangely endearing during my first stay. Now he laughs and hugs me once again.

In my room I lay the pills on a table, inspecting the tiny markings on their sides. One set is Flagyl, a strong antibacterial used to treat giardia. A second set is labelled "DS," which I assume means it is a double-strength antibiotic. The third type of pill remains a mystery. Unsure of what to do, I ask other travellers staying at the guest house for their thoughts.

"Throw the whole lot in the rubbish," Daniel, a dreadlocked German hippie who has been avoiding military service by staying on the road for five years, warns. A group of Israelis agree. A strong mistrust of Western medicine permeates the traveller's circuit, where carefree attitudes and conspiracy theorists abound. The consensus around the dinner table is to let my body heal itself.

"Just eat lots of yogourt and you'll be right," a British climber called Rob advises. Already feeling better, and concerned about taking unknown medications, I decide to put the pills aside and wait.

In two months' time, at a back-alley lab in Pokhara, Nepal, I will receive a double diagnosis of giardia and bacillary dysentery. The same cocktail of pills will be handed to me. This time I take them, and apart from a strange aluminum taste that lingers in my mouth for several days, I am completely cured. I can eat anything I want, whenever I want. I sleep at night. Biking quickly becomes a lot more fun. I no longer have to fill my panniers to the brim with toilet paper. But this revelation is still two months away.

⤫

At midnight, on August 14, 1947, an imaginary line was drawn through the deserts and plains and jungles of the Asian subcontinent, separating the Hindu-dominated state of India from the newly created Muslim state of Pakistan. After 350 years of British rule, two nations were born within the space of an hour. "A tryst with destiny," declared Jawaharlal Nehru, India's first prime minister. Celebrations quickly disintegrated into catastrophic rioting and appalling violence. Fifteen million refugees were uprooted by the split, forced to migrate across the borders. Over half a million people lost their lives; raping and looting were commonplace. "Ghost trains" began to arrive on the new border, carrying disembowelled corpses sent from the neighbouring nation. Some wagons were filled with only severed breasts, bawling infants crawling in their midst. Elders were occasionally spared, but only after having every limb amputated. Such inhumanity is difficult to imagine, and the deep hatred it spawned has never dissipated.

After a week of recuperation at Mr. Beg's cottages, I set off again with Nepal in my sights. A change feels like it will do me good. Travelling by bus, jeep, and bike, I slowly inch toward the Indian border. From Lahore, I pedal across the Punjab's deserted plains where the death toll of Partition was horrific. In the cool of predawn, the land lies silent; roads deserted, fields of barren red earth cracked by the sun. Silhouetted lorries sit along the shoulder. Sleeping drivers huddle underneath, tucked against tread-bare tires. A lone boy appears in the mist, driving a herd of mud-splattered water buffalo. Black drongos hop nimbly across the cattle's backs, pecking at insects. The sky shudders, and without warning, a shimmering orange sun floats up from the horizon.

The physical manifestations of Partition soon appear ahead: barbed wire, cement guard towers, watchful soldiers. The passage proves tedious, three hours of head-scratching and form-filling by a dedicated team of we'd-rather-be-doing-nothing officials. It is illegal to leave the country with Pakistani currency I am told. All my currency must be converted to Indian rupees, and a stiff commission paid before a stamp slams down in my passport. I bike alone across an ominous swath of no man's land only to find at Indian immigration that entering India with Indian rupees is also illegal. An appropriate bribe is negotiated, and I am on my way. Pedalling away through luxuriant forests, unknown India lies ahead.

Across this man-made, arbitrary line, everything is different. Instead of the ubiquitous *shalwar khamis*, the men here wear shorts and faded Western T-shirts. Their shaven faces and bare legs are a shock. A group of unveiled women, washing clothes in a roadside ditch, leap up and wave as I pedal by. With every passing kilometre the land grows lusher. Families work in the fields, harvesting wheat, driving oxen ahead of wooden plows, collecting damp dung that is plastered in geometric patterns against the outside walls of their homes to be dried and used as fuel.

While planning the bicycle trip in Canada, I had no interest in India itself; the country simply provided a route to the mountains of Nepal. Now I find myself absorbed. The country is ablaze with colour, saturated hues of red and orange: spices, chilies, bricks, and betel. A fiery sun sets over dusty plains. In busy markets garlands of marigolds are stacked shoulder-high and graceful women drift by in saris of crimson and gold.

In Amritsar, amidst the riotous fervour of colour and crowds, poverty is inescapable. Beggars lie on street corners, amputated, dirty, scarred, burned, or rotting. When I stop for a Coke, a shadowy woman comes to stand beside me. Her arm, a withered stick of skin and bone appears to have an extra joint, and extends like a crane toward me, her hand shaking a small tin cup. A tiny infant, its belly distended by malnutrition, is wrapped within her robes. A crowd of locals turns to watch my reaction.

I feel torn, and stare straight ahead. The woman cries louder. If I give her anything, beggars will materialize from all directions, each more insistent than the first. But how can I not give her a coin or two? At home I have been taught never to give money to panhandlers, better to buy them a coffee or sandwich, my mother advises. For almost ten minutes I try to ignore the beggar's presence, but I can sense her staring directly at me, noisy at times, silent otherwise. Finally, unable to withstand the pressure, I dig several rupees from my backpack. I stuff them in her can and then look up, smiling. The woman looks straight past me. One eye is solid white, opaque like a cooked egg. The other socket is hollow and raw. Flies crawl about the pink flesh.

From Amritsar I catch a night train to Delhi. Louts crowd the platforms of Central Station, following on my heels, striking up conversations, chasing off competition, and then returning to continue their story. Hands enter my pockets with such frequency that it is almost comical. I capture one wrist and raise an eyebrow at the perpetrator before releasing him. A dog, covered in blisters and sores, nips at the food in my backpack. I step over rows of sleeping bodies. Amidst the mayhem an animated platform vendor catches my attention, waving me toward a cart laden with metal urns and jars of coloured syrup. I glance at the hand-painted sign overhead, and decide there is no way I can explain to this poor gentleman the gravity of his spelling error, for he is advertising "Cum, Flavored Milk!"

And onward to Varanasi, where piles of tangled firewood sit beside funeral pyres that burn day and night. Cars wind through the crowded market streets with stiff bodies lashed across their roof racks like skis. Grieving is not private here; death not separate from life. I watch a foot and lower leg drop from one blaze, only to be tossed back in the flames without ceremony or callousness. Tourists rush past, paying one U.S. dollar to take a photograph. A father, shaking with grief, crouches over the body of his tiny baby, wrapped in white sheets and laid by the water's edge. While millions make an annual pilgrimage to bathe in the holy waters of the Ganges, thousands more come to die, for to pass away here carries the promise of *moksha* or enlightenment.

A week later I lie on the roof of a speeding bus destined for Kathmandu, having just confirmed a flight to Thailand for December. In the New Year I'll meet up with friends in Australia for a month of surfing and there are plans for biking in New Zealand after that. I watch monkeys swing from branches high overhead; the sun is warm on my shoulders and face. Crisp mountain air tussles my hair. We pass the border into Nepal and without realizing it, I reach down and adjust my watch to local time.

Immaculately hand-scripted on rice parchment, the following letter arrived in Canada a year after my return from travelling.

My Dear Kirkby,

Please recall your recent visit to Northern Pakistan and your stay at the Tourist Cottages, Gilgit. While leafing backwards in my diary, my sight met your name, and some inner force urged me to write you to say hello and know about your good health and well being of your family members.

For some moments you might have been left thinking who could be this strange writer. Well, I am Afrazullah Beg, your well wisher in Gilgit, where we delighted in exchanging news and views. From my stack of letters I retrieved your missive of March 1991, written after six months stormy travels. I do thankfully acknowledge you for your good impressions of your stay, and our after dinner table talk which I also equally enjoyed.

This card reminded me of your jovial, broad smile, and your ardent love of your illustrious mother. Your mum must have been very elated to have you at home after six months of separation. We, in our part of the world, highly esteem our mothers. It is a great bounty for children to have the warmth and love of motherly affection. If one can do anything good for his parents, it is here in this world, for we do not return this way again.

It has been said by sage people, "One time seeing is better than hundred times of hearing or reading." You are very fortunate to undertake such a long journey at such a tender age, which I am sure will be of immense value in your good years ahead. All I can advise you now is to press forward your further studies to widen up your horizons of thoughts.

Mr. Ali and Mr. Akbar send greetings, remembering you with dedication and respect. With my very profound regards, I combine my best wishes for your good health, prosperity, and a successful life,

AFRAZULLAH BEG

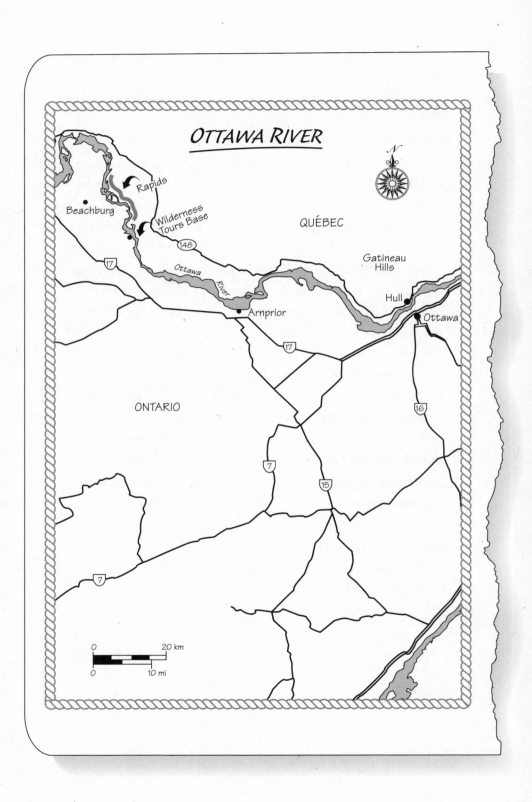

two

Escape from Engineering

BUNGEE JUMPING AND RAFT GUIDING

It came down to a choice between two lifestyles. One where I paid $500 per month rent for a noisy apartment, commuted an hour through traffic to work, punched in at a job I hated but kept only so one day I might retire so to enjoy a brief time pondering how I had wasted my one and only life. The alternative being this: a life of repose and adventure, of pretending that our time here is to be enjoyed and explored, of trout fishing whenever I am so inclined or sleeping in until the tipi glows warm with the morning sun, a lifestyle wherein my only chore is to breathe and my only hobby to witness the sun hurdle across the horizons and the moon be nibbled through its phases by that unseen mouse.

Robert P. Johnson, when asked why he chose to live alone in a tipi for a year, THIRTEEN MOONS: A YEAR IN THE WILDERNESS

Ottawa,
1991/92

EMPLOYMENT WAS NOT hard to find upon my return from Pakistan. A software development firm in Ottawa hired me within weeks. Only the seventh employee in a small consulting company, the heady atmosphere of growth and self-reliance lured me onward. Work was challenging; visions of future riches danced on the horizon; I was happy.

Everything about the professional existence was new and captivating. I had my own office, a sprawling desk, even a nameplate on the door. For the first time in my life I had voice mail to check and a leather Daytimer to fill. Clearly important things, for I felt myself swell with pride while attending to them. I was free to manage my own projects, with the unspoken expectation that I work long hours and bill the client for every one of them. Best of all, I was paid a staggering salary.

For the first time in my life, I had the freedom to buy things: a stereo, CDs, new cross-country skis, even an old pickup truck. Despite these extravagances, I maintained a relatively frugal existence. I shared a cheap downtown rental house with a university classmate, Shawn, and we furnished our home with milk crates and scraps of lumber. In need of suitable office attire, a trip to the Salvation Army produced five white shirts, ten ties, and a sports jacket, all for less than one hundred dollars. I was shocked to learn that a colleague, hired at the same time as I was, had purchased a four-thousand-dollar "Young Businessman's Wardrobe" at a tony downtown boutique. He would have to pay for his clothing through forty-eight monthly instalments. I instinctively stayed free of debt, avoiding a mortgage or car payments.

With no homework and lots of money, the days and months passed in a dizzy, exciting blur: long weekends, road trips, mountain biking in the nearby Gatineau Park, skiing, beers and wings, concerts, movies, dinners – basically the standard twentysomething existence. And then there was bungee jumping.

⁓

Shawn bursts through the front door of our house in downtown Ottawa, an enormous cardboard box in his arms.

"Check this out!" he yells, dropping to his knees and tearing open the lid.

I join Kolin and Jeff, two friends visiting from university, as they press close and peer in. Swirls of white elastic band fill the box to the rim, like a jumbled pot of overcooked spaghetti. Jeff kneels and runs his hands through the thin strands, stirring up clouds of chalk dust.

"Holy crap, that's a lot of elastic."

"Twelve kilometres in total," Shawn smiles. "The exact stuff that is sewn into the waistbands of women's underwear. Gentlemen, this is going to make us rich."

A month earlier my three engineering buddies had been on New Zealand's South Island, where they witnessed the exploding popularity of bungee jumping. Upon returning home and realizing there was nothing similar in Canada, they decided to start their own company.

"You've seen it yourself, Kirkby." Shawn gets excited whenever he talks about the project. "In Queenstown tourists are lining up for hours and paying one hundred dollars each, just for the chance to jump off an abandoned bridge with nothing but elastic cord attached to their ankles. There can't be many overhead costs. I think we've stumbled on a gold mine."

The few bungee companies already in existence around the world carefully guard their secrets. Bungee cords are simply not for sale, anywhere. There are no "how-to" manuals or training courses. In fact there is no public information at all, so experimentation is going to be required.

Shawn grabs the box and disappears into the basement, Kolin and Jeff in tow. For hours they work, weaving strands of thin elastic back and forth between two carabiners. Eventually they create a cord as thick as a baseball bat, fifteen hundred individual strands in total. Before dinner they allow me a sneak preview. The white worm they have constructed does not instill confidence. It looks like a floppy, springy, fraying firehose. I feel no inclination to jump off a bridge with it tied to my ankles.

That weekend, as dawn breaks over Eastern Ontario, a group of friends secretly gather at an abandoned railroad trestle. Kolin loads a backpack with weightlifting plates; thirty-six kilograms (80 pounds) in total. He throws in a few rocks for good measure. It's not even close to body weight, but he decides it will do. One end of the rubbery cord is lashed to the bridge railing, while the other is clipped to the heavy pack, which is then heaved up onto the railing with a clunk.

"Three . . . two . . . one . . ." Everyone tenses. ". . . Go."

The pack topples over the edge and for a few heart-stopping seconds it plummets. Then bit by bit the cord begins to stretch, and the pack slows. Eventually it stops, well before hitting the water, and then . . . boing! . . . it bounces back up, almost reaching the railing again. Boing, boing, boing. Finally the bouncing and swinging stops and the pack is lowered to Shawn's younger brother, who waits on the shore below. The cord is set up again. It is time for a human test pilot.

"OK. Who's first?" Shawn asks.

No one comes forward.

Jeff, who is sleeping in the back of the car, is nominated. Soon he appears, wide-eyed. There is silence as Shawn wraps a towel around Jeff's ankles to pad them. Next, a loop of webbing is run around the towel and cinched in a tight girth hitch, securing Jeff's ankles. The webbing is clipped to the bungee cord. Jeff hobbles to the bridge railing, and with help, clambers up. Shawn gently lowers the thick bungee cord so it hangs in a loop below. Weighing twenty kilograms (44 pounds), it tugs Jeff toward the edge. After a few deep breaths, Jeff asks for a count.

"Three . . . two . . . one . . . JUMP!" we yell in unison.

The water below is perfectly calm. Jeff bends his knees and launches forward, arms outstretched, a textbook swan dive. Thirty metres (110 feet) below him is a shallow river. All that is attached to his ankles, and keeping him safe, are fifteen hundred elastic cords, the waistband material of women's underwear.

The jump goes perfectly. Jeff shouts with exhilaration and pumps his arms in the air as he is lowered to the shoreline. Shawn volunteers to go next. And then Kolin. Excitement starts to build and a lineup forms.

Suddenly a siren echoes in the distance. Local residents have called the cops. We scramble toward the cars and pack up the ropes and cord quickly. The gathering dissolves.

Two days later. Monday morning. 5:45 a.m. Alarm buzzes. Hit the snooze button, hoping a few more minutes of sleep will help.

Shit. Slept for twenty! Stumble from bed into the shower. Tearing through my closet, I find my only remotely clean shirt lying crumpled on the floor. Sniff the armpits. *It'll have to do.* Stuffing a bagel in my mouth, I dash out the front door and run along crowded sidewalks. Don't see a red light and am almost hit by a taxi.

Through the revolving doors of my glass building, flash a security pass, then join a crowd waiting for the elevator. Waiting, waiting. Doors open. Crush to get in. Too many people. The doors can't shut. We shuffle closer. Okay, close enough. Going up. Staring at my feet. *Why don't people look at each other? Why don't I look at them? Why does no one talk?* Up, up . . . bing . . . Ninth Floor. Smile at the cute, new receptionist. Try to sneak past the boss's door.

"Mornin', Bruce. Good weekend?"

"Oh . . . yeah . . . pretty good, you know. And you?"

Slump into desk. Time check. 7:30 a.m. Made it. Another workday begins.

Every weekend during that summer I joined Shawn, Jeff, and Kolin as they travelled to different highway bridges across the province, covertly arriving in the early hours of the morning. A flurry of calls the evening before would ensure that a crowd of friends converged at the same location, all slightly nervous, nursing coffees, lining up to become human guinea pigs.

The trio quickly realized a length of climbing rope needed to be tied between the bridge railing and the bungee cord, to reduce bouncing. Through experimentation, they learned how to adjust this rope's length – taking into account the jumper's weight, the bridge height, and wind conditions – so that every jumper's fingertips just grazed the water below before they were yanked skyward.

No one was ignorant of the dangers, and the trio was meticulous about safety. Every piece of equipment was inspected and re-inspected. Protocols were established, old cords retired, and new cords produced. Despite these efforts, a simple miscommunication almost proved tragic.

When Jeff took a weekend off, Shawn and Kolin changed their routine, deciding to wrap the climbing rope around the bridge railing three times, and simply have the "jump-master" hold the loose end in his hand rather than tying it off. It made things faster, and with three wraps, there was almost no tension on the free end. When Jeff returned the following weekend, he missed this critical update.

To start the day, Shawn set up a rope for his own jump, and then asked Jeff to be the jump-master. Jeff secured Shawn's ankles, clipped him to the cord, helped him up to the railing, but he did not take hold of the loose rope end. Instead, he incorrectly assumed it was tied off. As Shawn jumped, and plunged from the bridge, a sickening sound of whistling rope echoed across the deck. Loops whirled around the railing, and Jeff instinctively slammed his hand down onto the spinning wraps. The rope stopped paying out. Shawn slowed, but still crashed hard into the water. After floundering around for a few seconds, he finally yelled up that he was fine. Only then did Jeff lift his hand from the rope, the palm burned through to the tendons.

Despite the accident they persevered, and as word of their guerilla operation spread, friends told distant friends, and soon strangers were driving from Toronto, Montreal, and farther, just for the chance to lob themselves off a bridge. With the arrival of autumn, Shawn calculated that the group had overseen more than three hundred jumps. Apart from Jeff's early season burn, their record was unblemished, and now there was talk of expanding the operation.

Throughout the summer, I had been leading a double life. The buoyant enthusiasm of bungee-jumping weekends was in stark contrast to the grey, lethargic languor that had seeped into my engineering office, along with a growing indifference. It was an insidious type of discontent, pervasive yet difficult to pinpoint, for the signs were relatively innocuous.

Though I was normally an early riser, prying myself from under the covers grew more difficult with each passing week. I dreaded the sound of my morning alarm. Soon I was arriving at work five minutes late, then ten; stumbling in with shaggy, wet hair dripping on my shoulders, unshaven. At my desk I felt constantly bored, visiting the drinking fountain often and staring absently out my cubicle window for hours. I tried drinking coffee, something I had never done before. For the first few days it gave me the shakes and made my heart race. Soon I "needed it," and was sucking it back by the gallon; morning, lunch, and afternoon.

My stomach rumbled constantly. It seemed no matter how much breakfast I ate, I was hungry by ten in the morning. My mind kept drifting to the lunch in my backpack, and inevitably I would pull it out for a "nibble." Minutes later I would glance down at the Tupperware, hoping for another bite, and realize both sandwiches were gone. Famished again by midday, I would devour a second greasy meal in the cafeteria.

Above all, I ached to be outside. The urge to move felt irresistible; to run and jump and swim, to carry heavy packs, to swing axes, it didn't matter what so long as I could huff and puff and sweat. I was twenty-three, and reasoned that thousands of years of evolution had prepared me to be active at this age, not to sit for hours at a time in front of a computer screen. Ironically, doing nothing made me feel perpetually exhausted. I looked at thickening co-workers, not much older than myself, with sunken eyes and resigned spirits, and felt a similar fate reaching toward me.

As fall descended on Ottawa, and battalions of tired government workers returned from summer vacation, Shawn approached a local rafting company with a proposal to open a bungee operation on their riverside property. Wilderness Tours expressed immediate interest, and with Kolin and Jeff back at university, Shawn suggested I tag along to the first meeting.

Rushing to a downtown bar in the ByWard Market after work, I found Shawn and a senior manager hunched over a mess of paper, beer pitchers, and wings. There was plenty to discuss, and Wilderness Tours wanted to move quickly. A competitor had opened on the West Coast, and there were fears other ventures might be underway closer to home. A tower needed to be constructed; safety procedures audited by a high-angle rescue expert. Securing insurance would be tricky. There would be staff to hire and train, and most importantly, advertising for the upcoming season needed to begin almost immediately. Within an hour, a preliminary deal was negotiated.

As he stood to leave, the manager turned his attention to me. "Hey Bruce, are you interested in guiding rafts for us this summer?" It was an afterthought, a polite nicety, but my heart skipped a beat. "We could use some help on the weekends. A training course starts in May. Do you want me to save you a spot?"

My first and only rafting adventure had taken place during high school, on the Ottawa River. At the time, our group's strong, tanned guide seemed almost superhuman. Every girl aboard our raft had fallen for him. Of course I wanted to be a guide!

"Sure!" I spluttered, not realizing how lucky I was to have the offer fall in my lap. Guiding positions at Wilderness Tours were limited, and every year reams of applications were received for just a handful of openings. Back at the office, my boss did not view the guiding opportunity with the same enthusiasm. My request for a two-week, unpaid leave of absence caused a major stir.

The sprawling grounds of Wilderness Tours's riverside resort lie silent and deserted. Green blades of spring grass are already poking up between fast-shrinking snow patches. Standing in the parking lot, along with nineteen other rookies, I feel like a child on the first day of summer camp, nauseating surges of anxiety, excitement, and nervousness welling up from within.

A gruff River Operations Manager begins barking out a military-style briefing. "No free rides here. You're gonna have to earn your keep by doing maintenance every morning. We'll start with a sweep of the grounds today. Pick up every single piece of trash you find, no matter how small. Cigarette butts. Bottle caps. Everything. I'm gonna check up on you later, so don't disappoint me. And don't be slow either, 'cause there are decks to stain, equipment to inventory, floors to mop, and a fence to build. Later in the week, if there is time, the buses will need a fresh coat of paint.

"Now, to the reason you are here, the river. Rain or shine, afternoons are gonna be spent on the water. But be warned. The runoff is huge this year, and rafts are going to flip. Be prepared to go swimming, and dress appropriately. The water is still freezing cold."

On my hands and knees, poking through the sodden ashes of last year's bonfire, looking for scraps of foil and glass, I am struck by the irony of the situation. This is crappy work and I am voluntarily here, not being paid a penny. Back in Ottawa, my friends who are programming computers will make two hundred dollars today. Yet there is not a moment's doubt where I'd rather be.

After a lunch of hot dogs and pop, a rickety school bus shuttles us twenty-five kilometres (15 miles) upriver. With sunshine warming our backs, we haul two heavy black rubber rafts to the water's edge and pump them up. Nondescript life jackets and helmets are handed out, the same stuff that is provided to guests or "Gorbys." (Good Old Rafting Buddies is the source of this acronym, a derogatory term widely used within guiding circles, typically to refer to guests who have no clue what is going on.) After squeezing into wetsuits, we tentatively clamber aboard.

Two senior guides accompany us, wearing sun-bleached clothes that reek of experience. Ian Stibbe and "Rougie" also carry complicated-looking safety equipment, and neither of them says much. They just grunt and point. Basically they are cool, and they know it. Every one of the rookies, myself included, wants to be like them.

The first few kilometres of river pass lazily, the waters wide and slow. Eventually we enter a labyrinthine maze of narrow channels and congested islands, where a growing current whisks the rafts along. Anticipation builds. Soon a rumble can be heard. Swinging around a corner, we can see the river ahead disappear over a blind drop, mist rising from below.

"Little Trickle!" Ian shouts over the roar. "Pull over. We need to scout this drop."

Paddling furiously, we claw our way into an eddy. After tying the rafts to an old pine, our group scrambles along the shoreline, gathering at a point where the dark waters of the Ottawa River plow over a ledge and enter a confusion of rocks, waves, and spray.

Now the real education begins. Yelling to make themselves heard, the senior guides carefully describe every feature we are seeing – holes, reactionary waves, tongues, eddies, and haystacks. They explain how each will affect our raft – slowing it, turning it, stalling it, flipping it. Next they detail the "line" we need to take in order to pass safely through, at the same time emphasizing that we should not simply memorize the route. "These rapids will change at every water level. The goal is to understand what you are seeing on the water, so that in time you can make your own decisions and navigate any obstacle you find yourselves facing."

I stare at the frothing rapids, trying to break the run down, but the tumult is overwhelming. The ground beneath me shakes, and I imagine myself falling from the raft to become flotsam, pummelled by the drop. As we head back upstream to the rafts in silence, butterflies flutter in my stomach.

Two trainees are assigned as "paddle captains," to sit at the stern of the two boats and steer a course through the rapid, using their paddles as rudders. They will also coordinate the crew by shouting commands such as "Forward!" "Back!" and "Ease off!" I am relieved not to be chosen for this first test.

Life jackets are double-checked for tightness and the bowline painters coiled. With a heave, the heavy boats drift from shore and I brace myself, sitting low, gripping my paddle tightly. There is no turning back now. Earlier Ian had pointed to a small curling wave on the lip of the drop. "You want the right-hand tube of your raft to run over that wave. That will put you in the perfect position for what lies hidden below."

We had all stared intently at the wave from shore, memorizing its position, but viewed from the raft the rapids look completely different. Where has the wave gone? Precious time slips by.

Suddenly we spot the curler, far to our right. The paddle captain screams a command, but I can't hear a word she says. Everyone begins paddling hard. We reach the wave, but have too much momentum and overshoot it, slamming into a midstream boulder. Spinning, we are drawn over the steep drop, backward.

Bodies fly about the boat. I glance down and see the paddle captain on the rubber floor beside me. Rocks scrape past the tubes, waves crash over us. I have no concept of where we are in the rapid. The boat is facing downstream, then upstream. Then it is over. We are spit out into a calm pool at the bottom. Counting heads, we are missing two but they are soon spotted, floundering in the water beside us, gasping and laughing.

All afternoon we do the same thing, over and over: stop to scout a drop, discuss our plan, and then run it. Everyone has a chance at the helm. There are plenty of mistakes – a raft flips, a shoulder is dislocated. The next day we try it all over again.

My early attempts at guiding the raft are marked by confusion. No matter how long I stare at the rapid beforehand, I always lose my orientation as the rubber boat is tossed by the first waves. *Where are we? Is this the wave where I need to turn? Or have we already passed it? Shit, why are we sideways? Was that a rock we hit?* There is no hint of grace, control, or finesse. As the raft bounces through the whitewater, often my only focus is on staying aboard.

With time the raft's path through the whitewater begins to slow in my mind. I develop the ability to distinguish between individual waves as we slam through them, and can maintain an understanding of the boat's position in the fray. Eventually I am able to anticipate the raft's reaction to approaching features and adjust its course accordingly. Ignorance and fear are slowly replaced by confidence in my abilities, and an ever-growing respect for the river.

Ten rafts sit by the water's edge. Mist slowly drifts downriver, winding through shoreline trees. Cool air nips at my fingers as I double-check my bowline and lash safety gear aboard. I am nervous. Today, for the first time, there will be no senior guide sitting beside me at the rear of the raft. No one to offer suggestions or help out in case of trouble. I alone will steer the twenty-two-foot rubber raft, carrying a group of complete strangers.

A convoy of dilapidated yellow buses bounces down the dusty road. Throngs of wet-suit-clad guests pile off, laughing and shouting, streaming toward the waiting rafts. The trip leader conducts a quick safety briefing, laced with bawdy humour, and then all ten rafts float from shore. My crew of middle-aged softball players is so intent on starting a water fight with another boat that they hardly ask my name, which is fine by me. Twenty minutes later, as we approach the first rapid, my jitters begin to fade. Concentration wipes all other thoughts aside. *You know this run like the back of your hand. Start wide. Aim for the third breaking wave. Straighten up before the hole.*

Although I navigate a textbook line, one of my guests is flipped overboard at the very first wave, her body instantly disappearing, swallowed by a large hole. Holes, or reversals, form when water flows over a sharp drop, and they can vary tremendously in size and strength. A large hole can flip an expedition raft and tear it to shreds, a small one may go unnoticed under the boat's floor. A "swimmer" – the rafting industry's term for a person thrown overboard – will occasionally be caught in a large hole and thrashed around, head over heels, a situation akin to being inside a washing machine, irreverently dubbed "Maytagging."

I leap to my feet and anxiously scan the waters. *Where is the woman? Why hasn't she popped up?* Each passing second feels like an eternity. The raft drifts onward. More waves are approaching. I begin to panic. Jumping up and down, I signal my worries to a safety kayaker, waiting in a shoreline eddy. The experienced paddler looks at me blankly, and then shakes his head in disgust, pointing to my feet. Just then I feel something through the raft's thin floor. Moments later a spluttering figure emerges. She had been drifting along hidden underneath, a normal result of falling out. My relief is immense.

That summer flowed blissfully by. I was addicted to the river. When I was not on it, I was daydreaming about it, counting the days or hours until I would be back on its shores. Fridays never came soon enough. When they did, I always slipped away from work early, cramming my pickup with paddling gear then heading north, windows down and a smile on my face.

I bought a whitewater kayak and started at the bottom of the learning curve all over again. The little boat manoeuvred like a race car compared to the tank-like rafts I was used to. Even tiny riffles and waves affected its course. On my first run, I fell out and swam through every rapid on the river. My roll was inconsistent at best, and it seemed I spent half my time upside down. I loved every second of it.

The first moment that I surfed a wave – managing to perch my kayak on its face, in a position where the force of gravity pulling downward was perfectly balanced by the current rushing upward – a new world opened before me. I didn't know what was going to happen, I was just copying what I had seen others do, but as the kayak found equilibrium, gently carving on the smooth face, all worries faded. The river rushed underneath me, but made no sound. A feeling of grace and ease passed over me. For just an instant, I was part of the river.

Seconds later I was slammed upside down and torn from my boat, but in that fleeting glimpse, I came to understand the addiction that causes a tribe of men and women to wander the globe, spending their lives in pursuit of such a ride.

As the months passed, my skills in the raft also continued to grow, although a humbling parade of mistakes kept me constantly aware of how much remained to be learned. Early in the season I was fiddling with a guest's life jacket above the biggest rapid on the river when my raft was drawn from shore without my realizing it. With only half my crew aboard, we bumped through the gauntlet backward, lucky not to flip.

Another time I fell out of the bouncing raft at the start of a huge drop. Everyone in the boat was facing forward, paddling for all they were worth, and although I swam madly after them, I could not catch up. I hollered at the top of my lungs, but the rudderless raft quickly left me behind, without any of the guests realizing that I was gone. Rescued by a safety kayaker, I was hauled ashore and reunited with my surprised crew far downstream, head hung low.

And then it was over. Fall colours streaked the forests of the Ottawa Valley. The number of guests arriving each weekend dwindled. Wilderness Tours packed away their rafts. I enjoyed a few last kayak runs down the deserted river, and drove back to Ottawa, the guiding days done.

At work I found myself constantly daydreaming of the crisp river mornings. I missed the camaraderie and jocularity of the guides. I yearned for the peaceful, worry-free times, living from dawn till dusk in shorts and sandals, lying shirtless on sun-warmed rocks, the smell of pine pitch and baked earth in the air, staring aimlessly into the deep blue of the afternoon sky.

Computer programming was tediously boring by comparison, but I was reluctant to quit my job simply because I didn't like it. I had done that once before, to go to Pakistan. Once again I felt conscience and societal expectations pulling me toward a career, a house, family, and retirement. But what about the interim? What if I do not enjoy the life that all this scaffolding is meant to support?

Although I was quickly becoming proficient in programming C++, and had just built an integrated work management system, could I light a fire in the rain? Which was a more important skill? Could I survive in the wild? Harvest enough food to last a winter? Butcher and preserve the meat of a deer? Watch the skies and understand the weather patterns? Weren't these fundamental life skills? I knew I was getting soft.

Like most children who grew up under the spectre of the Cold War, buried somewhere in my psyche was the need to plan for the survival of Armageddon. The vast and undeveloped Canadian northlands lured me, offering the perfect escape, far from the heavily targeted cities of America. For years I had half-jokingly claimed that if the worst ever unfolded I would commandeer a vehicle, grab an axe, a gun, and my girlfriend, and head north. Now I found myself wondering if I could survive once I got there.

As all these struggles clouded my thoughts, one simple truth lay at their core: I knew I could be happier. I was trading my time for money, and it was an exchange I was no longer willing to make.

With no plan for the future, I quit.

Using two-by-fours, sheets of plywood, and Plexiglas for windows, I built a camper on the back of my pickup. There was a sleeping berth on top, and room to pack gear underneath. After tarring the roof to make it waterproof, I painted a gruesome skull and crossbones over the cab. My mother was appalled, and in an attempt to appease her, I covered the symbol with the word *SKI*. My sister adorned the whitewashed caravan with doodles and cartoons. Then I packed what I could inside. Kayak and skis were lashed to the roof, my bicycles suspended from the front bumper. Everything else was left behind. Whoever moved into that rental home found a bed, dresser, and desk waiting for them.

My co-workers gathered for a farewell party, staring in disbelief at the ungainly vehicle. Using a thick black marker, they scribbled messages of luck along the sides. "Blue skies and tailwinds all the way," wrote my boss.

With that I was gone. Westward.

MY BABY DON'T LOVE NO ENGINEER
by J.T., SC191

CHORUS

My baby don'd love
No engineer
that's why she ain't here
So I'm headin' on down
To 'OL CLARK HALL
WHERE THE BOYS
SWILLIN' BEER
there AIN'T NO USE IN TRYING
TO KEEP HER LOVE FROM DYIN
HERE'S THE NEWS,
I GOT THE BLUES.
MY BABY DON'T LOVE NO ENGINEER

Her Daddy he a told her
when she was just ten years old
whatever you do my do
My darling stay away
from a man
whose leather is bad
He'll do you wrong
he'll make the blues your favorite song
here's the news
I got the blues
MY BABY DON'T LOVE NO ENGINEER

German / blred with from Greenmonth to Hirakson?
→ in Hamilton F13/1c Rd 2 RD
MARTIN GRAB
141 PROPSTHOF 111 Centura Agriculture
D-53x Box Center Horticulture HAMILTON, NZ
Germany HAMILTON, NZ
1

- pick up mail
- write to Chronicle
- look for a flat
- photo booth
- shampoo
- buy mattress
- 3 sets shirts
- call Steve on ...
- call Allan on ...
- washing

Mary Barbra's Brother
John? Catherine Spencer
Les Cresaunt (?5)
Brawford
Helen: Selby Spencer
77 avocet St Hamilton
ph 064 68 368

"Mary Barbra's something?
Selby Spencer
77 avocet St Hamilton
85

1ID in Brisbane

fastPOST
PAR AVION

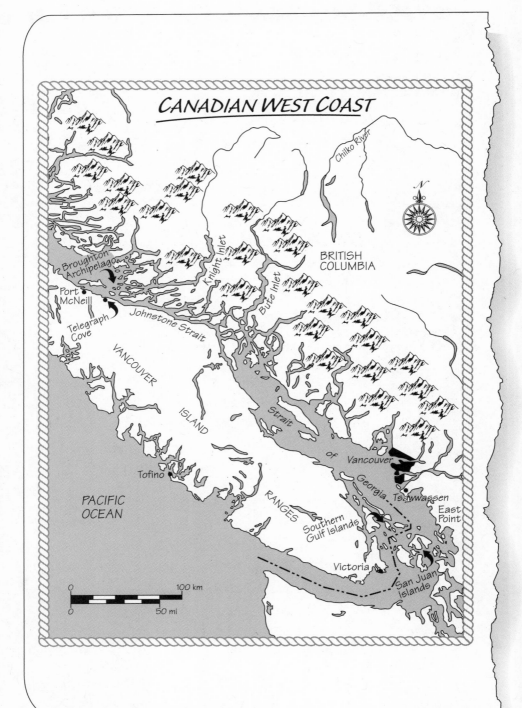

CANADIAN WEST COAST

Chilko River

BRITISH
COLUMBIA

N

Broughton
Archipelago

Knight Inlet

Bute Inlet

Port
McNeill

Telegraph
Cove

Johnstone Strait

VANCOUVER

ISLAND

Strait

of

Georgia

Vancouver

Tsawwassen

East
Point

Tofino

RANGES

Southern
Gulf Islands

PACIFIC
OCEAN

Victoria

San Juan
Islands

0   100 km
0   50 mi

three

Un-Natural History

A SUMMER OF SEA KAYAKING

When you jump over the edge, you are bound to land somewhere.

D.H. Lawrence

Canadian West Coast, 1993

MIST STEALS THROUGH the deserted streets of Vancouver's trendy Granville Island. Rows of yachts yaw gently in the harbour, and two sluggish workers prepare for the day, hauling away dew-laden tarpaulins that cover market stalls. I shiver and pull my thin fleece close.

Ten aspiring guides have gathered in the grey light of predawn, each hoping to secure a summer job with a local sea-kayaking outfitter. After a five-day training course, only one will be hired. We eye each other warily, feigning friendliness, sizing up the competition. Duffel bags are lashed to the roof of a large white passenger van, and then the group piles aboard. Long before rush hour traffic starts to build, we are speeding off, down grey streets, past grey buildings, toward the ferry terminal at Tsawwassen, and from there on toward the nearby Gulf Islands.

Driving the van is Jim Allan, the owner of Ecosummer Expeditions. Toweringly tall and built like a linebacker, Jim is one of the pioneers of the Canadian sea-kayaking industry. Black, wavy hair hangs to his shoulders. Jim's hazel eyes have already been noticeably bleached by years in the sun, although he is only in his forties.

The would-be guides packed in the back of the van begin a tentative round of introductions, and one attempts to include Jim. "Hey Jim, Ecosummer sure is a great name for your company. You must be pretty stoked. I think it is the best of any on the coast."

Jim turns and glares back. There is a momentary, uncomfortable silence. "Everything is goddamn 'Eco' these days," he finally grumbles. "Eco-this and Eco-that. Back in the seventies, I picked it as an acronym: *Education* and *Challenge* in the *Outdoors*. Makes me sick to see it so popular now. If I had my way, I'd change it. The last thing I want to do is seem trendy."

A tough-as-nails adventurer with a wildlife biology background, Jim established Ecosummer Expeditions as a means of introducing high-school students to the world of coastal ecology. The school programs were a success, but more significantly, Jim noticed an extraordinary number of parents volunteering to accompany their children on the journeys, and expanded his operations to include commercial trips. In the space of one summer a successful business was born. In the years since he has organized and undertaken a formidable series of trips – sea-kayaking expeditions to Tonga and Greenland, dog-sledding odysseys across the High Arctic, and a traverse of Belize's Maya Mountains. As Jim begins to grill the group on their background, I sit silently in the back row, hoping to avoid notice. Amongst the group of hopeful guides, I am by far the least experienced.

After driving away from my engineering job in Ottawa, I spent the winter near Nelson, British Columbia, sharing a backwoods cabin with five others. It was a simple existence, centred on skiing. None of us had much money, so we brewed our own beer in the basement, gathered firewood from clear cuts, and even created a sauna in a nearby abandoned bus. Shortly after my arrival, one of my housemates dragged home the carcass of a deer – road-kill. Although I was initially shocked, we ate its meat all winter, along with other cheap staples; bok choy, noodle soup, and oatmeal.

A trip to the local dump produced a pair of discarded downhill skis and some flimsy leather telemark boots. Using plastic cuffs, duct tape, and wire I managed to reinforce the boots, and with the addition of a pair of second-hand bindings, I had a workable backcountry rig. Day after day I followed more experienced skiers though forested valleys and up nearby peaks, searching for powder, spending most of my time tumbling hopelessly downhill.

It was a heady time. Everything I encountered was new, and I only wanted more; more experience, more skills, more knowledge. I sensed new worlds waiting beyond the horizon, and I wanted things I could not yet imagine. The word "No" was not part of my vocabulary.

One crisp morning, as our group clambered up a ridge, we abruptly broke through mists into sunlight. I stood transfixed. Soft, puffy clouds filled the valleys below. Above rose ice-rimed rock. In the distance another long fin of jagged peaks arched up through the clouds like the backbone of a whale. I had entered a world I had seen only in glossy magazines. That moment alone was enough to justify quitting my job.

As spring slowly warmed the mountains and the alpine snowfields began to shrink, I moved on to the coast. Living in an aunt's basement, I bided my time by picking up a sales job at a camping goods store, remaining determined to find a job in the outdoors. It didn't take long to notice a display of glossy sea-kayaking brochures sitting beside the cash register. The sport had enjoyed a recent explosion of popularity on the coast, and fifty-three outfitters were clambering for business. One of them must need a guide, I reasoned, and despite never having been in a sea kayak before, I called every outfitter represented in that store-front rack.

My inexperience proved an almost insurmountable handicap. With hundreds of other eager applicants, no one was interested in a newbie without ocean skills. The only glimmer of hope came from Ecosummer Expeditions; but there was a hitch. To be considered, I first had to take their sea-kayaking leadership course, offered at the astronomical fee of six hundred dollars. And even then, only one of the ten participants would be hired as a guide. The office manager seemed optimistic about my chances, but I suspected she was just trying to fill the course. With no other options, I signed up as soon as my next paycheque arrived.

⁘

"Who wants to keep the official bird list for our trip?" Jim interrupts the back-seat ruckus, and our group falls silent.

Bird list? I have no idea what Jim is talking about, but around me nine hands shoot into the air. *I can't believe it. What a bunch of brown-nosers!*

I thought this was a sea-kayaking leadership course, not some bird outing. Do they actually care about identifying birds, or are they trying to kiss Jim's ass? I choose to keep my hand in my lap, and some excited eager beaver on the front bench gets the job.

"You should get in the habit of keeping your own personal bird-list whenever you're in the field. It's a great way to learn," Jim continues. "Natural history interpretation. That's what these trips are all about. Every one of my senior guides is an expert. You'll need to be one too if you want to stick around."

I don't know what he means by "natural history," and begin to sense the other participants are more in tune with Jim's interests. Although I feel a mild twinge of inadequacy, birding seems beside the point. I have come to learn the fundamentals of sea kayaking, to discuss leadership, safety, and navigation. I am eager to immerse myself in maps of the region, study tide charts, practise rescues, attempt surf landings, and plan emergency strategies. I will happily leave the birding to the others.

Jim returns his attention to the road, but I am saddled with a niggling suspicion that he noted my lack of interest and disapproved. As we race past fields of cranberries en route to the ferry terminal, bird names begin flying around the van at a dizzying speed. It seems everyone wants to impress Jim by recounting exotic species they have once seen. I don't recognize any of the names.

Several hours later, I approach Jim on the deck of the ferry, confused by the expression he used.

"In the van you said something about 'natural history.' What is that?" I ask sheepishly, my engineering studies never exposing me to the subject. "I haven't heard the term before."

"What?" Jim stares at me in disbelief. "You're joking, right?" It will be the only time I see him at a loss for words. After a long pause, he draws breath. "It is the study of everything to do with the ecosystem . . . animal life, plant life, geology, weather patterns. How can you possibly have never heard of it before?"

"I understand the 'natural' part, but why is the word 'history' in there?" I continue digging myself deeper. "The two just seem an odd combination. I mean, is there such a thing as 'Un-natural History'?"

"No!" Jim runs his hands through his hair in exasperation.

Then his thoughts are interrupted, and his gaze sweeps out to sea as he raises his binoculars. "See those?" he says after a pause, pointing to a line of small black birds skimming along ahead of the ferry, just above the water. "Pigeon guillemots." Jim carries on talking without lowering his binoculars. "You see lots of them on the coast at this time of year. They're nesting."

The guillemots turn and streak past us. With a flurry of high-pitched calls, they slow, extend tiny webbed red feet, and come to a splashy, water-ski-style landing. Almost instantly the group disappears beneath the dark water.

"Members of the Alcid family. That means they use their wings to fly underwater," Jim notes as he lowers the binoculars and strolls off to join the rest of the group.

What? Birds flying underwater?

I linger, waiting for the birds to reappear, and soon spot them bobbing along behind the ferry. Half an hour later, as we enter the narrow channel of Active Pass, more pigeon guillemots whisk by, their small wings beating rapidly, chirps echoing from the rocky shores. I am surprised I recognize them, and feel a twinge of pride. I never would have noticed the birds before.

❦

The Gulf Islands are a cluster of over two hundred tranquil and pastoral islets, tucked into the southwestern reaches of the Strait of Georgia, in the lee of Vancouver Island. Sheltered from the storms of the open Pacific, the islands bask in a mild, Mediterranean-style climate, the driest zone along Canada's entire west coast. Vancouver's moisture-laden North Shore, only sixty kilometres (40 miles) away and clearly visible across the Strait, receives double the precipitation.

(Above) *"The Confluence" of the Tatshenshini and Alsek rivers, at midnight on summer solstice, where* **(right)** *four great valleys meet in the heart of the St. Elias Mountains, forming a natural cross. During my first three summers of northern guiding, I spent two hundred days on the Tatshenshini, and it was while lying cruciform on these gravel flats that a deeper understanding and appreciation of true wilderness began seeping into me.*

(Top Left) *Eagerly testing brand-new gear in the family back garden before departure for the Karakoram Highway.*

(Top Right) *Heading westward after quitting my engineering job. This rusty pickup and homemade canopy were my home for years.*

(Above) *Kathmandu street scene, 1990, on first journey abroad.*

(Left) *A decorated bus on the Karakoram Highway, northern Pakistan.*

Early Days

(Opposite) *Guiding sea kayaks on the Canadian West Coast provided my first exposure to natural history. An early morning view from the cockpit; camera case and coffee mug rigged on deck.*

Tatshenshini

(Above) *Rafts moored at Confluence camp, during my first northern guiding season.*

(Left) *A six-metre (18-foot) expedition raft is dwarfed before the toe of a glacier calving into Alsek Lake.*

(Main) *An arctic tern protects its nest by attacking a photographer who has crawled too close.*

(Below Left) *Sun slowly sets on the Alsek Range.*

(Below Right) *The first frosts of August have brought colour to a grove of fireweed, growing amongst riverside poplar.*

River

(Main) *Sea kayaks anchored on shallow flats atop barrier reef.*

(Below Left) *Pappy, a Garifuna fisherman who accompanied our trips, with the kayaks on Glovers Reef Atoll.*

(Below Right) *Jonesy, the legendary Carib hunter and jungle guide.*

Belize

(Above) *Exploratory descent of Soldier Creek.*

(Right) *A mating pair of osprey that often shared tiny Manta Ray Cay with our guided groups.*

(Following Page)
Mt. Everest base camp, with the west shoulder and lower Khumbu Icefall illuminated by moonlight. Karsang's operation took place in the red-and-white dome tent.

Here one finds thick stands of Douglas fir soaring above sandstone cliffs. Arbutus and Garry oak – distinctly southern trees – dot grassy headlands. Prickly pear cacti grow amidst south-facing outcrops, and sandy beaches fill quiet bays. In the shallow channels woven between islands, continual tidal flushing creates the perfect environment for marine growth. Warm, nutrient-rich waters bring schools of fish and vast numbers of seabirds and waterfowl. In turn this abundance brings larger predators; harbour seals, stellar sea lions, and pods of orcas, all of which forage in the islands' sanctuary.

It is misty and cool when we arrive on Mayne Island, just before noon. Only three other vehicles bump off the ferry with us, and we follow them through Miners Bay, a town of a dozen rustic shops, before veering away and heading across the island to a farm where Jim's kayaks are stashed. Tents, stoves, food bags, rescue gear, and our duffels of clothing are dragged from the van and heaped in a daunting pile on the beach. Our first job is to pack the boats, which appears impossible. After only a few terse words of instruction, Jim leaves.

Dropping to our knees, we begin to haphazardly cram, shove, and stuff gear in the narrow hatches. Quickly space starts to get tight. Before long nothing more will fit, and we have hardly made a dent on the gear piles. Craning our necks and peering awkwardly in the holds, we struggle hopelessly to jam in just one more bag, tearing skin from knuckles and cursing. No one knows what to do next, and we argue amongst ourselves while rearranging the loads but making little progress.

Jim returns after half an hour, clearly disappointed that we have not done better. "There's lots of room in the cockpits," he snaps. "Try packing stuff behind the seat backs, and in the spaces beside them. Waterproof bags can be lashed on the decks. The really big stuff – water jugs, stoves, the pot set – these will have to squeeze in between people's legs."

We continue cramming, shoving, and stuffing. Eventually everything is aboard and Jim gives a brief safety talk. Then we lug the heavy boats to the water's edge, climb in, and tentatively paddle away. Jim is quickly out in front, and the group gravitates after him. A few of the more experienced paddlers pepper him with questions. "Do you prefer feathered paddles, or straight ones? What percentage of your stroke's power comes from trunk rotation, and what percentage from the arms?"

"Just put the damn thing in the water in front of you and pull it behind you," Jim yells back. "Sea kayaks are a means to explore the coastline. Nothing more. Don't get caught up in silly little details."

Despite gusty winds and turbulent waves, Jim hugs the rocky shoreline. Mats of sea stars cling to nearly every boulder. Edging nearer, Jim plucks one from a crack and flips it over, holding it out to us, upside down. "Purple Ochre stars. You'll find them everywhere."

"Sea stars operate on an internal hydraulic system," he explains after a pause, running a finger along one of the rays, suddenly seeming less crusty. As he does, hundreds of tiny, translucent tube feet reach up, flare, and retract like miniature periscopes. "When the sea star wraps its arms around a mussel, it can keep pulling and pulling, almost indefinitely, because when one foot gets tired, another takes over. Eventually the mussel will tire and open, just a crack, but this is all the sea star needs. It'll push its stomach out and digest the mussel right in its own shell."

We pass the sea star around. I expect it to be soft and jelly-like, but instead it is stiff and hard. Before continuing on, Jim carefully places it back in the crack where he found it.

Within the first half-hour Jim has talked about the growth rates of bull kelp, the mating rituals of bald eagles, the politics of oyster and salmon farming on the coast, and the evolution of harbour seals. He points out colonies of aggregating anemones, a bright California sea cucumber, and several spiny urchins. We taste different seaweeds he pulls from the surface – rock kelp, red laver, and bright green sea lettuce – and Jim describes how to use them in salads and other meals.

After pausing to watch a pair of Harlequin ducks scoot through the chop ahead of us, Jim spots something on the bottom of a sandy bay. "Sunflower star," he yells out as he lands, rolling up his pants and wading out into the cold waters. Using a paddle, he carefully lifts the large star and brings it over to show us. It is thirty centimetres (12 inches) across, and has more than twenty soft, slimy arms which droop from Jim's hand like goo. The flesh is a bright orange-red, almost iridescent in intensity.

"These can get pretty big, up to a metre (3 feet) across," Jim explains as he flips the soft star over onto its back like a pancake, gently placing it upside down on the deck of a kayak. The entire underside is a moving sea of tube feet, perhaps as many as fifteen thousand. Gradually one side of the upside-down star begins reaching upward, soft arms quivering in the air, stretching even higher. Then with a sudden flop, the star folds in half and gently slides right-side up. "If they couldn't do that, they'd be as good as dead if a storm or predator flipped them over," Jim notes as he returns the star to the bottom.

Grey skies darken and a steady drizzle settles in as we stop for the night at the Belle Chain Islets, a long, narrow stretch of eroded sandstone rising from Georgia Strait, just offshore of Samuel Island. Windswept and barren, the outcroppings are tufted with dried grasses. A sprinkling of weathered and gnarled firs rises in the centre. After unloading the heaviest equipment – water jugs, sacks of food, and a tank of propane – we struggle to heave the double-fibreglass kayaks up a steep, rocky embankment to a point above the high-tide mark. Tents are erected and piles of food set out.

Jim suggests we pair off. "There are ten of you, and five nights. A different group can cook every night. Veggie chili is on the menu for tonight. You'll find everything you need in the bag marked 'Dinner 1.'"

As partnerships form Jim disappears to investigate an eagle's nest at the far end of the islet. There are no further instructions, and apparently no recipe. The first two volunteers are left staring at a pile of fresh vegetables, cans, and dry goods.

"Why hold students' hands all the time?" Jim explains to me later. "They are perfectly capable of figuring things out on their own. And it is better for them."

The cooks cobble together a fine, although slightly burnt dinner, and as we huddle underneath a tarpaulin to eat, Jim outlines his plan for the week. Each day a new pair will be assigned the task of leading the group, with only the travel objectives to guide them. Every decision will be up to the student leaders, and Jim pledges to step in only if safety becomes an issue. "You'll have to manage the group and deal with whatever sea conditions arise. It's pseudo-leadership, as close as you can get to the real thing. If nothing else, I want you to go home with an understanding of what it is like to actually lead a group in the wild."

I end up partnered with red-headed, freckled Scott, a real keener who is clearly Jim's favourite. Solidly built, Scott is the son of an Ontario undertaker, and hopes to do anything in life but take over the family business. I like him, for he is clearly competent, but find his eagerness off-putting. I tell him I'm interested in photography. He confides he has already arranged to sell his prints at Jim's store. I mention I guided rafts for a season. He has been doing the same for five years, all over the country. I admit I am not particularly interested in birds. He tells me he is planning to write a bird identification handbook, creating the index not by family, but by wing movements during flight. "It is absurd no one has done this yet," he spouts. "What could be an easier way to pick out different species? Some flap once and rest, some flap twice, others beat constantly. Wing-beat patterns are very distinctive."

"That's nice," I nod, tuning out to the sounds of my Walkman.

The next day our group paddles along the arrow-straight northern shore of Saturna Island, working our way toward the haven of Cabbage Island. I am thankful Scott and I are not put in charge, for the leaders have all types of problems. *How close should we stay to shore? When should we have lunch?* By noon everyone is hungry, but steep slabs make it impossible to land. *Should we pass around a snack? Where are the snacks? Are they accessible?* On and on it goes. What should be simple proves confounding. Jim watches, but says nothing. Apart from an hour-long explanation of tides and currents, he is silent all day. In camp he notes only that leading a group is harder than it looks.

The planning of the second day falls to Scott and me, and it is getting dark by the time we finish dinner and start looking at the maps. East Point lies ahead, a thin, rocky promontory protruding far into the open waters of Georgia Strait. The charts indicate that powerful currents and tidal rips form along this headland, building four times a day – twice as tide waters race in and twice as they ebb back out to sea. Scott and I agree we should try to pass the headland at slack water, just as the tide turns. Studying the charts, we find a period of slack falls conveniently at 11:15 in the morning, giving us plenty of time to cook breakfast, pack the boats, and be on the water.

As we begin to fold up the charts, Jim ambles over. "What's your plan?" We explain, and watch for Jim's reaction, but he betrays not a hint of a smile or a frown.

"Does that make sense?" I finally ask.

"Well, it's not what I would do."

After a long silence Jim uncharacteristically offers some advice. "East Point is dangerous. Sheer limestone cliffs line the opposite shoreline, and there is not a single landing for three kilometres." Then he points to the chart. "All this open water nearby means that big waves are common. Do you know why this is significant?"

We stare at the chart but remain silent.

"Because of the strong currents," Jim finally explains. "Waves coupled with current can be a deadly mix. When current flows with waves, it flattens them deceptively. But when it flows against them, the waves will rear up and start breaking. Given the wrong conditions, calm seas at East Point can suddenly leap into a mess of whitecaps when the tide turns."

Scott and I stare at the maps, wondering how to change our plan, but Jim is not done. "It gets worse. Waves and cliffs are also a bad combination. Swells rebound and head back out to sea, where they slam into the oncoming waves, doubling in height and exploding upward."

"So, you think we should change our plan?" I ask.

"You are free to do what you want tomorrow, but I do think you should be cautious. In 1983, a sea kayaker died off East Point, and just last year a kayak on one of my trips capsized. That boat sank, and the occupants were slammed into the cliffs. They lived, but that guide is not around any more." With that Jim wanders off to his tent.

Shit. Scott and I stare at each other. What can we do differently? After going over the charts and tide tables again, we note there is an earlier period of slack water, at 5:15 in the morning. Will it be light enough to paddle then? Neither of us knows. What are the advantages of leaving early? If we arrive to find that conditions are unfavourable, we can wait six hours for the next slack tide and hope things improve. Also, the ebbing current following the early slack will help speed us past the cliffs. Reluctantly we agree the safer option is trying to pass East Point at 5:15. Working backward, that means being on the water no later than 4:45, and rising at four.

"Are you serious?" the group moans when we tell them our plans.

"Do you think it will be dangerous paddling in the dark?" Jim asks.

I feel my confidence in our decision erode, but rather than vacillate, we suggest that the group will stay close together on the water and wear headlights. Jim says nothing else.

A flashing lighthouse guides us across dark waters, toward East Point. We reach the end of the long promontory just as the soft luminescence of dawn begins to light the sky. The waters are glassy calm, and there is not a whisper of current, so Scott and I decide to keep going. We paddle in silence, past towering limestone walls etched by waves and wind. Soon a gentle rain settles in, and while Scott takes the lead position, I drop back to sweep. Lingering beside Jim, I ask about our decision.

"It is not a case of right or wrong, but I would have left early too. It might not seem like much, but it always gives more options." I am about to ask more, but Jim is already pointing to a colony of pelagic cormorants that caw noisily as we pass.

"Can you see them holding their wings out?" he yells forward to the group. "Cormorants have no oil on their feathers, which makes them great underwater swimmers. The downside is that after coming up, they have to dry their feathers before they can fly again."

A short time later we pass a cove, and Jim notices telltale streaks of guano on a distant wall. A peregrine falcon has nested on the cliffs above. The others eagerly follow Jim into the bay for a closer look, but I dawdle behind, not interested in paddling out of my way to see a nest. Only when Jim fires me an angry glare do I reluctantly tag along.

By the time we arrive at the first possible landing beach, the drizzle has become a downpour, and everyone is soaked. Lips are blue, teeth chatter, and fingers fumble with zippers. Scott and I decide to stop, light a fire, and prepare soup. As food is pulled from the hatches, some group members dash off to seek driftwood while others gather kindling, but getting a fire going proves difficult. Matches fizzle and go out. Everyone has a different strategy. Teepee builders argue with log-cabin builders. Fifteen minutes later we are still struggling, and have created nothing more than a pitiable whisper of smoke.

Jim, who has been watching the unsuccessful efforts without comment, finally comes to our assistance. He carefully selects two pieces of driftwood, and drawing a long knife from his belt, carves a curling sliver from one. As the grey exterior peels away, a red, aromatic wood is revealed.

"Sniff this," Jim holds the piece out. "Western red cedar." As he creates a pile of shavings, sheltering them from the rain under one knee, Jim teaches us how to recognize cedar by its straight grain, and explains that natural oils help keep the wood dry, even after years of exposure. "Everything else that has drifted ashore here will be sodden."

As he talks Jim chops the second piece of cedar in half with an axe. The wood splits easily along the grain, and Jim quickly splinters the rest into pencil-thin slivers. After arranging these on top of the dry shavings, he pulls a candle from a life-jacket pocket. Sheltering it with one hand, he lights the wick and then gently inserts the candle into the heart of the shavings. Within minutes, a fire is crackling. Jim pulls the candle from the fire, blows it out, and stuffs it back in his life jacket. Soon the group is huddled close, sipping mugs of hot chocolate, steam rising from the legs of our damp pants.

On the water we practise endless rescues, flipping boats, rafting the others together, righting and bailing the upset craft, and getting the immersed paddlers back into their cockpits. Jim shows us how to rig masts and sails, and we race along in the afternoon sun, enjoying easy kilometres. Each night we spend hours poring over the maps, and Jim explains how to take accurate bearings, how to use our fingers to estimate distances on the horizon, and how to navigate by dead reckoning. He discusses the cause and effect of the region's strong tides, and explains standard safety protocol, such as the use of marine radios and emergency locator beacons.

Jim takes a hard line about his guides' responsibilities. "No matter what the circumstances, if something goes wrong on a trip, it is your fault. If someone starts a fire that gets out of control, it's your fault for not watching. If someone cuts their finger open while preparing lunch, it's your fault for not teaching them to use a sharp knife. Even if you instruct your guests not to do something, and they go ahead and do it anyways, it is your fault for not stopping them."

Jim's most fundamental rule: There is no excuse for losing a boat. Ever.

"If you are unsure how high the tide will come during the night, carry the boats higher. If the winds might change direction while you sleep, and bring up waves, carry them even higher. If a guest ties up the boats and they come free, it is your fault. If you don't double-check the knots securing the boats at night, it is your fault."

These words will resonate in my head, and during a decade of guiding, not a day passes when I don't inspect the anchors and lines securing my craft before collapsing into a tent, no matter how exhausted I am.

The five days melt away quickly, and too soon we head back to Vancouver, tired out, with clothes reeking of smoke and salt water. I have learned a lot from Jim, but overall I feel disappointed. The sea-kayaking trip seemed tame and uninspiring compared to the thrill of whitewater rafting. I still hold out hope that Jim will offer me work as a guide, even though I am not sure I'd really like it.

Returning to my job at the camping goods store, I hear through the grapevine that Scott has been given the sole guiding position, just as everyone expected. So it comes as a complete surprise when Jim calls a week later. There is no small talk, and he cuts straight to business.

"Bruce, I want to ask you something. Does the idea of paddling around the Gulf Islands all summer, following exactly the same route we did, week after week . . . does that excite you?"

"Well . . . I suppose it might get a little repetitive," I understate my feelings.

"You just don't get it yet, do you? At your age I would have given my left arm for the opportunity to paddle around outside all summer. Forget being paid, I would have done it for free." There is a silence, and then he continues. "I'm in a jam. I need two new guides this summer. I have already hired Scott, but who else?"

More silence.

"You know that you are not my ideal candidate. You have no sea-kayaking experience, and show no interest whatsoever in natural history. But you have the potential for good judgment and strong leadership. Choosing new guides always requires a balance between hard skills and soft skills. Technical stuff, like paddling and lighting a fire, even natural history interpretation, these can be learned quite quickly. On the other hand, soft skills – how you handle a group, your attitude to adversity – these are a culmination of life experience. You can't just pick that stuff up overnight. You are OK with the soft stuff, and I can see no other option but to gamble that you will take interest and learn the rest . . ." Finally, he spits it out. "I guess what I am saying is that I want to give you a chance."

"Thanks," I reply, not really knowing how to interpret Jim's comments. This was his style – hire you and in the same breath tell you that you were not quite good enough for the job.

I always wanted to know Jim better, but he was an elusive character. He would disappear for weeks on end, and then suddenly show up when you least expected him. He drove a fast Audi, and appeared one day while I was cleaning gear on his front lawn with a million-dollar cheque. "Not from Ecosummer," he nodded as he flashed the seven figures before my eyes. Jim's other company – a manufacturer of quickly erectable, semi-permanent structures used in war zones and relief missions – was booming, and he had just been voted Canadian Entrepreneur of the Year. The next day he bought a plane. I think hiring me as a guide was another one of his experiments, and whether it worked or failed, Jim knew he would find it entertaining.

Four days after Jim's call, I picked up the company van at first light, already stuffed with food, water, paddles, tents, and gear. Fighting my way through early morning rush hour traffic, I arrived at the airport just in time to greet a group that had flown up from Texas. Hastily scribbled notes, describing the route to the ferry terminal, were hidden under a map atop the dashboard. On Mayne Island it took an hour to find the barn where the sea kayaks are stored. Fortunately, no one asked why we were driving in circles. As we took to the water, I consciously avoided telling the group that it was my first trip as a sea-kayaking guide, or that my total ocean experience was five days. Instead I pointed out a group of pigeon guillemots that darted over the water, feeling surprisingly proud that I had this knowledge.

While Scott was sent north to the Queen Charlotte Islands, a prestigious appointment coveted by all guides, I was assigned to "The Grind." For the next two and a half months I ran Ecosummer's relentless schedule of back-to-back Gulf Island trips. Every Monday morning I collected twelve guests from their hotels and shuttled them to the Gulf Islands. On the beach at Mayne Island, I started afresh, carefully explaining the routines for packing, paddling, setting camp, eating, going to the washroom in the intertidal zone, and so forth. Friday night the group returned to Vancouver, sunburned and exhausted. After dropping the tired participants at their hotels, I would race to Jim's house, clean and repack the gear, pick up a fresh supply of food, fill ten hefty jugs with water, and steal a few hours' sleep in the back of the van. At the crack of dawn on Saturday I met a new group for a two-day, weekend trip. Out to the islands by ferry, some quick instructions, a rushed paddle, and then back to Vancouver late Sunday night, where I stumbled through preparations for Monday's trip.

Initially I possessed pitifully little natural history knowledge to share with my guests. I was able to introduce them to the kayaks, cook their food, and keep them comfortable in whatever weather was thrown our way, but I came to feel self-conscious that I could not offer more interpretation. There were often long and uncomfortable pauses when I was asked about a plant species or a passing bird. Luckily for me, many of the guests knew volumes about the ecosystem and I sponged it up. Every tidbit got locked away and regurgitated in the future. I jotted down every question I couldn't answer, and started making rushed visits to the library between trips to search for the information. As the weeks passed my confidence grew, and one day I came to the startling realization that even if I tried, I could not impart everything that I had learned about the area in the space of a single trip. With time I learned to tailor what I taught to suit the group and its interests.

Because of my repetitive schedule, I found myself at the very same campsite on the windblown Belle Chain Islets twice a week, every Monday night, and every Saturday night, and it was here that a subtle yet profound shift in my awareness was born. As we approached the islets on my third trip of the season, I was surprised to see brilliant yellow wildflowers adorning rocks that were barren just five days earlier. Bouquets of gold star had flowered, sprouting from thin cracks above the spray zone. A month later they disappeared, and were replaced by a bloom of delicate purple sea blush. In the clearing where we camped, lush grasses were already shooting up through last year's trampled crop.

As summer passed, the pigeon guillemots grew less common as the flocks headed offshore to feed. The loons disappeared altogether. In their place came congregations of marbled murrelets, tiny squeaking balls of fuzz that landed with awkward splashes and dove at the approach of our kayaks. Four mergansers spent a week around the island, and just as I grew used to their presence, they disappeared. I never saw them again.

One sunny morning, I noticed a large driftwood log washed ashore near the southern tip of the Belle Chain and paddled over to investigate. My kayak was only metres away when the log suddenly reared up. I was face to face with an enormous stellar sea lion. The bull's eyes met mine and his mouth slowly opened, a purplish-red cavern, large enough to swallow a television. There was a momentary silence, and then a powerful roar erupted from deep within the beast. Strands of saliva sprayed outward, and the smell of rank breath washed over me. Heart pounding, I beat a hasty retreat, trying to act casual before my guests.

In July, a dead harbour seal washed up near camp. It had been shot through the head at point-blank range, likely by fishermen concerned that it was stealing their catch. It took weeks for sandhoppers, ravens, and eagles to clean the carcass. The skeleton that remained bore an uncanny resemblance to a beagle, which is not surprising, for seals and dogs have evolved from a common ancestry.

Each trip brought something new, and slowly my eyes grew attuned to previously hidden subtleties. A summer I worried might be boring changed the way I saw the world.

⁓

I rarely see Jim during the busy summer months, but when our paths do cross, I begin to sense that I have earned his begrudging approval. This is confirmed in mid-August when a note appears in my mailbox. As a reward for my efforts, I am being sent to Johnstone Strait, where I will finish the season as an assistant guide on orca whale–watching trips.

Taking a Greyhound bus to Port McNeill, and then hitching a ride on a stubby, stinky fishing boat to the offshore Broughton Archipelago, I stumble into a wild and raw land. There are towering forests, misty waters, craggy shores, majestic eagles, and most noticeably, salmon. Everywhere salmon. The ocean is alive. The pink run is in full swing, so strong it looks like a light rain is falling across the silvery waters. Fish constantly launch themselves skyward, fluttering in the air before splashing down. Such abundance is staggering. Occasional carcasses wash ashore, bringing bears and other scavengers. The orcas have been drawn by the migration, and so has the commercial fishing fleet. Trawlers, longliners, and purse seiners bob offshore, waiting for an "opener" (permission to fish). Each morning, Jacqui Goldsby, the senior guide I am assisting, trails a small hoochie lure behind her boat, and within minutes we have landed dinner. We eat so much salmon that after three weeks I pray I never see another.

Blue-eyed and strong-willed Jacqui has spent four years as a sea-kayak guide, and I fall for her instantly, her petite frame, her hands calloused from hard work, her twinkling eyes and Québécois accent. Unfortunately, she has a boyfriend, who follows us to the dock at the start of the trip and sternly watches us paddle away, but this does not stop me from wanting to impress her. I work extra-hard around camp, and am careful to watch everything she does. Jacqui knows a multitude of tips and tricks – how to fix a sticky tent zipper, how to rig an anchor and moor the boats offshore, how to keep vegetables fresh in the holds, how to repair broken rudders and seal leaky bulkheads.

Thick fog is common here, and Jacqui's compass is always handy, hanging around her neck. Mine, conversely, is buried in a waterproof case, where it does me little good. I notice Jacqui never leaves shore without taking a bearing on her destination, and when I mention how much I am learning by watching her, she smiles and tells of other guides, mentors who once taught her. In the Gulf Islands I had been working in isolation, solving problems on my own. For the first time I sense the fraternity of guiding – the shared struggles, the exhaustion, the endless cooking, the laughing fits, the love of a simple life.

My education is continuous. We carry white plastic cutting boards with our kitchen, for chopping and serving food, and after our first lunch I amble down to the ocean to scrub them with gravel and a dash of soap, just as Jim showed me. Jacqui almost has a hernia. She has brought a small green scrubbie pad specifically for the boards. "Don't let me catch you using this on the pots," she laughs, shaking the scrubbie at me as she cleans up the mess I have made. But she is dead serious. That night she soaks the cutting boards in boiling water and then bleaches them. Anyone else I would have labelled as anal, but I am under Jacqui's spell. I think back to my Gulf Island cutting boards, stained black from ground-in dirt and sand, and wonder if my guests cringed as tomatoes and cucumbers were sliced and laid out for lunch. As the days pass and Jacqui's cutting boards remain sparkling clean, I find myself adopting another of her ways.

Jacqui is also an unstinting recycler. Cans are placed in the fire, to burn off residual odours, and then crushed with the axe head. Glass is collected and stored separately. Aluminum foil is rolled into a ball. Paper and cardboard are burned. Only plastic is put in the big black trash bags we carry. This frustrates me because it seems much easier just to throw all our rubbish into one bag and forget about it. One day, exhausted, I hurriedly throw a mess of tins and paper in the trash, thinking Jacqui isn't looking. Later that night a noise causes me to peer from the tent door, and I am ashamed to see Jac sorting through the garbage by the light of her headlamp, redressing my laziness. After three weeks on the coast we return with three small bags – one of crushed tin, one of glass, and one of plastic – which Jacqui carries to a Vancouver depot for recycling.

The single most important lesson I learn from Jacqui that summer is this: no sign of our passing should ever be left behind. When I arrived in Johnstone Strait, the wilderness seemed unending to me. There were new beaches around every corner. Why worry about a few logs arranged as beach furniture, or a lost bread-bag tie? But Jacqui is meticulous with details that I have never considered. All of our fires are built on the exposed beach, below high-tide line, no matter how inconvenient, and she uses four carefully selected stones to support the corners of our cooking grill. Before leaving camp, Jacqui hides these fire-blackened stones in the forest, and if she ever stops at the same spot again, she reuses them. Without her guidance I would have left a ring of ashes at each place and never thought twice about it.

"Everyone deserves the same experience," Jacqui insists. "There was nothing here when we paddled up to the beach, and we should leave it that way."

Her message sinks in when we arrive at a remote island to find meadows we stayed at only a week earlier now scarred by a firepit, half-burned beer cans, and other refuse. I am dismayed by the mess, and work with Jacqui late into the night to clean it up, surprised at how much pride and pleasure I feel upholding this "no trace" principle. Slowly such actions become integrated into my own way of wilderness being.

The tension of attraction that marked my early days of guiding with Jacqui slowly eases, for she is clearly not interested, and instead we develop a playful, joking, supportive bond. We are a team within a team, helping each other survive the drudgery of endless cooking, cleaning, and perpetual questions from the group.

Wilderness experiences have a way of magnifying personal dynamics, and as the end of the season approaches, I am occasionally overtaken by flashes of nostalgia, the same peculiar blend of anticipation and melancholy that accompanied the end of the school year as a child. It will soon be over; the chilly pancake-over-the-fire mornings, the damp paddling clothes, the brain-numbingly-cold gravel-beach shampoos, the routines we developed, our inside jokes. Maybe they will form again, somewhere else, with another crew, another summer. Maybe Jacqui and I will even guide together again, sometime, somewhere, but it will never be the same.

A German film crew tags along on our very last day, shooting a documentary about women working in the outdoors. As our group arrives at the Sophia Islets, gear is unloaded, kayaks carried above the high-tide line, damp clothes hung out to dry, and a large salmon placed to roast over the fire. As the sun slowly sets and high cloud banks blush orange, the film crew requests a sunset paddling scene. Jacqui needs a partner in the front seat of the double kayak, and when the tired guests decline, I happily jump in. Soon our boat quickly races away from the island, through the tranquil waters.

A sense of calm has settled on the Strait. The sun slumps toward the horizon, a fiery ball growing larger by the minute. We angle toward the nearby shore, and a bald eagle, silhouetted atop a weathered snag, watches us pass. For the first time in over one hundred days, there are no other boats to worry about, no clients to watch. I am totally absorbed, and even forget about the film crew following somewhere behind.

"You know what would make this moment perfect?" Jacqui whispers when we take a break. "To see a whale."

We paddle on, the darkening shoreline rushing by. Several minutes later a boom reverberates across the glassy waters, loud as a shotgun, the powerful blow of an orca.

"I can't believe it!" Jacqui giggles. Straining to turn and look behind, we spot a lone dorsal fin in the distance, moving our way, and without speaking we race to position ourselves in the whale's path. After rising three more times, the orca submerges and does not reappear. A long dive. The Strait is silent. We stop paddling and glide forward, waiting, holding our breath. Waiting. Waiting . . .

Suddenly, I become aware of something massive directly below our boat. Seconds later a black fin breaks the water ahead of our bow, rising until its full two metre (6 feet) height is exposed. Then the whale arches and its back breaks the surface. The blowhole snaps open and closed. Spray erupts. I can feel the reverberation of the orca's lungs, only then sensing the true enormity of the animal below us. Slowly and gracefully the whale submerges, disappearing from sight.

We race after the orca, and it rises again and again before us, the mist from its breaths glowing pink in the last rays of sunlight. Eventually we slow and come to a stop, hearts pounding. I wipe the dampness from my brow. The eagle launches from its snag, passing by us, the powerful beating of its wings fading into the distance.

Two days later I sit in a van packed with dank, mildewed gear, slowly grinding through stop-and-go traffic on Vancouver's Lions Gate Bridge. The bright lights of the city ahead feel foreign. Behind us I watch feathers of green dancing above Grouse Mountain, the most brilliant display of northern lights all summer.

"What time will the moon rise today," I wonder, but can't remember. Fifty-two minutes later than yesterday, but when did it rise yesterday? Again, I can't remember. Just days ago such things were instinctive to me, akin to breathing. Now I have no idea.

A muted sense of sorrow, of separation, is growing. It is not just the camaraderie and lifestyle of guiding I miss. There is also the realization that I am no longer in tune with the outdoors, that its unconscious rhythm is seeping from me. Once again I live behind glass, metal, and concrete, looking out on the world.

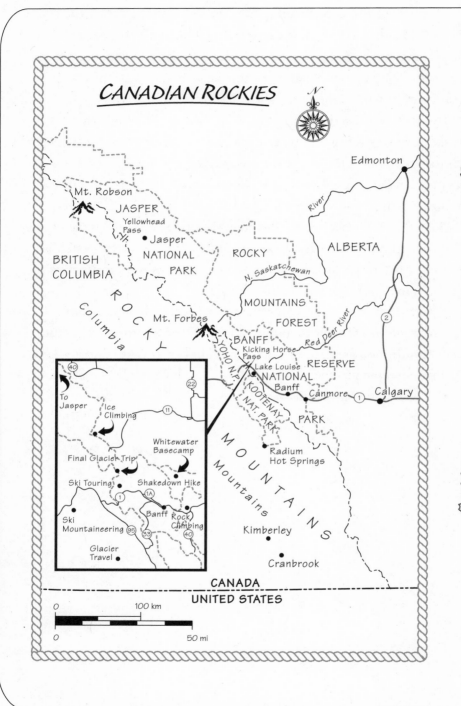

CANADIAN ROCKIES

N

Edmonton

Mt. Robson

JASPER

Yellowhead
Pass

Jasper

BRITISH
COLUMBIA

NATIONAL

PARK

ROCKY

ALBERTA

N. Saskatchewan

River

R
O
C
K
Y

Columbia

Mt. Forbes

MOUNTAINS

FOREST

Red Deer River

2

YOHO N.P.

BANFF

Kicking Horse
Pass

Lake Louise

RESERVE

NATIONAL

Banff

KOOTENAY

Canmore

1

Calgary

To
Jasper

40

Ice
Climbing

22

11

Whitewater
Basecamp

Final Glacier Trip

Ski Touring

1

Shakedown Hike

1A

NAT. PARK

PARK

M
O
U
N
T
A
I
N
S

Ski
Mountaineering

95

Banff

33

Rock
Climbing

40

Radium
Hot Springs

Glacier
Travel

Kimberley

Cranbrook

Mountains

CANADA

UNITED STATES

0   100 km

0   50 mi

four

The "All-Boys Choir"

A MOUNTAINEERING EDUCATION

*At the heart of the matter is a battle between wish and fear.
Fear generally proves stronger than wish, but it leaves a taste of disappointment on the tongue.*

George Packer, THE NEW YORK TIMES MAGAZINE

Canadian Rockies, 1994

JOHAN WAS IN Vancouver when I got back from guiding, and we met in a smoky Granville diner. His engagement didn't last, and another tree-planting season was over. "I've been thinking about a new adventure?" he smiled, mop of blond, curly hair shaking as he flopped down at a bench.

A cold, grey rain fell outside, and dishes clinked as the Saturday morning breakfast crowd sipped black coffee. In one corner a grainy television was rattling off cartoons, but I hardly noticed. My attention was riveted to Johan's finger as it traced a sprawling loop on a tattered map of British Columbia, through fjords, mountains, and rivers.

"OK, here's the plan. We launch our sea kayaks right here, from downtown Vancouver. We're gonna have to go light, pack just the basics – a tarp, an axe, a bag of rice, some fish hooks, perhaps. Then we paddle north, up the Inside Passage for about three hundred kilometres, to Knight Inlet (the longest fjord on the coast), and follow it to the end. Now we jump out and go by foot, following these glaciers up and over the peaks. If we use plastic kayaks, we can rig them as sleds and haul them behind us over the mountains. Then on the far side we put our boats back into these little creeks, and check it out, these flow into the Tatla River . . . which feeds the Chilcotin River . . . which eventually joins the Fraser. We'll be able to paddle all the way back to Vancouver!"

It was a fifteen-hundred-kilometre (900-mile) loop around British Columbia's southern Coast range, a daring plan. Johan's eyes sparkled with excitement. Full of youthful bravado, we thumped our chests and shook hands, agreeing to give it a shot.

But the autumn was not the right time. Fall storms were coming, and the high mountains had already received their first snows. Plans got pushed back. Johan moved to Rossland, B.C., where he began hand-crafting furniture. I fell in love and flew to Europe. We lost touch.

Midway through the season with Ecosummer, I had returned from the Gulf Island "Grind" to my aunt's basement for a rare day off, and spotted a bright yellow envelope on my pillow. Even from twenty feet away I knew it was from Cecilia. Sent to the wrong address, somehow it had found me.

Cecilia, a Rotary exchange student from Sweden, and I had fallen in love at the age of seventeen, during the last month of high school. I had never known anything like it. The sky, the flowers, the grass; everything was brighter when she was around. When she flew home just weeks after graduation, it was a teary, heart-wrenching departure. Sweden seemed as far away as the moon to me back then, and in a time before e-mail, when parents forbade overseas phone calls and a plane ticket cost more than an entire summer's work, we wrote.

Letter after letter, year after year, we somehow stayed in touch. For eight years we wrote, always avoiding mention of other girlfriends or boyfriends, never admitting we were anything other than good friends. We recorded cassettes of our favourite songs, and decorated envelopes with carefully chosen ephemera. I posted heartfelt scratchings to addresses in Greece, Switzerland, and northern Sweden, and replies followed me to Pakistan, Ottawa, Nelson, and now Vancouver.

Cecilia was planning a visit to Toronto. In three days! "Can you come and meet me?" she asked. She had no idea I was on the other side of the country. It didn't matter. Of course I would.

I begged Ecosummer for a week's holiday, but the office manager refused. "Impossible," I was told. "You'll lose your job." The job I had dreamed of, struggled to get, and was now enjoying immensely. On top of that I was broke. With less than six hours to make a decision, I quit my guiding job, used a credit card for the very first time in my life (to buy an exorbitantly expensive last-minute plane ticket), and flew home.

It was like we had never been apart. Cecilia and I spent three blissful days together, and then came another goodbye. I returned to Vancouver, and luckily Ecosummer gave me my job back (none of their senior guides wanted to do "The Grind"), but after two more months of paddling, after Jacqui and the wild lands of Johnstone Strait, after Johan and his crazy schemes, nothing could stop my mind from drifting back to Cecilia. So I flew to Stockholm. Taking my bike and a tent (in case things didn't work out, I thought I could pedal south through Europe), I showed up with less than a week's notice on the doorstep of Cecilia's one-room apartment. We spent every minute of the fall together, wandering cobbled streets, lazing in cafés, eating salty candies and cod caviar. During the days, while Cecilia worked at a bookstore, I studied Swedish, the first foreign language I made an honest attempt to learn.

By Christmas my money was gone, and I returned to Ottawa to program computers. The price of the path I had chosen was starting to show. The co-workers I left behind three years earlier now drove fast cars. Hardwood floors, contemporary furniture, and big-screen televisions filled their new homes, which sat in fields of identical boxes, all around the outskirts of the city. Most had married, many had babies. Conversely, I tossed my mattress on the floor of a Hull flophouse, dug my musty Salvation Army suit out of storage, walked to work, and drove the same rusty pickup whenever I ventured out of the city.

While this didn't bother me at all, it certainly concerned others. "You are wasting your life," a friend's father told me. "Why not take pilot training. Then you can travel and do respectable work at the same time."

Although aware of my growing divergence from the "standard path" (and the associated lack of material acquisitions and savings), I was far too consumed by my interest in outdoor activities to really care. There were occasional twinges of concern about what it meant for my future, but to sacrifice the bulk of my life simply to secure an unappealing retirement seemed ridiculous. Instead I plastered my bedroom walls with pictures, spray-painted *This is only for three months!* on the ceiling above my mattress, and waited for Cecilia to arrive.

When she did, we packed the pickup and headed west, planning to spend the summer together in Whistler. "As long as we have ice cream and each other, there is nothing else we'll need," she laughed as we sped away from Ontario, smoke pouring from the pickup's tailpipe. After forty hours of non-stop driving, fuelled only by Tim Hortons coffee and doughnuts, we were both dizzy from travel. As Cecilia slept, the mountains inched closer, and the Trans-Canada Highway funnelled into the tightening Bow Valley. A green highway sign flashed by, marking the exit for Canmore. As it did, the word *Yamnuska* burst into my consciousness.

Yamnuska? What is *Yamnuska*?

Then I remembered. Yamnuska. A Canmore-based mountain-guiding company, renowned for its rigorous, one-hundred-day mountain skills semester. I had first heard of Yamnuska from Ian Stibbe, the guide who trained me on the Ottawa River. An exceptional paddler, uncannily nonchalant in the most daunting whitewater, Ian was a god to the rookies. He had described Yamnuska's gruelling semester as the toughest three months of his life, so it unquestionably lay beyond my abilities. I had a paralyzing fear of heights, and dismissed the course as something I was incapable of attempting. For two years I never thought of it again.

Now I felt curious. Over the past three years I had developed skills on rivers and oceans, but mountains represented a great unknown. Fear still nagged at me, but the idea that I might now overcome what had previously seemed insurmountable was seductive. Leaning over the steering wheel, I peered up through my windshield at the snow-covered peaks flanking the highway, imagining the exhilaration of standing on their summits – the solitude, the beauty, and the gut-wrenching exposure.

In Banff I pulled over to search for information on the mountaineering course. Finding a Yamnuska brochure pinned to a bulletin board on Main Street, I called from a payphone.

"The semester program is offered twice a year," the receptionist explained. "Once in the spring and once in the fall. This year's spring session has already started, and there is only one position remaining this fall. If you are serious about enrolling, you should place a deposit. That spot won't last long. We'll need a thousand dollars to hold it."

I thanked her, hung up, and wandered back to the truck. As we drove on toward the coast, Cecilia slept while I pondered what to do. The course was expensive, over seven thousand dollars. The equipment would cost another thousand dollars. That was 90 per cent of what I had in my bank account; twice the value of my pickup. Enrolling would leave me penniless.

What of my fear? Pictures in the brochure made me anxious. One showed a group of students perched atop a granite spire, hundreds of metres above the ground.

Most difficult was what the course would mean for Cecilia. After Whistler, there would be another season apart. We talked about it, and while she was supportive, she was also hurt.

I anguished. Was I becoming too self-absorbed? What was this elusive path that I proclaimed to chase all about anyways? Was it just thinly veiled immaturity and aversion to real work? Where could guiding possibly lead in the long term? I knew I didn't want to end up like the older guides I had seen at Wilderness Tours; forty-five-year-olds who still acted eighteen, sporting greying ponytails, chasing college girls every weekend, trapped in a whirlpool of partying that was going nowhere.

I didn't know the answers, but there was no way I was ready to admit defeat and return to engineering.

A day later we reached Tofino, pulling over to sleep in a deserted parking lot. Rain pelted the back of the pickup as the last of the spring storms lashed the coast. The vast beach beyond lay deserted. Through the Plexiglas window we watched salty air blow in from crashing Pacific rollers, and fingers of froth reach up to lick away the footprints of earlier visitors. As gulls soared and dived in the gale, their shrill cries rising above the rumble of surf, I wandered to a nearby pay phone and called.

"Hurry up, lads," George Reid pulls at his wiry moustache in exasperation. "We've not got all day." The lanky Scottish mountain guide gathers our group of twelve under a tall pine, but only a few of the students are listening. After a moment of waiting, he loses his cool. "If ya 'ave come fur a vacation, YA CAN LEAVE RIGHT NOW."

Someone at the back snickers.

"Would ya mind telling me what ya think is so funny," George erupts, his eyes dark. He is not in the mood for nonsense.

Earlier in the day, thirty-six nervous participants arrived at the Alpine Clubhouse in Canmore for the start of Yamnuska's Mountain Skills Semester. Some are fresh out of high school. Most are in their early twenties. The oldest is a thirty-seven-year-old aeronautical engineer on leave for three months. There are twenty-seven men and nine women. After a quick introduction, the program coordinator announces we will be split into three groups. Each of these groups will spend the entire one hundred days together, working and learning as a team.

"I know some of you will be disappointed," the coordinator continues, "but we have made one of the groups entirely male." Groans and moans erupt around the room. "It is only the second time we've done this in seventeen years, but the numbers simply work better that way."

Names are called, and lines form. I joined eleven other young men in what has already been dubbed "The All-Boys Choir." At twenty-six, I am the oldest member. As we trudge from the meeting hall, I suspect everyone feels somewhat dismayed, but George, our section leader, has no time for such trivial matters. He has a knots lesson planned for the afternoon, but first there is an icebreaker to get through.

"This is a wee bit touchy-feely for me, lads," George notes apologetically, "but it's in the curriculum, so I 'ave to do it."

Dividing the group into pairs, George asks us to learn a few things about our partner — name, where he is from, previous mountain experience, and his biggest fear about the course. After reconvening we are asked to introduce our partner to the group. "Don't get used to the chitty-chatty stuff boys. It is for dart players, and we are here to climb."

Eventually my partner, Ken, stands up and gives a quick sketch of my background. He wraps up by explaining that my fear of heights will be my biggest challenge.

"Haa!" a young, punky-looking kid laughs out loud.

What a complete asshole, I think. He has been goofing off all morning and George glares in the kid's direction before peering at me over the top of his wire-rimmed glasses. "Just exactly how scared are ya, laddie?"

Oh shit. Now the instructor is concerned?

"It's no big deal, I'll be fine," I nod, wanting to move on quickly.

When Brad, the punky kid, is introduced, his partner announces that his biggest fear is that "he has no fear." Brad jumps up and down, pumping his fist in the air. Everyone laughs. A few guys give Brad a high-five. *Three months of this?* I have the sinking premonition that we are not going to get along.

The semester is broken down into ten-day units of study: rock climbing, glacier travel, whitewater canoeing, mountaineering, alpine ski touring, waterfall ice climbing, wilderness first aid, avalanche awareness, and outdoor leadership. We begin with a shakedown hike, traipsing through the backcountry of Banff, travelling by compass and map, scrambling up peaks along the way. The purpose of the week is to ensure that everyone has a solid base of fundamental skills: knowledge of food packing and preparation, a familiarity with stoves and tents, an ability to read topographical maps and competently navigate through untracked land, an understanding of synthetic clothing systems and the principles of layering.

Although it is review for most, George constantly pushes the group, grilling us with questions and scenarios that test the depth of our understanding. A strict and dedicated teacher, he expects complete commitment and effort in return. There is no room for tomfoolery. When half the group develops bad blisters on the third day, George only shakes his head. "I told ya boys to stop the instant ya felt a hotspot and tape it. Now what are ya going to do? The rest of us can't be waiting while you're limping like a bunch of grannies." With that he presses on through the dense undergrowth. Complaints are silenced, and everyone manages to keep up.

Successful mountaineers are meticulously thoughtful, and George is no exception. Nothing is left to chance or happenstance. A vast amount of our learning comes from following his example. Every morning he is ready to leave camp at precisely the arranged time. His pack is loaded, water bottles are filled, and snacks are handy in a front pocket. There is no last-minute fiddling or adjustments to be made. George always begins the day dressed lightly, knowing he will warm up once we start moving, not wanting to waste time by pausing to remove a layer later.

"Laddies, how many times do I have to tell ya?" he grumbles in exasperation when forced to halt for someone to peel off a jacket. "Ya need to be chilly when you start a day in the mountains. You're going to warm up as soon as ya start movin'."

When one of the boys drops his pack at a stream and stoops to fill water bottles only minutes after leaving camp, George fumes straight past. "You're doing last night's chores this morning. Why should we all wait for ya? Everyone else already has their water!" We disappear down the valley, leaving the boy scrambling to catch up. After that no one ever begins a day without his water bottle filled.

Although it seems finicky, George wants to instill good habits, which in more demanding environments will become very important. Constantly halting a rope team on a windy glacier so that climbers can change clothing is more than a minor inconvenience. Despite his gruff exterior, George is kind and thoughtful. His stern nature reminds me of my father, and I like him immensely. As the only member in our section who has paid for the course on his own, I want to learn all I can, and am thrilled by his no-nonsense attitude.

I notice quickly that no one can keep up with George. He is in his fifties and greying. We are all fit and young. How does he move so fast, I wonder, never before considering walking a skill. It was something I took for granted, but watching closely as George ambles across loose, ankle-twisting scree without breaking stride, I realize that strategy and planning are involved. George never looks down at his feet, but always a few steps ahead, judging which rocks are stable, planning where to step. Sometimes his boots find the spaces between rocks, at other times it clearly works better to leap from top to top. Experience has taught him when to kick a heel into loose gravel and when to jam a toe on a tiny crack. He seems to know which steep surfaces will grip his boot, and which will let go. Without trying to, he leaves our group of twelve young men panting far behind.

A rock-climbing unit follows the shakedown hike. Each morning my heart pounds and my palms grow sweaty as our group packs helmets, ropes, and harnesses into the back of the van. Thankfully, George methodically explains everything, the use of ropes, protection systems, and anchors. He shows us how to create a belay device from carabiners, how to tie a bowline with one hand, how to create a Münter hitch or a clove hitch with a simple twist of the rope. We are bombarded with new skills and information. Every night I practise what we learned during the day, until it becomes second nature.

Most of the others are experienced climbers, and while they easily scamper up the faces, I struggle to even get off the ground. Soon I learn that fear always proves worse than reality. Once underway, my focus is on the rock before me, seeking good handholds, moving my feet up, and I forget about the drop below. The worst part always comes at the top, when I have to lean back and let the rope take my weight as I am lowered. Then my fate is out of my hands.

"Trust," George yells up. "Trust the rope, trust your anchors. You've inspected them, haven't you?"

As the weeks roll by, the "All-Boys Choir" slowly gels. While the other groups battle problems of discipline, drinking, drugs, and thievery, George will not stand for any nonsense, and continually presses us to our limits. No one wants to let him down, and even the jokesters in our group clean up their act.

We spend a week whitewater canoeing and practising rescues on the

Red Deer River. Then Barry Blanchard — one of the world's great alpinists, and a legendary figure of Canadian mountaineering — joins us for ten days of waterfall ice climbing. A "solo experience" follows, and we are each dropped off alone in the woods, with only a tarpaulin, a sleeping bag, and meagre provisions. Instructed not to move anywhere for three days, the experience is meant to slow down our minds, and open our eyes. I am skeptical and can't understand why I am paying almost one hundred dollars a day to sit on my ass. As soon as the instructor leaves, I pack some food and head off, following the creek I am camped beside toward its headwaters. Despite daily outings, and the chance to relax, practise photography, and read, the three days pass slowly. I have a hard time doing nothing. When the time comes to finally break down my bivouac, I spot a wolf's claw in the brush by my feet. It has been sitting near my campfire for seventy-two hours, and I had never noticed it before.

In late October, our group travels to the Columbia Mountains of southeastern British Columbia for an introduction to glacier travel. Parking the van at the end of a deserted logging road, we hike upward, following switchbacks through rain-drenched forest. The rain turns to sheets of snow at dusk, and we stop to set up a base camp on the toe of the Catamount Glacier. For the next week George teaches us the fundamentals of glacier mountaineering: walking with crampons, using an ice axe to self-arrest, travelling in a rope team, and crevasse rescue. Finally, we are ready to put the skills to use, and the group sets out for a five-day traverse of the region's ice fields, carrying all our gear and supplies on our backs.

The landscape we enter is both enticing and formidable. Fields of untracked snow, silent and vast, stretch before us. Footprints trail behind, a thin black thread draped across the rolling slopes. Countless crevasses block our path, some wide enough to swallow a bus. As we cautiously wind past these dark abysses, I often steal a glance downward, dizzied by the depths before a tug from the rope returns my focus to the placement of my feet.

Passing beneath a great buttress of rock, a clattering causes everyone to look up. Suddenly a stove-sized boulder launches outward from the cliff overhead, whistling as it picks up speed. For one sickening moment it looks as if the rock will smash into our midst, and everyone freezes. Instead it lands with a thud fifty metres (160 feet) away, and rolls down the slope, soon disappearing from sight.

The travel is exhausting. We carry heavy loads and are often breaking trail through deep, soft snow. At other times we crunch over wind-hardened crust and ice, nervously aware that a tumble could send the entire group spilling downward.

On the last morning we pack camp hurriedly. Our topographic maps show an easy glacial descent to the forested valleys below. We should be down by lunch, and visions of beer and warm showers dance in every-one's heads. Instead of seeing the gentle ice slopes we expect at the edge of the glacier, we find our way blocked by steep cliffs. The glacier has retreated more than four kilometres (2.5 miles) since cartographers first mapped the land, and we face a difficult, if not impossible, descent.

Hoping to find a route through, we scramble downhill, tentatively crossing boulder fields and traversing narrow ledges. Several hours later, nerves frayed, we have almost made it. Easy forested slopes lie just ahead. Only one final cliff blocks our way, a steeply angled slab of grey rock. There is no way around it. A narrow crack traverses the face, just wide enough to hold the toe of a boot. The drop below is frighten-ing. If anyone slips, they will plummet sixty metres (200 feet) into a narrow gorge. The sound of powerful rapids drifts up from the dark-ness. Because the cliff is north-facing, it has been in the shade for hours, and water trickling down from above is already freezing into sheets of black ice.

George gathers us. "It's a difficult decision, lads. We can turn back, but it will take three, if not four days to retrace our route. We have almost no food or fuel left. Traversing this rock band is not terribly difficult, but any slip will be your last. Let's have a show of hands. Who wants to go back? Who wants to cross the cliff?"

It is unanimous. We'll move ahead, across the narrow ledge.

When we first arrived, the cliff crossing had looked impossible to me, completely out of the question, but slowly I began to realize it was really just a case of controlling my fear. Now, as my turn approaches, I feel surprisingly calm. Edging outwards, my mind is clear, every thought focused on moving smoothly. *Don't look down. Don't move one foot until the other is solidly in place. Take your time.* Little by little I move across the face, the heavy pack tugging at my back. Moments later the obstacle is behind, and soon the last of the group has followed.

Later that night, as I clean gear at a mountain hut, Brad, the punky kid, joins me. During the glacier trip we shared a tent with Cory, a struggling member of the group and the target of constant joking and harassment. On the glacier I expected Brad to lead the sarcastic assaults, but to my amazement he took Cory under his wing, helping him with daily tasks, encouraging him when he became dejected or frustrated, and even subtly stepping in when others picked on him. I was impressed. Brad was a jerk when he first arrived at Yamnuska, but glimmers of a more complex, caring personality had emerged from beneath the bravado. Still, nothing could have prepared me for what he said next.

"Bruce," Brad sighs, leaning against the wall and looking earnest, "I was scared shitless today."

What? I almost fall over. *This is the arrogant, loud kid who claimed to have "No fear." Eight weeks ago he was a complete jackass.* How can someone change so drastically, so quickly?

Brad's growth mirrored changes that swept through the entire group as we struggled together. We had come with a consuming rush to get extreme, to be radical. The true value of outdoor endeavours – the depth of the bonds formed, the opportunity to trust others with your life, to do things you never thought possible, the understanding of the land's rhythms – were not what had drawn us to the course. I had anticipated nothing more than three months of hard mountaineering, but before the course was half-done I could sense that I was being changed indelibly.

During the final month, George continued to push us. We learned to dig snow pits and assess the stability of avalanche slopes. "Victims" were buried under six feet of snow and sought with probes and beacons. We slept in snow caves and igloos, hiking up and skiing down immense bowls of deep powder, linking turns, tumbling, and trying again. As Yamnuska's director pledged at the first meeting, we became "unconsciously competent," repeating the same tasks over and over until they became second nature: tying into ropes, setting up belays, building anchors on rock and snow, rappelling, analyzing the snow pack.

Our final trip was spent exploring ice caps straddling the British Columbia–Alberta border. After seven days of glorious sunshine, we descended and gathered for one last photo. After lashing our packs to the roof of the van, we drove back to Yamnuska's base camp and I gazed out the window, at the same peaks I had stared at through my pickup's windshield six months earlier, remembering my gut-wrenching worries. The course had given me the confidence to travel safely in the mountains, and amidst camaraderie and sweaty exhaustion, I felt grateful for that special freedom.

Less than six hours later I began the marathon drive back to Toronto, to visit my parents, and then travelled on to Switzerland, where Cecilia and I had plans to spend the winter skiing. But first there was a wrap-up dinner. That night, the "All-Boys Choir" presented George with a picture of our group gathered on a summit, along with an inscription thanking him for his efforts. Normally stoic, George's eyes grew misty as he stepped on stage to accept the gift.

"It's been bloody special, lads," he began with a quivering voice, and then recovered quickly. "But don't go getting all soppy on me now. I know you Canadian men like to hug each other, but if ya try that on a Scotsman, you'll get a Dublin kiss [a head-butt]."

five

Marcel's Mother

THE DIRTBAG LIFESTYLE

Do not imagine that the journey is short;
And one must have the heart of a lion to follow this unusual road, for it
*   is very long.*
One plods along in a state of amazement,
Sometimes smiling, sometimes weeping . . .

Farid ud-Din Attar, THE CONFERENCE
OF THE BIRDS (12th Century)

Swiss Alps, 1994/95

A BLIZZARD HAMMERS Saas-Fee on Christmas Eve. Staggering outside into heavy winds and darkness, I begin a search for a Christmas tree. Drifting snow makes it impossible to see more than a few feet in front of me, and small trees prove difficult to find. After almost an hour I stumble upon the perfect specimen, and lop it down messily with a penknife. At the time I think I am in the woods marking the edge of town. In reality I have just chopped down the sole tree decorating the front lawn of the town's most exclusive hotel. I discover my error the next morning, while strolling to the bakery. A group of angry Swiss men are gathered around the stump, swearing loudly.

"Unbelievable!" Cecilia whispers, elbowing me in the ribs. "This is a tiny village. Everyone knows everything that happens. We're doomed!" We hustle home, tear the tree from the window where it stands, stuff it in a bag, and dispatch it to the dump.

It is not the only unbelievable occurrence marking our first week in Switzerland. I also find a job.

"You'll never get work here," our landlord warned as I lugged a heavy duffel up to the loft Cecilia and I would share that winter. "This is a very tight community. I've lived here fifteen years, and am married to a local, but they still refer to me as a visitor. If you can't speak *Schweizerdeutsch* (Swiss-German, the gravelly local dialect), no one will ever hire you. And without a working visa? You may as well give up. Spend the winter skiing. Enjoy yourself."

Luckily, Cecilia has a job, which is the reason we have come to Saas-Fee. Just as the Yamnuska Mountain Skills semester finished, another distinctive handwritten letter arrived in the mail. "Do you want to spend the winter in Switzerland?" she asked. A restaurant she wait-ressed at years earlier had invited her to return. "You can share my room. Don't worry about work. My tip money will be enough. We can survive on bread and cheese, and ski all day, every day." I didn't need any more convincing.

But after a few evenings of sitting alone in our dorm room, I grow restless and begin to weigh the standard options available in a resort town: washing dishes, busing tables, hotel housekeeping, ski school, working in a rental shop, retail sales, bartending. My lack of *Schweizerdeutsch* rules out most. Of all the possibilities, waxing and tuning rental skis, with its early-morning and late-afternoon shifts, away from customers, makes the most sense. It would leave Cecilia and I free to spend the daytime hours of sunshine together, skiing and exploring. There is just one problem with the plan. I have no idea how to wax skis.

Wandering through the town's maze of narrow streets, I discover six shops offer tuning services. One has a large window opening onto the workshop, and inside two technicians are attending to a pile of skis. I pause to watch. One of the workers runs the skis through a grinder, which sends a great shower of sparks flying. The other uses a smoking hot iron to apply wax to the freshly ground bases. It is not long before the young men notice they have an audience, which they apparently don't appreciate. Both vehemently wave for me to move on. I wave back and keep watching. After an hour I have a fairly good idea of what a ski technician's job entails, and while I cannot apply at that store, there are still five others in town.

The next afternoon I rush about Saas-Fee, visiting the other ski stores and offering my services as a trained ski technician. The first three attempts prove disastrous. As warned, no one wants to hire a foreigner. One impatient owner turns as red as a ripe tomato when I speak English. "*Git ooout*" is all he says, shaking a thick finger in the direction of the door. Number four is more hopeful. Marcel Burgener, the owner of Burgener Schuh und Sport pauses momentarily.

"Jah, I could use some help," he admits, lighting a cigarette and taking a deep drag. Smoke gently drifts from his mouth and is sucked back in the nostrils. "But no *Schweizerdeutsch*? This is a big problem."

"I can try to learn," I offer, knowing it is unlikely.

"Are you crazy? You won't learn *Schweizerdeutsch*. Not in one winter. Anyways, it's not me who cares. It's my mother." Marcel rolls his eyes and then falls silent. "OK, OK . . . we'll try. You come back, no? Today at four o'clock."

I bite my lower lip and nod with excitement.

Tucked high in the eastern Swiss Alps, the village of Saas-Fee is set in an amphitheatre of rock, ice, and snow. Jagged peaks encircle the tiny town, thirteen in total, all soaring above four thousand metres (13,300 feet). For centuries this remote valley existed in peace and tranquility, its alpine pastures the seasonal home of shepherds and their herds. With the arrival of a road, in 1948, and the subsequent development of cable ropeways on the mountains, Saas-Fee was plunged into the twentieth century. Today gondolas, chairlifts, and even an underground funicular railway give year-round access to a staggering swath of glaciated terrain.

Despite its rapid transformation into a holiday destination, Saas-Fee has managed to preserve some of its rustic past. Hotels and restaurants have been constructed in traditional Swiss mountain style. Hay storage lofts and goat stockades remain in the narrow alleyways, tucked between fashionable boutiques and upscale galleries. Cars are banned from town. Visitors must park outside, either walking the cobblestone streets or shuttling to and fro in electros (battery-powered carts). Overshadowed by Zermatt, the famous ski resort that lies one valley to the east, this spectacular enclave remains a treasured secret, known to the locals as *Die Perle der Alpen* (the Pearl of the Alps).

As long shadows stretch across town and temperatures begin to plunge, I sprint back to Marcel's shop, through narrow streets, past patios crowded with giddy vacationers. Bursting in, I come face to face with a large, grim woman. Marcel's mother. She glares at me, and launches into a bitter tirade, of which I understand nothing. Smiling, I duck between her and a towering pile of shoeboxes, and dash upstairs.

The backroom workshop is an absolute mess. Distinctly un-Swiss. Decrepit wooden shelves are piled with tools and gadgets. Overstuffed drawers spill from under the workbench. Screws, old bindings, and spare parts litter the floor. Generations of dilapidated boots are heaped waist-deep in the back closet. Everything is covered in curls of sticky wax and the fine dust spewed forth by the grinder.

Marcel has already begun grinding the bases of rental skis returned that afternoon, creating a pile of skis ready for me to wax. I take my place beside him at the bench and look around. The skis are clearly meant to go in a pair of clamps, so I secure the first pair and then pause. Marcel notices my hesitation. Grabbing a square of wax-impregnated cloth from a supply bin, he clips it to a heated iron that runs along a set of tracks over the clamps, lowers the unit to rest on the skis and presses a glowing green "Start" button on the control panel. Voilà, the rest is done automatically. The iron glides along the skis, lifts off, and returns to its starting position. Marcel continues grinding bases. I begin working on the pile of skis. Three hours later we are done.

As I sweep the floor and prepare to leave, Marcel's mother lumbers up the stairs from the shoe store below. Pointing her finger in my direction, she falls into a heated exchange with Marcel. He lights a cigarette and continues closing the cash register, yelling back without looking up. His mother slams her fist on the counter. He keeps counting. Eventually his mother retreats, but not before levelling a long, hard glare in my direction.

"Should I come back again tomorrow?" I ask meekly.

"Oh, yah yah," Marcel nods absently. "She is just a little upset that you don't speak *Schweizerdeutsch*. Don't worry, I told her that you were learning."

The next afternoon Marcel rushes into the workshop with a brand-new pair of Salomon skis, racing bindings, and boots. "I've just sold a package. The customer is waiting. Quickly!" he yells, motioning for me to mount the bindings. Then he dashes out.

I stare at the skis. They are colourful and loud, with shaped tips and fancy graphics. Probably worth eight hundred dollars, maybe more. I pull the protective cellophane wrapping off and secure the skis in the clamps. Next I open the binding box, and spread parts across the workbench. *What next?* There is no way I am going to drill holes in the brand-new skis. Instead I stall, pretending to busy myself with preparations. Marcel runs back in. "Ready?" he asks impatiently.

"Would you mind showing me exactly how you like this done?" I stammer. "Just in case we do things differently in Canada. I want to make sure I am doing everything the way you like."

Without hesitating Marcel grabs a mounting jig from an overhead rack, adjusts the contraption for the boot size, aligns it with the centre point of the ski, clamps it down, quickly drills eight holes, removes the jig, dabs a touch of glue in each hole, places the bindings in position, and uses a power drill to drive the eight screws rapidly into place. Everything takes less than a minute. He says nothing, simply running out of the workshop and leaving me alone with the second ski.

I nervously check and recheck the jig before drilling. I hate to scar the gleaming surface of the new ski. My father always told me you can measure as many times as you like, but you cut only once. Tentatively I position the drill and squeeze the trigger. The drill bit slices into the ski like butter. With growing confidence I zip through the rest. Moments later, glue applied and screws tightened, the ski is ready.

Within a week I can competently complete all the repairs, mountings, and adjustments that come in over the course of a day. In the mornings I drop by to prepare rental skis going out for the day, adjusting the release settings on the bindings and sizing them for the boots. After a full day on the hill, I return in the late afternoon, mounting bindings on ski packages that have been sold, repairing any broken equipment, and servicing the returned rentals.

The only part of the job I dread is the hour I spend restocking the shoe store with Marcel's mother. If she isn't yelling at me, she is yelling up the stairs at Marcel and shaking her fist at me. I cannot understand a word she says, and feel like more of a hindrance than a help. When sent to the storeroom to find shoes, I bring back the wrong boxes, and Marcel's mother grows angrier and angrier with me. Eventually I begin repeating everything she says in the hope of somehow calming her fury. The effect is almost immediate.

"*Acht und dreißig*! (Thirty-eight!)," she thunders, holding up a shoe and pointing to the supply room. I nod my head and shuffle off.

"*Acht und dreißig, acht und dreißig*," I repeat, having no idea what it means. I return with several boxes of size twenty-six. "*Acht und dreißig*?" I hold them out. Marcel's mother pauses, looks at me sideways, and then shakes her head. Grabbing my sleeve, we shuffle to the storeroom together.

"*Acht*," she says slowly, pointing to the number eight on a shoebox. ". . . *und dreißig*," she continues, pointing to thirty.

Acht und dreißig. Thirty-eight! It is a painfully slow way to learn *Schweizerdeutsch*, but with time I can get any shoe she asks for. Eventually our shared vocabulary grows to include words such as *broom* and *ladder*. While Marcel's mother may never actually like me, she does grow to tolerate me, although I suspect she considers me as dense as a doorknob.

The icy peaks towering over town are a constant temptation. Since arriving I have wanted to venture into the surrounding high country and practise the skills I learned at Yamnuska. As soon as an extended forecast of clear weather finally arrives, Cecilia and I decide to have a go at climbing Allalinhorn. The summit rises 4,027 metres (13,211 feet) directly outside our dorm window, and we have stared at it for weeks. The undertaking feels serious. Allalinhorn will be the highest peak Cecilia or I have ever attempted.

George was fastidiously strict whenever our group travelled on glaciers. No one stepped onto the ice unroped, and everybody carried a full complement of safety and rescue gear. Although the route on Allalinhorn looks straightforward, I want to be prepared. The evening before our climb, Cecilia and I review the use of our safety equipment and double-check everything.

Long before the sun rises we catch the first gondola of the morning. The slopes of the ski hill lie in shadow, completely deserted. Setting out from the upper station, we find the route only moderately steep, and are able to climb most of the way up using skis and skins. We leave our skis behind at a high col, scrambling up the final, windswept ridge on foot, arriving before noon at a small summit adorned by a simple iron cross.

The view is spectacular. To the north rises the pyramidal bulk of the Matterhorn. Farther east the peaks of Italy are silhouetted against clear blue skies. In the valley far below, we can make out tiny dots, the hotels and restaurants of Saas-Fee. There is not a breath of wind in the air, and in no hurry to get back, we lay down and linger on the sunwarmed rock. Soon we have drifted asleep.

I wake with a jolt some time later, to the sounds of laughter and the clink of wine glasses. Jumping up, I see almost one hundred people have joined us on the summit. Others are winding their way up the ridge. Many wear straw hats, some are in T-shirts. None are roped. Very few have either harnesses or ice axes. Blankets have been spread out; cheese, bread, and schnapps are being passed around. I am completely speechless. During the one hundred days of Yamnuska, we never saw another climber.

In Switzerland, vast numbers of locals and tourists set out for the high country during the sunny weekends of late winter and early spring. The detailed Swiss mountaineering maps show ninety-eight routes emanating from Saas-Fee. As the weather grows warmer, hordes of climbers can be seen departing from the gondola each morning, working their way up the slopes of surrounding peaks like long lines of ants. Far from being a frustration, this allows me to explore the Alps more than I would have ever dared to alone. There are always tracks to follow, and help nearby should problems arise. With no shortage of challenges awaiting, I throw myself at the mountains.

The season passes slowly and peacefully, one day running into the

next. Cecilia and I live in magical exile, isolated from the worries and
rush of the modern world by the tall peaks surrounding us. Sharing
this existence with us are transient workers from around the globe,
Norwegians, Germans, Japanese, Kiwis, Chileans, and others, all of
whom have converged on Saas-Fee, part of an endless planet-wide
migration in search of powder. With raccoon-tanned faces and clothes
held together with duct tape, these searchers are easy to pick out. They
stand in line for the first gondola of the day, and swoop down out-of-
bounds slopes beside us. It is a tribe united by a common quest, and
friendships form quickly; they are strong, but transitory, for with the
end of the season comes the inevitable journey onward.

Money is always short for ski bums, but it doesn't take much to
scrape by, and the clan takes care of its own. Cooks and dishwashers
save unfinished meals each night, passing them out the back door of
fancy restaurants. Bartenders pour unnoticed drinks in crowded bars,
and hotel doormen look the other way as Cecilia and I sneak into the
sauna room. In return I wax their skis and repair their bases. No one
keeps score, it is beside the point. As long as there is fresh snow on the
hill, everyone is happy.

As storm after storm rolls across Europe, shutting down airports and
closing cities, Saas-Fee and its underground tribe are in their glory. An
infectious enthusiasm abounds in ski towns during winter, especially
ones getting lots of snow. Skiers and non-skiers alike are swept along by
a collective euphoria. Life becomes a series of ear-to-ear grins. At night,
in smoky bars, the day's runs are relived over jugs of beer, the tales
growing ever taller. Alarms remain set for dawn. No matter how tired,
everyone wants to be on the first lift. The jubilance in Saas-Fee is pervasive. Even Marcel's mother begins to smile.

I awake with a start, breathing heavily. Our tiny dorm room is in complete darkness. Snow softly patters against the window by my feet. I had
been standing in the desert, a warm wind blowing with such weight and

substance that I could lean against it and brace myself on its force. In the distance a long train of Arabic men appeared, weaving toward me through the gentle dunes. At the head of the procession, hoisted upon a platform borne by four bare-chested men in flowing white robes, sat my sister. Draped in embroidered red cloth, she swung her head from side to side, dispassionately announcing to the world "Peter Kirkby is dead, Peter Kirkby is dead!" I ran up and shook her litter.

"What are you saying?" I screamed. "That is our father."

"I know," she turned to me with clear blue eyes, "it's sad, but it is true."

I lie awake for what seems like hours, soaked in sweat, my heart racing. In the morning I still feel ill at ease. The memory of the dream and its intensity will not leave me. That evening, before making tea on the small hot plate in our room, I call my parents. They are not at home, so I try the farm where as children we spent every weekend. Mom answers on the second ring. With only one phone, Mom and Dad hold the receiver between them, taking turns speaking into the mouth-piece. I tell them of the fabulous skiing, my evenings at work, my new friends, remembering to thank them for the *Guidebook to Adventure Photography* that recently arrived in the mail, a belated birthday present. I don't mention the dream. As always, "I love you" are the last words I say before hanging up.

A week later Cecilia bursts into the backroom of Marcel's shop, still wearing her waitress' clothes. I pause over the waxing machine. One look at her face tells me that she is distraught beyond words. With Marcel yelling at me to return to the workshop, we walk straight through the crowded store and I follow Cecilia downstairs to a narrow laneway outside. It is pitch-black out. Large snowflakes float down from above, softly landing on our shoulders, hair, and eyelashes, melting in seconds. I watch Cecilia's back as we walk. Time creaks by. I know something ter-rible has happened; I suspect either to someone in her family, or someone in mine. I don't want it to be either. I don't want to find out, and I know that in seconds I will. Around us a sea of noisy vacationers walk awkwardly past, many half-drunk and wearing unbuckled ski boots, skis balanced on their shoulders, swinging in dangerous arcs. Cecilia turns and looks me in the eye.

"Your father has been in a terrible accident at the farm."

A shiver washes over my body. I feel dizzy. My mind starts to go black, but then comes back. "Is he still alive?"

Cecilia shakes her head and cries.

My head screams but I'm silent. Every cell of blood slows in my veins, my breath stops, I can't move. And then it explodes. A million thoughts, and no thoughts. My kids – if I ever have kids – will never know their grandfather. It can't be right. I know it is. It's not fair. Dad had so much to teach; about tools and handiwork, writing, and science. He is gone?

In a dim underground restaurant I wait for my mother's call, beside a black phone on a deserted bar. "It was a glorious day . . ." is all she gets out before words leave her. I don't even ask what happened. "Mom, I am coming home," is all I say.

Half an hour later I have packed my duffel bag, taken leave of my job, and staggered to the bus station. I catch the very last coach of the evening. As the bus swings through the wide switchbacks leading to the valley below, the world around me recedes. I stand amidst a crowd of exuberant skiers, in tears. I see forms and hear muffled sounds, but I am not there.

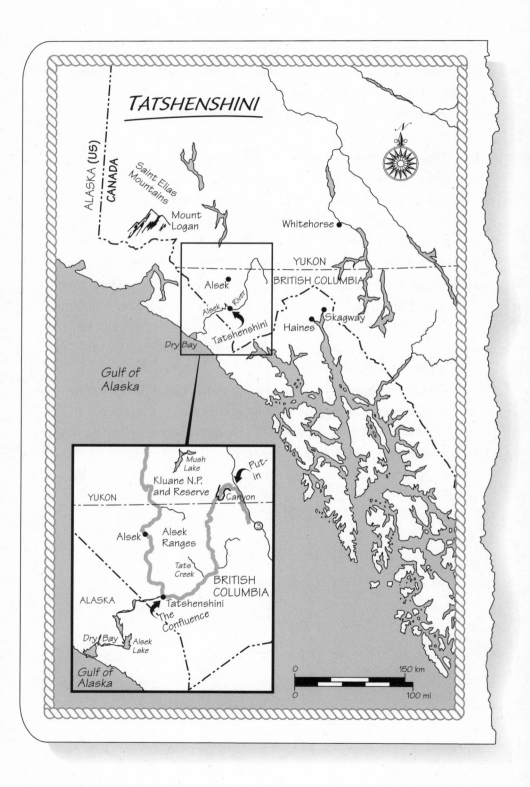

six

Shifting Frontiers

NORTHERN GUIDING

Summer in the North is a dramatic, urgent affair.
The flowers, the birds, the closer sun all seem to broadcast the message . . .
Live this moment well and true before it burns down to a softly glowing
*   ember,*
sheltered close against the wind, and carried into the long cold night of
*   winter.*

Brian Payton

Tatshenshini River, Yukon, 1995

FOR A MONTH after my father's death we huddle at home – brothers, sister, and mother – reminiscing and grieving, laughing and sharing, digging out old slides, sorting through endless ephemera, drinking so many pots of chamomile tea that I swear I never want to taste it again. If anything good comes from my father's passing it is my family's strengthened bonds.

With the bloom of spring I return to Cecilia and Saas-Fee. There is one last month of work at Marcel's, and then the inevitable farewells to our temporary friends. Cecilia has a job in Sweden, and I spend six weeks with her there before returning to Canada, where Ecosummer has offered me a guiding position on the coast. I call their office to check in, just before boarding my homebound plane. The manager doesn't seem happy to hear from me. After some hemming and hawing, she tells me they were not confident I was going to show up, and have found someone else to fill my spot. I have no work for the summer.

By the time I land in Toronto I am plagued by all the old doubts and worries. *Is it time to return to engineering? Am I just on an extended vacation? Where is all this taking me?* I have no job. No house. Nothing solid to hold on to. Is it time to accept that while it has been a good ride, I need a real job, a normal life? *What is a normal life?*

I am twenty-seven, the eldest son of a recent widow. Friends who studied engineering at the same time as me are getting promotions, becoming managers, buying houses. Some are already producing grand-children. I have been living out of duffel bags and staying on stranger's couches for four years. Is the black hole of office life the inevitable and unavoidable conclusion to all this? I hear discouraging voices whispering, "I told you so."

At a crowded downtown newsagent I buy every single adventure publication I can find, returning home with a heavy bundle in my backpack. There are glossy volumes on travel, independent works on kayaking, backpacker rags, newspaper travel sections, and more. I tear through them all, scanning advertisements in the back, making an enormous list of potential employers. Then I start calling – canoe trippers, wilderness lodges, rafting companies, summer camps, sea-kayaking outfitters. At the same time I dredge my memory for contacts, networking with everyone I can think of.

It is disheartening work. There are not many jobs, and hundreds, if not thousands, of eager applicants. Each promising lead seems to evaporate in a dead end. Summer is just weeks away and my hope is fading when the canoeing instructor from Yamnuska returns my call. Randy leaves a scratchy, cryptic message on my mom's answering machine. "*Hey Bruce, try Nahanni Neil in Whitehorse . . . I think he is looking for a raft guide . . . Tatshenshini River, maybe? Good luck.*"

I have heard of the Tatshenshini. During high school I chanced upon a lavish picture book at the local library, compiled by an environmental group struggling to preserve the river corridor from development. The river – born in the interior of the Yukon, running through northern British Columbia, and then out across the Alaskan panhandle – cleaves a green corridor through the coastal St. Elias Mountains, the only break in hundreds of kilometres of rock and ice. I recall the book's stunning images, showing a raw, untouched wilderness, and call Neil immediately.

"Yup, Randy is right, I need a Tat guide," he confirms. "One of my veteran trip leaders just joined the fire department. I have five fully booked trips on the river this summer, and no one to run them. They are twelve-day wilderness rafting expeditions. This is big-time stuff. What is your experience? Are you qualified for something like this?"

I tell Neil it sounds like a perfect match, promising to send him a resume that afternoon, and hang up.

There is no doubt that I am grossly underqualified. I have never been on a multi-day rafting trip. I have never rowed a heavy oar-rigged expedition raft (the lighter passenger rafts at Wilderness Tours were controlled by a paddle at the stern). I have never been to Canada's North. And I know nothing about the region's ecosystem or history. Although I am sure I can master the new skills and knowledge quickly, it seems a long shot that Neil will view my situation the same way. I fax him a resume anyways. Days tick by as I anxiously await a reply.

I have almost given up hope when the phone rings. It's Neil. "I need you up here next week. Your ticket is in the mail." The canoeing instructor's strong recommendation coupled with Neil's pressing need to fill a position created my lucky break. After hanging up, I race to the back garden, throwing my arms around Mom in a giant bear hug, unable to stop dancing at the good news.

I arrive at the peak of the pre-season rush, and Neil is consumed with office work. His company, Nahanni River Adventures, will operate fifty trips during the summer, on rivers all across the Arctic. In an act of blind faith, he hands the reins of the Tatshenshini program to me and Kevin, another rookie guide. After giving us a basic overview, Neil leaves us alone. "If you have a question, my door is open. Otherwise, figure it out yourselves." Over the next two and a half months we will be responsible for running five expeditions, each twelve days long, down the Tatshenshini River.

Dark-haired, athletic Kevin has just graduated from a two-year outdoor leadership program that makes Yamnuska pale in comparison. He represents the newest trend in guiding: structured school learning rather than mentorship. Classroom courses ranging from entrepreneurial strategies to hospitality management, endless field trips, and a fistful of certifications have led Kevin to the Tatshenshini. Although his background is intimidating, Kevin is clearly focused on the "coolness" factor of guiding, and we get on tentatively at first. Not until we discover our shared incompetence – a complete lack of knowledge surrounding northern natural history – does our friendship cement.

Starting from scratch, we immerse ourselves in the staggering logistics required to organize multi-day rafting expeditions. Our existence is centred on lists. There are food lists, gear lists, packing lists, repair lists, shopping lists, "to do" lists, client lists, and emergency contact lists. There is a list of equipment needing repair, and a list of batteries needing charging. Lists of things to pick up and lists of things to drop off. Kevin and I even create a list of our lists. Forgetting just one thing – say toilet paper for example – can cause turmoil on a twelve-day trip.

In Neil's garage we pack hundreds of kilos of dried food. On his front lawn we clean and sort equipment that has grown stale from winter storage. We study maps of the region, review emergency plans, and discuss every conceivable eventuality. At nearby Miles Canyon we familiarize ourselves with the rafts, purposely flipping in the gentle current of the Yukon River and then righting ourselves. We complete a swift water rescue course, spending five days tumbling down the rapids of nearby rivers, repeating rescues over and over.

Two weeks before the first trip is scheduled to depart, an Alaskan rafting company calls. One of their Tatshenshini guides has fallen sick and they desperately need a replacement. "Sure, I have a guide right here. I'll put him on a bus this afternoon," Neil quickly agrees, failing to mention my inexperience. "It's the perfect opportunity to complete your training!" he smiles after hanging up. An hour later I am on my way to the bus station. My only instructions: Upon arrival in Haines, look for someone called Joe Willy Jones.

❧

With the simple motion of coiling the bowline and pushing away from shore, we commit ourselves to the journey. There is no turning back; no roads, exits, or shortcuts exist in the wilderness ahead. The ocean lies two hundred kilometres (124 miles) away, and the river will drop six hundred metres (2,000 feet) before reaching it. The only way out is through. A strong current grabs hold of the rafts. For a moment everyone sits quietly, surrendering to the magnitude of the trip ahead.

"Hey Canada, stay right behind me, OK?" Joe Willy Jones shouts back. The heavily muscled (and heavily moustached) trip leader was not impressed when I arrived in Haines with a shiny new river bag slung over one shoulder. "A rookie? They sent me a rookie? And not just any rookie!" he moaned, before a sliver of a smile betrayed him. "A bloody *Canadian* rookie. You know how to spell that, *eh*? C-*eh*-N-*eh*-D-*eh*." After that, no one on the crew bothered to learn my name. Country of origin would do.

Joe Willy is a man's man, raised in Alabama, resident of Alaska. He has guided for fifteen years, regularly leading expeditions to exotic locales, including Kenya, Chile, and Russia. The rest of his crew – Pat, Dan, and Beth – are experienced – very experienced. We spent two dizzying days in preparation: buying food, packing gear, loading a half-ton truck (careful to bury shotguns at the bottom of the pile, far from the eyes of curious customs officers at the border), racing to the river, inflating the rafts and rigging them. Despite his tough-guy facade, Joe watched me from a distance, only helping when required.

Now, as we drift downstream, I struggle to follow Joe's every move. The heavily laden rafts are sluggish, each carrying five hundred kilograms (1,000 pounds) of food and gear, enough to provision twenty-five people on a twelve-day journey. The coolers are crammed with fruit, vegetables, cheese, and frozen meat. Dry goods are stuffed into mammoth waterproof boxes: sixty loaves of bread, one hundred bagels, two hundred eggs, twenty jars of mayonnaise, and ten kilograms of coffee. Barrels full of cookies and snacks are lashed to the frames. Cases of beer, wine, and liquor are nestled in the holds. Big waterproof sacks on the rear deck have been loaded with pasta and rice. The first few kilometres are winding and gentle, but I have to work to keep my boat from banging into the outside corners.

Less than an hour downstream burnt-orange cliffs appear, signalling the entrance to "The Canyon," the most continuous stretch of whitewater on the Tatshenshini. At first the river flows peacefully through a narrowing gorge, and I feel relieved. *This isn't too bad.* Then the water begins to pick up speed. *Oh boy.* A faint roar can be heard, which grows louder as we rush forward, and then our boats swing around a final corner. In the distance the water drops from sight. *Holy shit!* Tilting forward like a roller coaster, the rafts race into an S-bend. Ahead the foaming water is squeezed between cliffs and boulders. Ricocheting off a headwall, it disappears around another bend. Joe Willy glances back one last time.

Waves smash off my bow. Canyon walls rocket past. Spray soaks me. An oar is yanked from my grasp, the handle smacking me in the gut, winding me. I grab it, gripping it till my hands cramp and my knuckles turn white. Standing up, I haul on the oars with all my might, focused on following Joe Willy's lead. Drenched with sweat, I hardly notice the exertion.

"Waahooo!" the guests in my boat scream as water crashes over the tubes, dousing them.

"Bail!" I scream, straining to see what is ahead. The rapids keep coming. The raft bends and folds, the frame creaks, gear bounces around. A barrel comes loose and rolls around the floor. With no time to tie it back up, I simply kick it aside. *Joe Willy is moving right. Gotta follow. What is coming next?*

Two hours later we drift from the bottom of the canyon. My run was clean; sheer luck. "Not bad, Canada," Joe Willy nods.

The others didn't fare so well. One of the rafts strayed too close to a corner, where an overhanging branch swept a guest overboard. The bobbing man was recovered quickly, safe but shaken. Another boat slammed into a canyon wall and has sprung a slow leak. As dusk falls we set camp on a gravel island mid-river. A salmon is baked over the fire and the exhausted guests are soon asleep. After patching the leaky raft, I linger with Joe and the other guides around the embers, passing around a bottle of corn whisky, finally beginning to feel like I belong.

Joe's cowboy crew operates on an "Alaskan" schedule, the opposite of the early-to-rise, early-to-bed regime George instilled at Yamnuska. Breakfast is a long-drawn-out affair. Pot after pot of coffee is brewed and the group straggles by the fire. We never get on the river before noon, and rarely stop for lunch before four. Not until eight or nine o'clock do we begin looking for a campsite. Dinner is served at eleven, or later, but it hardly matters as the sun never sets. Time becomes irrelevant. Watches are packed away, and the group surrenders to a quasi-circadian rhythm.

Each day we drift deeper and deeper into grandeur. At first the river meanders slowly through a maze of lowland bogs and beaver marshes. Here mammoth blocks of rich brown earth droop from outside banks, slowly cleaved by the incessant current, secured only temporarily by feathery roots. By the end of the second day, the grey bulk of Carmine Mountain rises in the east, pressing the Tatshenshini toward the rugged Alsek ranges. Swollen tributaries crash down from these peaks, bringing massive fans of alluvium that spread across the valley floor, benches of rounded stone kilometres wide. The volume of the river grows by the hour, as do its speed and power. The expedition rafts race along, dwarfed beneath shale cliffs, ancient sedimentary seabeds turned on edge and rising from the water, folded and confused.

The river, a translucent tea-brown at the start of the journey, has grown steadily cloudier. Soon it is a rich, chocolatey brown, carrying a heavy load of glacial silt. I hear a hissing from my raft, and search the tubes for a leak.

"That is just silt hitting your floor," Joe yells over the roar of the water. "Try putting a paddle to your ear and holding the blade in the water. You'll hear it better." When I do, I can hear the heavy thumps of boulders bouncing along the bottom below us.

After a week the river breaks through the Noisy Range, and spills out across "The Confluence." Four great valleys meet here, forming a cross in the heart of the mountains, a natural cathedral more than twenty kilometres (12 miles) in width. The horizon is wreathed by peaks. I count fifty-eight glaciers plastered to the impossibly steep rock faces. At the centre of the cross, the Tatshenshini's muddy waters are swallowed by the larger, milkier Alsek, and the boats now float on a moving ocean.

Every evening, huddled by the campfire, I cover my maps with notes, describing routes through the rapids, marking the trails we hiked that day, and highlighting hidden trickles of fresh water Joe has shown me. He always selects his campsites carefully. Which way is the wind blowing? What will happen to our boats if the river rises? Is there a corridor along the shore where wildlife can pass? Are there flat, private spots for tents? Is there driftwood nearby for a fire?

We leave no trace of our passing. Fires are built in shallow aluminum boxes, the ashes dumped in moving river water. Solid human waste is carried out in portable toilets. Organic garbage is burned. Plastics are packed out. Aluminum and glass recycled.

"Most of the popular sites on the river get visited every day of the season," Joe tells me at Walker Camp, one of the busiest, where a blue tongue of glacial ice stretches right to the water's edge. "Think about it. Groups of twenty, or more, every day. Last night someone stayed here, and the night before that. Two thousand probably camped here last year. And look around. There is not a single sign." All we find are footprints, and one forgotten tent peg. No fire scars, no garbage, no little shit bombs hidden in the forest, no toilet paper spread about by rodents, no ashes along the shore. Joe is clearly proud of what he and his fellow trip leaders have accomplished, and I am impressed.

The trip is not without incident. On the third day we are hiking along a high ridge when Joe spots a grizzly heading toward camp far below. Tearing off his shirt, he straps a shotgun across his back, and races to divert the bear, leaving me and the rest of the group open-mouthed. A week later, nearing the coast, we find a jam of icebergs blocking the entrance to Alsek Lake. For three exhausting hours we drag the rafts along the shoreline, chopping away small bergs with an axe, prying on larger ones with oars, wading in to push floating chunks. Eventually it becomes clear we will never make it through. With our last reserves of energy we portage the heavy rafts across a series of gravel flats, using the oars as rollers. The sky is flushing a watermelon pink as we finally reach clear water, and set camp. It is one-thirty in the morning, and a full moon is rising over the curtain of snow-capped peaks surrounding us.

"The Tat is like a symphony," Joe tells me that night by the fire, his eyes dancing and warmed by wine. "The Canyon is the opening violin, a kinda crazy, lonesome, energetic solo. Every day the river keeps getting bigger and bigger. As new rivers and tributaries wash in, they are like new sections starting up. The scenery gets crazier and crazier. When the O'Connor River arrives, that's the strings. The Tkope, that's the brass. And the Confluence, that's huge, it's the bass. Walker Glacier gets the percussion going. By the time we reach Alsek Lake, clogged with icebergs, and Mount Fairweather rising thousands of metres above, that, my friend, is the full Alaskan symphony. You can't beat it. There is nowhere in the world like this. You are gonna love this river."

Joe is right. I spend the entire summer on the Tat, drifting its waters and sleeping on its banks; six trips, seventy-two river days. The work of a guide is exhausting, and often frustrating, but I am happy to the core. Day after day I fall into my sleeping bag feeling satisfied and calm, my cheeks sore from smiling. I am in the right place at the right time doing the right thing.

Jocular banter and deep unspoken comradeship bond fellow guides. There is a surprising calm and purpose amidst the perpetual lifting, carrying, loading, and oaring. At the beginning I struggle to effectively lead the groups. Northern rafting trips are not cheap. The vast majority of participants are several decades older than me, and well established in successful careers. In retrospect, it must have been difficult for some to follow the direction of a young and clearly inexperienced guide. But I enjoy the company of nearly all guests – even those requiring abnormally high maintenance – viewing them as friends for two weeks rather than clients. Some I form closer bonds with, and remain in contact with for years to come. Although the bombardment with questions often seems endless, and the cooking incessant, I return for three consecutive years, and by the time I move on, I have spent more than two hundred days travelling through the Tatshenshini wilderness. It is here that I learn how a person can fall in love with a spot on the planet and love it with all their soul. I never see the natural world through the same eyes again. There are others after the Tat. For nine straight summers I journey north, rafting a spectrum of different Arctic rivers. All are special, but for me the Tat is different. It is, I suppose, my first true love.

During the glory and intensity of an Arctic summer, the midnight sun does not set. It simply scrapes low across the horizon, and the immense northern sky is showered with an ever-changing palette of mauve, ginger, and cherry. The stark shadows of daytime recede and a soft luminescence lights the land. For just a moment, the explosive fecundity that marks the breeding season pauses, catching its breath before launching into the frenzy of a new day. Peace descends upon an incomprehensible vastness.

Four years after leaving my job as an engineer, I find myself lying flat on my back amidst sprawling fields of locoweed and sweet-vetch, resting in the boulder-strewn flood plains at the union of four grand northern valleys. A flash of pink lingers on distant peaks. I am alone, a mere speck in the enormity of the landscape. The sediment-laden waters of a frigid river rush unremittingly past at my feet.

Resting cruciform atop a bed of sun-warmed, river-smoothed pebbles, I drift slowly to sleep, lingering in the netherworld between dreams and desire. Arms stretched outward, face toward the sky, I can feel the world beneath me. Not just the rock and dirt, but the entire planet, gently arching away in the periphery of my vision. For one enchanted moment I am at one; neither a visitor nor an observer, passerby nor interloper, but rather part of the land, indistinct and inseparable from the greater whole.

This is wilderness.

For the first time I sense what the word means in my heart, not just my head. Primal and vast, wilderness can never be defined by words in a dictionary or colours on a land-use plan. It has to be felt, and that takes time, for you can't rush a union with the land.

Just upstream of Towagh Creek, if you look carefully along the Tatshenshini's right-hand bank, you will find hidden gravel benches tucked into the alder forest. They are easy to miss unless you know they are there. It is a spot that Joe Willy showed me. Whenever I visit, I can't help but think of the copper mine.

Our group stops here on the fourth trip of my first season. After unloading the heavy gear from the rafts, I spot Kevin entertaining the guests by juggling oranges, and decide to steal away for a moment of solitude.

Crawling atop a house-sized boulder on the crest of a nearby gravel embankment, I watch the Tatshenshini rush past below. Its muddy waters are wide, so wide that a strong person couldn't throw a baseball halfway across. Heavy waves surge and break in the channel, engulfing each other and speeding on. The sound of their crashing blankets the land. A massive tree trunk floats past, dwarfed by the flow, whisked out of sight in seconds. Rugged mountains rise across the valley; snow lingers in their high gullies, unbroken forest carpeting the lower flanks.

Something catches my eye on the opposite bank. A dark spot. Moving fast. *Grizzly!*

Through my binoculars I watch the bear bound along. First it sprints, then it meanders. Soon a cub appears behind, a rolling ball of fur that chases its mother, bouncing along between her hind legs. Abruptly the sow rolls onto her back and twists, as if scratching an itch. Up she leaps again, sniffing at a stump and pushing on it with one paw before losing interest and loping off. Baby follows. Soon they have melted into a dense swath of purple fireweed.

I reflect on where I stand. In six days our group has travelled one hundred kilometres (60 miles) down the river, and in that time we have not passed a single sign of human presence or development. We will travel another hundred kilometres before reaching the coast, all of it untouched. This may not sound significant, until one considers that nowhere in the lower forty-eight states is more than twenty-seven kilo-metres (17 miles) from a road. On a continent transected by an expand-ing web of freeways, the Tatshenshini Valley represents something rare and precious. It is easy to imagine (as I long did) that such places exist in abundance, endlessly lined up beyond the northern horizon, an eternal frontier awaiting exploration, but they do not. They are finite, and one by one they are being lost.

During the late 1980s, Geddes Resources quietly applied for permis-sion to exploit a massive copper deposit – 1 per cent of the world's known reserves – that lies buried in the heart of the Tatshenshini wilder-ness. If that development had been approved, trucks would now be rumbling through the forest at my back, and pipes carrying slurry to the coast would criss-cross the shoreline where the bears had just played.

Geddes's plan involved ripping the top off nearby Windy Craggy Mountain, and digging a three-kilometre- (2-mile-) wide open-pit mine. To contain the thirty thousand tons of tailings that would be pro-duced daily, massive earthen dams needed to be built, flooding side valleys to create enormous storage ponds. A permanent town site would provide housing and services for five hundred workers, and a road carved through the mountains would allow year-round access.

Just a single gravel road would have changed the nature of this wilderness irrevocably. Sportsmen, hunters, poachers, prospectors, vacationers, and dirt bikers would all follow its course, bringing with them inevitable garbage, noise, and pollution. Migration routes would be disrupted and nesting grounds disturbed. Noxious seeds and weeds would arrive, hitching rides on vehicle undercarriages. Gall bladders of bears would be hidden in coolers by poachers and smuggled out along the same path. When considering the effect of access to a wilderness area, there is no partway or in-between. An area is either wilderness, or it is not. And altering it is akin to dropping dye into a bucket; once done, you can never go back to the original state.

But the mine represented a far more dangerous proposition than simply bringing access to this previously hidden valley. Copper samples, taken from the heart of the Windy Craggy deposit, were found to be high in sulphides. If the giant tailing ponds ever leaked, sulphuric acid would be released into the ecosystem, an agent notorious for the leaching of bedrock heavy metals. Once the leaching process has begun, there is no known technology that can stop it. Roman mines still bleed acid into English country streams today, two thousand years after they were abandoned. Any spill would not just devastate the Tatshenshini's salmon-rich waters for a season, but would instead ripple down to affect every living thing in the valley for millennia to come. The earthen dams could not afford to leak for ten thousand years, and given that the St. Elias Mountains experience four times the seismic activity of the San Andreas Fault, a disaster seemed inevitable.

A battle quickly began, and as the well-financed and fiercely determined mining industry courted the government, declaring that the Windy Craggy mine would become the next pillar of the floundering British Columbian economy, concerned scientists, politicians, naturalists, and celebrities fought back. There were public awareness campaigns, legal actions, and court injunctions. Eventually Al Gore and Pierre Trudeau waded in, lending their voices to the outcry as tensions continued to escalate.

On June 22, 1993, the Province of British Columbia called an unexpected news conference. To the surprise of many, it decisively saved the region, creating the 2.4-million-acre Tatshenshini "Class A" Provincial Park. Joining Kluane National Park (Yukon) and Glacier Bay National Park (Alaska), this park was the final piece in 23 million contiguous acres of fully protected wilderness, an area twice the size of Switzerland. A year later the United Nations declared the region a World Heritage site.

As I watch through my binoculars for another sign of the bears, I wonder how many would have ever known the extent of the loss had the mine been approved. Without the chance to see the mother grizzly and her cub, wandering carelessly through fireweed, without the chance to lie on sun-warmed rocks, and sense the mysteries of the wild, how could they? If I had not spent a summer on these banks, I know I would never have cared so deeply myself. Until now such issues had never concerned me.

Before heading back to camp I bow my head in silent thanks to those who fought to save the river, wishing they could know that at least one person's life has been changed as a result of their struggle.

A layer of innocence was lost during that first summer on the Tat. Never again was I able to look out over the planet's wild places with wonderment alone. There would always be a faint whisper of concern lingering on the periphery of my thoughts, but perhaps this is not so bad, for a powerful drive comes with the realization that what you love may not last forever.

A veteran river guide joins Kevin and me for the final trip of the season. Standing six-foot-eight (203 cm) and weighing 240 pounds (110 kg), Neil Hudson is an intimidating monster of a man, with one wonky eye, a scraggily beard, and hands larger than baseball mitts. A snowplow driver during winter and raft guide during the summer, Neil's passion is song. His partner on stage is a tiny woman named Marge – their band's name: Marge and the Barge. On the river Neil Hudson is simply known as "Griz."

Fall is in the air when Kevin, Griz, and I arrive at Alsek Lake. The river is low, and strong winds have blown blocks of ice across the main entrance. Forced to drag our rafts through shallow side channels, we camp on the lake's remote western shore. Piles of driftwood dot the sandy flats. Beyond, groves of aspen shimmer, their yellow leaves quivering in gentle breezes. A brilliant display of red-and-orange fireweed marks the shoreline, the dying plants flaming with the arrival of the first frosts.

As the lasagna cooks in big Dutch ovens, and our guests huddle around the fire, I join Kevin by the water's edge. A deep tiredness slows me, a satisfying exhaustion that comes from a season of hard work.

Resting against my raft's soft bow, I gaze out across the iceberg-dotted waters. The setting sun is turning Mount Fairweather's summit salmon pink. A white shape darting along the distant shore suddenly catches my attention.

"Do you see that!" I whisper and point.

It's a wolf, silently trotting through grass-tufted dunes, unaware of our presence. I can't believe it. All summer Kevin and I have marvelled at the abundance of wolf tracks along the banks of the river, for elsewhere in the world they are rare. I often suspected that the elusive animals were nearby, silently watching our group as we drifted past. But we have never caught a glimpse of one. Before we can alert the group, the wolf catches our scent and melts into the underbrush. After scanning the shore with binoculars, we join Griz and the others, enjoying the warmth of red wine in the flickering twilight.

Much later the lyrical moans of a howling wolf pack drift across the dark land. In a sleeping bag beside me, Kevin stirs. Without rising, I quietly unzip the tent door and peer out, my warm breath billowing into the frosty night. Northern lights float high above, streaks of green reaching across the sky. Occasional strands of pink erupt upward from the horizon, arcing across the blackness before dissolving into a swirl of cotton candy. The howls of the pack grow more distant. Zipping up and lying back, sleep soon overcomes my weary body.

A blood-curdling howl splits the night.

I sit bolt upright. *Wolves! Right outside our tent!* My heart pounds. Frozen, I struggle for breath. I want to laugh, cry, spring from the tent, and bury myself in my sleeping bag all at once. Kevin is also awake and our eyes meet, wide as saucers. We both remain still for what seems like an eternity, straining to hear another sound.

Very slowly a muffled snarling grows. Growls drift across the sand flats surrounding our tents. *Is the whole pack in camp, raiding the kitchen?*

"Kev, did you clean up the kitchen?" I whisper.

"Can't remember," he rubs sleep from his eyes.

We have been fastidiously careful and clean all summer. Constantly aware of the presence of bears in the valley, Kevin and I always put away every scrap of food, scrubbed the dishes, and locked the group's toiletries in an aluminum box before collapsing in our tent. But tonight, after a few bottles of celebratory wine, neither of us is sure if the job was done properly.

The snarling continues. There is no option. We are the guides; we need to defend camp.

In complete darkness Kevin and I don headlamps, take the safety latches off canisters of bear spray, and pull river knives from their sheaths. I can imagine quivering lips and rows of jagged teeth as wolves fight over scraps of food. On the count of three we unzip the tent door, turn on our headlamps, and leap out wearing only our underwear.

Nothing? Camp is deserted. We stand unmoving, mystified. Then we hear it again, the same frightful snarling. *Where is it coming from?* Tiptoeing forward, we hold our knives before us, bear spray at the ready.

The kitchen is clean and empty? Nothing is moving near the rafts? The guest's tents appear undisturbed?

Rounding a final clump of willow, we come to the campfire. There, lying on his back beside the dying embers, is Griz, snoring.

We haul down the tent in the soft light of dawn. Kevin creeps away to cook oatmeal while I struggle to fasten my bulging river bag. There in the sand, right beside the compacted tent spot, is a fresh wolf print. It is enormous, almost the size of my hand.

"So the howl wasn't your imagination?" Griz laughs when I drag the others back to show them. "Well, I bet it was my snoring that scared the wolf off. You guys should thank me!"

"I bet it was your snoring that attracted it," Kevin retorts.

Slowly we begin packing camp for the last time. Our time in the north is done, and the parting will be bittersweet. Although I have daydreamed of the end – of clean clothes and hot showers, of lattes and weekend newspapers, and other southern comforts – I still mourn the loss. No gesture can capture the enormity of debt I feel to these lands. As our rafts drift from shore, I take one long last look up the river. I know I will be back.

PACKED   9 oars   3 clips
                    6 locks

10 veggie boxes

5 drop bags / do we want a 6th?

feed bags / canvas bags? (cover pelicases.)

grate? stove?
seats.
biffy?

Condaments bag / kit / box
w jars → coffee
          → sugar
          → milk pow

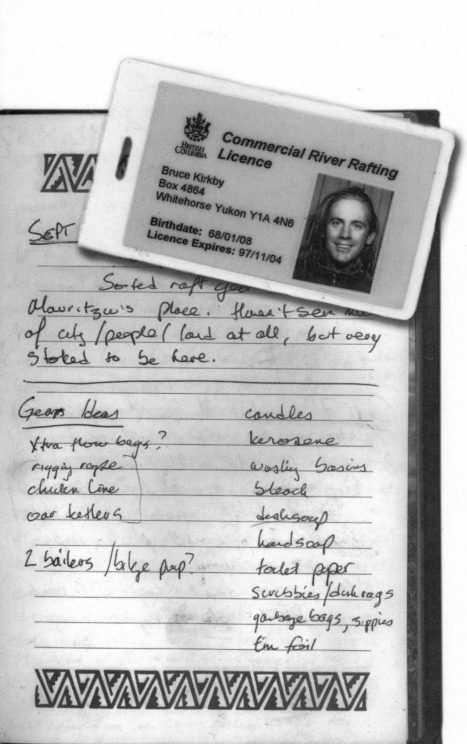

Commercial River Rafting Licence

BRITISH COLUMBIA

Bruce Kirkby
Box 4864
Whitehorse Yukon Y1A 4N6

Birthdate: 68/01/08
Licence Expires: 97/11/04

SEPT

Sorted raft gear
Mauritzw's place. Hasn't seen much
of city/people/land at all, but very
stoked to be here.

Gear Ideas

Xtra flow bags?
rigging rope
chuck line
oar kettles

2 bailers/bilge pmp?

candles
kerosene
washing basins
bleach
dishsoap
handsoap
toilet paper
scrubbies/dishrags
garbage bags, zippies
tin foil

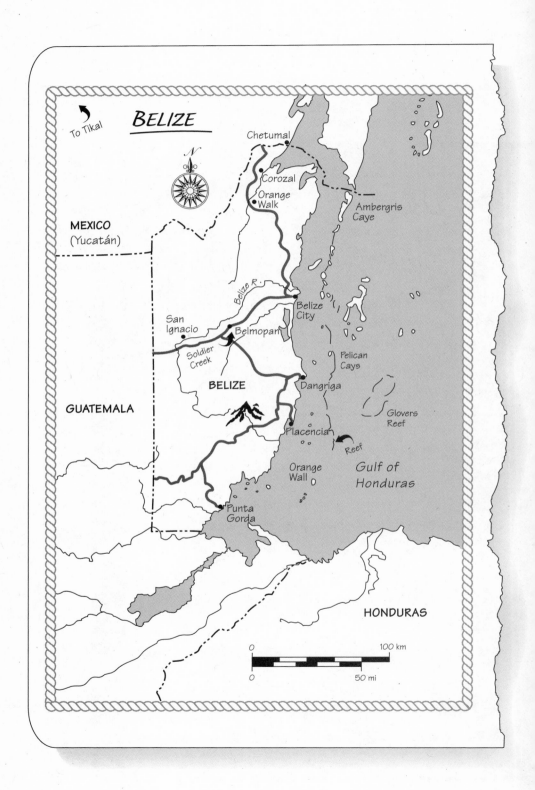

seven

"Da White Mon Mek Bad Fisha"

REEFS AND RAIN FOREST

We are children of our landscape; it dictates behavior and even thought in the measure to which we are responsive to it.

Lawrence Durrell

Belize, 1995

"DON'T TOUCH ANYTHING unless you see me, or another one of the guides, touch it first," Brian, the trip leader, warns. "Plenty of things living on the reef pack a ñasty bite, or sting."

Then he swings both legs out of his kayak's cockpit, slides into the azure water, and swims away, four guests following close behind. Pappy, the dreadlocked local Belizean fisherman accompanying our trip, sets off in another direction with an English couple and their two children. I am left with three men, vacationing pilots from Continental Airlines, anchored on the edge of vast coral shallows. After straining to cram on the awkward flippers, I spit in my mask to prevent it from fogging. Then all four of us flop from our kayaks and splash off. It is my very first day of guiding in the Caribbean. I don't have a clue what is safe to touch and what isn't.

We drift lazily through the sun-drenched waters. Schools of tiny fish dart before our masks, moving in unison like sparkling sequin sheets. Shafts of light, cutting down from above, create never-ending patterns that dance across the colourful reef below us. There are yellow tube sponges, orange anemones, purple sea fans, banana nudibranches, and bristling red fire-worms. A spotted eagle ray rises from a sandy patch ahead and speeds away, wings flapping gracefully. I point, and glance back over my shoulder, exchanging snorkel-contorted smiles and slow-motion nods with the swimmers behind.

As we float, a pair of elegant French angelfish engage us in a game of hide-and-go-seek. Swimming within centimetres of our masks, they dart away, disappearing into clefts in the coral before cautiously approaching again. We pass a school of grazing parrotfish, chipping away chucks of hard coral with their beaks of fused teeth, constantly expelling white puffs of fine sand from their back ends. (These are key contributions to the white beaches of the Caribbean. A single parrotfish can produce up to a ton of sand each year!) With fins flowing like a schooner at full-rig, a queen triggerfish rushes by, and behind, horse-eyed jacks chase schools of blue-headed wrasse in sudden, frantic starts. I stop to lift a sea star from the bottom, turning it over to show the three men its thousands of tiny tube feet.

As we explore I lose track of time, eventually raising my head to search for the kayaks, now distant specks on the blue horizon. I am preparing to gather the men and start back when an unusual sea fan catches my attention. Growing on the edge of a large coral patch, it is brown and leathery, markedly different from anything we have yet seen. Ignoring Brian's warning, I reach out toward the fan, overtaken by a desire to run my fingers down its soft, fluttering length. As my fingers brush the edge of the fan, which feels like a dog's tongue, I realize that something is not right. An unmistakable form lies hidden in the coral ahead. My heart skips a beat. This is no sea fan that I am stroking, it is the tail of a large shark.

The shark rests inside the hollow centre of the coral head. It must be eight feet long, or more. I can see its gills gently opening and closing. Looking closer, I see there is a second shark, lying motionless beside the first. They both face away from me, and show no sign of moving. Fighting the urge to gasp for breath, I back up silently. Twisting my head, I spot the others on the far side of the coral patch and wave, giving a thumbs-up signal, indicating I want to talk above the surface. Placing our flippers awkwardly on the sandy bottom, we all stand at once, leaving the peaceful world of water behind.

"Let's head back to the kayaks," I splutter, spitting out my snorkel. "But swim as slowly and calmly as you can."

"Why?"

"Well . . . there are two big sharks in the coral between us."

The three men slam their snorkels back in and plunge underwater to look. I follow, just in time to see the tail before me flicker and disappear. Our motion has disturbed the sharks, and they emerge from the far side of the coral, intimidating creatures with tawny hides and blunt heads. Their beady eyes appear unmoving, and for what seems an eternity, the sharks simply float. Then slowly they begin moving toward my guests. I can't believe it. My very first day of guiding in the south, and three of my clients are about to be eaten. All I can do is watch. The sharks continue toward the frozen men until they are almost face to face. Just a metre (3 feet) separates them. Then, with a single flick of their tails, the sharks angle away and speed off across the flats.

My heart is still racing when we arrive back at the kayaks. The pilots are bubbling with excited stories, but I feel guilty. It seemed way too close for comfort. Sensing my concern, Brian takes me aside and gently explains that the monsters we encountered were nurse sharks, generally docile and harmless creatures.

"*Wha-da-go-on, mon?* (What's going on, man?)," Pappy swims over and asks. Hearing the story, he laughs till his dreads shake, then playfully berates me. "*What mon? What! Dem was sleepin'! Ya coulda ridden dem like ponies! Boy, next time ya betta try. Ya need ta hold dem tight with ya knees, cause dey git vera angry. Da skin is rough, mon. First time I try, ma legs a bleedin' afta. Jaaa, we mek ya Belizean yet.*"

After finishing the season on the Tatshenshini, I left the Yukon and flew to Toronto. Neil had offered me a guiding position for the next summer, but what to do in the interim? For years I had listened with envy to the stories of senior guides who travelled south during winter, following the sun and finding employment in places like Chile, Mexico, Costa Rica, and Kenya. While it was usually just the veterans that got southern assignments, I decided to give it a shot, employing my "call-every-advertiser-in-the-back-of-every-magazine" strategy. After only two weeks, the owner of Island Expeditions, a Vancouver-based company that ran sea-kayaking trips in Belize, called me. That first informal, unplanned phone interview was brutally difficult.

"So, you spent a season kayaking on the Canadian coast?" Tim, the owner, began. "Then show me what you learned. Give me a life-cycle sketch of the five Pacific Salmon species, highlighting their differences."

Dredging my memory, I regurgitated a list of facts.

"Not bad. How about a species profile of a marine invertebrate. Any one, your choice."

My mind raced back to Jim Allan, and the sunflower sea star he pulled from the bottom of a sandy bay on our guide's course. I started talking. Questions about tides, weather patterns, and navigation followed. There were two more phone interviews and a quick meeting at the Toronto airport when Tim's business partner passed through town. I was not hopeful, and busy searching elsewhere, when the call came: "We need you in Vancouver next week. You are going to drive our company van south to Belize. Your girlfriend can come down for the season too if she wants, and help manage our base."

Cecilia instantly agreed to join me for six months in the sun. Looking back now, the sacrifices she was making to accommodate my nomadic lifestyle were enormous. At the time I was blind. I couldn't imagine why anyone would want to do anything else. Three days later, full of anticipation, we arrived together in Vancouver, greeted by a West Coast autumn – grey clouds, incessant drizzle, and streets littered with brown leaves.

With the help of two other guides, we crammed a twelve-person passenger van with supplies. Crates of non-perishable foods – baba ghanouj, hummus, olives, miso soup, sushi leaves, pasta, rice, and spices – were hidden beneath seats, to avoid the prying eyes of customs inspectors. Paddles, tents, sails, ropes, and hammocks were piled on top, filling the van to within a foot of the roof. There was just enough room to slide in a thin mattress and create a sleeping berth. Six sea kayaks were lashed to roof racks; a trailer towed behind carried ten more.

As mist turned to icy rain we pulled across the Washington State border and began the seven-thousand-kilometre (4,400-mile) drive south. For four days and four nights we drove, stopping only for gas and snacks. Oregon, Nevada, and Arizona passed in darkness. Temperatures rose as we sped across the dusty plains of New Mexico and Texas. At the crowded Mexican border a mind-numbing trail of paperwork led from office to office. Eventually, an appropriate bribe was agreed upon, and we were waved past.

Half an hour later, *federales* stopped us on a deserted stretch of tarmac, and searched everything again. Another bribe was negotiated. We rolled on. Palms began to spring up along the roadside, then rainforest. We climbed along winding roads, into rumpled green hills, passing roadside stands of pineapple, banana, and papaya. Darkness came and went. The sun pried itself from the horizon, spraying streaks of gold across misty forests. At Chetumal, on the Belizean border, there were more worried glances, handshaking, and paper signing. Then in a final, caffeine-induced haze, we rumbled past swamps and karst mountains, at long last arriving exhausted in the sleepy coastal town of Dangriga.

⁓

"*Nefa leaf ya fingas in da wata, mon!*" the local Garifuna guides like to warn new guests at the start of each week. "*Dem Belizean barracuda ar vera hungra ya know, an' ya finga mek some good eatin!*"

These dreadlocked and enviably relaxed men then throw their heads back and roar with laughter, gleefully relating the details of a shiny wedding ring (and the finger it was on) that was bitten clean off a kayaker's hand trailing in the water beside the cockpit.

Garifuna history can be traced back to 1635, when two heavily laden Spanish slave-trading vessels sank off the coast of St. Vincent, a Caribbean isle. Arawak and Carib Indians inhabiting the island gave refuge to the African slaves that survived, and the people that sprang from this unlikely union are today known as the Garifuna. For more than a century the Garifuna coexisted peacefully with French settlers on St. Vincent, but conflict erupted when English colonists began arriving and demanding land. The Garifuna put up a fierce resistance but were hopelessly outnumbered. After being soundly defeated by English forces in 1797, all surviving Garifuna were rounded up and deported to

Roatan, an island off the northern coast of Honduras. Thus began a diaspora that still endures today, as the Garifuna slowly spread outward, establishing settlements and fishing villages along the coasts of Belize and Nicaragua.

The Garifuna men that accompany our trips are all expert fishers, and they spend their days diving for conch and lobster, hunting jack fish and grouper with spears, and trolling for barracuda. This allows us to carry just the staples, rice, flour, oil, and beans. The rest comes from the sea.

Early in the season I fall under the mistaken impression that I can contribute to this harvest, and confidently set off from camp with a Hawaiian sling (a handheld spear propelled by a loop of surgical tubing) in search of dinner. Hours later I return, exhausted, carrying a single angelfish, embarrassingly small and impaled through the eye. Tiptoeing from the water, I try to sneak past hammocks strung between shoreline palms.

"*Wat es dat mon?!*" Pappy looks up, exploding with laughter. "*A lee, lee fish! Da white mon all mek bad fisha, I say! Alwes dem comin wit da pretty fish, nefa da eatin fish!*"

One of the napping guests peers up from her hammock and suddenly bursts into tears. Jumping to the ground, she disappears in the direction of her tent, sobbing. I hand the spear over to Pappy and go to investigate.

"I have two angelfish as pets at home," the teary-eyed woman explains. "They are very intelligent fish. Each has its own personality and quirks. Mine are like friends. Now you want me to eat one?"

Pappy returns fifteen minutes later with two triggerfish and a big grouper, more than enough to feed our group of twelve. He is still laughing as he throws the fish down and starts cleaning them.

"*Bruce, mon. It is easy ta catch a fish. Ya onla need ta do two tings. Ya need ya hook in de wata, and ya need ta be patient. It's like if ya want a coconut. A mon sit long enough unda da tree, an one will fall. I guarantee you dat!*"

Pappy (or Hugh Buller as his Creole parents named him twenty-nine years ago) is always joking. Thin, dark, and with long sun-bleached dreadlocks, he looks the quintessential Rastafarian.

"*When da first kayak guides come ta Dangriga ta do some exploring, mon, dey sleep on ma family beach. I come down and say, 'What-a-go-on?' De say, 'We going to da cays.' What?! In dem lee boats? Are ya crazy? I laugh at dem. Dat was ten years ago, mon, and I guide wit dem eva since.*"

As we scale the fish I ask him about a curious bald spot on his forehead. "*Oh mon. Dat was a big problem,*" he rolls his eyes and laughs till tears come. "*Look at me. I am a lee, lee mon. Now my girl, Lucy, she be a big, big lady. Tre hundra pounds. One time I come home from a kayak trip smellin' like fancy perfume, and Lucy she blow her top, mon. Noting had happened, mon, I swear, but she no be listenin' to me. Instead, she be draggin me round the house by my dreads. Finally, they just rip out, an I run mon, scared for ma life!*"

"Are you still together?"

"*Oh yah, mon. Da Belizean, mon, he alwas like a big woman, wit a BIG bum! Not da lee girls ya Canadians like.*"

Each night, over a coconut husk fire, we cook a different feast: conch fritters, roasted lobster tails, shark ceviche, grilled fish, and seafood curry. On special occasions we gather coconuts, grating the meat and mixing in condensed milk, orange rind, ginger, and toasted almonds. This thick concoction is heated over a fire and stirred until our forearms ache. Slowly browning, it eventually caramelizes into a delicious, gooey lump known as *tableta*.

Our kayaking journeys wind south along the barrier reef, weaving through turquoise waters, coral reef, and mangrove cays. Even when no islands are in sight, vast, sandy shallows allow us to stop for lunch. We prepare supper on folding tables while the guests wade through the warm, knee-deep water, chasing schools of needlefish and hermit crabs. Each night we camp on idyllic white-sand isles, many no larger than a football field and tufted with a handful of coconut palms. As dinner cooks, tents are raised on the sand, and hammocks strung between trunks that sway gently in evening breezes.

Unlike my sea-kayaking experiences on Canada's West Coast, where cold waters made hypothermia a constant threat, in Belize the ocean is our playground, we are free to wade, swim, dive, snorkel, and splash at will. On the first day of each trip, we teach our guests how to slide out of the kayaks while in deep water, and more importantly, how to get back into them. Then masks and snorkels are kept handy on deck, and whenever an interesting patch of coral appears beneath our hulls, we jump out and explore, towing the boats behind on tethers.

The gentle and steady trade winds that caress Belizean waters during winter allow us to sail the kayaks with ease and consistency. Although the water occasionally gets rough, the consequences of a flip are not severe, and I became increasingly confident travelling under adverse conditions. When the kayaks are "catamaran-ed" together (a single kayak held firmly to the side of a double as an outrigger), they cut through intimidating chop and swell, and we sail in all but the roughest of gales.

Doldrums are rare, but when they do descend, the sea grows glassy calm and progress slows to a crawl. Sound carries for kilometres in the uncanny stillness. An oppressive humidity spreads, and while water fights help ease the discomfort, we spend most of our time right in the water on the hottest days, just swimming and towing the kayaks behind us.

Dolphins occasionally race up to investigate as we float, their ghostly white bodies often giving me a start as they rocket unannounced out of the green. Usually they do not linger, but occasionally a pod will swim close, diving below us and turning upside down to peer at the strange human swimmers, the clicks and chirps of their echo locations chattering in our ears. These brief moments bring a joy that lasts long after we have arrived at camp and settled beneath sheets and mosquito netting.

At first glance, the tiny country of Belize appears an anomaly; a misplaced burp of Caribbean island culture lying on the doorstep of Latin America, an English-speaking country encircled by Spanish neighbours. And who exactly are the Belizeans? It is difficult to define. As a long-standing haven for refugees, the young nation has been inundated with successive waves of immigration – colonial settlers, Carib slaves, Mestizos, East Indians, Chinese labourers, Garifuna exiles, Mexican Mennonites, and Latin American refugees. All have been accepted, and to varying degrees, absorbed, creating today's unique and diverse population.

The great Mayan civilization that once carpeted Meso-America was already in decline when the first Europeans began arriving in the early sixteenth century. Disease, slavery, and ferocious persecution quickly devastated what remained. One million Mayans once lived in the lands encompassed by Belize. Less than twenty-five thousand survive today. While Spanish settlers quickly overran the surrounding regions, the swampy backwaters of modern Belize were deemed undesirable and left alone.

It was not until the second half of the seventeenth century that a group of British settlers known as the "Baymen" settled along the coast. These rough buccaneers, forced to find a new profession when the age of state-endorsed piracy ground to a halt, came to exploit the logwood and mahogany. The value of their hardwood harvest quickly drew Spain's interest, and skirmishes over control of the region began to flare up.

The conflict reached a head in 1798, when a determined combination of Baymen, armed slaves, and British navy battleships defeated the Spanish at St. George's Caye. Shortly afterward, a sliver of land just three hundred kilometres (180 miles) long and one hundred kilometres (60 miles) wide was formally declared the Crown colony of British Honduras. Not until two centuries later, on September 21, 1981, did Belize finally become an independent nation.

Within Belize's confined borders lies an incredible diversity of natural habitats. Rain forest cloaks the mountains of the interior, where an estimated 70 per cent of old growth still remains intact. Ocelot, tapir, peccary, and puma roam these dark woods, as do jaguars, the highest concentration found anywhere on the planet. Mangrove swamps stabilize lowlands and estuaries, while offshore one finds the perfect conditions for coral growth – clear, warm seas, plenty of sunlight, perfect salinity, and a constant circulation of well-oxygenated water. Belize's great barrier reef has been developing for 450 million years, and represents the second largest coral growth in the world.

Hundreds of different coral species exist in the world's seas, but these are easily divided into two major groups. Hard corals are the reef-builders, secreting a sturdy exoskeleton of calcium carbonate. Soft corals appear plantlike, using spicules of calcium carbonate to produce a flexible axial skeleton. Although hard corals are often misperceived as lifeless rocks, and soft corals as marine plants, both are in fact colonies of living animals, comprised of millions of individual polyps connected by a thin layer of living tissue.

Both types of coral are voracious hunters. Each individual polyp living in a coral colony captures passing zooplankton with tiny stinging tentacles, and colonies are so effective at capturing micro-organisms that wash over the reef (90 per cent or more are removed from the water) that they leave the sea completely devoid of nutrients, turning it a glorious tropical blue. Herein lies the great enigma of tropical seas. The plankton present in the water can provide only 10 per cent of the coral's nutritional needs. Where does the rest of the energy come from?

Viewing the ecosystem as a whole, one notices a greater paradox. There are a vast multitude of fish (secondary consumers), just a few snails and worms (primary consumers), and almost no sea weeds or sea grasses (primary producers). The pyramid of life appears to be inverted. This is analogous to great herds of lions roaming a desert, sustained by just a few zebra that live on grassless plains. How can this be?

The answer to the riddle lies with an algae known as zooxanthellae, a highly specialized, single-celled organism that lives symbiotically inside coral polyps. Zooxanthellae contains chlorophyll and through photo-synthesis produces a supply of food for the polyp. In return the coral provides protection for the algae and certain waste products, such as ammonia, which the algae requires for growth.

It is zooxanthellae that gives the coral its colour, and it is also this sensitive algae that defines the conditions under which reefs may grow, as colonies react to even small perturbations in the environment by expelling their zooxanthellae. This process, known as "bleaching," quickly leaves the reef colourless and dead from starvation, making coral a canary species, a harbinger of change.

Sixty-four kilometres (40 miles) offshore, far beyond the protection of Belize's barrier reef, lies Glovers Reef atoll. After two months of leading kayaking journeys through the cays, Cecilia and I are transferred here, to run trips from a comfortable base camp. Each week a new group of tourists arrives, shuttled out by powerboat to spend seven lazy days paddling the inner lagoon, fly-fishing, windsurfing, beachcombing, and diving. At night we walk reef crests exposed by low tides, the beams of our flashlights illuminating hundreds of reflective eyes. It is not hard to find crabs, octopi, even small sharks and crocodiles. Later we sit around flickering coconut-husk campfires as our Garifuna guides drum long into the night.

Belizean atolls have formed on top of massive bedrock blocks, thrown up along ancient fault lines (unlike their Pacific cousins, which have grown around the calderas of extinct volcanoes). Consequently, the edges of these atolls are precipitously steep, dropping thousands of feet to the ocean floor. The nearby Eastern Wall of Glovers Reef quickly becomes one of my favourite areas to investigate. Whenever I have free time I paddle here, jumping from the kayak and floating face down, fifty feet above forests of staghorn coral and giant basket sponges, gently tugged to and fro by the swell. Black-tipped reef sharks pass below, as do the schools of barracuda that hunt along the flats. The water is so clear that vertigo plays tricks with my mind, making me feel as if I am floating in thin air, about to tumble down and crash onto the coral below.

Then there is "the Wall," an abrupt line where the coral suddenly falls away into an abyss of nothingness. Drifting near the edge, I feel my stomach tighten. One moment there is reef just fifty feet below me, and the next there is nothing but a black void. I swim for hours along the edge, watching for rays and turtles that occasionally appear from the depths, soaring up the sheer wall and setting off across the flats.

The depths are inviting. I practise swimming deeper. I learn to relax, slow my heart rate, and take several deep breaths before sliding under the water. Soon I can equalize the pressure in my ears without using my hands, allowing me to continue stroking downward the entire time. Over these clear flats I discover the concept of negative buoyancy. On the surface, a human body floats (more or less) and effort must be exerted to descend. As divers know, the deeper a person goes in the ocean, the more their chest and lungs are compressed. There comes a point – about six metres (20 feet) below the surface, depending on the person – where the lungs have been squeezed enough that the body will sink under its own weight.

After swimming down to this point, I can simply relax and spread my arms. My body soars downward without any effort, like a giant bird. There is a momentary glimpse of weightlessness and tranquility. Then fear grasps my heart. *Have I gone too deep? Can I make it back up?* Turning toward the surface, I frantically claw upward. Lungs scream; heart pounds; pressure builds in my ears. Moments later I explode at the surface, gasping through my snorkel, the sun warming my back. Within minutes I find myself wanting to dive again.

In the lee of a nearby islet I find a steep, sandy slope that drops from the beach to unseen depths. After passing the point of negative buoyancy, I can soar headfirst down this underwater dune, centimetres above its surface, arms angled back. As the weeks pass I return whenever I have a spare minute, almost always alone. I begin carrying small shells down with me, dropping them as I turn, marking my downward progress on the sloping sand surface, testing myself. Deeper and deeper I go. When I roll up toward the surface, I can see only a shimmering, translucent light, far, far above. Perhaps it is the silence and serenity, but I feel pleasantly altered after diving deep, and am constantly enticed back.

One day I arrive to find a lone barracuda sharing the slope with me. Accustomed to swimming near barracuda, I do not give the fish a second thought, and it appears disinterested in my efforts. After half an hour my body is in tune with the water and diving has become effortless. I drop my deepest shell yet and roll into an ascent. For a second it looks as if my way to the surface is blocked. A school of barracuda has appeared, and hundreds of fish circle directly overhead. The water is thick with their bodies blocking my way. There is no time to think. My only option is to swim straight through them. With lungs bursting, I thrash to the surface. Somehow I pass directly through the middle of the school, without touching a single fish.

Floating on the surface, my chest heaves as I stare downward. The barracuda are still below me, circling, and I am overcome with the unshakable feeling I have pushed too far into a realm where I do not belong. Although I plan to come back, I never do. During the weeks and months ahead, a chaotic whirlwind of sickness, jungle explorations, and reef trips keep me away from Glovers Reef. I never return to the barracuda slopes, and I never dive deep again.

❧

Thick rain forest carpets the interior of Belize. Between kayaking trips I catch occasional whispers of this languid world – the pungent scent of tropical decay, a foul-tasting bark-and-root tea delivered to my sickbed, iguanas strung over the shoulders of short Mayan men who emerge from hidden trails behind our house in Dangriga. I feel drawn to the jungle, but keep my distance. It is not the place for a casual stroll. I am busy on the ocean and there is no one to teach me about this dark realm, until the day Jonesy arrives.

Jonesy is a sixty-two-year-old Carib who has spent his entire life in the rain forest. Tall, heavily muscled, gentle, and usually silent, this legendary hunter is respected throughout the southern provinces. His aura can silence a room; his knowledge of plants and animals is encyclopedic. A renowned healer, Jonesy is always collecting barks, roots, and leaves. His carefully dried and preserved collection exceeds five hundred specimens. It was Jonesy's fever-grass tea that appeared by my bedside at the height of an unknown illness, brought by one of his seven sons upon the request of Tim (the owner of the sea-kayaking company). It was Jonesy who accompanied Jim Allan of Ecosummer on a crushingly difficult traverse of the Maya Mountains, carrying heavy camera gear and finding water when the team's supplies ran dry. Now it is Jonesy that Tim turns to when he needs help in the jungle.

A new itinerary of jungle-river trips has been advertised and sold. The guests are due to start arriving in less than a month and the pressure is on because we have not yet found a suitable river to run. Tim sends word through Jonesy's children that he is planning an exploratory descent of Soldier Creek, a small river draining the inland Maya Mountains, north of Dangriga.

Three days later Jonesy appears at our door, on his way home from gathering plants in the nearby Cockscomb Basin, the world's only jaguar preserve. His enormous palm envelopes mine when we shake hands. He says nothing, just sits and listens. I watch him from the corner of my eye as Tim explains our plan. Jonesy's skin is dark black, his face deeply creased. He doesn't smile, but his eyes are lively, and his body appears to be that of a twenty-year-old athlete. With a simple nod, he agrees to help us slash and crash our way down the overgrown river.

Two days later, the company van halts at the end of a rough dirt track. Before us is a languorous, tobacco-brown stream. Emerging from one wall of forest, it passes across a clearing four and a half metres wide (15 feet) and disappears into another curtain of bush. Tim, his brother Bill, Jonesy, and I will try to follow this river all the way to the ocean, which lies thirty kilometres (18 miles) away, somewhere on the other side of this green barrier. Everything in between is a mystery to us. We pump up two inflatable ducky-style kayaks, loading them with barrels of food, a dry bag of tents and stoves, one chainsaw, and four machetes.

"*Ya betta wear long pants and a hefa (heavy) shirt,*" Jonesy breaks his silence. "*Da bush it's scratchy. And ya will be wet da whole time.*"

Pushing the kayaks from shore, we jump in and float downstream, passing through a curtain of vines. Sunlight fades behind us. As our eyes adjust, I see we have entered a dim, cavernous realm. Delicate ferns and moss-covered rocks line the shores. Decomposing leaves litter the forest floor beyond. High above us, the canopy blocks almost all direct sunlight. Only a few rays break through, shining down like spotlights on an empty stage. Woody vines and epiphytes (aerial roots) hang from branches, others creep and curl around thick buttressed trunks. The air is moist and stagnant, smelling of decay.

Jonesy and I run in the first kayak. Vines, prickly bushes, and leafy plants constantly block our way. Jonesy sits in front, slashing madly with a machete, cutting a path as fast as the current carries us. I steer from the back, aiming for the least congested areas. Whenever a big log or tangle of branches blocks the flow, we simply drag our boat over it or wade around. Tim and his brother follow behind, using a chainsaw to clear these bigger obstructions. Commercial clients will find it easier to make the descent a week from now, but the luxuriant growth of the jungle will quickly cover signs of our passing. It is tiring work, and feels, at times, futile. The humidity is oppressive, and sweat soon soaks our clothes. Jonesy is thin on patience.

"Right . . . Jesus, mon, RIGHT, I said. What's wrong? Faster. Left now . . . Quickly! Left!"

Jonesy doesn't mean to rude, he is just focused. He reminds me of my father that way, so caught up in what he is doing that he hardly realizes he is being brusque. The others roll their eyes and quietly express their sympathy, but I don't mind. I like Jonesy, and feel lucky to be paired with him, despite his temper. I learn by watching him and listening to his mutterings.

"*Chicle tree*," he points with his machete. It is a giant sapodilla, criss-crossed with ancient machete slashes as high as the eye can see. The tree's milky sap – known as *chicle* – was once one of Belize's leading exports. Hard-working *chicleros* combed these rainforests in the early part of the century, harvesting the thick substance, a key ingredient of chewing gum (hence the brand name "Chiclets").

"*I nefa seen a chicle tree without dem cuts*," Jonesy notes. "*And I nefa seen a chicleros with all his arms and legs. Everee mon he got bit by de tommy goff.*"

"Tommy goff" is the colloquial name for the fer-de-lance, a deadly pit viper common in the Belizean jungle. The snakes can grow to more than eight feet in length, and their hemorrhagic poison causes profuse internal bleeding. It is the lucky *chicleros* who lost just an arm or leg. Many others faced agonizing deaths.

An afternoon cloudburst chases us from the water. Although already soaked, we take shelter under the thick fronds of a cohune palm. Before letting us settle, Jonesy rakes a stick through the jumble of oily nuts that spread beneath its trunk. "*Dis mess mek a perfect home for da tommy goff*," he warns. I fidget nervously, wearing just a pair of river sandals that sink ankle-deep in the soft black mulch.

"*Yes, mon!*" Jonesy yells in triumph. To my horror and amazement, a fer-de-lance slides from amidst the debris. As thick as a forearm and a metre and a half (5 feet) long, its olive skin is marked with diamonds of tan and black. It races toward the creek and Jonesy chases after with his stick. He returns minutes later, having killed it. I felt saddened by the needless waste. I think of speaking up, and suggesting that simply frightening the snake away would have been enough. But who am I, on my first jungle trip, to counter Jonesy's years of experience? I feel conflicted, but hold my tongue.

The downpour ends, and as the sun bursts out above the canopy, a hammer of humidity crashes down inside. Steam rises in wisps from the forest floor. Sweat beads on our brows. Continuing downstream, Jonesy spots a collection of water vines hanging above the river. With a quick slash, he chops a woody section, which he holds above his head as if he were playing a trumpet. Clean, clear water drips into Jonesy's mouth. "*Da best wata i Belize,*" he smiles.

The old Carib hunter peels off his sodden shirt. Thick pectoral muscles wrap around his chest, meeting at the centre like knotted fingers. His biceps, perfectly round, look like tennis balls that slide easily under jet black skin. Only the greying of his hair betrays his age. Two years ago, when his beloved wife, Emma, passed away, one half of Jonesy's closely cropped afro suddenly turned silver. Split exactly down the centre, the other half remains perfectly black. We rarely see this though, for Jonesy always wears a red bandana, pirate-style, pulled tight across his head.

For the first day and a half Soldier Creek is playful, splashing through smooth limestone channels like a giant waterslide. By the second afternoon its mood changes. The water slows. Growth chokes the passage. We are often forced to lie flat in our boats and slide beneath tangles of branches, shielding our eyes as beetles and spiders drop from above. Elsewhere we must get out and wade, dragging the boats, feet gripped by squelching, thick muck.

Bamboo quickly becomes a reviled adversary. Giant groves erupt along the banks, with stalks reaching more than a hundred feet. Tangled piles of deadfall lie at their bases, spilling into the river and choking the passage like a mess of pick-up-sticks. Dry and sinewy, the dead stalks are too strong to be cut by machete, yet too flexible and yielding for the chainsaw. We must laboriously bulldoze through the floating jams, pushing the stalks under our kayaks with paddles and machetes as we pass.

Jonesy and I grind to a halt in the centre of one particularly thick pile.

I haul on nearby stalks and Jonesy paddles hard, but we don't move. Eventually we are forced to get out and balance on the slippery bamboo, using our weight to submerge an entire floating platform of deadfall. Waist-deep in the dark river, we carefully edge the kayak forward. Suddenly the entire lot shifts, and our feet drop out from underneath us. Flailing in the stagnant pool, grasping for the kayak, we both struggle to keep our heads above water. I can feel bamboo poles rising all about me.

"*JESUS!*" Jonesy yells, thrashing madly. I think his patience has finally snapped, but soon I notice a tickling on my shoulders, and looking around, see the surface of the water is covered with tiny grey spiders. There are thousands of them, each no bigger than a tick. I feel them swarming up my neck and over my scalp. They crawl under my clothes, in my ears, even on my eyelids. I duck underwater and shake my head, but as soon as I come up I am covered again. The toppling bamboo must have submerged their nest. Jumping and lunging, we frantically tear the boat free of the obstruction, leap in, and paddle away. Hours later I still find spiders crawling from nooks and crannies in the kayak. The sensation of itchiness refuses to abate, plaguing me through the night.

My first impression of the rainforest was one of emptiness, of abandonment. There seemed to be no life. With patience and Jonesy's coaching, I begin to notice more. There are bright flowers hidden amongst the branches. Heliconia, orchids, and bromeliads play host to butterflies and hummingbirds. We spot colourful parrots, green and yellow trogans, even a keel-billed toucan, which thrills me, for it is the "Fruit Loops" bird. There are turtles in the large pools, and Jonesy finds the spoor of peccary, tapir, and ocelot along the riverbanks. A paca – or gibnut as it is commonly known – wanders into camp one evening as we cook. This large rodent is considered a delicacy, and was served to the Queen on her visit to Belize.

But more than anything else, it is the ants that amaze me. They are everywhere. Unbroken highways of leafcutters stream across the forest floor, carrying shards of foliage above their heads. Their nests, marked by mounds of earth bigger than Volkswagen Beetles, are home to millions. The leaf fragments streaming in are carried to underground farms where workers grow fungus that feeds the colony.

On the third day Jonesy stumbles on a colony of army ants, spilling like oil across the forest floor. Rushing through decaying litter, they raise spiders, snakes, beetles, and anything else alive. As we watch, a black tarantula bursts up from beneath the leaves, hopping about desperately, trying to avoid the stinging ants, but to no avail. Slowly, the life drains from the tarantula's body, and its hairy legs fold. Immediately, it begins moving back along the column, passed between workers as if on a conveyor belt, food for the queen who travels far in the rear.

"*Dem ants a always welcome in ma home,*" Jonesy whispers as we watch the melee. Three years earlier, when Emma was still alive, they woke up to a strange sound. Moonlight revealed their ceiling was covered in a moving layer of ants. "*We run screamin from da house,*" he laughs. "*We 'ave ta wait tree days for all dem ants ta be gone. But afta dat, da house was sparklin clean! No more spidas, no bugs, no geckos, no flies. Emma say she neva seen da house so clean!*"

We hang our clothes out overnight, sweaty and sodden, but they only grow mildew. Nothing dries in the rain forest, and I crawl naked into a damp sleeping bag, inside a damp tent. By morning my fingers and toes have shrivelled like prunes. I notice clear blisters are beginning to appear on my arms and legs. Tim and Bill have the same problem.

"*Dem a wata blistas, mon,*" Jonesy mutters when I ask. "*Dis riva wata no good.*" He says nothing more. Ticks and chiggers are common in the brush, and they attack our legs, leaving red welts. Sitting by the campfire, Jonesy squeezes a boil that has grown on his shoulder. A botfly larva pops out.

At noon on the fifth day we round a corner and find our way blocked. A cliff of sheer limestone runs across our path. Soldier Creek disappears into a dark cave at its base. We immediately pull over. Jonesy declares he has heard rumours of the cave, and believes fishermen from the ocean have dragged their boats upstream, through this obstacle.

No one knows what to do next. If we commit, and paddle into the cave, the current will make it impossible to return. We peer into the cave with our headlamps. The passage narrows, and in its depths we can see the water pouring over a small drop, disappearing around a bend. Jonesy is confident that we can make it through, and seeing no other options, we decide to trust him.

The river drops over a series of small falls, gurgling and splashing. As our eyes adjust, we find we have entered a smooth, water-carved channel. The air around us is cool, and the stench of guano strong. Sounds echo, and vision is restricted to the beams of our headlights. On and on we go, eventually drifting into a large cavern where stalactites and travertine glisten on the roof and walls. It appears we have come to a dead end, but after some swearing, Jonesy discovers a low, keyhole exit. Lying flat in our boats, we push ourselves into the shallow slot. The ceiling is low, only centimetres from our faces, and hand over hand we go. Eventually the faint glow of daylight appears ahead. Breaking through a curtain of leafy vines, we paddle into the sunlight.

Six days after entering the rain forest, the blue waters of a coastal lagoon open before us. The company van is waiting for us on a sandy beach. Tim and his brother drive north toward Belize City. Jonesy and I jump out and wait by the coastal highway, hoping to hitch a ride back to Dangriga. I carry our wet clothes, wrapped in a ball and slung on a machete over my shoulder, while Jonesy holds a worn rifle, his constant companion.

As the setting sun casts shadows across the dirt road and the shrill cries of cicadas begin to fade, a decrepit pickup slows. We clamber up into the back. Standing side by side, grasping the roll bar, Jonesy and I lean forward into the cool evening air. Glancing down, I catch a glimpse of my reflection in the rear window, hair messy, face covered with stubble. With the beard, I look shockingly like my father. But it is my eyes, shining from behind the grime, that surprise me. I have never seen such raw happiness in them before.

I prepared to leave Belize as summer arrived. Far to the north, great swaths of arctic tundra were slowly warming, and soon I would return for my second season on the Tatshenshini. A letter had arrived in Dangriga from Nahanni Neil, listing me as a "Senior Guide" for the upcoming season. I was shocked at the title, albeit very pleased. For four years, no matter where I had gone, I had been the beginner.

The seven months of tropical luxuriance – sun, snorkelling, sailing, diving, and paddling – broadened my ecological understanding, and helped me to sense the natural world, the entire earth, as an interconnected web, and not a set of disparate pieces. One year later, high sea-surface temperatures around the globe would lead to an unprecedented and severe bleaching of corals. Reefs throughout the Indian Ocean, the Caribbean, and Pacific were affected. From the Maldives to Mauritius, the Seychelles to Sri Lanka, along the Indonesian and Philippine coasts, in Papua New Guinea, Galapagos, and elsewhere, staggering numbers of corals expelled their zooxanthellae and headed into a spiral of death. Researchers estimate worldwide coral mortality from this single event at 20 per cent. In Belize a mass mortality of lettuce coral, the most abundant species in the central lagoon, represented the first complete collapse of a Caribbean coral population in three thousand years. The waters I swam through will never be the same, at least not in my lifetime, or many more to come.

I squeezed Cecilia's hand as we took our seats aboard an American Airlines flight bound for Miami. The bonds between us were strong, for we both believed in true love and felt we had found it in each other. While the constant responsibilities and regular departures that guiding demanded were beginning to take their toll, one advantage of the lifestyle was that it provided extended chunks of free time. In the years ahead I would return to Sweden twice, and Cecilia would travel north for a Yukon summer.

While Cecilia understood my passion for the wilds, her friends and family back home struggled to see where it was leading. It didn't conform, and Cecilia was left precariously balanced between my unusual path and the regular life of someone in their late twenties. Although she never once suggested I should settle, the long on-again, off-again stints would eventually prove too much. If we had been on the same trajectory perhaps it could have worked, but we weren't. I never blamed guiding, because I never saw it as a choice between *my lifestyle* and *our love*. Feeling young and immortal, I was just too consumed with my search to imagine any other way. There was never a clear single decisive moment; just endless fretting, plenty of tears, painful phone calls, and no shortage of doubt.

The relationship, as the Swedes would say, eventually washed away in the sand.

Two other events occurred during my season in Belize – both seemingly insignificant – that would change the course of things to come.

First, my waterproof "pelican" case – containing all of my camera gear and twenty rolls of exposed film – was stolen. I left the equipment in the company van for no more than a minute on a major street in Belize City, taking care to lock all the doors. But my short absence provided enough time for a thief to smash a side window and remove my hidden camera case. For days my mood ranged between disbelief, sorrow, and rage. Months later, insurance provided a replacement. The Nikon system that I was sent was far more advanced than my previous amateur rig. The lenses were tack sharp. The body featured auto-focus, spot metering, and programmable modes, allowing my photography to take a giant leap forward. Over the next six years, I shot twenty-five thousand images on the new camera, building a nascent portfolio, embracing a burgeoning photographic passion. At the time, I could never have afforded such a system myself.

And the other serendipitous event? I met an undercover narcotics officer called Snake.

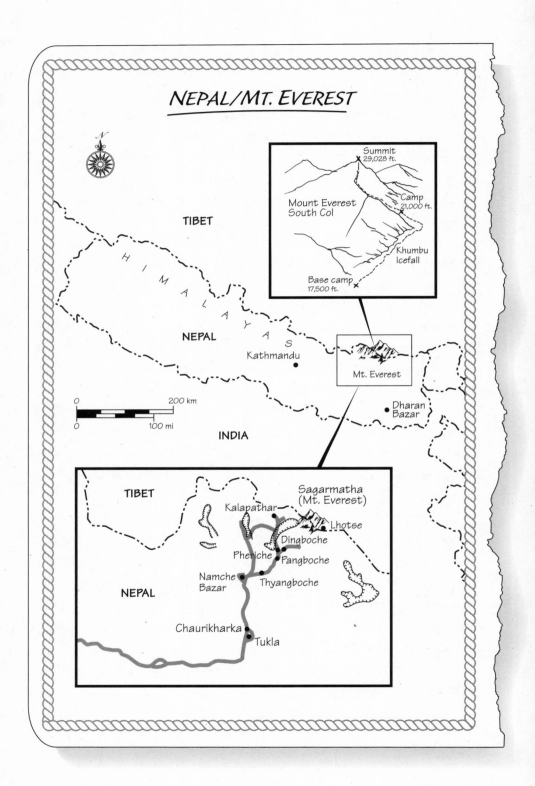

NEPAL/MT. EVEREST

Summit
29,028 ft.

Mount Everest
South Col

Camp
21,000 ft.

Khumbu
Icefall

Base camp
17,500 ft.

TIBET

HIMALAYAS

NEPAL

Kathmandu

200 km

100 mi

INDIA

Mt. Everest

Dharan
Bazar

TIBET

Sagarmatha
(Mt. Everest)

Kalapathar

Lhotse

Dingboche

Pheriche

Pangboche

Namche
Bazar

Thyangboche

NEPAL

Chaurikharka

Tukla

eight

"All this, and Everest Too"

THREE MONTHS IN THE HIMALAYA

Maybe true, maybe not true; better you believe.

Sherpa saying

Nepal,
1997

"SNAKE" WAS A hulk of a man, with shaved head, bristling goatee, and expressionless scowl. He looked like one mean biker, although in reality he was an undercover narcotics officer. And a very loud one. He arrived at the Glovers Reef base camp in Belize on New Year's Eve.

The Tilley-clad ecotourists sharing the trip with Snake – doctors, dentists, and massage therapists in search of a relaxing Caribbean escape – exhibited little interest in his lewd and outrageous accounts of crack busts gone bad, bawdy house raids, dead bodies, stolen guns, and smashed-down doors. So Snake hung out with the guides, becoming a de facto member of the crew for the week he stayed, lending a hand on the water and in the kitchen. Pappy and the other Garifuna fishermen loved his jokes of questionable taste.

By coincidence, Snake had once been a raft guide, a veteran of Wilderness Tours, the outfit on the Ottawa River where I first began guiding. We grew to be fast friends, often lingering late by the fire under starry equatorial nights, vying to outdo each other with outlandish and absurd tales. Although a memorable character, Snake was one of hundreds I met during the Belizean winter, and after he left, I doubted our paths would cross again.

Five months later and seven thousand kilometres away, I was standing quietly on the bank of the Ottawa River when someone snuck up behind and wrenched my arm into a half nelson. Warm breath and whiskers rasped against my ear.

"I don't like your type, hippy boy," the unseen assailant whispered. "You are a granola-eating, crystal-gazing, tree-hugging no-good fruitcake."

It was, of course, Snake. When I mentioned that I was heading north for a second season on the Tatshenshini, adding as an afterthought that a few spots still remained open on the first trip, Snake signed up the same day. A week later, as my raft drifted toward the first canyon, he sat perched on the front tube, yipping about his plans to wrestle a bear.

Snake fit in much better with the sort of tourists who go north. On the fifth day, as I covered a Dutch oven in embers from the fire, I spied him entertaining the crowd with an impromptu interpretation of yogic flying. Between snippets of stories about pimps and shotguns, I heard the word "Everest" float across the clearing.

"Yup, a good buddy of mine is organizing an expedition to Everest next spring," Snake yelled back when I asked. "Kirkby, you should call him. There might be a spot for a big, mindless guy like you on the team. In fact, I think they are looking for a cook."

My mind reeled. Everest, the icon of adventure. For the rest of the trip I could think of nothing else. Back in Whitehorse I prepared a detailed resume, compiling letters of reference and calling the expedition organizers to let them know a package was in the mail. The receptionist seemed optimistic about my chances and I left for my second Tatshenshini trip of the season brimming with anticipation.

Twelve days later, when I returned to Whitehorse, a single pink slip sat inside my mailbox. The hastily scrawled phone message read, "Sorry, decided to hire Nepalese cook."

What? Nothing else! No further explanation? My enthusiasm drained, and I slumped across a chair. Unwilling to give up, I called the office, relieved to hear the receptionist's voice and not the answering machine. I was bursting with questions. "Are there any other positions still open? What else needs to be done? Surely there is some way I can help out?"

Mary hesitated before conceding that one final spot remained. "It is for a satellite communications *expert*," she enunciated carefully, as if that somehow spoiled my chances.

"Perfect!" I exclaimed.

Mary, who later admitted a soft spot for my foolish tenacity, had her doubts. "The raft guide from the Yukon, the one who applied to be the team cook, now thinks he can build a satellite communications system and implement it at base camp?" Reluctantly, she agreed to fax me the job description.

The three-page document was designed to boggle any aspirant. The requisite "Hard Skills" included a detailed knowledge of satellite communications hardware, telephony interfacing equipment, remote DC powering systems, and gasoline-powered electrical generators. An understanding of the effects of mountain topography on radio signal propagation patterns would be useful. The ability to adjust carburetor jetting in a gasoline generator to account for the atmospheric effects of altitude was mandatory. On top of that, "The applicant should possess the ability and willingness to maintain and repair any and all aforementioned equipment in all weathers at any time of the day and night."

The mind-numbing list went on and on. It was followed by an exhaustive inventory of "Soft Skills." Mental, physical, emotional, and spiritual toughness; commitment, self-discipline, innovativeness, creativity, resourcefulness, focus, maturity, high self-esteem, attention to detail, honesty, integrity, a good sense of humour, equanimity. *Equanimity? What is that?* How can you apply for a job when you don't even understand its description?

I had a smattering of background in the hard-skill areas. Engineering physics had given me the fundamentals of communications and electronics. I had grown up with a dirt bike at my farm and could take apart a carburetor without much difficulty. Years of guiding had taught me to jury-rig almost anything with the right combination of wire and duct tape. Whatever I didn't know, I was sure I could learn.

I compiled another resume, this one focusing on my technical background, and faxed it just as I left for the third Tat trip of the season. This time I returned to a glimmer of hope. The expedition organizers, Jamie Clarke and Alan Hobson, were considering me. I called Mary between every trip that summer, ensuring the Everest team did not forget my interest. Eventually I was able to wrangle a telephone interview with Jamie and Alan. It went well. After the rafting season finished, I passed through Calgary in order to meet the two men. Our brief exchange was encouraging, but my optimism collapsed a day later, when I talked with Steve Matous, a seasoned Himalayan veteran from Colorado in charge of expedition logistics. Steve was not interested in having a young and inexperienced tagalong on the trip.

"Have you ever lived outside for a long time?" he started. I began by describing my guiding seasons, but Steve was not impressed.

"No, no. Not that at all. I mean a long expedition. Have you ever spent a substantial amount of time away from civilization? You've got to understand that one sixty-day trip is completely different from six ten-day trips."

I saw his point but was confident I could handle the new challenge. "Well, I've spent four hundred days in the field over the last two years."

Steve remained unconvinced. He had an old friend in mind for the communications position. I mulled over his comments as I flew home. Not content to let things sit, I faxed the office several pages addressing the issues Steve had raised. Two weeks later, after a notable period of silence, Jamie called back.

"It was a really tough decision," he started. "We considered both candidates long and hard. You were both superbly qualified . . ."

I felt the air spilling from my sails. *Just tell me straight, you bastard. Get to the point. I'm not going to be invited.* I was on the verge of breaking in on Jamie's unceasing elaborations.

". . . but in the end our team concluded that you would be the best man for the job, and we want you to come with us."

The phone dropped from my hands. My ears went numb and my nose began to tingle. For the first time in my life, I thought I was going to faint. It seemed unreal, but I was going to Everest.

❧

Beep . . . beep . . . beep . . . I can hear the phone ringing, clear as a bell.

"Hello?" my mother answers. The connection is perfect, she could be next door. Instead our voices are travelling across seventy thousand kilometres (44,000 miles) of open space.

I am standing on the roof of a downtown Calgary office tower, beside a small antenna pointing at a geosynchronous satellite far overhead. The signal is being beamed to my mother in Toronto, and there is not a single strand of wire connecting us. It is the first time I ever use a satellite phone, and it boggles the mind.

In preparation for the Everest expedition I move to Calgary, where Jamie and Alan, both successful public speakers, have comfortable offices. This will be their third trip to the mountain. In 1991, both were support members of a large team attempting a route on the north face of Everest. When that effort failed, Jamie and Alan organized their own north face expedition in 1994, which was turned back by storms. For three years they have been fundraising and planning for another attempt, this time on the south side of the mountain. Colliers International, a commercial real-estate firm, and Lotus Notes, the software giant, have signed up as sponsors.

Jamie is charismatic, my age, and once a top Nordic ski racer. From the moment we meet I know we will be great friends – he is just easy to be with. Alan is harder to read. A seven-time all-American gymnast, his consuming drive is never far from the surface, even in relaxed moments. Returning from a training climb together, I ask him how he would feel about failing to reach the summit for a third time.

"Black, Bruce. All I can see is black." His answer chills me.

The two have built a powerful team to aid in their quest for the summit. Top climbers Jason Edwards from Washington State and Jeff Rhoades from Utah will travel with them on the upper mountain and oversee the Sherpa crew. Dr. Doug Rovira, also an experienced climber, will be along in case of any emergency. Schoolteacher Dave Vavre-Rodney will send updates to a group of children following the climb. My responsibility is to design, install, and maintain a satellite connection system that will allow a website to be updated with messages and digital images.

After three months of work I am almost ready. Producing and delivering the power at base camp will be relatively simple. High-performance

Kala Patar

From the summit of Kala Patar (5,545 m/18,200 feet), starstreaks over Mt. Everest, the lights of base camp visible below. As darkness fell, I set my tripod, locking the camera's shutter open. 3:00 a.m.: first tinge of sunlight warms the eastern sky. To my horror the shutter is frozen open. With only seconds to react, I slam a lens cap on, bury the camera in my backpack, and head for base camp. After rewarming the camera, I heard the faint click of the shutter closing. Two months later, when my film was developed, the result was one of my favourites from the expedition.

(Main) *Dzopkyo, an infertile cross of cow and yak, arrive in base camp after a ten-day trek.*

(Below Left) *Pilot Col. Madan peers into the cockpit of his helicopter, which crashed just beside our tents. Miraculously, no one was injured.*

(Below Right) *Dr. Doug Rovira injects morphine into Karsang's cheek. Seventy stitches were placed in the monstrous gash.*

Everest

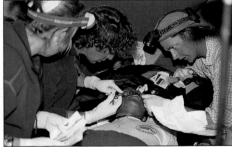

(Main) *Jamie leads camels before the setting sun.*

(Below Left) *The caravan crosses large dunes in the core of the wastes.*

(Below Right) *A three-day sandstorm forced our Bedouin companions to don goggles. Eventually the team took shelter.*

Arabia's

Empty Quarter

(Main) *Raft dwarfed below basalt cliffs.*

(Below Left) *Creek crossing during the five-day trek to the river. Minutes after this image was taken, the stream flooded, washing away a team of men and mules.*

(Below Right) *Curious Gumuz villagers, living on the plains near the Sudanese border, surround the rafts as we pull ashore. No boats had descended this section of river for thirty years.*

Ethiopia's

Blue Nile Gorge

(Above) *A Gumuz farmer on the Blue Nile. The spear is used to plant pepper, maize, and sorghum on the muddy banks of the receding river.*

(Right) *An Amharic muleteer from the Ethiopian highlands. Note the zipper pull hung on copper wire as an earring.*

(Following Page) *Tissisat Falls, engorged by a long rainy season. Here the Blue Nile thunders over a volcanic shelf and plunges into a deep gorge. Perpetual mist from the falls creates a lush pocket of rain forest, and a thunderous sound can be heard for kilometres. This is a sight that has entranced visitors to the region for centuries, but will no more, for the falls now run dry, the water diverted to nearby turbines.*

Abush, the young orphan boy who accompanied our team on the trek along the Blue Nile. Abush had travelled 600 kilometres (375 miles) by foot in the two years since his parents died. His only possessions a soiled sheet and a tattered pair of shorts, he survived by stealing crops from farmer's fields, yet remained courageously joyous and optimistic.

solar panels (and a gasoline generator for backup) will charge a bank of deep-cycle batteries. Regulators and inverters convert this DC source to AC, providing steady power to laptops and VHF radios. We have been given specially configured laptops from a sponsor in Boston, with data transmission ports, fax software, and a customized database. I ensure that every system has a backup, and that whenever possible, this redundancy is three layers deep.

The only problem I have is with sending e-mail. The laptops will connect to our server in Boston over landlines, but not by satellite phone. After weeks of fiddling I discover the phone unit has not been configured to transmit data. I return the phone to the factory for repairs, and wait impatiently. Three weeks later it arrives back, and I head up to the rooftop again. This time a tiny red warning light pops on as the phone powers up. Digging through the manual, I discover that this time something is wrong with the internal electronics. As I package the phone up once again and call a courier, a gnawing worry begins to grow in my stomach. My flight to Nepal is only a week away.

An entirely different rental unit is sent to me, and unbelievably it does not work correctly either. The situation is getting dire, and I worry the team will lose faith in my abilities. Stress keeps me awake at night. The supplier promises to courier me a brand-new phone, straight from the production line, and it arrives on a rush shipment only twelve hours before my flight to Kathmandu.

Customs impounds it. After a frantic series of calls to a manager in Ottawa, the rarely used E460 clause is invoked, allowing for the temporary importation of personal goods for diplomatic use. I still have to test the unit, and making matters more complicated, a winter storm has descended on Calgary. It is past midnight as I take the elevator back up to the top floor of the downtown office tower. Snow cascades through the trapdoor when I heave it open and crawl out into the blizzard.

The phone functions properly on every test. *Thank god.* I am starting to pack it up, desperately needing an hour or two of sleep, when the same red light flickers on.

My heart sinks. I can't believe it. I pull the system apart and drive out of the city, into the foothills, where a crested rise provides an unimpeded shot at the satellite. The error light remains on. The twenty-four-hour support line has no explanation. It is 2:30 a.m. My bags are packed and waiting in my truck. Check-in for my flight begins at 5:45 a.m. With every airline office in North America closed, I finally find an agent in Australia who cancels my reservations. Three days later an embarrassed phone company sends me their most recent prototype. After testing it in every condition and configuration, and finding it works perfectly, I jump on the last possible plane to Nepal.

⁓

The Sherpas meet us at the Kathmandu airport, waiting patiently beyond Immigration. "*Namaste*," they whisper with lowered heads. Each short man carries an armful of silky white scarves, which they drape around our necks. While the cheery countenance of the Sherpas is legendary, nothing has prepared me for their gentle, disarming presence.

There is butter-skinned Tashi, who stares at his feet, too shy to look up. He left his life as a monk three years ago to pursue climbing. Already he has been to the summit of Mount Everest five times. Happy Lhakpa Tsering, no taller than my shoulder and thin as a rail, throws three heavy duffel bags on his back. He first reached the summit with Canadian Pat Morrow in 1982, and has returned to the mountain seventeen times since. Cousins Norbu and Gyalbo, who have climbed Ama Dablam, Makalu, Cho Oyu, and Mount Everest together, speak so softly I cannot hear what they say. Crammed in the back of the lurching tuk-tuk, we sit with arms draped across each other's shoulders, as if we have known one another our whole lives.

Kathmandu has changed drastically in the six years since I first visited, after biking the Karakoram Highway. Traffic is madness. The streets are crowded with hawkers, salesmen, beggars, and louts. Taxis honk impatiently and bicycle rickshaws, pedalled by raw-boned men with legs no thicker than cobs of corn, fight their way through the throngs. The red-brick walls lining city streets have been painted with exhortations to eat noodles, relax with Anbguri Liquor, and use Dhaal condoms. Above are billboards urging drivers to drink Coca-Cola, Limca, and Juicy Fruity. Racks of fake Patagonia and North Face clothing stand between tikka-daubed statues of Hindu deities. Dreadlocked holy men, their foreheads caked with thick yellow tikka, wander the streets, charging tourists a fee to photograph them.

At a busy intersection, Tashi grasps my hand and points out the open carriage door. A group of monkeys swing from a banyan tree. One dashes down and steals an orange from a distracted street vendor who angrily shakes his fist and throws a stick up into the tree. Two monkeys begin to copulate directly over the man's head. The Sherpas fall over each other with laughter. "Sauce making!" they proclaim. "Jiggy-jiggy!" Sherpa colloquialisms for such antics.

One week later, an aging U.S.S.R. M17 transport helicopter carries us into the mountains. A tangled nest of wires hangs from the ceiling. Warnings in Russian are spray-painted across the windows. Everest's distinctive summit can be seen briefly, floating in a sea of snow-covered peaks, but it soon disappears as we drop into the deep valleys of the Khumbu and land at Lukla. A sheer precipice marks one end of Lukla's dirt runway, a cliff the other. Passengers on fixed-wing planes must endure a gut-wrenching approach, but our hovering Goliath settles down with ease and quickly begins disgorging people and gear. Base camp is still a ten-day trek away.

The team has brought several tons of equipment, and Ang Temba, the expedition *sirdar* (Sherpa leader) divides the gear into standard loads of thirty kilograms (66 pounds). Barefoot porters and yak herders swarm as loads are checked for weight to the sound of shrill bargaining. Ang Temba rearranges some piles to make them lighter, shaking his head and walking away from others. Caravans of *dzopkyo*, the infertile cross of cow and yak, must carry the heaviest gear. Handcrafted bells jangle from the necks of the protesting animals, and red woollen tufts hang from pierced ears. Eventually an agreement is reached, and swarms of spidery-legged men begin hoisting the conical wicker baskets, called *doko*, to their backs and disappearing down the path. Before my eyes a fortune of specialized climbing gear and communications equipment melts into the hills. Ang Temba keeps no list. Business in the Khumbu still operates on word and trust alone.

Porters are the backbone of this high country's economy. No roads penetrate the steep valleys of Nepal's Solo Khumbu region. Every construction beam, television set, toilet bowl, and case of beer must be carried in on bent back. Sherpas generally do not stoop to perform such work; it is left to the Tamang, Gurung, Newar, and other lowland tribes. These thin men and women sleep under threadbare sheets, rise long before bed tea has been delivered to the trekkers, and struggle off in chilly air under the weight of luxuries they will never know. Every year, exhausted porters succumb to altitude sickness, snow blindness, and frostbite. I watch a group of well-equipped and well-dressed trekkers from Europe battle mercilessly over wages with the dusty porters that linger by the airstrip. Although their reward will be but a few dollars a day, every one of the barefoot men who hoist the trekkers' packs smiles luminously and waves as they shuffle by me.

I rush about in excitement, taking photographs of everything, but soon Jason, the team leader, comes to find me. "This is going to be a long expedition," he politely notes. "You should rest. Let your body acclimatize to the thin air gradually. There will be plenty of time to take pictures later."

Leading me back to the garden of a quiet teahouse, Jason and I join Jeff and Alan at a small wooden table where they are devouring heaping piles of small boiled potatoes. The four of us, along with the Sherpa team, will hike into base camp together. Jamie, Dave, and Dr. Doug will follow a week later.

I have spent only four days with Jason and Jeff in Kathmandu, but I hold both men, and their extensive Himalayan experience, in high regard. Jeff is a laid-back, self-deprecating, "free-flowin'-Idahoan," who has spent decades as a raft guide in the deserts of the southern States, and I felt an instant kinship upon meeting him. The clothes Jeff wears, the sun-bleached visor, the flip-flops, even his slow drawl, remind me of other guiding friends from the same region.

Jason, the schoolteacher from Washington State, is slightly more solemn, and although excited to be back in the Khumbu, being the team leader also clearly weighs on his shoulders.

"Remember to eat all you can, whenever you can," Jason notes between mouthfuls. "You never know when you are going to be able to eat again." He is serious, and his words always stick with me, particularly on extended trips in foreign locales. "Anything could happen on this expedition: diarrhea, food poisoning, altitude-induced nausea, interruptions in supplies. Best to take advantage of every opportunity you get to give your body some nutrition." Jason, just like George from Yamnuska, is meticulously thoughtful.

⤜

Mist and cool fog slide down the mountainside as we began our trek into the high Himalaya. Winding through terraced fields of mustard, barley, and corn, we pass stone huts daubed with clay and painted white with lime. Sun-bleached prayer flags flutter above roofs of thatched bamboo and *Sherpani* women stand in darkened doorways with grubby children clinging to their knees. Others sort piles of *aloo* (potato) in muddy courtyards.

"*Namaste Didi!*" Jason yells out.

"*Namaste Daju-bhai,*" the women call back, placing their hands together in prayer and bowing their heads.

Didi means older sister, and is a term of respect and warmth. *Daju* is older brother, and *bhai* younger; combined they form a familiar greeting. These terms are used commonly by the Sherpas, and always spoken with genuine affection. *Bahinee* means little sister, and when I use the greeting to address Pasang, a quiet teenage *dzopkyo* driver accompanying us on the trek, she wraps her arms around my waist in delight.

An hour after leaving Lukla the trail begins to drop into the tight valley of the Dudh Kosi River, and we pass between two house-sized boulders. Tibetan script has been carved across the entirety of their grey surface, each letter carefully detailed in white paint. A jumble of colourful prayer flags are draped between the boulder's crests, representing the Buddhist elements of earth, wind, fire, water, and consciousness. Although no sign lauds the crossing of a border, and no map shows a division, there remains the unshakable certainty that we have entered the Kingdom of the Sherpas.

Nyingma Buddhism, practised throughout the Himalaya, is inseparable from the daily existence of its followers. Life is religion, and monuments to the Sherpa's deep faith spring up everywhere. We stumble upon prayer wheels, metal drums as large as refrigerators covered with colourful murals, spun by the rushing water of mountain streams. Rocky outcrops have been carved and painted with depictions of Buddha; prayer flags are strung across open fields and hidden amidst the forests of rhododendron and cedar; and *Mani* stones, ancient tablets etched with prayer and scripture, are piled along the trail. Anywhere else such bright displays might seem gaudy, especially when set amidst the splendour of a natural landscape, but here they inspire reverence, even in non-believers.

Swaying suspension bridges lead back and forth across the Dudh Kosi River. Weather and wear have polished their rickety planks. Occasionally there are gaping holes, where emerald waters rush over flood-smoothed boulders hundreds of feet below. The *dzopkyo* always skitter at the approach to such bridges and try to turn back, but from far behind the handlers throw stones and urge the beasts forward with guttural cries of "*Kgchaa, kgchaa!*" The sting of sticks against leathery backs can be heard.

News of our coming travels down that trail before us. Quiet Kami glows with excitement as we approach Pangboche, the village where he was raised. His elderly mother meets us on the path, bent double like a fish hook, spinning a prayer wheel braced against her bony hip.

Grasping our faces with knotted hands, she pulls each of us close and looks into our eyes.

Her single-room home is built above livestock pens, where the rising warmth of animals helps ease frosty mornings. We crawl up a narrow ladder, finding the interior pitch-dark, apart from the glowing embers of a dung fire. Smoke stings my eyes, and the thatched ceiling is blackened from decades of cooking. Benches along the walls double as beds, and are piled with yak-hair blankets. A small shrine holds two faded photographs of the Dalai Lama, Tibet's spiritual and political leader-in-exile. Sherpa culture closely mirrors Tibetan, and the inhabitants of the Khumbu are believed to have origins on the high plateaus, crossing passes and settling in the foothills just four hundred years ago.

As we settle, Kami's mother places grimy glasses before each of us. From a wooden barrel in one corner she retrieves a jug of *chang*, the sour Tibetan beer brewed from barley and rice. The milky liquid is warm, and bears a sharp taste of yeast. Having been warned about ailments contracted from the unpurified beer, I take just a sip. As my glass settles to the table, hardly a mouthful gone, Kami's mother rushes over and refills it to overflowing.

"*Shey, shey*," she insists, nodding her head vigorously and waving an open palm to make it clear that I should drink more. I sip a little more, and am quickly topped off again. No one is spared. It is Nepalese tradition to force food and drink on guests, whose polite attempts to decline are destined to be unsuccessful. Soon our Sherpa teammates have control of the *chang* jug. Merrily they "*shey-shey*" us through the afternoon. By the time we leave to visit the local lama, I am stumbling and dizzy.

Young monks with shaven heads and maroon robes peer at us as we shuffle down the monastery's barren corridors. Ushered through a low doorway, we enter a dark room illuminated by a single yellow bulb. Intricately woven mandalas hang from the walls. Statues of bronze and silver Buddhas fill nearby shelves. The lama is seated cross-legged amidst piles of cushions, flipping loose sheaves of rectangular scripture laid out before him and quietly chanting.

Silently the Sherpas take places on the floor, and indicate we should join them. With eyes closed they begin to mouth the familiar mantras. Occasionally the lama strikes a skin drum that hangs beside him, highlighting crescendos in the reading. At other times he jangles finger cymbals and tosses rice in the air. An hour passes and I hardly notice. A feeling of deep peace is pervasive. Eventually the lama motions us forward, laying a finger on our foreheads and then tying red string necklaces, known as a *sungdhi*, around our necks. These have been blessed for our protection. They are not to be removed under any circumstance until long after we have left the slopes of "Chomolungma" (the Tibetan name for Everest, meaning Mother Goddess of the Earth).

Dark clouds pour across the sky as we climb past the lonely stone huts of Pheriche. A group of aging *Sherpani* stand in one doorway, spinning yarn between calloused fingers. We are now only two days from base camp. A few *goraks* (ravens) soar in the gusty winds. Otherwise the valley is desolate, barren, and grey. People do not live here year-round, it is too high and too cold. We have climbed above the realm of man.

I awake the next morning to a crushing headache. Placing a finger on my neck, I measure my resting heart rate at one hundred beats a minute, extraordinarily high. Snow falls steadily outside the tent. I feel dizzy and wretched. Breakfast brings little relief, and as we set off again, climbing higher, I worry about my state. Being the youngest and least experienced on the team, I want to prove myself. I would rather silently suffer than slow the group down, but altitude sickness can be a quick killer and I know I have to be honest. I catch up with Jason, who is puffing like a steam engine.

"Pressure breathing, that's what you need," he gasps between breaths. "Purse your lips and pretend you are blowing out the candles on a birthday cake, over and over. Pressure breathing helps to raise the partial pressure of oxygen inside your lungs. It also increases your respiration rate. Both will help."

I gave it a shot, but feel a little silly, sounding like an over-zealous yoga instructor.

"Faster," Jason prods me. "Like this . . . phhh . . . phhh . . . phhh."

Within ten minutes my headache has evaporated. Earlier in the trek I had noticed that both Jeff and Jason, the two most experienced climbers, were always breathing laboriously. *Out of shape*, I had assumed. Ridiculously I had prided myself on the ability to control my gasping. Now I feel like an idiot for trying to act tough all along.

The final kilometres of our trek wind across the Khumbu Glacier, a tossed and confused ocean of ice. The great southern face of Nuptse soars above us, a fractured sheet of granite plastered with rime. The trail traverses magical forests of ice pinnacles. Each strange formation is topped with a stone or pebble, and has formed as the high altitude sun melts away the surrounding ice. Although none can be seen collapsing, a steady chorus of tinkling echoes across the glacier.

Soon the Khumbu Icefall comes into view, pouring down from a narrow gap between Everest's west shoulder and Nuptse. Minutes later the prayer flags, tents, and satellite antennas of base camp appear. Thirteen teams have already arrived, and more are due soon. This year over three hundred climbers will attempt to reach the summit from the south side alone. There are commercially guided groups, national efforts from Malaysia and Indonesia, and an expedition financed by the CEO of a Japanese cosmetic company. A miniature city has grown amidst the rubble of the glacier; the sounds of generators and radios echo across the moraine. It has not been this way for long.

Just one year earlier, Nepal changed its mountaineering rules and began allowing more than a single team on a route each season. Despite skyrocketing peak fees (from US$3,000 to US$70,000) and a tragedy in that first season (that took fifteen lives and grasped the world's attention), a mad rush has set in. Other climbers wander over to greet us, sizing up their new neighbours, comparing backgrounds and experience. Despite being genial, these initial interactions feel unnatural, and I sense an undercurrent of anxiety. Looking at my watch, I realize it is April Fool's Day and wonder if the date is prophetic.

Our Sherpas have laid claim to a stretch of ice and rock on the outskirts of the burgeoning tent city. A square, shoulder-high monument marks the centre of camp, painstakingly pieced together from chiselled stone. Each face of the *chorten* is flawless and flush. Sprigs of juniper smoulder on an altar at its base, the purifying smoke wafting over camp. Beyond stands an equally impressive kitchen shelter. The rectangular building has thick, solid walls of stone. A blue plastic tarpaulin, held taught by ridge poles, forms the roof. Inside, a dining space has been constructed around a massive flat-topped boulder which serves as a table. Benches made of rock line the walls, creating enough seating for the entire team. Our cooks, Pemba and a crew of three "cook-boys," have built this by hand. Looking around I see other teams have constructed similar structures.

"They will be gone by next season," Ang Temba explains. "Destroyed by winds, storms, and the movement of the glacier. We'll have to build a whole new set for the fall season."

Before any climber can set foot on Mount Everest, a *puja*, or blessing ceremony must be performed. This sacred tradition pays tribute to Chomolungma, asking the mother goddess to accept the intrusion on her flanks and praying for the safety of all climbers. The faith of the Sherpas runs deep, and to ignore this ritual would be unthinking and divisive. The wait stretches on as *sirdars* consult the Tibetan calendar, weighing the merits of auspicious days. The concepts of a "lucky day" can be difficult for impatient Western minds to accept. To some it feels as if years of work and million-dollar projects are on the line, and rumblings of impatience can be detected. Some *sirdars* chose to move ahead quickly with a *puja* for their team, while others wait.

Finally Ang Temba settles on a date and sends word to Tengboche. Three days later an aged lama shuffles into camp, wearing a tattered cowboy hat, Coke-bottle glasses, and a heavy sheepskin thrown over one shoulder. He has travelled by foot for two days with only a small sack of supplies. The team gathers in a semicircle before the *chorten*. Settling onto a blanket, the lama unravels his cloth sack, extracting a drum, cymbals, several aged books of scripture, and a heavy brass *dorje*.

Earlier our Sherpa teammates prepared an army of small figures from *tsampa*, the stiff porridge of ground barley and butter tea that is their sustenance. As the lama begins to chant, these statuettes of birds, yaks, mountains, and monsters are placed atop the *chorten*, along with crampons, ice axes, and other climbing equipment. Pemba, the head cook, circles the group, filling mugs with *chang*. Ang Temba follows with a smouldering bough of juniper, wafting the purifying smoke over the team. Streaks of *tsampa* are smeared across our foreheads. Thin thread necklaces, taken to Dharamsala by Ang Temba's uncle to be blessed by his holiness the Dalai Lama, are tied around our necks. As the ceremony reaches a crescendo, a tall pole is raised atop the *chorten*. Streaming lines of prayer flags run from its apex to the four cardinal points. Handfuls of rice are thrown in the air. More *chang* is drunk. Then, very slowly, the gathering fades. Hungry *gorak*, which have waited patiently on the periphery, swoop in to peck at the statues.

Several hours later, as dinnertime approaches, I wander past a storage tent near the back of camp, and hear the lama chanting inside. Ducking into the kitchen, I ask Pemba what is going on.

"Oh, Mr. Bruce, we have rented the lama for twenty-four hours," he explains earnestly. "We want to get all the praying we can from him."

As the climbers sort gear and prepare loads, I set to work on the communications equipment. Antennas and solar panels are erected and secured to boulders. Inside the communications tent a mess of electronics and circuitry covers the floor. A cheer goes up from the team as the first e-mails are exchanged, and for almost a week everything works perfectly.

Then without warning, our data connection is lost. I try everything I can think of to get the system working again – altering the software configurations and circuits, moving the antennas all across the glacier, and rewiring the power. Staying up late into the night, I huddle inside the frigid communications tent, waiting for support desks to open in North America. Around me, panels of tiny red, green, and yellow lights blink like the controls of a jumbo jet, and I can hear avalanches thundering down the slopes of nearby Khumbutse. Finally, at 2 a.m., someone answers the phone in Newfoundland.

"Must be the Hale-Bopp comet, boy," a friendly but uncertain technician declares. "Don't worry, the problem will be gone in a few months."

That won't do much good. I call technicians in Australia, Norway, and Paris to no avail. For a week I test every possible combination of configurations, and nothing works. The rest of the team has lost faith that the system will ever work again.

Then the Japanese team pulls out. Their leader has collapsed from exhaustion, only metres outside of base camp. It was clear from the start that he was in way over his head. Rather than allowing the extraordinarily powerful team of Japanese climbers and Sherpas he had assembled to continue working toward the summit, the $5-million project is scrapped. The waste is senseless.

Teams of yaks begin streaming up the valley, retrieving immense piles of equipment that arrived only weeks earlier, including portable showers, crates of sushi and noodles, even televisions. I watch two of the hairy animals pass, large satellite dishes strapped to their backs. An hour later I try our communications system again, just as I have every hour for the last week. This time it works. I will never know if those powerful transmitters were jamming our signal, but from that moment on we never have another e-mail problem.

Each morning the climbers and Sherpas rise early, departing long before the first rays of sun hit the Khumbu Icefall and loosen its precariously balanced towers of ice. The Khumbu Icefall would be classified a "non-route" on almost any other mountain, too dangerous to consider passing through. Blocks of ice, some the size of apartment buildings, regularly break away and crash across the route. It is riddled with crevasses that shift daily, yawning open and close. Aluminum ladders, identical to those found in garages across North America, are used to traverse these gaps. Often five or more of the three-metre (10-foot) sections must be lashed together and lowered in place like a drawbridge. These bend and bow with each step, and climbers must look straight down in order to place their feet on the rungs while trying to ignore the drop below. There are no handrails. Only a loose section of rope is secured to both sides, which climbers clip a short tether to.

Ferrying loads, climbers establish a series of camps higher on the mountain while allowing their bodies to acclimatize to increasing altitudes. Although I know my role is one of support, I always feel a twinge of jealousy watching them leave. When I joined the team, it was made abundantly clear to me that I would not have an opportunity to climb during the expedition. My name was not on the permit, and my role was at base camp. Nonetheless, I trained with demonic intensity in the months prior, harbouring the secret wish that a chance to climb, even just partway up the mountain, might arise.

That dream evaporates the day Mr. Bhuddinath Bhattarai, a senior member of the Ministry of Tourism, arrives at our cook shelter. Nepal has instituted a strict US$100,000 fine for any non-permitted climbers travelling beyond base camp, and Liaison Officers (L.O.'s) are sent to watch over each team, ensuring rules are adhered to. Plenty of L.O.'s never make it to base camp, and those that do generally hibernate in their tents, but "Bhuddi" is different. Quick to smile, interested in what is going on, and very personable, for all practical purposes he becomes a part of our team, sitting in on planning meetings, sharing meals, staying up late into the night under the light of butane lamps. I resign myself to months of stagnant base-camp existence, and do all I can to enjoy that experience, focusing on photography and exploring the nearby glacier. But as the weeks wear on, Bhuddi must sense my impatience, for he occasionally mentions before retiring that he plans on sleeping in the following morning, till perhaps noon, and if I were to for any reason be away during that time, but back before he rose . . . well, no one would have to know. Those few brief forays into the icefall, crossing deep crevasses by aluminum ladder and ascending huge ice blocks by rope, kept my spirits high during the long months of the expedition.

Despite its general stagnancy, life at base camp is constantly intriguing, and nothing is a more astounding joy than living amongst the Sherpas. Their cheery nature never falters, even in the heat of expedition politics, and their unstinting generosity is humbling. Although every one of them can climb faster, and carry more weight, than the fittest Western climbers, such things matter little to them. Praise is always deflected to others, and a deep contentment marks their being. They possess a "kind of merry defencelessness that is by no means common," Peter Matthiessen writes in *The Snow Leopard*. "Their dignity is unassailable, for the service is rendered for its own sake – it is the task, not the employer, that is served."

"Bed tea, Mr. Bruce!" the cook staff whispers at my tent door each morning as the sun rises. "*Tato pani* (hot water)? *Chai* (tea)?" I implore them to stop this embarrassing tradition, a remnant of British colonialism, but they will hear nothing of it. I try rising at 5:00 a.m. in the hopes of beating them to the kitchen, but find this is where they sleep on thin sheets laid over rocky ground. Soon they are up, cold fingers fiddling with kerosene stoves. Water needs to be fetched from a distant spring, carried back to camp in twenty gallon-jugs. Nine times a day young Ang Dawa trots the path. I follow him and insist on carrying a load. He laughs but moves aside. A tumpline across my forehead strains, and it is a struggle even to stand under the weight of the water. I totter into the kitchen ten minutes later and collapse on a bench, out of breath. Ang Dawa grabs the jug and skips off to retrieve another load.

Privacy and personal space appear to be foreign concepts to the Sherpa, their need for solitude rare. These caring and courteous men clearly enjoy each other's company, but their communalism is never exclusionary, and I always feel welcome in their midst. During the trek to base camp they often shared the same large tent, sleeping naked, cuddled together under piles of blankets, prone to riotous sessions of horseplay.

On days when they are not climbing, the Sherpa laze together in the sun, sprawled on the rocks outside their tents, arms across each other's shoulders, heads resting in friends' laps. Their spirited dice games echo across the moraines, a polished wooden cup slamming down on a leather pad, a shrill and prolonged cry predicting the result of each throw. Pocketfuls of cowrie shells are exchanged in lieu of currency.

Physical contact is a sign of genuine friendship, and carries none of the same stigma it does in the West. At home the accidental brushing of hands with a stranger in a crowd is often followed by a rush of apologies, lest it be interpreted the wrong way. The Sherpas walk happily hand in hand, and it is a privilege to witness such camaraderie. One day I notice Kami and Pema Temba, another Sherpa, drop their grasp upon my glance, and I feel a rush of guilt. Have they sensed some judgment from me? It was not implied. *"Don't learn from us"* I want to yell out. *"Teach us your ways instead."*

Days later I am in a neighbouring camp, crowded around a three-inch television screen with an American film crew and more than twenty climbing Sherpas. The screening of *Casablanca* garners little response. *Leaving Las Vegas* comes next. Silence passes through the tent as Elizabeth Shue's blouse comes off. I glance about and see several of my Sherpa friends wide-eyed, not knowing how to react. Shock slowly turns to tentative cheering. A sense of nervous momentum builds, like uncertain college kids at their first strip club. Soon the crowd is roaring and slapping each other on the back. I feel that I have witnessed the ending of a small piece of innocence.

❧

As the weeks roll by, life at high altitude begins to take its toll. Weight drops from my frame; cuts and scrapes never heal; a hacking cough brings up wads of bloody phlegm. Constantly thirsty, I curse our drinking water, which is boiled for purity and kept in thermoses; every morning I forget it is scalding and burn my chapped lips. Soon they are little more than scabs. The quality of our food also deteriorates. Water buffalo steaks and spinach give way to pasta. When our canned tomato supply runs out, ground sardines become the sauce. Night after night of ground sardines on penne.

After six weeks, camps on the upper mountain are established, and the climbers have acclimatized. All that remains is to wait. Each spring the Asian monsoon forms over the Bay of Bengal, and then sweeps northward, pushing the jet-stream winds off the summit, presenting a brief window of opportunity for climbers before the heavy snows start. Some years there are two clear weeks, others there is not even an hour.

Team leaders weigh countless variables. It is a complicated game, and everyone knows the stakes are high. Millions of dollars are invested, and soon people's lives will be too. Climbers who spend too long resting at base camp risk losing their acclimatization to higher altitudes, but conversely, staying too high on the mountain threatens to exhaust them. If they shuttle partway up the mountain and are on their way back down when the weather clears, they could be too exhausted to make an attempt at the summit. Satellite phones are used to retrieve weather forecasts. Alliances form. Some teams share their information; others prefer to remain guarded. The mood grows increasingly tense.

On our team, Jamie and Alan begin to show signs of the pressure to reach the top. Usually the life of every party, Jamie grows curt, even with the Sherpas, which is unlike him, for he has an enormous heart. Alan is downright unbearable, withdrawing into his own world, eating team meals with his head down, saving every ounce of energy for the effort ahead.

One morning, I awaken to the thundering sound of a freight train. The jet stream has slammed into the mountain, and a plume of spin-drift fills the sky overhead. Torn from the summit, it races away toward the horizon like a never-ending conveyor belt. Frantic radio calls can be heard. A single gust of wind has flattened over sixty tents at Camp II. No one is hurt, but the camp is destroyed and everyone must retreat.

The next morning, our Sherpas set off with more tents and the waiting begins all over again.

Helicopter traffic at base camp has continued to increase all season, and with summit bids now imminent, it reaches a fever pitch. Teams requisition last-minute supplies; some climbers descend to lower altitudes for rest; reporters and inquisitive tourists crowd inbound flights.

Choppers can be worrisome at the best of times, and in the thin air of base camp their struggle to stay aloft is frightening. Specially oversized rotors provide only marginal lift, and hovering is not an option. Flight at this altitude requires forward motion.

Takeoffs and landings are the most unsettling moments. When approaching the pad, these stripped-down machines scream in low and fast, flaring their nose at the last instant. Tail booms frequently brush the rocky ground, and the landing skids thump down without a hint of grace. Getting aloft is equally dramatic. Pilots must red-line their engines before the wobbling helicopters begin to painstakingly claw their way upward. Sometimes the attempt is aborted and the machine thuds back to the ground. Invariably the cabin door opens, duffel bags are jettisoned, and the pilot tries again. If the unstable craft manages to gain sufficient altitude it banks sharply forward and accelerates, skimming away over the surface of the descending glacier.

May 20 dawns clear and warm. Most of the climbers are at an upper camp. With little to do, I set up a table outside for breakfast. Jeff, who is sick and can't climb, and young Ang Dawa join me. We laze in the sun, eating boiled eggs and sipping sweetened milk tea, inured to the steady stream of helicopters landing on a rough pad hewn from the ice just a few hundred metres away.

Morning slowly melts into afternoon, and as it does, Nepal's Colonel "K.C." Madan, one of the world's most famous helicopter pilots, begins a continuous shuttle of flights back and forth between Tengboche and base camp. (Col. Madan's heroic rescue of Beck Weathers and Makalu Gau from Camp 1 during the 1996 disaster represents the highest helicopter rescue in Himalayan history.) Time and again his green army helicopter rattles up the valley, nothing more than a tiny spec against towering walls of rock. The approach path brings the noisy chopper directly overhead, no more than thirty metres (100 feet) off the deck, and with each pass we cover our ears and avert our eyes from blasts of dust. We have grown so accustomed to this that we hardly notice the intrusions.

"Oh god," Jeff whispers, sitting across the table from me, his eyes suddenly as wide as saucers. An inbound chopper has just passed overhead, and I spin around. The craft is faltering. As it decelerates, it lists ominously to one side, and then abruptly drops from the sky, disappearing behind a jumble of boulders, only a hundred metres (300 feet) away.

A split second later three distinct events occur in rapid succession. First, the main rotor shatters. With only a faint crack, thousands of fragments spray upward from behind the rise, filling the sky with shards and dust. Then a mighty crash reverberates through the glacier, shaking us in our seats, followed by an eruption of smoke and fire that fills the sky.

Jeff and I look at each other with stunned disbelief. Our camp is closest to the crash site. "Grab the trauma kit," Jeff yells, and together we sprint toward the column of rising smoke. I feel light-headed, and steel myself for the grisly sights – dismembered or burned bodies. Surely no one has survived.

Cresting the rise we run head-on into the two pilots who are walking calmly toward us, their green flight suits unruffled. Behind them lies a smouldering hulk of metal, crumpled in the boulders. All around us concerned climbers are streaming across the moraines, advancing on the crash site like an army of ants. There are a million questions. "What happened?" "Are you OK?"

It is not clear what precipitated the accident, but during the skidding crash, momentum flipped the helicopter over, shattering the tail boom and spraying oil into the super-heated exhaust, creating a plume of flame and smoke. Astoundingly, the only injury on either man is a minor cut to the co-pilot's baby finger. Oxygen bottles arrive and masks are placed on the pilots' ashen faces. Because their bodies are not acclimatized to the elevation, supplemental oxygen and quick evacuation are crucial, otherwise the thin atmosphere will kill them, possibly within hours.

I wander over to the helicopter, which is lying on its side. It's surprisingly large, the length of several cars placed end to end. Film crews buzz about and photographers scramble over the wreckage. Souvenir seekers scavenge among the debris that has been strewn for hundreds of metres. I pick up a splinter of the main rotor blade and bounce it in my hand. The size of a baseball bat, it is as light as a paperback novel, nothing more than foam sandwiched between two thin layers of fibreglass.

The Italian team brings their satellite phone, and a call is placed to Kathmandu, requesting an evacuation flight. When the handset is passed to Col. Madan, a rushed conversation in Nepalese follows. At one point he puts his hand over the receiver and turns to the crowd. "They won't believe that I have crashed. They think that it is a joke of some sort."

He continues yelling into the handset, and eventually hangs up. "Help is on the way. They asked about the condition of the pilots and the aircraft," he smiles. "I told them we are all in operating condition ... more or less."

An hour later, a second green army helicopter rattles up the valley and carries both pilots back to Kathmandu.

Just hours before the helicopter crashes, Jamie, Alan, Jason, and six Sherpas depart base camp for a bid on the summit. It will take them four days at least, and I rise early to see them off, knowing my teammates will face extreme levels of danger before I see them again. Historically, Everest has extracted one death for every ten climbers who reach its peak. Jamie in particular has become a close friend, and while I am excited about his opportunity, I feel a knot of worry. Walking with the group until the path begins to rise, I linger and watch their slow progress through the icefall above.

Three days later the men reach the South Col, at 7,930 metres (26,000 feet), site of our team's highest camp. We chat by radio that afternoon, confirming plans. The climbers will depart for the summit at midnight, under a full moon. To reach the top before 1 p.m. (the team's agreed turnaround time), the climbers must ascend at least seventy-five metres (250 feet) every hour, and they plan to call in on the hour, so I can advise them of their progress. As midnight approaches, Ang Temba builds a pyre of juniper beside the base-camp *chorten*. The moon rises over Lhotse, casting a ghostly white pall over the icefall. The radio crackles. Thousands of metres above us the climbers are underway.

There is no call at 1 a.m., our first arranged contact. I suspect the men are too busy climbing. Two a.m. comes and goes. Then three o'clock, four o'clock, five. Still silence on the radio.

It is 7:10 a.m. when the radio finally crackles. Jamie is standing on the summit, along with Gaylbu and Lhakpa. I can hear the excitement and joy in their voices. I try to imagine what my three friends must be feeling as we talk, and the scene they look out across. I feel a powerful surge of elation, and am slightly surprised, for I wondered if I might feel jealousy. But I simply feel satisfaction for having played a small part in the moment.

<hr />

But there are others to think about. Jason was forced to turn back below the summit when retinal hemorrhaging left him partially blind in one eye. Norbu accompanied him, and no one knows where they are. Alan is somewhere below, still grinding upward.

An hour later Jason calls from the South Col, safe but disappointed. Shortly after Alan reaches the top, exhausted and overcome with emotion. I worry about his descent, thankful that Kami and Tashi, two of the team's most powerful Sherpas, are with him. After a nervous wait, we receive word that everyone has returned safely to the high camp.

Other teams are not so lucky. It seems the same situations are evolving all over again, just one year after tragedy on the mountain caught the world's attention. That evening I sit silently in the American camp as the team doctor explains over the radio how to perform a tracheotomy using only a Swiss Army knife and a syringe. A climber's throat has swollen to the point where he is choking on his own saliva. As his partner battles to save his life, several stunned members of a commercial team stumble into the tent. They have just received news that one of their clients collapsed from exhaustion at the South Summit. The Sherpas were unable to raise him, and high winds have turned back a rescue effort. Spending a night out at such an altitude is a veritable death sentence, but to everyone's astonishment, the climber survives, hobbling down under his own power the next morning, hands and face badly frozen.

What took our team two and a half months to ferry up the mountain takes only two days to strip down. Everything is piled at Camp II, and eager to be done, the Sherpas elect to carry it all back to base camp in one single, colossal effort. Hoisting double and triple loads, they stumble toward the icefall and begin delicately inching their way downward.

Lhakpa, Gaylbu, and Tashi are the first to reach the bottom. We meet them with thermoses of hot lemonade and cookies. An hour later Alan comes into view, his steps slow and tired, his face burned by the high-altitude sun. The effort has devastated him. His eyes are sunken, his voice is gone, his chin grey with stubble. We hug, and the Sherpas pile on top, laughing, hugging, and rolling in the snow.

The mood around base camp is festive. Over forty people have summited in the last four days and only one team still has climbers on the upper mountain. Jamie and Jason should be down any minute. Everyone else is celebrating. Temperatures soar, Walkmans play pop music through tiny speakers, and a party begins to unfold. Pemba bakes a cake. Precious bottles of pop and beer are being unearthed as the radio crackles to life.

"Doug! Doctor Doug. It's Jamie here. Do you copy? Over."

Doug grabs the handset. "Go ahead, Jamie. I read you loud and clear. Over."

"We've got a Sherpa here from another team. He's fallen down a cre-
vasse. Pretty bad facial trauma. We're going to need some help. Over."

Doug sprints to his tent, gathers a backpack of basic medical supplies, and within minutes has left for the icefall. The rest of us alert the
other teams in base camp, enlisting the musclepower that will be
required to transport the injured Sherpa down the mountain. Then we
follow Doug into the icefall.

Jamie and Jason have almost finished their descent of the icefall
when three Sherpas from the Italian team race past them. Minutes later
they round a corner, and find two of the Italian-team Sherpas standing
at the edge of a wide crevasse. Faint moans can be heard drifting up
from the depths. Their partner has fallen from the bridge, and apparently was not clipped to the safety rope. While Jamie makes a radio call
for help, Jason sets up a rope and rappels into darkness. He finds the
stricken Sherpa thirty metres (100 feet) below, slumped on an ice ledge,
and rigs a line to haul him out.

By the time Dr. Doug arrives, the injured man lies beside the crevasse. His right cheek bears a monstrous gash. A slab of flesh – running
from the eye, down to the corner of the mouth, and back up to the ear
– has been peeled back, revealing bone and glands. The right eye, which
was out of its socket when Jason found the Sherpa, has since reseated
itself. The young man moans and twitches weakly, fluttering on the
edge of consciousness. Bulky clothes make it difficult to assess other
injuries, but no breaks or other major traumas are obvious. His friends
tell us his name is Karsang.

Doug sets up an intravenous drip to deliver fluids and morphine.
Oxygen is administered. The limp body is transferred to an aluminum litter and strapped down. By this time more than fifty people
have arrived to aid with the laborious task of transporting Karsang to
base camp. Gently, we hoist the stretcher and a procession slowly
starts winding downward through narrow passages of ice and snow.
Only four can effectively bear the load at a time, so we trade off in
quick succession.

Two large crevasses block the route back to base camp, both at least six metres (20 feet) wide and bridged by narrow ladders. Upon reaching the first, ropes are attached to the stretcher, allowing climbers on the far side to slowly drag Karsang's litter across. The balance is precarious. The ladder bobs and shakes over the twenty-metre (60-foot) drop, and as it does, Karsang moans. Little by little the stretcher slides forward, until at last a climber on the far side is able to reach out and grasp its handle.

Because of the seriousness of Karsang's fall, there is concern that he may have suffered a brain injury, and so it is imperative he not slip into unconsciousness. As the procession slowly winds down through the icefall, one climber stays beside Karsang's head at all times, talking to him, reassuring him, preventing him from drifting off.

When my turn comes, I stumble alongside as close as I can. There is not much of Karsang to see. His body is bundled in bulky down jackets. An oxygen mask covers his nose and mouth. Gauze lies over the injured eye. Tape runs across his forehead. Only a solitary eye stares out, dark and scared.

And the eye speaks. One moment it pleads, the next it cries. Often it flutters on the verge of an abyss. I can feel Karsang slipping back inside himself, and redouble my efforts to connect with him.

"You are doing great, Karsang . . . Blink if you can hear me . . . We are almost there now . . . We are passing the Indonesian camp . . . Karsang! Look at me if you can hear me."

Suddenly we are at camp. Our dining tent has been cleared and transformed into a makeshift hospital. Karsang's stretcher is laid across a folding table. A small group remains inside to help Doug while the rest of the rescuers mill around outside, waiting anxiously. As gauze is peeled from the wound, a distinctive odour spreads through the tent; the smell of raw human flesh, and death. Karsang is deteriorating, writhing weakly in a delirious state. His cousin and uncle, both climbing Sherpas, stand by the bedside, faces bent with grief.

Doug stares at the mess of exposed glands in Karsang's cheek as he swabs the area with iodine. "I'm a goddamned oncologist. I know about cancer. What the fuck am I supposed to do with this? Get the SAT phone in here."

As the phone comes to life, Doug recites the phone number for Denver General from memory. I place the call on the speaker phone. Six of us hold our breath, huddled around Karsang in a red-and-white dome tent, perched under the west shoulder of Everest, as the blips and bleeps of call processing proceed.

"Emerg," a female voice answers.

"This is Doug Rovira. I am calling from Everest base camp. I need to talk to Dr. Ben Eiseman right away. It is an emergency."

"One moment, please." Through the phone we can hear the bustle of an emergency room. There are muffled conversations and intermittent static. I can hear Dr. Eiseman being paged. The wait stretches on. Suddenly, Dr. Eiseman is on the line.

"Ben, it's Doug. I'm calling you from the south side of Mount Everest. I've got a Sherpa here who has fallen thirty metres [100 feet] into a crevasse. Trauma to the right side of the face. He is losing consciousness. There are a shitload of glands and ducts exposed. Should I sew the wound up now or leave it for doctors in Kathmandu? It will be at least twelve hours before a chopper can evacuate him."

There is no pause. The answer comes clear and quick. "Clean it and sew it. Now."

We hang up. Jeff digs through a barrel of medical supplies and finds sutures. Doug uses a large hypodermic needle to inject a local anaesthetic in the wound. Karsang screams out in pain. Doug points to the intravenous. "More morphine." Then he loosely threads one stitch in the centre of the wound. For several agonizing minutes he works to align the edges. Finally the jagged tears match like a jigsaw and Doug pulls the knot tight. Stitches go in quickly, twenty to close the wound toward the eye, another thirty back toward the ear.

Karsang's face is suddenly recognizable, and the transformation is miraculous. I know the man. We met two months earlier in the village of Lobuche during the trek to base camp, and spent an evening laughing and joking together. Around base camp he always greeted me with an enthusiastic *Namaste*. His injuries had been so traumatic – the caked blood, the torn flesh, the limp body – that I never recognized him, even for the eternity that I held his eye in my gaze.

The mood in the tent lifts. The smell of death is gone. After half an hour Karsang sits up and sips a bowl of soup. His cousin and uncle hug him over and over, crying.

The next morning, Karsang is able to stand up, and with help, limps to an awaiting helicopter. I meet him several weeks later in Kathmandu, preparing to return to his wife and two children in the Khumbu. The wound has healed well, the scab already gone.

Without Jason and Jamie's rescue, and Doug's interventions, Karsang would have surely died. While these efforts feel insignificant compared with the Sherpa community's commitment to our expedition, I find immense satisfaction in being able to return something. To see the eyes of Karsang's uncle as he realizes his nephew will live, to consider the grief and loss that Karsang's village has been spared; these moments represent the most meaningful part of the entire expedition for me.

The burning rays of the high-altitude sun weaken my tent walls. After two months the bleached nylon is no stronger than tissue. My hand goes straight through a panel as I dismantle what is left. A notable depression in the ice underneath shows where my sleeping body melted a little deeper into the surface of the glacier each night.

Within hours our small community has dissolved. Trails, trodden smooth from countless boots, now lead to eerily deserted camp spots. As the last yaks jolt away, we hoist our packs and set off down the valley. Each step brings the memory of forgotten pleasures – the smell of grass and moss, the sound of burbling streams, the stillness of rhododendron forests.

Before leaving for Everest, I would have done almost anything in my power to secure a spot on the climbing team, despite an utter lack of experience. I felt strong and confident, and the summit represented a pinnacle of achievement, recognized the world over. What more could a young person enthralled by adventure ask for?

But the time at base camp jaded me. While the mountain was no less majestic, its aura felt sullied by a carnival-like atmosphere. It seemed everything I had hoped to escape by leaving home had been boxed up and brought with us. There was an underlying sense of desperation, of being rushed, and stressed. Colossal sums of money had been invested, and egos were on the line. The perceived benefits of reaching the summit, that little pinnacle of rock and snow, both personal and professional, seemed oddly inflated. And this obsession came at a cost. Lost was an appreciation of living amidst nature, and the constant exposure to its beauty and power. Lost also was the opportunity for immersion in a foreign culture, for rather than Westerners learning to live as Sherpas, the opposite occurred.

The experience forced me to question my own motives for pursuing adventure. My interest in going places that others weren't, in exploring lesser-known areas, was steadily growing. With the number of Everest summiteers exponentially increasing (less than 150 people reached the peak in three decades after Sir Edmund Hillary first stood there; recently one hundred stood on the summit in a single day), looking up from base camp left a palpable sense of following, of joining a jostling line. Also, there was so much literature available, and so many pictures published about the South Col route on Everest that it almost felt like familiar ground. This lack of the unknown made it feel more like a tick on a list than a journey of discovery. Fundamentally, I asked myself if Everest were not the highest mountain in the world, and if others did not attach such unnaturally inflated significance to reaching its peak, would I wade into the fray that had gathered around its base? The answer was clearly no; yet as I boarded a plane leaving Kathmandu I found myself wondering if I would be drawn back to the mountain, despite these misgivings, for the attraction it exerted was still strong.

Back in Canada I began to edit hundreds of rolls of film and prepare for a third season of rafting in the Arctic. A year had passed since the tragic events of May 1996, but Everest-mania was still in full swing. *Into Thin Air*, Jon Krakauer's bestselling account of that climb, meant that many people were intimately familiar with the mountain. There was an inevitable outburst of excitement when strangers learned I had just returned from Everest, usually followed by clear disappointment upon realizing my time there was spent in base camp. I sensed a constant hunger for stories of famous climbers, accidents, or controversy, while tales of our Sherpa teammates and the beauty of the land garnered little interest. More than a few acquaintances confided that they hoped to climb the mountain in the years to come. While I admired their enthusiasm, I found myself worrying about our unbalanced obsession with the summit. No one ever told me they wanted to spend more time outside, undertake a long apprenticeship in the mountains, or climb a single other peak.

A year later, when an opportunity arose for me to return to Everest, this time as a climber, I was shocked at how easily I turned it down.

"Don't you realize what I am offering you?" the expedition manager exclaimed, losing his temper when I told him I had other plans. Of course I did, but there was already a new project on the horizon, one that was consuming my heart and imagination.

He didn't see it the same way. "You are going to cross a desert? Big deal. Who's gonna care?"

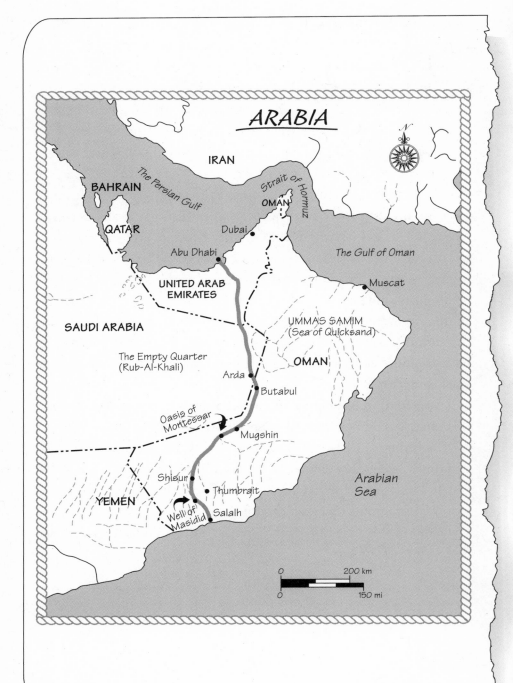

nine

Al-Rub al-Khali

Branded by the Empty Quarter

A cloud gathers, the rains fall, men live; the cloud disperses without rain, and men and animals die. In the deserts of southern Arabia there is no rhythm of the seasons, no rise and fall of sap, but empty wastes where only the changing temperature marks the passage of the years. It is a bitter and desiccated land which knows nothing of gentleness or ease.

Wilfred Thesiger, Arabian Sands

Arabia,
1999

IN THE HEART of Arabia lies a land so arid and forsaken, so bleak and foreboding, that even the great Bedu tribes, the past, unchallenged masters of the peninsula's deserts, trespassed only tentatively on its periphery. It is a dead and empty land, where dunes rise like mountains, built of sand finer than flour. Woven between these peaks are unending salt flats, surfaces as hard as rock and sharper than a grater. During the hot season, surface temperatures soar above eighty degrees Celsius (175° F), and the incidence of rain is measured in decades, not days. Until recently, no men lived here year-round, and those who had crossed the wastes could be counted on a single hand. To the forefathers of today's Arabs, this was *al-Rub al-Khali*, "the Empty Quarter" of their world.

The spell of the desert is strong, and even now, years after our journey, it is a land that I can recreate in my mind as if I stood there now: the heat that makes breathing laborious and eyelids sag, the gentle afternoon breezes that bring unimaginable relief, Bedu companions kneeling in prayer as a purple glow fades on the western horizon and night plunges down upon the wastes. The monotony, the silence, the isolation. The joy upon spotting a single blade of grass, and the elation of arriving at the oasis that inevitably lies beyond. The surprise of seeing a gerbil or hawk after days of solitude. The crunch of sand underfoot, the patterns of the wind.

I remember the camels; their towering size, their power and ungainliness, the fear they invoked, the respect and love they engendered. I remember my own steed, Crazy Dancer, on whose back I rode for seventy days. The way his ears swivelled back to listen whenever I talked in the saddle. The dates I fed him by hand each night before bed, and the ticks, swollen larger than grapes, that I plucked from his coat and squeezed until viscous purple blood splattered out (lest their progeny survive to infest the herd). I can feel the tight curls of hair running up Crazy Dancer's neck, and his muscles rippling underneath me with each stride. Tears would stain his cheeks whenever he grew tired or stressed, and with time he allowed me to gently clear away these sand-encrusted accumulations, all the while staring back unquestioningly. The ache of our parting remains as fresh as the day I drove away toward the airport, eyes glued to the rearview mirror, losing my own battle with tears.

More than anything else, I remember life amongst the Bedu. The unaffected warmth of their smiles, the depth of their faith, the contra-dictions of their existence. How we walked hand in hand across the bleak flats, even while disagreeing, sharing gritty bread baked in the sand beneath our fire, sipping water from rank goatskins. Laced with rotting hairs and the colour of chocolate milk, that precious liquid tasted as sweet as anything I have known. They taught us the ways of the desert, the rhythm and rhyme of the camels, and their unflinching codes of generosity and manhood. Sitting in the shade of acacia trees, afternoons would melt away as we shot distant cigarette butts with their ancient rifles. They infuriated us with unpredictability, clinging to their past with pride and ferocity, yet insisting pickup trucks laden with food and water follow us every step of the way. Without them the journey across Arabia would have been meaningless.

I went to the Empty Quarter following a hunch, a feeling, my instinct; and in return it shaped me, and my views of adventure, more than any previous experience. It is a land that changed everything.

⤜

During the months of preparation for Everest, my friendship with Jamie had grown strong. There was a natural connection between us, an easiness that is not common. Although we could banter incessantly, words were not necessary. Quick to smile and charismatic, Jamie was a shrewd businessman and an extremely successful public speaker, employing a team of four to manage his busy office. He introduced me to a world I knew little of, and I learned constantly in his presence. Our time in Nepal only strengthened the bonds between us.

Upon our return to Canada, life felt strangely empty. I missed the meaning, focus, and direction that the intense preparations for Everest had lent to the months before departure, and yearned for another grand undertaking. Jamie felt the same. While public interest in "extreme" endeavours was exploding, we knew we could not compete in this arena, nor did we want to.

"There is always gonna be someone crazier, willing to risk more, willing to lob themselves off a higher cliff," Jamie felt, and I concurred. My interest in long journeys to remote areas had been steadily growing, and the time with the Sherpas had reinforced for both of us the delight of experiencing another way of being. We envisaged an ongoing series of adventures to aesthetic, environmental, and cultural environments; a river run perhaps, a long island-hopping ocean crossing, and first of all we set our sights on a desert traverse. But which desert?

After weeks of researching different options, I chanced upon Wilfred Thesiger's classic book, *Arabian Sands*, in a local bookstore. This account of his travels in the *Rub al-Khali* (Empty Quarter) is, above all else, a stirring tribute to the Bedu he travelled with. In closing he wrote, "I shall always remember how often I was humbled by those illiterate herdsmen, who possessed, in so much greater measure than I, generosity and courage, endurance, patience, and light-hearted gallantry. Among no people have I ever felt the same sense of personal inferiority." Lost in the poetic words, entranced by gritty black-and-white photographs, puddles slowly forming around my winter boots, I knew we had found the desert we would cross.

Everyone said we could never do it, the reasons we were given were endless. There would be no camels strong enough, for in the fifty years that had passed since the onset of oil production and Arabia's renaissance, camels had been relegated from caravan beasts to sedentary livestock. There would be no Bedouin willing to travel with us. The elders of today had once known the fear of raiders, the pain of thirst and hunger. Now settled in cement dwellings, driving Toyota Land Cruisers and chatting with friends in neighbouring tribes by cellphone, why would they ever ride to Abu Dhabi, a difficult thousand-kilometre journey, when they could fly there in an hour? Most significantly, we would never get permission. The heart of our proposed route lay through Saudi Arabia, and there is no such thing as a travel visa to the Kingdom. Foreigners can go to Saudi Arabia for work, but not as tourists. The BBC had been trying for nine years to secure permission to film in the desert, to no avail.

We ignored the pessimism and charged ahead, studying Arabic, seeking sponsorship, courting the support of sheiks and ambassadors, and physically training. One year and seven days after finding Thesiger's book, Jamie, his brother Leigh, and I flew to Arabia. Living in a desert camp, we adopted Arabic names, struggled to saddle and ride unruly camels, and slept in the sand beside three Bedu men who, for a short time, became our family. On February 2 our caravan departed the southern Omani coast, headed toward the Arabian Gulf, more than one thousand kilometres (600 miles) away, across the sands of the Empty Quarter.

By the time Jamie, Leigh, and I rode along the skyscraper-lined streets of Abu Dhabi, completing the traverse and dipping our feet in the blue waters, we had spent seventy days in the desert. During the entire year of preparations and travel, I never once questioned my path. Just like my first season on the Tatshenshini, you might not be consciously aware of it when you are doing the right thing at the right time, but you sure feel it inside.

⁓

The desert journey affected me deeply, in large part due to the time I had invested in preparations. The ability to speak Arabic opened a previously unimagined window into another culture, and my understanding of the region's rich history lead to a depth of experience that would not have been the same had we simply flown to Arabia, jumped on camels, and ridden across the desert.

Perhaps most significantly, the journey renewed my confidence.

Before going to Arabia I had been struggling with the same old question, *Where was this all leading?* It had been six years since leaving engineering, and at times it seemed I was mired in no man's land. My office existence continued to disappear further into swirling fog behind me. Even if I wanted to go back, would I be able to? Would I have forgotten too much? Was I digging myself ever deeper into a penniless future?

The price of the path I had chosen never bothered me. While others my age made far more money and had much nicer "things," I didn't mind. I was happy with simple food, a spot on the ground to throw my sleeping pad, and a rusty truck that got me from place to place. The uncertainties of daily life while travelling suited my nature. Many asked if it was a lonely existence, spending long stretches on the road, but I found the opposite. Continually thrown into intense situations with like-minded souls, a web of friends was slowly growing around the world; the type of friends that you could fall out of touch with for a decade, and then show up on their doorstep, picking up right where you left off.

Also, with its long off-seasons, guiding provided plenty of free time, allowing unusually long visits with these distant friends and family. During the year after my father died, I spent twenty-one weeks with my mother (in Toronto, Belize, and the Yukon), far more than any of my nine-to-five, office-bound friends could have managed. Although Cecilia and I had faltered, I didn't blame the unsettled lifestyle, for deep inside I knew that we could have made the relationship work if it had been meant to be.

No, what nagged at me most was the lingering doubt my search was in vain.

The belief that life could be, and should be, a wondrous journey is what dragged me from my office and continued to fuel my decisions. I didn't want to just exist, I wanted to live. I had no interest in jumping in a rattling tin can each morning and crawling through gridlocked traffic, only to sit at a desk, pushing piles of paper, staring at the clock, feeling deflated, longing for a weekend, enslaved by the need to pay for endless things I didn't want, as months and years ticked by. Yet it was more than just good times or an active lifestyle that I sought; it was a feeling, a fleeting memory of childhood, a state of being that I intuitively felt was possible. And in my weakest moments, I worried such ambitions were unrealistic, that I was severely afflicted with Peter Pan syndrome, or worst of all, I was chasing something that didn't exist. *Be realistic*, a voice whispered. An oil-and-gas company offered me a head office job with a lucrative salary. I felt a momentary temptation. Six years after quitting engineering and I was still just a hair's width from slipping back into the life I was trying to escape.

Thankfully Arabia refreshed my enthusiasm, and upon returning home I resolved to write a book, chronicling the adventure. Everybody warned it would be impossible to get something published. As an unknown and unproven writer, I would be competing with thousands of other aspirants. Engineering had given me no literary background, and I very nearly failed English in high school (my mother was twice summoned by appalled teachers to be lectured on her son's shortcomings).

Undeterred, I retreated to a friend's cabin in the woods and in ten days pounded out a rudimentary hundred-thousand-word manuscript. After visiting a bookstore, and jotting down the addresses of publishers whose books seemed close to my vision for *Sand Dance*, I submitted proposals and sample chapters to every one of them.

To my delight a letter of offer arrived within a week. I asked a local editor to review my work, and his first suggestion was not to go with that first offer, but to find an agent. I navigated that process, and after accepting competing bids, the agent placed my manuscript with a top Canadian publisher. Soon there was a book contract to sign and an edit to undertake. With the release of *Sand Dance* came promotions, a tour, and media interviews. A month later the book had reached number one in the local charts. I spoke to book clubs and attended author luncheons. The entire experience was extraordinarily satisfying, but on occasion I found myself stricken with the guilt of an imposter.

I was so enthusiastic about sharing memories of Arabia that public slide shows became two-hour, non-stop, babbling monologues that left the audience exhausted. Before long corporations were asking me to present at conferences and meetings, and were willing to pay for the service. For the first time since leaving engineering, I generated enough revenue in one year to actually owe the government income tax.

After running an excerpt of *Sand Dance, Outpost* magazine offered me a position as a contributing editor, and sent me on assignment to Hong Kong. There were editorial deadlines to meet, photo shoots and sponsor meetings to attend. As my schedule grew busier, I became aware of how easy it would be to get distracted from actually getting out in the field. My prevailing interest remained tough, human-powered voyages through remote lands and cultures, and I promised myself not to let the *business* of adventure take over.

Amidst all the excitement, one painful note existed. After surviving journeys to Everest and Arabia, and being strengthened by all the associated stresses, my friendship with Jamie was unravelling, over something as petty and silly as photo rights. We argued endlessly and became entrenched in our positions; I felt sick to my core. I knew both Jamie and I placed the value of human bonds, especially those forged in the intense arena of an expedition, above business, yet we seemed powerless to stop clashing.

For three years I had occupied a tiny space in the basement of Jamie's office, plans for new adventures cluttering our whiteboards, jocularity and giddy joking marking our time together. Now that had changed. Although we still rubbed noses whenever we met, a remnant of our time amongst the Bedu, the levity had faded. Instead we were guarded, always sizing the other up, weighing their actions. While the bonds the desert had formed between us could never be broken, much in the same way that brothers will always be blood, something deep had shifted. We each believed passionately that we were right, and could find no compromise. Soon lawyers were involved. One morning I woke up and realized it was over. Two hours later I had moved everything out of the office. Suddenly, I was on my own again.

"A wealthy American wants to cross the northern Tibetan plateau, an area known as the Chang Tang." Steve Matous, the organizer of our Everest expedition, who initially argued to keep me off the team, has called out of the blue. "Once you look at the maps, you'll realize that this is a really tough undertaking."

"The whole area is at high altitude, and very isolated. I'm going to help with logistics, but with a new baby, I can't go. Three months is just too long for me to be away from home. The group needs someone experienced with remote communications and navigation, and I've suggested you. I hope that's all right. Give Nevada Weir a call. She is the expedition photographer, and should be able to explain their plans better."

I rang Nevada right away. Plans for the Tibetan trip, still two years away, remained vague. As we discussed the challenges of the proposed journey, Nevada noted that she could not afford to spend much time thinking about the Chang Tang as she was swamped with preparations for a trip of her own, on the Blue Nile.

The Blue Nile? For a moment I completely forgot about our Tibetan discussion. There was something familiar about that name and I wanted to know more.

"The political situation in Ethiopia has stabilized recently," Nevada explained. "For the first time in decades, travel in the Blue Nile Gorge is a real possibility." She had recently pitched the National Geographic Expeditions Council with the proposal of following the entire length of the Blue Nile in Ethiopia, from the river's source in the highlands all the way to the Sudanese border. "It is a journey that has never been completed before. In fact, the majority of the river has not seen any travel for over thirty years," Nevada noted.

Council liked her pitch, and had given an elated but nervous Nevada her first photographic assignment with the magazine. A writer and videographer would be sent along to document the trip, and Mountain-Travel*Sobek, the world's most prestigious rafting company, had been contracted to convey the team down the river.

"Hey, Steve mentioned that you spent some time guiding rafts," Nevada paused. "Would you be interested in coming along and rowing one of our boats?"

Interested? That was an understatement. I would be ecstatic.

However arranging for me to join the expedition proved difficult. MountainTravel*Sobek rebelled vigorously against anyone but one of their elite guides working as an oarsman. The journey was Nevada's creation, and she battled tirelessly on my behalf. Eventually, the company relented, allowing me a spot on the team, but instead of paying me a salary like the other guides on the journey, they demanded $10,000 U.S. fee.

Ten thousand dollars was everything I had in the bank, every single penny and then some. It would have been easy to say "no," but thinking back to Yamnuska, I knew the value of such experiences can never be measured in dollars. With mixed feelings and some second thoughts, I dropped the massive cheque in the mail, considering it an investment in myself, and flew north for a fifth season of guiding.

Once again on the northern rivers I loved, the turmoil surrounding my dispute with Jamie faded behind. The days rushed by, filled with anticipation; Africa lay crouched on the horizon.

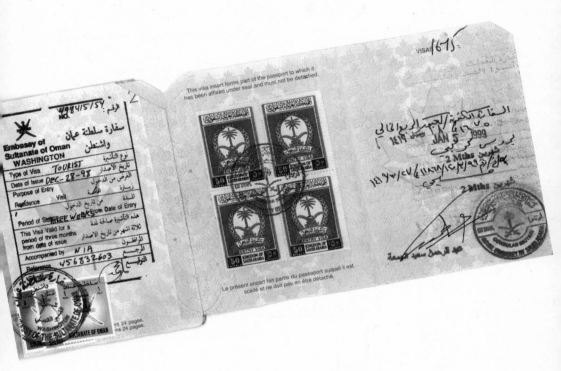

VISA 1615

Embassy of
Sultanate of Oman
WASHINGTON

الرقم 498415/54
NO.

سفارة سلطنة عمان
واشنطن

Type of Visa TOURIST نوع التأشيرة

Date of Issue DEC - 28-98 تاريخ الأصدار

Purpose of Entry الغرض من الدخول

Residence Visit زيارة

Period of Stay THREE WEEKS من تاريخ الدخول

This Visa Valid for a
period of three months
from date of issue ثلاثة أشهر من تاريخ الأصدار

Accompanied by N/A المرافقون

Reference 456832603 المرجع

التوقيع

nt 24 pages.
ns 24 pages.

JAN 5 1999

2 Mths

2 Mths

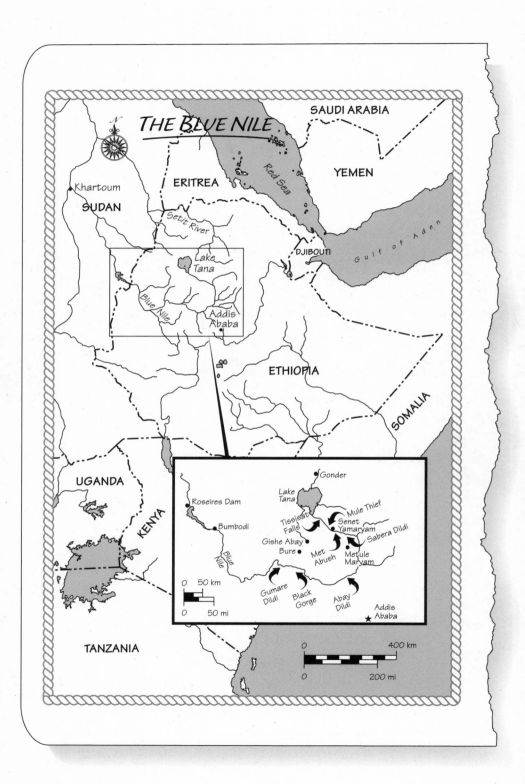

ten

Abay Wenz

RAFTING THE BLUE NILE GORGE

Of the gladdest moments in human life, methinks, is the departure on a distant journey into unknown lands. Shaking off, with one mighty effort, the fetters of Habit, the leaden weight of Routine, the cloak of many Cares, and the slavery of Home, one feels once more happy. The blood flows with the fast circulation of childhood. . . . A journey, in fact, appeals to Imagination, to Memory, to Hope – the three sister Graces of our moral being.

Sir Richard Francis Burton, ZANZIBAR

Ethiopia, 1999

MICHAEL SPEAKS, the leader of the Blue Nile expedition, waits for me outside a warehouse in Addis Ababa, Ethiopia's capital city, where our expedition gear is stored. A tattered T-shirt hangs from his muscular shoulders, and wire-rimmed glasses are perched on his angular face. We have met before, just briefly, on the banks of the Tat, and I like Speaks, at least the little I know of him. He is the embodiment of tough; a stoic man of few words, he lives alone in a hand-hewn cabin, lost somewhere in the Alaskan mountains. For twenty years he has been guiding the world's most demanding rivers, and while gracious, I have the feeling he will be hard to get to know.

"You're the first to arrive," Speaks nods. "The others will be here in a few days. For now, why don't you start by packing food into dry bags."

Then he leaves to make some phone calls, and I settle in the sun, silently loading pasta and rice into indistinguishable black plastic sacks, carefully labelling each one. Twenty minutes later Speaks reappears.

"Jesus Christ! What are you doing using duct tape on the dry bags? Goddamn, the things you Canadians do. It'll never come off without leaving a mark!" Speaks runs his hands through his hair, but within seconds has softened. "Jeez, if a swamper (junior rafter) did that on the Big Ditch (Grand Canyon), they'd be scrubbing groovers (toilets) for a month."

"Hey, see this," Speaks wades through a tangle of dusty equipment and hoists a crumpled aluminum tube. "Used to be a raft frame. Hippo bit my rig on the Omo last year. Opened her mouth and just like that, sucked in an entire tube. One of her tusks got caught on the frame. She shook us about like a mouse." He tosses the useless piece onto a pile of garbage in one corner. "Finally had to jam an oar into her mouth to get her off."

"I only got here yesterday," he continues, finally getting to what is stressing him, "and as far as I can see, none of our permissions are in order. I've just arranged visits with the Water Ministry, the Tourism Department, and Communications this afternoon. Tomorrow we meet the Ministry of Defense, and that will be the most important visit of all. Without their approval this trip is off."

For several months Ethiopia and Eritrea have been battling over a disputed triangle of land, blasting away at each other with rocket launchers, bombs, and jets. Our route along the Blue Nile passes beneath the only bridge connecting Addis Ababa with the war front, and it is a critical supply link for the army. Rumour has it that the bridge is crawling with soldiers whose orders are to shoot on sight.

"They'll have itchy fingers all right," Colonel Kenny, the U.S. military attaché confirms when we visit him later that night. "Just last week the army shot down a civilian flight within Ethiopian airspace when it deviated from its flight plan. Bit of a screw-up. The plane was carrying a load of European businessmen." Although friendly and helpful, Col. Kenny does not like our plans. "Even if the Ministry of Defense approves your expedition – which I doubt they will – what are the soldiers on the bridge going to do when three strange rafts come floating down the river? Think about it. There is a fair chance you'll be shot right there."

I feel a twinge of anxiety, and glance over at Speaks, who appears unmoved. "Typical bureaucratic African jive," he grunts when I ask him later, not even looking up from the supply list he is tallying.

That night, long after the warehouse lights are turned off, I lie awake, riddled with anxiety. Sweat pours from my body, but despite stifling humidity, the faint buzz of mosquitoes keeps me cowering beneath a scratchy blanket. I fidget nervously, unable to fall asleep, slapping at tingles on my neck and shoulders, growing convinced that each of the persistent insects carries a virulent strain of malaria. Apart from the occasional sound of a barking dog, Addis Ababa is silent. In the darkness, alone and far from home, I am starting to freak out.

There are always moments of worry before an expedition, but this is worse than usual. My stomach is in knots. Everything I have learned since my arrival in Africa makes the trip seem more dangerous than I had anticipated. It is more than just the war. The rainy season has been heavy, and the Blue Nile is in a raging flood. No one really knows how big the rapids will be, as no one has been down the river for decades. Then there are crocodiles, a serious problem if we flip a raft. Not to forget hippopotami that swim up and bite rafts. Most frightening of all are the ongoing rumours of *shifta*, East Africa's nomadic bandits. For centuries the Blue Nile Gorge has been their exclusive domain, and while the new government claims to have deputized the *shifta*, no one really has a feel for the situation on the ground. Over dinner Speaks casually mentions that one of the world's pre-eminent rafters, a man with decades of African experience, has declared the journey too risky.

I try to rationalize my fears, to understand my panic. Perhaps I am simply overwhelmed by my first visit to Africa. Addis has been shocking, an assault of poverty, heat, and crowds. Or maybe it is the Larium speaking, the powerful anti-malaria prophylactic I take. There are widespread reports of the drug's psychotropic side effects, which include delusion and paranoia. My heart races. My head aches. It was a struggle to gain a spot on the expedition, but if it comes down to a question of safety, I'll follow my instinct and back out.

Roosters are already heralding the arrival of dawn when I finally doze off. But the sleep is short and fitful, broken by visions of unnavigable rapids, raft-eating crocodiles, and gun-toting brigands.

Within days the other team members begin to arrive. Nevada jumps from a taxi, hauling waterproof boxes of camera equipment behind her. A weathered visor holds back blond hair, lightly streaked with lines of grey. Despite the pressure of her first *National Geographic* assignment, Nevada laughs and jokes easily, and I look forward to learning more about photography by watching her at work.

Kate, a paramedic, and Virginia, the *National Geographic* writer, arrive together. Kate is from Michigan, and has never been on a long expedition before. Enthusiastic and overwhelmed, she talks a mile a minute. Virginia is reserved and harder to read. When she does speak, her wit is sharp and sarcastic, and I keep my distance.

"G'day, g'day!" Mick Davie, a young, lanky Australian videographer, is the last to show up. With long, wavy hair falling to his shoulders, Mick looks like a surfer but talks like an earnest and eager high-school student. "Can I help? What can I do? Can I finish packing that bag of food for ya, mate?" I shake my head, almost done the job. "How 'bout a tea then? Anyone want a tea if I put the kettle on?"

At twenty-four, Mick is something of a prodigy, *National Geographic*'s youngest field producer. Only two years earlier he hitchhiked from Cape Town to Cairo, producing an independent film en route that covered an array of controversial subjects, including police brutality, land-mines victims, and child prostitution. It was that film, shown around the world, which launched his career and made him a quasi-celebrity in Australia.

We are the youngest two on the trip, and as such we already share a kinship. Mick spreads his gear beside me and peppers me with questions; I can tell immediately that we are going to get along.

Over the next days the pace of preparations accelerates, and my emotions continue to swing back and forth between fear and acceptance. One moment, I am completely convinced that the expedition is a safe and reasonable undertaking. Then some tidbit of information surfaces that reveals a whole new set of dangers, and I slide back into the depths of indecision.

I'm not sure if I ever make a rational decision to continue or not. In the end I think I am simply swept along by the excitement.

The Blue Nile – or Abay Wenz as it is known locally – carves a semicircular gorge in the Ethiopian plateau, a deep trench that first heads south, then curves west, and eventually turns northward as the river spills out onto the hot plains of the Sudan. Deceptively peaceful at its origin, the water leaving Lake Tana will drop fourteen hundred metres (4,600 feet) on its journey to the sea. After only thirty kilometres (18 miles) the river thunders over a volcanic shelf, at Tissisat Falls, and disappears from view.

"This marks the end of all peace on the Blue Nile," Alan Moorehead writes in his definitive history of the river. From here on "it tears and boils along too fast for any ordinary boat to live upon the surface." For the next nine hundred kilometres (540 miles), the great river lies hidden in a gorge that grows to be a kilometre (1/2 a mile) deep and twenty-four kilometres (15 miles) from rim to rim.

After exiting the gorge, the Blue Nile meanders across the Sudanese desert until it meets the White Nile at Khartoum. Named for the colour of their respective waters, these two great rivers flow side by side for kilometres, mixing in slow spiralling swirls, a sight Arab poets have called the longest kiss in history. The White Nile is the better known of the two, and it was on its waters that Sir Richard Burton, John Hanning Speke, and others staked their lives and reputations in a consuming search for the source of the world's longest river.

All but ignored by the outside world, the Blue Nile is no poor relation. Each summer, heavy rains drench the Ethiopian highlands, and the ensuing chocolate-brown flood that crashes down the Blue Nile represents 80 per cent of the entire Nile River basin's annual flow. The current is so great that it blocks the White Nile at Khartoum, causing its waters to pile up, and even flow back upstream, until the deluge has passed.

For centuries the inhospitable and naturally fortified gorge of the Blue Nile has remained shrouded in mystery and myth. Its stagnant backwaters are a breeding ground for malarial mosquitoes, the sandy beaches home to hordes of aggressive crocodiles. Evil *jinn*, or spirits, are said to inhabit the Abay, lurking beneath the surface, waiting to reach up and grab unsuspecting prey. Few settlements exist in the gorge, for local tribes have long avoided venturing into the humid depths, preferring instead the expansive horizons of the plateau above. Historically, it was only the *shifta*, East Africa's bands of roaming highwaymen, who inhabited the canyon, their camps hidden by thick jungle.

W.N. McMillan, a wealthy American big-game hunter, organized the first major expedition on the Blue Nile, in 1902. The journey was barely underway when one of McMillan's heavily laden boats flipped in turbulent waters, losing all of the team's food supplies and ammunition. A runner was sent for help, leaving the crew behind, subsisting on meagre rations of chickens and flour. While awaiting rescue, one of the Somali porters was mauled in his sleep by a crocodile. Shortly after, a member of the press accompanying the expedition was castrated in nearby Danakil country. (The ritual of gelding is historically common through the African Horn, its roots linked to derision of the victim and prevention of future parenthood.)

Three years later, Norwegian explorer B.H. Jessen attempted to trek up the river's shoreline from Khartoum, but travel along the banks of the Blue Nile proved impossible. Steep headlands and sheer gorges kept sending Jessen's party into the jungle, where mosquitoes, stinging fleas, and insatiable fire ants plagued the heat-stricken men. More than twenty of their pack animals died of exhaustion. A porter was murdered and mutilated by local tribesmen, his genitals taken as a trophy, and chunks from his upper arm used as fish bait. The few portions of river that the team actually managed to scout contained powerful cataracts. "Dangerous for navigation at any time of the year," Jessen concluded.

A series of abortive, and often tragic, attempts followed. In the 1930s an Austrian couple brought canoes to the river. Their excursion ended in minutes. The husband capsized just metres from shore and was eaten by a crocodile as his wife looked on. Four nudists took to the river in collapsible kayaks in 1955. They found the waters clogged with crocodiles, which attacked persistently, slamming into the bottom of their boats and crunching down on the hulls with open jaws. Wisely, the naturalists abandoned their attempt. A decade later six Swiss kayakers arrived on the banks of the Blue Nile. Their team managed to travel for an entire week before *shifta* attacked their camp at night. Two members of the party were shot dead in their sleeping bags. The others managed to escape only after a pitched gun battle. A lone kayaker attempted the river in 1966, but he lost his boat and equipment in a violent cataract, and returned to Addis Ababa wearing only a swimsuit.

The British Army was the last group to explore the most remote reaches of the gorge. In 1968, the notoriously tough Colonel Blatchford-Snell led a hand-picked team of servicemen down the Blue Nile, during the era of grand military-style adventures. The well-documented expedition endured intense gun battles with the *shifta*, countless crocodile attacks, and a drowning – all of which did little to diminish the river's mystique.

From this litany, two names stand out. The first, Kuno Stuben, was an idealistic twenty-year-old German who arrived in Ethiopia in 1959. Well-versed in skills of survival, Stuben built a seventeen-foot raft from eucalyptus logs and oil drums on the banks of the Abay, and then pushed off carrying only a handful of fish hooks, one rifle, and meagre supplies. He was forced to run most of the rapids without scouting, for the shorelines were packed so thickly with crocodiles that it was impossible to land.

After two weeks of leisurely, unrushed travel, Stuben's journey was interrupted by thieves, who robbed him of all his possessions save the rifle. Undeterred, the young German pressed on, hunting antelope, wart hog, and monkey for sustenance. Three weeks later, as he sat idly by a campfire, four tribesmen wandered into the clearing. Friendly at first, they suddenly turned and attacked Stuben, stabbing him in the side and back. Convinced they coveted his genitals as a prize, Stuben fought desperately and managed to escape. For several days he drifted downriver, bleeding heavily, wavering in and out of consciousness. When his strength returned, Stuben stopped to pan for gold, but within days an infection and fever set in. He lost consciousness again, to awake in a village on the high plateau where his rescuers were offering one of their daughters as a bride. Politely declining their offer, the young German returned to Addis by mule.

The other name of distinction belongs to Arne Rubin, a tough Swede who canoed from the river's midway point to the Sudanese border in nine days, during the height of the 1965 rainy season. With little bravado he recounts driving off crocodiles with his paddle, and failing this, blows from an empty Coke bottle. At one point Rubin lingered too long while filming an approaching crocodile, and its sharp teeth perforated his bow. After running many difficult rapids, Rubin's boat was upset in a tiny riffle just short of the finish. Tragically the cine-camera, film, and notebooks he so treasured were lost.

Despite these horrors, it was political events, not banditry, which put a halt to exploration in the Blue Nile Gorge. On September 12, 1974, His Imperial Majesty Haile Selassie 1 was unceremoniously deposed. The Emperor of Ethiopia, *Negusa Negast* (King of Kings), Elect of God, Conquering Lion of the Tribe of Judah, the returned Christ, the Jah, the One and Only for the faithful, the last and longest reigning ruler in a dynasty stretching back three thousand years, a lineage rumoured to have sprung from the celebrated love affair between King Solomon and the Queen of Sheba, was gone.

A revolutionary Marxist-Leninist council assumed control of the country, promising reforms to the outdated feudal system. Sadly, in a sequence of events bearing uncanny resemblance to George Orwell's *Animal Farm*, the liberated soon found themselves ruled by a cruel dictator. Mengistu Haile Mariam's regime mercilessly quashed all opposition, and Ethiopia descended into a period known as the "Red Terror." For twenty-five years, the country was devastated by corruption, bloodshed, war, drought, and famine. During this time the Blue Nile Gorge was all but forgotten by the outside world.

A ragtag team of porters, muleteers, and armed guards accompany us on our trek to the river. They are Amharic, a Semitic, light-skinned people of shared Arab-African ancestry who inhabit the central highlands. They wear scant shorts and old suit jackets, trudging the muddy trails barefoot, emerald blankets thrown toga-style over their shoulders. Dark strings around their necks mark them as Christian, adherents to Ethiopian Orthodoxy. I can hear whispers of Arabic in their language – *bet* (the word for house) echoes the familiar *bait* used by the Bedu of Arabia – and I find comfort in the strange sounds of their native tongue.

Our expedition has been timed to coincide with the end of the rains, when surging waters will bear the rafts along quickly. During the dry season, the Blue Nile is a mere trickle, its lower reaches a trap of stagnant, boulder-choked pools. But with the floods, the initial fifty kilometres (30 miles) of the gorge become an impassable cauldron of whitewater, a certain death trap. We must trek past this section, following the course of the Blue Nile by foot over a rumpled patchwork of hills. Michael Borcik, the third raft guide, will meet us at the ruins of an ancient bridge, bringing the heavy rafts and frames down from a nearby village by donkey.

Several of the guards carry AK-47s, assault rifles capable of firing more than five hundred rounds a minute, remnants of past wars. Others sport Springbanks, heavy bolt-action rifles of Second World War vintage with wood stocks. One of our guards, Kes, is also a priest, which seems a little contradictory. I can't picture the minister at my childhood church delivering the sermon with a machine gun slung over his shoulder. Many travellers we pass on the trail recognize Kes, and bow before him. Swinging his Kalashnikov aside, he pulls out a heavy brass cross from under his robes, gently touching the metal to their foreheads and showering them with a litany of blessings. The travellers raise their heads, kiss the cross, and continue on.

The sounds of grunting and hundreds of tiny hooves wake me from a deep sleep. I roll over in my sleeping bag and sit up, rubbing my eyes, disoriented. It is pitch-black outside.

Suddenly gunfire erupts, deafeningly loud, just metres away.

What the fuck is going on? I can see muzzle flashes through the thin tent walls. In an instant everything comes back: I am in Ethiopia, trekking toward the Blue Nile Gorge with a team of men and mules. The region is notoriously lawless, and we are travelling with armed guards. More gunshots ring out. I try to envisage the terrain surrounding my tent, but can't, for we set up camp in the dark.

During the afternoon, our team was wading across a shallow tributary when it suddenly flash-flooded, washing away a group of men. They barely managed to reach shore before being swept into a section of violent whitewater. It was dusk by the time our team regrouped. Tents were erected hastily in a muddy field and everyone quickly collapsed in exhaustion.

Bursts of automatic weapon fire continue to rattle camp. Deep voices ring out and there is the sound of footsteps. Someone runs past my tent.

Where would a person aim if they were shooting into a dome tent? How should I position myself to reduce my chances of being hit by a bullet? Curled up in a tiny ball in the middle of the tent, or stretched out like a plank against a wall? More people rush past. An eerie silence follows.

"Jesus Christ! What is going on?" someone yells from a nearby tent.

"Is everyone OK? Was anyone hit?" Tents are unzipped nervously, and panicked faces peer into the night.

"A thief has raided camp," Zelalem, our Amharic interpreter explains, rushing from tent to tent, whispering through the walls. After successfully stealing one mule, the man came back for a second. In the confusion of darkness he accidentally took a nursing mother, and the bleats of her distressed baby caused the herd to stampede. At the time our armed guards had been contentedly snoring on the floor of the kitchen tent, an empty bottle of *arekie*, the strong locally distilled spirit, at their feet. Disturbed by the commotion, the eight half-clad men leapt up and dashed into the night, guns blazing.

Everyone is out of the tents now. The moon has yet to rise, and it is very dark. Speaks flips on a flashlight, scanning the black fields with its narrow beam. We can see the guards prowling beyond our tents, spread out in a fan, searching the uneven terrain. Shouts ring back and forth in Amharic. Guns are held at the ready. Suddenly, the flashlight beam catches a shadow lurking amongst distant shrubs, and the guard's guns erupt. Speaks immediately extinguishes the light. Despite feeling no allegiance to the robber, we do not want to see him killed.

Eventually, the guards return. The mules have been found, but the thief got away. I collapse back into my tent, where for hours I can hear the guards around the fire, keeping watch and reliving the events of the evening with animated shouts.

⁓

Two days after the mule thief's visit we camp atop Genete Maryam (Mary's Heaven), a wide, fertile ridge reaching down from the plateau above, into the depths of the gorge. A storm passes during the night, and sunbeams are streaming through morning mist when a group of armed men enter our camp abruptly. I count fourteen, each carrying a rifle, and they surround our group, leaning against trees, looking impatient.

The leader, a large, unsmiling man with an indigo turban, demands our papers. Speaks and Zelalem produce the permits, and quickly become embroiled in a loud discussion. I glance at the two men standing closest to me and realize that they are boys, not men, fifteen years old at most. Whispering with each other, they eye our group, fingers resting on their triggers. I pray they have some common sense.

"These men do not believe we have permission to be here," Speaks explains in a hushed voice during a break in negotiations. "They think our papers are forged. The leader wants us to walk to a police station. It is six hours away on a jungle trail." Speaks has refused. "Who knows what they could have in mind. We don't have much power now, but if we leave the river and our rafts, we'll be completely marching to their terms."

The discussion drags on for over an hour. Farmers watch nervously from nearby fields as voices are raised. Finally, a bribe is arranged, and minutes later the men melt away into the forest, climbing a trail toward the canyon rim. Speaks suggests we eat quickly and move on in case they decide to return.

Returning to our breakfast, I notice a young boy wrapped in a tattered blanket on the periphery of camp, hiding behind some shrubs. A series of badly infected cuts mars one of his legs. The boy reminds me of a beaten dog, sneaking closer when he thinks no one is looking, averting his eyes and cowering whenever I glance in his direction. It is clear that he is desperate.

I hold my bowl of oats out, but the boy remains motionless. I beckon and he scurries back to the bushes. Rising, I carry the bowl forward, placing it on open ground between us. He watches closely, and only after I retreat does he edge closer. Without taking his eyes off me, he sits down and starts eating spoonful after spoonful of oats. He does not pause until the bowl is clean.

After a second bowl of oats he joins the group by the fire. The armed guards – a rough and intimidating crew – seem especially fond of the boy, throwing extra blankets over him and stroking his matted hair. He sits on their laps, tugging playfully at their beards and answering questions. Whenever he speaks, the others fall uncharacteristically silent and listen. I ask Zelalem to translate.

The boy's name is Abush. He does not know how old he is, but after a moment's consideration he guesses twelve years. Both his parents died when he was ten. They lived in a poor village and no one could afford to take an orphan in. With no brothers or sisters, no aunts or uncles, Abush was left to wander the countryside alone. He has survived for two years, sleeping in the open, begging for food and stealing crops from farmers' fields.

"I know of his village," Zelalem whispers. "It is in the Wollo region. He has travelled more than six hundred kilometres (375 miles) by foot."

Abush's only possessions are a tattered pair of shorts and the dirty blanket he wears across his shoulder. The wounds on his legs are from a farmer's dog that attacked while he was stealing corn. He was wandering on the canyon rim when he spotted our tents. Thinking there was a wedding taking place, he descended, hoping to scavenge some food.

As Abush continues to talk, I stare at him with amazement. For someone whose situation is so dire, he exudes an astonishing joy. For a person so young, he is extraordinarily confident. I try to envisage an orphaned twelve-year-old in Canada, left to wander the streets for two years, surviving alone. It is incomprehensible.

Teno Amashi, the leader of our guard team, a wiry man with greying stubble, takes the boy's hand and looks into his eyes. "Abush, would you like to come to Bahir Dar and live with my family?"

Zelalem gasps as he translates, for Teno is very poor and his offer is generous. The old man continues undeterred. "After we take the *ferenjis* (foreigners) to the river, you can walk home with me. You will be welcome in my house. My wife will take care of you. There will be food to eat, and a bed to sleep in. We have two young children. You can attend school with them."

There is a silence around the fire as we await Abush's response.

"Thank you," the young boy smiles after a short pause, "but my destiny is to be a wanderer."

Everyone is silent. Shocked. Stunned.

Abush continues. "I want to see all of Ethiopia by foot, and when I am done, I will travel to Addis Ababa, where I will buy shoe-shining equipment, and shine lots and lots and lots of shoes. I will save all my money until I have enough to buy a house. Then I will shine more shoes, and save more money, enough to buy a bed. And then . . . ," Abush's face breaks into a broad smile, "then I will be ready to find a wife."

"Ahhhh!" The guards burst out laughing. "Abush! You are an orphan," they cry. "You will never have enough money for a house or a wife." Abush ignores them.

"I will buy a very small bed," he continues, holding himself in a hug, "so that my wife will have to sleep close to me at night, and keep me warm."

"Never!" the guards roar, lying back on the ground, convulsing in hysterics. "It is not possible. Abush, you are an orphan. How will you buy shoe-shining equipment? With what money? You will never have a wife."

Although their joking is playful, there is dangerous truth to their words. Six million people live in Addis Ababa, hundreds of thousands of them homeless and desperate. Drug use, disease, and child prostitution are rampant. Abush is clearly undeterred.

The midday heat is rising as we negotiate switchbacks descending into the depths of the Abay's central gorge. Abush has travelled with us for two days, and now he runs barefoot over the rocky path, darting in and out between the mules, whistling happily. The sun is hidden from view as we carefully pick our way down into a land of shadows. Through the thick jungle I catch intermittent glimpses of a silt-laden river below, and by two in the afternoon we stand on its banks.

The power of the Blue Nile is immense. Constrained by black volcanic rock, it careens through a slot less than thirty metres (100 feet) wide. Waves surge upward and then drop away, engulfed by folds that follow.

"The water here is fifty feet lower during the dry season," Zelalem yells over the roar. "Men test their strength by trying to jump across." Now it is an impassable, raging torrent.

The ruins of a bridge stand in upstream shadows, one of only four ways across the Blue Nile in Ethiopia. Constructed in the seventeenth century by Portuguese labourers from the court of Emperor Fasiladas, it is now slowly collapsing. Brick and mortar abutments rise from both banks and stretch toward each other, but never meet. The central arch was destroyed during the 1930s, when Ethiopian loyalists attacked the structure with picks and shovels, an attempt to slow the advance of Mussolini's Fascist army. Forty men drowned when the span gave way, their bodies washed out of sight by rushing waters. Known as Sabera Dildi ("The Egg Bridge"), it is rumoured that when cement ran out during construction, a sticky mixture of eggs and flour was used to secure the final brickwork. Whatever holds the pilings in place, it has withstood the river's violent current for more than four centuries.

A hemp rope spans the ten-metre (30-foot) break, and teams of men haul locals across the gap. Standing on opposite abutments, one group of men lets the thick rope out, hand over hand, while the other takes it in. Passengers trace a path over the whitewater, suspended only by a loop around their chest.

Our rafting gear has arrived on the opposite shore. Mike Speaks and I need to cross the river, inflate the rafts, and row them back with all the supplies aboard. I wander out on the bridge, and peer over the lip. It is a long way down. A young mother standing beside me tosses her baby into the folds of a robe, and slips a loop of the heavy rope over her shoulders. With a yell from the men on the opposite shore, the rope comes taut and she lurches out over the abyss. Minutes later a man carrying a goat under one arm is slung back the other way.

When my turn arrives I struggle to squeeze my shoulders through the tight loop. Using body language, I try to explain to the ropemen that I am likely twice as heavy as an average passenger. They laugh and wave me to the edge, and soon I find myself sitting, feet dangling over the drop. Cautiously I give the men a thumbs-up signal, a river knife held firmly in one hand in case I need to cut myself free.

The rope yanks forward. I slip over the edge and plummet. Quickly the men slow my fall, and bit by bit I swing outward. I can feel the rope being passed hand over hand, and with each pass I drop a little lower. Hanging from my armpits, I can sense the whitewater getting closer beneath me. I swing my feet up and hook them over the taut rope but still the sound of rushing water grows closer. A few splashes hit my sunburned arms. Finally my feet bump into the opposite piling, just centimetres over the waterline and I am dragged upward over loose bricks, until moments later, I stand atop the crumbling deck.

Michael Borcik, the third oarsman on the trip, greets me on the bridge with a smile. Borcik is solidly built, with a few days' growth of thick stubble on his square jaw. A straw sombrero shades his bare shoulders, and a slow, southern drawl betrays an easy manner. Speaks comes across on the rope after me, and the three of us work through the afternoon, rigging the rafts in a surging eddy. It is unusually difficult work as explosive water tosses the rafts to and fro. At dusk we finally finish and ferry the heavy rafts back to the far side.

"Where is Abush?" I ask, clambering up the banks.

"Didn't you see him on the other side?" Mick peers up from his video camera. "He was really keen on going across after you guys."

Before taking the rope across the river, I asked Abush to stay with us one more night, promising to pay his toll (thirty cents) across the river the following morning, something he could never afford himself. He must have misunderstood, for now I see him on the far shore, waving and yelling.

"He cried with fear when they put the rope on him, but was totally determined to cross," Mick adds. "Now it looks like he wants to come back. But he can't. The rope is down for the evening."

It is impossible for us to ferry the rafts back to the far shore, for the current would sweep them kilometres downstream. Abush stands on the rocks on the opposite bank, whistling for our attention. I wave back, but there is nothing I can do. The Blue Nile, swollen by a long rainy season, lies between us.

As long shadows stretched across the river and the canyon falls into darkness, I glimpse Abush at one of the scattered fires on the far side, sitting amidst a group of soldiers. In the morning he is gone.

Abush never wanted sympathy; he did not feel sorry for himself. Nevertheless, I had wanted to give him something; money would only endanger him, so I had packed a T-shirt, a good-luck necklace, and a small handful of coins in a Ziploc bag. Now it lies uselessly on the floor of my raft.

We cast off the bowlines and instantly the river grabs the rafts, the brown waters heaving them downstream. In seconds the broken bridge has disappeared from view. The jungle presses in on the banks, and arcs overhead. We race down a hot, humid tunnel of green. Great white egrets and crowned cranes dance along the shores. Occasional water-falls tumble from the leafy walls surrounding us. The river is fast and for the most part flat, although a few violent, crashing waves force us to row hard, and I remain alert.

Abruptly the tunnel of green ends and the rafts float out into a widening valley. Cliffs rise above, plastered with ferns and vines. Pillars of columnar basalt, more than one hundred metres tall, lean together like toy blocks, dwarfing our rafts as they pass beneath. These are rem-nants of a thick blanket of lava spread across the horn of Africa 30 million years ago, creating the Ethiopian plateau. The Blue Nile has cut through these layers, forming a gorge a kilometre and a half (1 mile) deep, and in the process carrying millions of tons of silt out toward the plains of Egypt.

The equatorial sun is hot and I can feel it burning my shoulders through my shirt. Reaching overboard, I douse my bandana in river water and drape it over my head, seeking relief. Nevada and Mick lie on the warm tubes of my raft, drifting asleep. We are lazily floating around a wide bend when I notice two dark eyes moving steadily and intently toward the raft. Without so much as riffling the water's surface, a croc-odile is on a direct course to intercept us.

Leaping to my feet, I drop the oars in their locks, disrupting Nevada and Mick. There is a stockpile of baseball-sized rocks beside my seat – "croc rocks" Speaks called them when he handed them to me that morning. I grab one and heave it at the oncoming crocodile. It misses by several metres and has no effect. Mick and Nevada begin backing away from the bow nervously just before my second rock lands centimetres from the crocodile's head. This time the water erupts, a thick tail arches into the air, and the reptile disappears into the muddy depths.

For a brief instant I feel heroic – I scared away a croc! – but the pride is short-lived, for it turns out scaring away crocodiles is not very difficult. With every passing kilometre more and more slide silently from the banks, making a beeline for our rafts, but a rock tossed in their general direction turns back most. Rafts have not travelled on this section of river for years, and I suspect our soft, grey hulls appear like attractive meals, akin to a bloated cow carcass.

A common rule of thumb used by herpetologists is that the distance between a crocodile's eyes, measured in inches, gives a rough estimate of the reptile's length in feet. By this test, most of the crocodiles we spot are relatively small, between five and seven feet long (1.5–2.1 m). We keep a running tally for the first few days, but after two hundred encounters we abandon the effort, for the exotic has become commonplace.

Only one interaction is not so innocent. It occurs on a grey, overcast day as we drift through a narrow section of river where tall hardwoods shade the flow. Rowing the second boat, I suddenly spot a massive crocodile surfacing behind the lead raft. Its head is roughly the size of a small refrigerator. Before I can yell a warning there is a hissing sound and its jaws slowly open. Taken completely by surprise, the passengers on the raft leap up, eyes wide, and begin pelting the crocodile with rocks. The jaws snap shut and the croc submerges, but not for long. Defiantly it rises again, just feet from the raft, to be bombarded with stones once more. Zelalem smacks the surface of the water with an open paddle blade. Speaks swings his long oar, narrowly missing the croc's head, and finally the beast submerges. For several seconds everything is silent. The river carries us along, its surface black and still.

Alone in the second boat, Mick and I scan the shorelines for a sign of the retreating crocodile. Suddenly its head begins rising from the water directly before us, mouth open, moving fast. Standing in the bow, Mick's only defence is a damp edition of the *Utne Reader* magazine, which he rolls up and begins slapping frantically against the raft tube. This is enough to scare off the huge beast, and it dives at the last instant.

Standing on the raft's thin rubber floor, I can feel the scales on its back as it passes beneath us. The crocodile surfaces one more time, far downstream, and then disappears for good. Speaks, who had the closest view of the monster, estimates it to be eighteen feet (5.5 metres) long.

The valley continues to widen and fields line the banks. We spot men tilling and planting under the hot sun. Some tend beehives, others drive herds of cattle. It would be extremely easy to miss the passing of our rafts, for the water carries us silently, but every one of the attentive farmers spots us. Leaping up, they sprint toward the Abay, faces alight.

"*Tenaystellegn!*" the men yell, waving rudimentary tools in the air. "May God give you health."

"*Endemen adderachehu,*" we wave back, "Good morning to you."

Many of them chase after us, shouting a slew of welcomes. Others drop their clothes and simply dive in, swimming after us. Whenever we pull ashore, a parade of men soon begins to emerge from the water. Most cover their genitals with a single hand, out of deference to Nevada, Kate, and Virginia it appears, but otherwise they show refreshingly little embarrassment at their nudity. Instead they eagerly pepper Zelalem with questions. One elder has been in our midst for fifteen minutes when Zelalem refers to us as *ferenjis* (foreigners). The man recoils with shock.

"These are *ferenji?*" he asks, staring us up and down. "I have never met a *ferenji* before. I didn't even know what they looked like." There is a long pause before the man continues. "This is a happy day. Now I can die. My children will tell their children of this meeting."

"He will never forget seeing you," Zelalem whispers as he translates our farewells and passes a gift of yarn.

"Where does the river go?" another sinewy farmer asks. He has lived on its banks his entire life, and is shocked to learn the water flows to Sudan.

"Do you have jackal poison?" a third demands, looking disappointed with the fish hooks we offer instead.

We pass a gathering of herdsmen, their bony cattle jostling in the mud by the river's edge. As we pull ashore, men and boys surround the rafts, excitedly explaining that their village has lost twenty cattle to crocodiles already this year. The stealthy leviathans have learned to linger in the shallows with only their nose and eyes protruding, waiting patiently for the cattle to come down to drink. When an unsuspecting cow lowers its head, the crocodile lunges forward and grabs the animal by its snout. Dragging it back into the water, the croc spins forcefully and breaks the cow's neck. I cannot think of a worse way to perish, dragged by the nose into the Nile by a crocodile.

Downstream we chance upon another group of men, working in the shade of a fig tree. They are returning from market, five days march away, with herds of livestock. The men lash bundles of wood to goats and donkeys, creating a rudimentary form of flotation. Eventually the bleating animals are pushed into the water, and the men jump after. Instantly the current sweeps them away.

I drift along beside one man as he struggles to cross the river. One arm strokes while the other grips three goats, tied together at the neck. Gurgling and choking with fear, the wide-eyed animals strain to keep their mouths above the water. It takes five minutes and every ounce of the man's strength to reach the other side, and for the entire way he is at risk of crocodile attack. I cannot help thinking of the differences in our existence. When his family needs meat, he must depart on a tiring, dangerous, ten-day pilgrimage. At home, I pop down to the local supermarket in minutes and can find almost anything I want, although I rarely contemplate the luxury of this convenience.

After seven days on the river, we near Abay Dildi, the highway bridge that leads to the Eritrean front. Rowing cautiously around the final bend, we stick close to shore, hidden by foliage. The bridge is about a kilometre (0.6 of a mile) away. Scanning the structure with binoculars, I make out soldiers strolling the upper deck, guns slung over their shoulders.

"Don't be a poofter, Kirkby," Mick whispers. "You Canadians are just like Kiwis, a bunch of pansies. For Chrissakes, go on and row to the centre. Any self-respecting Aussie would. Besides, I bet the boys are expecting us."

"You better hope so, partner," Borcik laughs from the next raft. "Otherwise you'll be the first they shoot, that ball of hair is a natural target."

We push away from shore, drifting tentatively into open water. They can't miss us now, three rafts floating down the centre of the smooth brown river. We are within range of the soldier's rifles, and I have decided I will dive straight into the water at the first report, but which way should I swim? I recall reading something about spear-hunters missing their mark when shooting from shore, because light bends as it passes from water into air. But which way does it bend? And is the path of a bullet similarly affected? I wrestle with these thoughts as the bridge draws closer, but despite our anxiety nothing happens after all, and the soldiers simply wave us past. We stop on the far side to pick up supplies, and twenty minutes later float onward.

Beyond the bridge we enter a land with no signs of human habitation. Wildlife grows noticeably more prolific. *Dik dik* and klipspringer – small antelopes with short pointed snouts and large eyes – drink by the water's edge. Black-and-white-pelted colobus monkeys swing in branches overhead. We are drifting close to a log when it suddenly exhales explosively. I heave backward on the oars, and a hippopotamus rises from the water, its eyes focused on mine. A small, grey baby surfaces by the mother's side and bleats. With a swirl, both disappear.

Emerald-green bee-eaters dart over the river, and a series of hoots that accelerate into peals of laughter reveal a giant hornbill. Entire colonies of yellow and black weaver birds rise in unison as we pass, racing off on shimmering wings. Their globular nests of mud and straw adorn riverside trees like Christmas ornaments. At sunset we spot a lone lioness trotting across distant plains. Baboon tracks litter the beach by camp, and beside my tent is the distinctive imprint of a crocodile's reptilian belly scales. As darkness falls, the unearthly cries of a bush baby echo through the jungle. Sometime later a distant hyena howls, a long unsettling laugh.

We have arrived at the mouth of the Black Gorge. Only two groups – the 1968 British Army expedition and a lone Swede – have navigated the waters ahead and reached Sudan. Neither left detailed descriptions of the rapids. In the morning Speaks, Borcik, and I take extra care rigging the raft, making sure that everything is firmly lashed in place. The next five days will hold the most sustained whitewater of the journey; not knowing what to expect, we will have to tentatively feel our way downstream.

The Black Gorge reveals itself to be not so much a canyon as a very steep V-shaped valley. Thick forest rises above our rafts, clinging to slopes almost too precipitous to climb by foot. Immense slabs of marble and gneiss lie jumbled along the banks, funnelling the river into a narrow passage. The uncertainty of what lies ahead heightens our senses and focuses our thoughts. Time passes in a slow, meditative trance. At the slightest hint of turmoil – a low rumble, a blind horizon line, or spray jumping upward from an unseen drop – we clamber atop piles of gear, peering through binoculars, straining to see more.

The first rapids we encounter are big and pushy, but straightforward. Formed by constrictions in the banks, water piles up and then pours over a smooth tongue into a confusion of haystack waves.

"Hey diddle-diddle, straight down the middle," Speaks yells back as he approaches, raising his arm in a charge signal. We press on our oars, accelerating into the heart of the roller coaster. Some of the waves explode upward more than five metres (16 feet) and are easily capable of flipping a raft that is in the wrong position.

We continue to edge cautiously down the gorge, evaluating every rapid we approach. Can we see a line? Is there any uncertainty of what lies over the lip? We simultaneously scan the shorelines. We cannot pass the "point-of-no-return" unless we are sure the rapid is safe to run.

There are plenty of blind drops and giant ledges that force us to stop and scout. Scrambling along shoreline rocks, scaring away thick monitor lizards that bask in the sun, we carefully plan our route. At one of the larger drops an immense eddy covers nearly three-quarters of the river's width downstream. The powerful hydraulic draws foam, flotsam and anything else it captures back up into the most violent section of the rapid. To avoid being caught by the eddy, we will have to run to the far left-hand side of the river, through a mess of rough waves.

As I stare at the eddy, an immense crocodile hauls itself up onto a sandy bank and settles to bask in the sun, its jaws creaking slowly open. The eddy is almost certainly this crocodile's personal hunting ground, where it feasts on dead and dying animals that float down the river. I have seen the power with which crocodiles explode off the bank. They hit the water like missiles, streaking after prey. As we trudge back to the rafts, I feel the weight of responsibility. No one can fall from the rafts here or they will be croc bait. And a flip is unthinkable.

After pushing away from the back, our three rafts line up one behind another and drift slowly toward the lip. On such a large river, it is easy to misjudge the size of waves from shore because there is nothing to lend perspective. As the first raft begins to slide over the drop, I realize the rapid is much larger than we estimated. Two glassy waves draw together into a long, V-shaped funnel at the entrance of the whitewater, and these dwarf Speaks's boat. Trying to escape this tongue of smooth water, Speaks rows hard at the left-hand wave, but only makes it halfway up the face. Then the raft shoots sideways, as if on a conveyor belt, directly toward the confusion we are trying to avoid.

With only seconds to prepare, I stand up and lean on my oars with everything I have. My boat slowly picks up speed, hits the steep wave, and only just pops over the top. Borcik follows closely behind. Downstream, Speaks fights his way through explosive whitewater, managing to manoeuvre his raft to the left side of the river and avoid the giant eddy. All three rafts shoot wide, and as we spin in the swirls downstream I look back to the sandy beach. The crocodile is nowhere to be seen.

Seventeen days after starting our journey we reach the second highway bridge crossing the Blue Nile, Gumari Dildi (The Hippopotamus Bridge). As the rafts pull ashore, Zelalem disappears up the bank in search of a translator fluent in local tongues. The highlands are now behind us, and ahead the river will slow, gently spilling out across grassy plains toward the Sudan. This is the land of the Gumuz, a mahogany-skinned, Nilotic people with oval faces and dark eyes. There are few reports of travel in this remote corner of Ethiopia, and no one knows what reception to expect.

Half an hour later Zelalem reappears, a tall, powerfully built man by his side. Shrunken blue coveralls pinch the narrow waist and broad shoulders of Melessa Sima. Extremely shy, he averts his eyes when introduced and then jumps aboard my raft. Melessa is clearly of different ancestry than anyone we have yet encountered on the river. His skin is dark ebony, his face rounded and nose flat. All he carries with him are an aging pair of purple flip-flops and a Kalashnikov.

"How long will we travel?" Melessa quietly asks Zelalem as we drift away from shore.

"Probably two weeks, maybe three, until we reach Sudan," Zelalem guesses.

Melessa turns and waves for the attention of men on shore. "Tell my wife I will be home in two weeks," he shouts as the rafts are swept away.

Ominous blue and grey thunderstorms darken the afternoon sky to the north. The last rays of golden sun sparkle off the river. We are drifting in silence, enjoying the grandeur, when I notice four men standing motionless on the bank ahead, spears in hand, golden robes thrown over black shoulders. All four remain perfectly frozen as our rafts drift closer. They neither smile nor appear threatening.

"*Nehgay! Nehgay!*" Melessa suddenly yells out, jumping to his feet in the front of my raft. ("Welcome! Welcome!" in the Gumuzina tongue.)

"*Nehgay! Nehgay!*" the men bounce up and down excitedly and motion us toward them. We land and are greeted with handshakes and bows that come from the shoulders and chest, not just the head. Melessa has not met these men before, but they quickly discover that they have mutual friends and hug again enthusiastically.

The Black Gorge, a natural barrier to travel, has created a sharp ethnographic split. Gone are the light skins of the Amhara highlands. Gone too are the ever-present guns, replaced by bamboo spears. Daggers are strapped across the men's smooth biceps, held in snakeskin sheaths. In the highlands, *teff* (a grain) covered every centimetre of arable land. Now it is nowhere to be seen. Instead crops of corn, cotton, flax, peppers, maize, and sorghum spring up along banks, planted in the mud of the receding Abay.

The Gumuz inhabit a land largely isolated from modern influence. The next morning we encounter a young girl walking along the banks. Upon seeing our rafts, she bursts into tears, drops the basket she is carrying, and sprints away. Minutes later a group of men appear, carrying spears. They are clearly shocked at the sight of our rafts, but despite their fear, wave us over.

"My daughter told us that giant geese were flying down the river," one man explains to Melessa.

"Are these airplanes?" another asks, pointing at our rafts. He has heard that *ferenjis* always travel in aircraft.

Soon the entire village has gathered on the banks, pressing closely around the rafts. Some clamber aboard, inquisitive and uninhibited. They try on our life jackets, rummage through the holds, and bounce happily on the raft tubes. Most of the men are shoeless and shirtless, wearing just tattered shorts held together by layers of patches. A few have faded T-shirts, threadbare from years of handwashing. I make out the words "AfricaAid 84" across one man's chest. The women are bare-breasted and wear colourful, decorative jewellery. Beads dangle from braided hair, copper bracelets have been hammered around wrists and ankles, long shafts of ivory and bone pierce nostrils. The discards of Western society are among their adornments; a Levi's zipper tag is used as an earring, a ballpoint pen – the clear, crystal type – pierces an earlobe.

Nearly every person bears intricate scarification patterns, raised markings created by packing hot ash into incisions in the flesh. Diamonds and chevrons cover the upper arms and backs of women. Men often bear circular markings around a cross on both cheeks. Some have filed their front teeth to sharp points. Ritualized mutilation is common in the tropical regions, where clothing is not always practical, and decorated skin is a means of affirming place within society.

Our interactions with these remote groups highlight an apparently fundamental difference between men and women. The men can hardly conceal their interest in the gear and equipment we carry. They slap the rubber tubes of our rafts, laughing out loud. One notes that the grey rubber is stronger than cowhide. They hoist our plastic oars above their heads, testing the weight and flex. Plastic and glass jars are tapped and held up to the light. The tents cause a stir. As we shake the light aluminum poles and shock-cords and snap them into long flexible spears, there is a gasp from the gathered crowd. Men test the tent fabric with their fingers. "How can a material be so thin yet so strong?" they mutter. Crowds gather outside our tent doors, crouching on their haunches and lingering for hours, peering in and saying little.

The women, on the other hand, appear interested only in our bodies. Initially most are too shy to approach, and hover on the periphery, eyeing us cautiously. Usually one or two hunched elders finally shuffle forward.

"Why do they wear such tight, white shirts?" asks one, tugging at the back of my hand.

Zelalem laughs when Melessa translates the question, and the old woman glares at him.

"Tell him be careful," she scolds. "He has already spent too long with the *ferenjis* and has caught their disease." (Zelalem's Amharic skin is far lighter than the Gumuz people's.)

"That is the normal colour of *ferenji* skin," Zelalem patiently explains. "They are not sick."

The women furrow their noses. "How can anyone bear the curse of being so ugly?" One traces the purple-blue veins on our forearms. "You can see inside them," she whispers with a look of revulsion.

The colour of our skin is forgotten the instant the women notice the hair on our arms. Then true hysteria sets in. Waving for nervous friends to join them, the women pull, pluck, and tweak at our hair. They can hardly believe it, for their men are completely hairless.

A crowd quickly gathers. New areas of our bodies are inspected. My arm is raised, and an air of gravity descends as fingers slide under my shirt to probe my armpit. Explosions of laughter and hilarity follow. Some of the women are unable to contain themselves, and run off holding their stomachs. Others fall to the ground in convulsions. A few just look into my eyes, completely speechless. Young children are dragged up to see for themselves.

With the floodgates open, nothing is out of bounds. The inquisitive crowd presses closer and a sea of hands begins to inspect every part of our bodies. Hands reach up our shorts, and grope down inside the waistbands. One woman tugs at my ponytail. Another looks carefully in my ears. The hair on my chest produces a reaction of horror and disbelief. Several hands reach down to tweak my nipples. One elderly woman appears utterly, completely confused by Mick's long hair, and finally yanks out the top of his pants to confirm his gender. Equally confusing is the fact that Nevada, Virginia, and Kate all wear pants. Are they men or women? As shirts are untucked, and hands reach inside to prod breasts, heads nod in a sisterhood of understanding.

There is nothing judgmental or invasive about these moments, since they arise from pure and untainted inquisitiveness. In the end it is clear that we all share similar equipment, that somewhere deep inside we are all the same.

Long, extended expeditions tend to be emotional flashpoints. Stress, lack of food, heat, physical exertion, uncertainty, even just the lack of showers and beds can often lead to tensions. The larger the group, the greater the chance for differing agendas and conflict.

A rift has been growing in our group since the start of the journey. Michael Speaks, charged with leading the expedition, always chooses to camp in secluded areas, away from villages and settlements. On previous Ethiopian expeditions he has lost equipment during the night. The visit of the mule thief, early in the journey, confirmed his belief that it is better to be hidden while camping.

Virginia, the writer, feels that cultural interactions during the daytime are not enough. She wants to spend as much time as possible with locals, and considers Speaks's desire to hide camp away as nothing more than racism. He quickly becomes the focus of her anger, which grows more vitriolic.

The bitter, veiled dispute begins to spill over into all areas of the expedition, fracturing the group. Nevada is under pressure to return with top images for *National Geographic*, and sides with Virginia. Michael Borcik is easygoing about everything, and tries to act as a mediator. As a boatman for Speaks, and his long-time buddy, Virginia considers Borcik complicit in the conspiracy and relegates him to the opposite camp. Mick initially manages to avoid any obvious allegiance, but as a member of the *National Geographic* crew, he is eventually approached by Virginia and Nevada to support their insurgence. When he declines, the dye is cast: he is a Speaks supporter.

I hardly know where I fit in. As a boatman, I both respect and follow Speaks, but it was Nevada's resolute belief in me that had earned me a spot on the expedition. I feel a loyalty to each. While I can understand some of Virginia's protests, she lacks diplomacy. Having struggled to lead groups myself, I am sympathetic with Speaks, and know how conflicted he must feel.

Unfortunately, the mess is left unresolved too long and personal feelings become deeply involved. Everything comes to a head late one afternoon when a group of villagers launches into an impromptu musical performance. Playing horns fashioned from gourds, elders and children dance along the banks of the Abay, lost in the drumbeat. It is magical, and no one is inclined to depart, but the sun is low and darkness nearly upon us. Several of the men have reddish eyes, and are becoming noticeably excited. Perhaps it is only the music, or perhaps they have been chewing quat, narcotic leaves popular around the horn of Africa. It is hard to tell. Speaks decides to push on and camp downstream. As he tries to pry the group away gently, Virginia becomes livid, her anger at last unconcealed.

The matter can no longer go unaddressed. After dinner I broach the subject at the campfire, suggesting that perhaps we can discuss the issues together instead of breaking off into small factions. Maybe there is a solution that can satisfy everyone.

"Solution?" Virginia jumps in. "The solution is that this is a *National Geographic* expedition and I am being paid to get a story. I intend to do that."

Speaks and Nevada add a few thoughts, generally conciliatory, but emotionally ridden. Nevada feels the purpose of the expedition should be clear to everyone; to get the story and pictures. Speaks is on his heels, torn between satisfying the crew's desires and following his instincts about the group's safety.

Mick pipes up. "This isn't really a *National Geographic* expedition. It's a MountainTravel*Sobek trip that Nat Geo has bought three spots on. What about Bruce and Kate [the paramedic]? They both had to pay a lot of money to be here. Shouldn't we hear how they feel? What do they expect from the journey?"

"Piss on them," Virginia hisses from the shadows, and with that, the discussion ends. It is clear we are not going to come to a resolution.

Three hundred kilometres (180 miles) remain to the Sudanese border, and every morning we rise with the sun, pack the rafts, and drift onward through hot, dry lands. We continue to pass sporadic villages, the largest of which has more than one hundred *tukols* (round huts built from eucalyptus poles with roofs of grass) and a rudimentary school. Here large crowds swarm around the cameras of the *National Geographic* team, and after securing my raft, I jump ashore and enter the melee, finding the village headman surrounded by notepads and flashing cameras. As he is peppered with questions, the interaction begins to feel like an inquisition, and tired of the perpetual group tensions, I wander off alone.

At the back of the village I chance upon three young boys playing with a goat in the shade of a thorn tree. Approaching softly, I kneel nearby and wait, but the instant they spot me all three burst into tears and run off. Before long curiosity brings them back. In no time they are sitting on my knee, tugging at my bracelets. One examines the contents of my camera bag while the other two take turns peering through my binoculars.

Suddenly, I realize someone is standing over us. Glancing up I find a teenage girl, naked apart from a small wrap of embroidered cloth around her waist. Her skin is smooth and oiled, her hair hangs in tight ringlets. I try not to stare at her full breasts, which are very close. Without a translator, and knowing little Gumuzina, I smile. The young woman smiles back, and then steps closer, her eyes locked on mine. The children run in circles around my knees, but I am oblivious, lost in the moment.

"Haaa-Hooooo." A leathery old man standing at the door of a nearby *tukol* breaks the spell, eagerly motioning us over.

The young woman scoops all three children into her arms and leads me by the hand to the hut. The interior is dark and dusty. Benches line the walls, fashioned from hardened mud and covered by dappled cowhides. As the old man gently pushes me inside, the young woman and children tumble onto the floor before me. In shadows at the back, a grey-haired woman is hunched over a hearth, blowing on the embers of a small fire. She fills a fluted clay pot with water, sets it in the flames, and then begins to roast coffee beans in a metal pan. I am witnessing the coffee ceremony, the traditional Ethiopian welcome.

The smoking coffee beans are ground with a pestle and tapped into the clay urn. As steam rises from the spout, the old woman retrieves small china cups from a folded skin and places them on a stone slab before me. After jamming a grotesquely dirty sponge into the urn's spout to strain the grounds, the coffee is poured. The old man passes me a cup. Everyone watches.

Common sense screams "*Do not drink this unfiltered, parboiled water that has passed through a grimy sponge.*" Good manners dictate otherwise. No one moves, all eyes are on me. I take a small sip and almost gag. The coffee is salted, a sign of great generosity, but it is a taste I have always found difficult to stomach. Only with considerable effort am I able to finish the small cup.

The old man and his wife are now pointing at me and prodding the younger woman. Slowly I begin to get the uncomfortable feeling that a union is being suggested. When the *National Geographic* team sweeps by, I take the opportunity to excuse myself, pulling a ball of yarn and two needles from my pack as gifts, offering my sincerest thanks, and ducking out. The old man and his almost completely naked daughter follow. Soon Zelalem takes me aside, confirming that the father has offered his daughter to me in marriage.

"The father has generously agreed that you can take her with you," he adds, suppressing giggles at my predicament. "That's good news. You won't have to stay here. And I have to warn you, it will be quite rude to say no."

"Come on, mate, be a sport!" Mick has overheard our conversation. "It'd be a shame to go home to Canada without a wife."

How do I explain to the man that I appreciate his offer, but it is not possible? That this is not my tradition? I feel ungrateful, and ask Zelalem to refuse as gently and respectfully as possible. The girl tosses her head back and laughs. The old man simply walks away.

Despite his banter, Mick is sensitive to the subtleties of Africa, having spent much of his childhood on his grandparents' Zimbabwean farm.

As the rafts drift through a tranquil dusk, we slip deep into hushed conversation, interrupted only by occasional whoops from the dark forest. Mick has been a pillar on the journey, constantly injecting light-hearted humour yet always ready to wade into a deeper discussion. We grew up on far sides of the world, experiencing diametrically opposed childhoods, but in Mick I can see all the same forces, motivations, and uncertainties that are shaping my own path, and it is reassuring to feel, for the first time, company on this unquantifiable search.

That night upon reaching camp, I am abruptly overcome by fever, the first single shiver so strong that it drops me to my knees; payback for the unpurified coffee. That night I toss and turn in my tent, deliriously wandering through a dream world, alternately sodden with sweat and then racked with chills.

Morning brings no relief. Speaks and Borcik decide to lash the three rafts together and clamp an outboard motor across the back. After leaving the highlands, the river has grown wide and sluggish. As we splutter away from shore, I lie asleep on a pile of gear, feverish and chilled, with cool drizzle beating against my face.

Waking some time later, I am vaguely aware that we have pulled ashore and a group of men are surrounding our boats, guns in the air. Speaks and Zelalem wave a sheaf of papers, and somewhere behind me I can hear Mick and Borcik whispering worriedly. The situation feels threatening, but I do not have the energy to raise my head. Soon I have drifted off to sleep again.

The men who have stopped us are members of a local militia, and they insist on taking us to their station, two days' trek away. Speaks refuses, but guns pointed in his direction leave few options.

"Are you supporters of the SPLA (Sudanese People's Liberation Army)?" the men demand. "Or spies for Eritrea?"

"Ridiculous," Zelalem counters. "We are here on the invitation of the Ministry of Tourism." He pulls a letter from his sheaf, but the men are not interested in reading it. Zelalem shows our approval from the

Minister of Defense and *National Geographic* endorsement to no avail. As a last resort he shows the signature of a policeman from the previous village who checked our papers.

"Oh . . . OK. We know that man." Tensions ease and we are free to go.

Five days later we spot gun towers looming on the horizon. It has been twenty-eight days since we left the shores of Lake Tana, and in that time we have travelled almost 1,000 kilometres (600 miles) on foot and by raft. Now the restricted border with wartorn Sudan lies ahead. We search the southern shores for any sign of Bumbadi, a village where we are to be picked up, but can see only thick jungle. A steady current draws us onward, toward the menacing bunkers.

We have almost given up hope of finding Bumbadi when a crowd appears on the banks ahead. Men wearing white robes and turbans clamber toward us. "*Salaam!*" they yell, the Arabic influence unmistakable. My fever has abated, and in stifling heat we de-rig the rafts, dragging equipment through fields of corn to six jeeps that wait beyond. Crowds sweep us away from the Abay, and in their midst, I turn to thank the river.

As our convoy bumps away from the hot, dusty town, beginning a four-day journey home along interminable corrugated tracks and muddy trenches, I think of Abush, remembering my last glimpse of the young boy, crouched beside a darkening fire. I wonder where he is now, and what fate awaits him.

While cleaning the rafts in Addis Ababa, I find the package I prepared for him, still sitting in the bottom of my dry-bag, never received.

One week after returning home from Ethiopia, I attend a black-and-white fundraising event in Calgary. During a lavish party beforehand I can think of nothing but the Nile. Days earlier I had been dragging rafts through fields of corn just a stone's throw from the Sudanese border. Children who would never know a proper meal, bellies distended by malnutrition, stared from behind the thin legs of shadowy mothers.

Now uncomfortable in the glare of opulence, it is clear how much I have to be thankful for. *Food, shelter, truth, freedom; these things truly matter.* I pray that time will not dull the immediacy of such thoughts, although I know how quickly a returning traveller grows accustomed to the world surrounding them.

Amidst the sound of laughter and clinking glasses, a book catches my eye from across the crowded room. It sits alone, on a square wooden table by the fireplace, and something draws me toward it. Pressing through the crowd of guests, I find an aged copy of Chris Bonnington's *Quest for Adventure.*

Fifteen years earlier, while attending high school in Toronto, I bought this book from a bargain bin in a local mall. At the time I chose it because it was cheap and had great pictures, but quickly I found myself absorbed by the tales of adventure and hardship. Eventually the book disappeared from my shelves, lent to a friend or left behind somewhere, forgotten.

Now I could no longer remember exactly what stories the book holds, and leafing through yellowing pages brings a pleasant nostalgia, each photograph triggering a flood of memories. As the book falls open to Chapter Seven, I am jolted to find it entitled "The Empty Quarter," a summary of Sir Wilfred Thesiger's journeys in Arabia. Two years earlier, when I pulled *Arabian Sands* from a bookshelf, I was convinced I had never heard of the Empty Quarter or Thesiger's journeys before. It was *Arabian Sands* that inspired Jamie, Leigh, and me to attempt our own camel journey across Arabia.

Alone amidst the noise of the party, I ponder what led me to the Empty Quarter. Had I been drawn to the desert by vagaries of childhood memories?

Then I flip to Chapter Eight, and my heart skips a beat. It is titled "The Blue Nile."

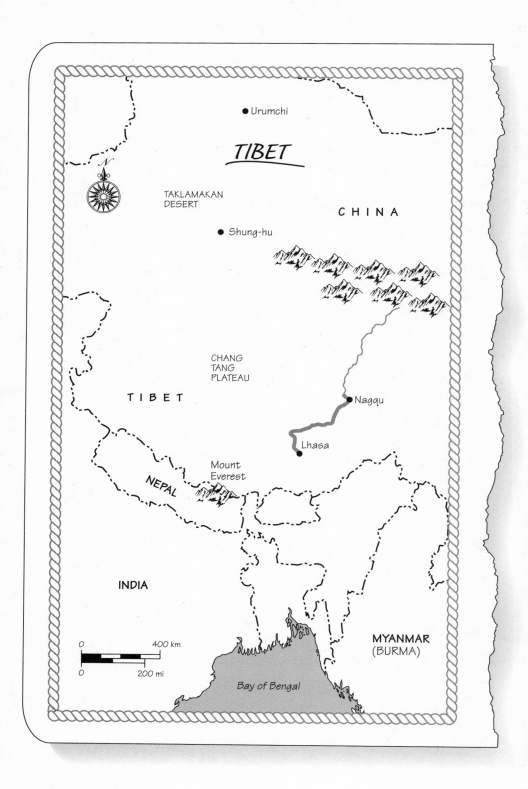

eleven

Stumbling Toward the Chang Tang

THE UNKNOWN PLATEAU

*T*here is another Tibet, much of it above fifteen thousand feet, with treeless steppes and windswept ranges where only nomadic pastoralists with
their herds of yaks, sheep, and goats can exist, and where there are vast
tracts so barren that even they cannot survive. This is the Chang Tang.

George Schaller, TIBET'S HIDDEN WILDERNESS

Tibet,
2000

WITH THE BLUE NILE behind me, and a successful book under my belt, the Tibetan project that Steve Matous introduced a year earlier began to dominate my thoughts. Soon I was seriously researching the Chang Tang. The more I learned, the more intrigued I became. The journey held all the factors that make an adventure meaningful to me: challenging wilderness travel through a land steeped in culture, history, and plenty of unknowns. I kept in close contact with Nevada Weir and the other members of the American team, but within a year their plans dissipated. By that time it was too late; I was hooked, and intent on making my own attempt.

The goal was simple: to cross Tibet's northern plateau. Between Shung-hu, the last nomadic settlement, and Tura, where the elevated plains dropped steeply to the Taklamakan Desert, lies 450 kilometres (280 miles) of no man's land. Over the centuries, many have tried to traverse it. None have succeeded.

It is an unforgiving land, where mistakes are paid for with lives. Without doubt, the journey across the wastes would be the toughest — physically and logistically — I had ever attempted, far more so than the Empty Quarter. The organizational challenges alone were staggering. Immense loads of food and gear would be required, and carrying heavy backpacks at high altitude is an exceptionally difficult task. Could we design a cart to be pulled behind us, or use mountain bikes instead? Pack animals were another option, but what animal? Tibetan horses? Yaks? Bactrian camels? How much could each carry? What would they cost? Would there be enough grazing along the way? Could we get assistance from indigenous nomads? Did any still travel in the far northern regions of Tibet? If so, would they be willing to travel with us, or sell us barley or meat at their camps?

The more I learned about the plateau, the more difficult I realized crossing it would be. The geography was formidable. What time of year should we undertake the expedition? After the monsoon, when water would be easier to find? Or at the end of the dry season, when the ground would be firmer? The route crossed several large rivers. Did they flood, and if so, when? Would we be able to wade or safely swim across them in the spring? During summer?

Permits, gear, and transportation for the expedition would not be cheap. Jamie had secured the sponsorship for Everest and Arabia, and raising funds presented a new challenge for me. During the long days of winter I threw myself at the effort, writing pitches and proposals, defining the benefits I could offer sponsors, targeting potential partners, studying their needs, and customizing my approach. Working with a graphic artist I designed a website and printed glossy information packages. Rather than finding the work wearisome, I was thrilled to be learning. Financing the expedition seemed an intriguing puzzle, one I was sure I could solve.

My sister, a recent Harvard MBA grad, offered her support. "Big deal that your Arabian website got 5 million hits. Who were they? Young, old, male, female? You can tell a company you will get 'media coverage,' but without details that means nothing. It is unprofessional. What media coverage? How much? How often? What audience and demographic? What were your past results? If the firm took the sponsorship dollars you are asking for and dropped them directly into a targeted public relations campaign, could they do better? You need to know these facts before you approach anyone.

"On the positive side, what you offer is unique content. What you need to determine is who needs it and who will be willing to pay? The dot-coms are scrambling for eyeballs right now. If you can help drive new traffic to their sites, the cost won't matter to them."

Calgary's Board of Education – excited by the results of our Arabian education project – expressed interest in building another online program, this one following the Chang Tang expedition. Having sensed the enormous potential of adventure to capture students' imagination, I was enthusiastic. Together we began work on a new website.

Classrooms would act as a sort of "mission control," helping the team with research and preparations beforehand, providing weather forecasts and monitoring progress once underway, and offering advice for challenges we faced in the field. Using instant translation tools, students could toggle between English, French, German, Spanish, Portuguese, Mandarin, Arabic, and Japanese, and every assignment built for the Chang Tang required children to work with classrooms in other countries, speaking different languages.

This education program did not go unnoticed, and three months after launching my fundraising efforts, a local communications giant became the first corporate sponsor, giving the expedition a badly needed infusion of capital and credibility.

Mick Davie flew up from Washington, D.C., to spend Christmas with my family, and over the holidays we worked together on a proposal for National Geographic Television. We also discussed strategies for including Australian schoolchildren in the online project.

With the start of the New Year, I began to train feverishly. Muscle is metabolized before fat at high elevation, and I needed to bulk up. A local sports centre offered to help, and assigned a top-conditioning specialist to oversee my regime. Shaggy-haired, surf-talking Kelly made each workout a dizzying, pain-filled experience; I loved it. There were ten-second, full-intensity sprints on a treadmill that inclined to forty degrees, and hours spent jumping up and down stairwells. I shuffled lead weights back and forth across the bottom of an Olympic swimming pool, until my lungs felt like they would burst, and then ran wind sprints in the gymnasium with refrigerator-sized wooden blocks dragging behind. The sports centre also provided a dietitian who designed a lightweight menu capable of providing the immense caloric requirements of the expedition. I met with a sports psychologist for an hour every week, discussing issues of stress, fear, over-training, and isolation.

For a full year I lived and breathed nothing but Chang Tang. It was all I talked about, and it was all friends asked about. I was fit and eager. With departure (now set for early summer) ten months away, seven sponsors had joined the team. Although I still needed more money (the hundred thousand dollars I had already secured would fund the children's program, but I needed that much again to pay for hard costs – animals, fodder, transport, permits, etc.), I was confident I could find it. Two other pressing priorities occupied my mind. I had learned in Arabia that while research was useful, nothing compared to a reconnaissance trip. I knew I had to see the land, talk to yak herders, wade through swamps, sleep out at night, to better understand the challenge ahead. Secondly, I had to get out and try a long, arduous hike closer to home, in order to fine-tune loads, menus, and routines.

Luck shone my way when Hugh McMillan, a local Calgary businessman, made a generous offer to support a Tibetan reconnaissance. Cleancut and clearly affluent, Hugh loved to travel. His only stipulation was that he accompany me on the fact-finding mission. Travelling with unknown partners is risky, for differing expectations and habits often lead to strife, and sometimes a complete fiasco. The reconnaissance would be gruelling, and I hardly knew Hugh, but what other choice was there? I agreed immediately, and in October 2000, we flew to China.

The brown smog of Beijing looms below, and the aircraft actually lurches as it passes through the palpable barrier. Outside the airport I spot a slender young woman holding a handwritten placard: "*Mr. Bruce & Mr. Hugh.*" Lee Ow Chen shakes our hands delicately, shepherding us toward a waiting car while whispering into her cellphone, arranging dinner. At the hotel Hugh and I gorge on the heaping platters of roast duck and bamboo shoots while Ms. Chen practises her fledgling English. She is clearly shocked by how much we eat. Staring at us with big, brown eyes, she flatly announces, "You are both very tasty men."

We fly on to Chengdu, where signs at check-in read: "*Please, no knifes, guns, bombs, radioactive material or other unfriendly items stipulated by the state.*" Three immense Airbus 340s wait on the dark, foggy runway, all destined for Tibet. An elderly Tibetan couple squeezes into the seats beside me, passing prayer beads through their fingers and muttering mantras. After takeoff I notice them intently watching the inflight movie, and slip on my headphones to see what is so absorbing.

"Those sure are a nice set of titties!"

The Nutty Professor is playing. I turn to watch the elderly couple, both staring unflinchingly at the screen and smiling, quietly passing their prayer beads. Four internal flights in China; four Eddie Murphy movies. I decide to sleep instead.

On October 7, 1950, thirty thousand battle-hardened Communist troops from the newly formed People's Republic of China marched on the poorly equipped Tibetan army. The "Liberation" of the long-sequestered, semi-mythical Buddhist kingdom had begun. Despite an appeal to the United Nations, foreign governments did nothing, fearful of incurring the disapproval of China, a powerful trading partner. Only little El Salvador was willing to condemn the aggression.

For the next three decades China kept the door slammed shut on Tibet, and only occasional whispers of devastation slipped out. But behind this curtain a systematic attempt at cultural genocide was underway, and the long-standing ethnic chauvinism (of Hans toward Tibetans), coupled with the madness of the Cultural Revolution, was inciting unspeakable acts of persecution.

It was not until the mid-eighties that the appalling facts began to emerge: 1.2 million Tibetans killed, 100,000 in exile, monasteries bombed, nearly every historical structure destroyed, widespread starvation, savagely deforested hillsides. There were chilling reports of degradation and torture; monks and nuns forced to fornicate in public, holy scripture used as toilet paper, weeping pilgrims made to denounce the Dalai Lama as a parasite.

While the horrors and brutality of those dark years have been well documented and are widely known, little has been done to intercede, and the Chinese assimilation of Tibet continues to grind on. Despite quiet foreign condemnation, policies encouraging massive Han immigration, exclusively Chinese higher education, and near complete Chinese economic control mean Tibetan dreams of independence slip ever further away.

Yet the Tibetan government-in-exile continues its struggle, providing a courageous example of how a culture, a people, and even a country can exist after its geographical home has been stolen. And rather than suggesting a boycott of Chinese-occupied Tibet, as one might expect, the Dalai Lama urges travellers to visit, believing that they will be moved by what they see.

After three days of flights and airplane meals, Hugh and I arrive to find Lhasa covered by a veneer of sadness. The Forbidden City has been Chinese-ified, now a mess of concrete and neon. Billboards demand "*Be a civilized citizen, and help build a civilized city.*" Pictures of the Great Wall and Tiananmen Square hang in storefronts beside towering piles of cheap consumer goods. We instinctively head for the old city, down narrow streets where eyes peer from behind hand-painted window frames. Here we find spirit. Hundreds of elders circumambulate the Jokhang Monastery, spinning prayer wheels balanced against their hips, muttering mantras.

"It is their job," Tashi, our government-issued guide, explains. "Once people get old, their duty is to pray and meditate. The elders make seven circuits around the temple, and seven around the old city, every day."

I watch an elderly woman, bent double by age, shuffle against the flow of pedestrians, trying to grasp at something on the ground. Vendors and tourists hurry past, a soldier almost knocks her over, but she totters on, one bony finger tracing a path on the cobblestone street. *What is she trying to do?* I wonder. It is a fly! She is trying to save a fly. Finally, she manages to get the tiny insect onto her palm, and carries it to the side of the road, saving it from being stepped on.

"Buddha teaches that humans should never harm, or kill, any living thing," Tashi explains. Now twenty-five, he escaped Tibet at the age of six, hiking over the Himalaya to find refuge in Dharamsala. "I went to school, and university there, but as soon as I graduated, the Chinese government forced my parents to write to me, begging me to return."

"'If you don't come back they will put us in prison, torture us,' the letters said. What could I do? I came back. And so did most of my friends, because they all got the same letters too. My mother cried for a month. She said she would rather die than have me live under the Chinese. The day I got back I applied for a passport. That was five years ago, but still nothing. I am a prisoner here. I can't leave, and this is the last year I can work as a guide. Next year all guides have to be Chinese.

"We can't talk about this any more," Tashi suddenly whispers. "There are spies everywhere. In monasteries. In teashops. On the streets. Some are even disguised as monks. People get thrown in jail all the time. I have to be very careful."

Climbing up to the Potala Palace, the historical residence of the Dalai Lamas, I pay my visitor fees and shuffle in, embarrassed to interrupt the streaming column of pilgrims. They have come from across Tibet, with wild eyes and sun-blackened skin. The men are wrapped in thick sheepskins, soiled from a generation of use. Women wear their finest clothes, beads of red and turquoise braided into long black plaits. They flow past in a never-ending line, crawling underneath shelves of holy texts that line the walls (believing the knowledge and prayers contained within will pour down on them like rain), prostrating themselves, silently rushing on. They carry pails of butter and bags of money, a lifetime of savings. The rancid yak butter is spooned into lamps that flutter and smoke, and crumpled bills fall like snow around me, thrown at statues, stuffed in picture frames, piled on offering plates. Caretakers walk past, sweeping the money into black plastic garbage bags as if they were raking autumn leaves.

A half-century of brutal repression has been unable to break the faith of the Tibetan people.

Our small convoy – consisting of one Toyota Land Cruiser, one huge Dong Feng lorry, two silent drivers, and our Tibetan guide, Tashi – leaves Lhasa at dawn, climbing upward into the southern fringes of the Chang Tang. Our destination, Shung-hu, the most northerly settlement on the plateau and the starting point for the expedition a year from now, lies five hundred kilometres (300 miles) away.

The Chang Tang is a high and desolate land, frozen for eight months of the year, a swampy bog the rest. The shallow lakes dotting the plains are brackish and salty. Fresh water is very scarce. Gusty winds rake the treeless steppes, which are higher than Mount Everest's base camp. Hands stuck into boiling water emerge unharmed, and heartbeats race at the slightest exertion. Empty, bleak, and barren, this is Tibet's northern plateau, an area of uplift spanning some 2.5 million square kilometres (half the size of the continental United States).

As the nineteenth century neared its close, exploration in high Asia reached a fever pitch, and the greatest jewel of all remained Lhasa, the Forbidden City. Strict isolationist policies had kept all would-be visitors at bay for centuries, and no foreigner had ever stood before the gates of the Tibetan capitol. The race was on, but potential interlopers faced an imposing array of geographical barriers; the Himalaya to the south; the tangled Karakoram, Kunlun, and Pamir ranges to the west; the deep, damp valleys of Sichuan to the east; and to the north, perhaps the greatest hurdle of all, the Chang Tang.

During the next twenty years, several groups attempted to reach Lhasa by crossing the Chang Tang, but none succeeded. Russian Nikolai Prejevalsky battled bandits and lost eighty pack animals to starvation only to have his party turned back by an army of monks. Frenchman

Jules Dutreuil de Rhins spent sixty days on the Chang Tang during winter and saw no one. Eventually he was murdered by unfriendly villagers, his body dumped in a river and never seen again. Englishman George Littledale set out with 250 animals, eleven tons of fodder, and six months of provisions. Difficult conditions decimated his herd and he staggered from the plateau with only four surviving animals. The legendary Swede Sven Hedin, made three attempts to reach Lhasa and travelled thousands of kilometres on the open plateau. He never reached the capitol. "The Chang Tang," he declared, "is a gigantic wall which nature has built up like a bulwark to guard the secrets of Tibet."

This era of exploration on the Chang Tang ended in 1904, when Sir Francis Younghusband invaded Lhasa from the south. The British general crossed the Himalaya in Sikkim, bringing with him ten thousand troops. When Tibet resisted, a modern force armed with machine guns met a medieval army that believed prayer made them bulletproof. The ensuing slaughter was horrific. After reaching Lhasa, Younghusband retreated, treating the wounded and paying for the supplies his forces had pillaged, but with his intrusion, the Forbidden City had lost its allure. The eyes of exploration turned elsewhere, and the Chang Tang was forgotten. For a century, no one attempted to cross it.

A flat tire in the first five kilometres (3 miles) does not dampen my spirits, but when one of the Dong Feng lorry's rear leaf springs breaks shortly after, the journey appears over. Without speaking the driver jacks the truck up, jams in a few spare pieces of steel, and bolts them in place. Two hours later the convoy limps forward.

We leave northern Tibet's only tarmac road at the muddy town of Nacqchu, where garbage fills the streets and the blood of butchered animals flows from dumpsters. Sheep are drinking from reddened puddles. Tibetan prostitutes, caked with makeup and looking like Michael Jackson, linger by the roadside, waving to Chinese truckers.

The dirt tracks beyond are hellacious. Our trucks jolt painfully slowly across bumpy plains, forced to stay in first gear for hours on end. At camp on the first night I calculate our progress. Sixty kilometres (36 miles) took six hours.

Day after day the rough tracks make our teeth clatter and kidneys ache. Barrels of extra gasoline stored in the rear begin to leak, giving everyone headaches. When we open the windows to get fresh air, the cab fills with so much dust that we are forced to close up quickly and suffer with the fumes.

Nights are freezing cold, the daytime sun burns our skin, and winds howl perpetually. On the fourth day, dark storm clouds arrive without warning, and a warm summer day changes to a blizzard in minutes. Ten centimetres (4 inches) of snow falls. When it melts, the meandering tracks become a soggy quagmire and we get stuck every few kilometres. Hours are spent digging, spinning tires, and yelling. Our efforts are uncoordinated and soon everyone is covered in mud. As night falls we give up, sleeping under the stuck truck. In the morning we dig a pit, drive our Toyota Land Cruiser into it, attach a steel cable to its bumper, and wrap the other end around the axle of the Dong Feng lorry. With the Toyota acting as an anchor, the huge truck drives itself forward through the mud, the cable winding around its axle like a winch. Finally, we are free.

We pass stream beds containing the skeletons of past convoys, frozen in a hopeless battle against the muck. Some of the vehicles have been abandoned. Others are surrounded by shovels, jacks, and sunburned drivers, sitting on the ground, devoid of hope.

A confusing web of tire scars criss-cross these grasslands, and the Russian military topographic maps I have don't help much. None of the trails marked on the maps seem to exist, and the ones on the ground lead in circles, constantly turning back on themselves. The scale of the land is so great that a wrong turn can waste half a day, or more.

It takes eight exhausting days to reach the Chinese administrative outpost of Shung-hu, a lonely jumble of concrete plunked in the middle of a shallow, windswept valley. Only a decade old, it already has drawn the majority of the region's nomads to settle in its confines. There is just one street, a dusty alley really, and it is jammed with people. Hardened men with windburned faces and empty eyes press around billiard tables. Families wander hand in hand, and young children swarm our Land Cruiser, chasing behind us as we inch down the street. A loudspeaker, suspended from a lamppost, is crackling with the State Radio's message of the day, broadcast from Beijing, five time zones away. Emerging from the mud-caked trucks, we stretch our legs and shake a hundred little hands. En route we have endured seventeen flat tires, five clogged carburetors, a broken distributor cap, one crushed muffler, and a broken leaf spring.

Almost immediately Hugh and I set off toward a barren hill rising behind town, hoping to catch a glimpse of what lies beyond, the uncrossed heart of the Chang Tang. Thirty dogs follow us as if we were two pied pipers. Most of the mutts are friendly but a few bare their teeth and lunge at our heels. We arm ourselves with rocks and begin to climb. A bitterly cold wind races down from the north, cutting straight through our Gore-Tex jackets. We are at 5,200 metres (17,000 feet) and the air is thin. Moving slowly, we rest often, bent double, trying to quell heaving lungs. Gradually the top comes into view.

A single wooden pole marks the rounded summit, and faded prayer flags snap in the gale. A vast grey-brown plain stretches beyond. In the distance, I can just glimpse the flanks of snow-capped mountains. Five hundred kilometres (300 miles) away, over unnamed ranges, past salty lakes and torrential rivers, the great plateau plunges downward and meets the Taklamakan Desert. My proposal is to walk from here to there.

Looking out over the plains, it is clear that if anything went wrong, we could never be rescued. It took eight days just to drive here. To find anyone in the great void that lies beyond would be asking the impossible. Helicopters couldn't reach the heart of the Chang Tang, not in such thin air, and there are no planes stationed nearby that could be employed in a rescue. Any team wandering out into the flats would be completely on their own. I always knew the journey would be a ball-buster, but for the first time I actually comprehend the true severity of the risk, and a shiver of fear passes through me.

Twelve hours later Hugh and I are in the trucks again, bouncing southward. The short visit has given me a better understanding of the challenges that will face us on the crossing. Local yak herders have agreed to organize beasts and supplies for next spring, and I feel optimistic. The undertaking seems at last plausible. By the time we return to Lhasa, Hugh is devastated. Two weeks of tooth-rattling driving have been enough. "I think I am going to fly to Thailand and mellow out for a few days," he announces at dinner. "The thought of getting in one more Land Cruiser is just too much."

I fly on alone to Urumchi, in China's remote northwestern Xinjian province, to glimpse the finishing point of the trek. Picked up by another silent driver, our muffler explodes an hour after leaving the airport and an entire day is spent in a greasy pit, welding it together. We set off again and the distributor cap blows. I feel my patience wearing thin when I need it most. Finally we roll on, over mountains and across the Taklamakan Desert, toward oasis towns lying in the shadow of the Tibetan Plateau, once stopping points along the ancient Silk Route.

"Very few tourists come here," my Chinese escort whispers as we enter Korla after five days of driving. "It is not a civilized place." Rows of poplars line the roads. Donkey-drawn carts clatter past, laden with firewood and hay. Bicycles are everywhere. A man in a business suit pedals by, a freshly slaughtered pig, perfectly bisected from nose to tail, slung over the back rack of his bicycle. There is only one hotel in town where foreigners are permitted to stay, and that night I eat alone, in a deserted dining hall. Salty tea and dumplings are served. Synthesized riffs of Canadian rocker Bryan Adams seep from hidden speakers, with Chinese lyrics dubbed over top.

By noon the following day the paved road ends. Ahead the plateau floats up from the desert, snow-capped peaks over sun-scorched sand. The silent driver turns onto a winding dirt track, speeding into badlands. It takes twenty-four hours to navigate a maze of narrow canyons leading to a wide fertile valley, carpeted in golden fields of grass. Sheep and Bactrian camels wander freely, and in the distance I spot Tura, a warren of concrete homes. Beyond rise the grey bulwarks of glaciated peaks. This is the very edge of the plateau. After dragging ourselves across the Chang Tang, this hidden oasis will offer the first opportunity of help or resupply.

The head of town, a Chinese army official from Urumchi, invites me to his office for tea. "Do you have any Canadian coins?" he asks. "My daughter is a collector."

I rummage through my wallet and give him thirty-one cents, which is everything I have. He seems very pleased, and offers me a camel ride in exchange.

As a groaning, bellowing beast is lead into the courtyard I begin to have second thoughts. Two years ago, after riding across Arabia, I could have steered Crazy Dancer through an obstacle course without blinking. Now I am petrified to even approach. The Bactrian camels (two-humpers) of high Asia are enormous beasts compared to the dromedaries (single-humpers) of Arabia, with backs as wide as a couch. I muster up my courage and then swing my leg high, trying to get it over the rear hump, but the camel gnashes its teeth and tries to rise, and I tumble awkwardly to the ground. The army officer hauls the camel down by the nose ring. Finally, I jump on, and the massive animal lumbers to its knees, and then its feet.

We follow a footpath along a clear, green stream leading up into the mountains. The sky is dark blue and cloudless, and the peaks soar before us. After an hour we turn back, but I have noticed a trail winding up into the barren mountains. It is not hard to imagine trundling down it next year, exhausted but exhilarated, after crossing the Chang Tang.

⁓

I return from the reconnaissance in high gear. The visit has given me the passion I need to see the journey through. Images captured in Tibet are plastered across glossy proposals and used to attract sponsors.

Diplomatic channels are opened with the Canadian embassy in Beijing, the first step in paving the way for permits. Requisitions for more detailed Russian military maps are filed. A communications expert in Boston begins designing a lightweight yet rugged platform of satellite phones, laptops, digital cameras, and solar chargers that can update the children's Internet program from the field. My phone rings incessantly. Several public-relations firms present proposals to secure media awareness. I fly to Toronto, Ottawa, Vancouver, and Edmonton to meet with partners, keeping enthusiasm high and efforts focused. A team of Calgary teachers begins designing and producing curriculum for the education program. After reviewing my initial pitch, National Geographic expresses interest in producing a video documentary of the expedition.

The journey will be expensive, and I need at least one more major sponsor. Two years earlier, before departing for Arabia, I exhausted myself with preparations and arrived in Oman sick. I know I cannot afford to make the same mistake again. The traverse of the Chang Tang will be too demanding; I must be 100 per cent, so I set a deadline. If the money is not in place by Christmas, I will postpone the expedition a year. But that is still six months away, which seems like plenty of time given how well things have been going, and it gives me no cause for concern. Another pressing issue is occupying my thoughts. I need to get out and go for a walk – a really long walk – with a heavy pack on my back, to help understand and prepare for the challenges waiting in Tibet.

Chris "Ferg" Ferguson and I were introduced by a mutual friend four years earlier, at a Calgary slide show. Both able to move fast in the wilderness, and happy to suffer the discomforts of exertion, we quickly became a regular team in the mountains. Within a year we had climbed Denali (North America's highest peak, more commonly known as Mount McKinley) together, a twenty-three-day expedition that cemented our friendship.

While our physical abilities were similar, it was clear from the start that we were opposite personalities. Ferg was serious, quiet, and reserved; his demeanour so intense that he was often intimidating, especially to strangers. As a purist and a stickler for details, he found my spontaneous and quick-changing plans sometimes dumbfounding, sometimes frustrating, and occasionally infuriating.

Growing up an Air Force brat on bases across Canada, Ferg followed his father through military college, working as a navigator on Hercules aircraft until the constraints of service life began to conflict with a growing desire to explore the wilderness. Now living contract to contract, and unemployed more often than not, Ferg shared one precious commodity with me: lots of free time. When I told Ferg I wanted to go on a long hike, he suggested the CANOL. A month later we met in Whitehorse, crammed enormous backpacks in his Subaru, devoured an all-you-can-eat Pizza Hut buffet, and headed north, toward road's end.

Bone-chilling clouds slide over the low foothills of the Mackenzie Mountains, and the intermittent drizzle of dawn has turned to a steady downpour. It is the wettest Yukon summer in recent memory. Ferg inches his Subaru through deep toffee-coloured puddles that obliterate the dirt road. Water sloshes against the doors and threatens to flood the engine. Fifteen kilometres (9 miles) shy of the border with the Northwest Territories a swollen creek washes across the road. We can go no farther. Ferg shuts the engine off, and we sit in silence. Raindrops patter on the roof. The windshield grows foggy. Neither of us moves.

"This is not the type of weather that makes me eager to depart for an eighteen-day hike," Ferg grumbles.

The great Victorian thinker John Ruskin once wrote, "There is really no such thing as bad weather, just different kinds of good weather." I generally agree. But leaving a warm car in the pouring rain? That just feels wrong.

We are going to get soaked, and delaying the inevitable won't help. Moving quickly, we jump out of the car and haul bulging backpacks from the trunk, retrieving anoraks, slipping waterproof covers on our packs, and tightening gaiters over leather hiking boots. After hiding the keys under the rear bumper, we edge across a slippery beam spanning the creek. Before us willow scrub stretches out in every direction. Apart from the soft patter of rain, the rolling land sits under a veil of silence; even the birds have taken refuge. With heads bowed, we stride off, side by side, down a solitary gravel track.

During the latter years of the Second World War, this quiet corner of Canada's north played host to the U.S. military's biggest construction job since the Panama Canal. The CANOL project, approved by Congress in 1942, was intended to deliver Norman Wells crude oil to the new Alaska Highway, insuring that any Japanese land invasion could be fought with a well-fuelled army. A quick and simple five-month construction was forecast.

Cloaked in secrecy and hidden in a vast wilderness, the pipeline slowly crept forward. Barges toiled around the clock, and two hundred thousand tons of supplies were shipped north. A refinery was purchased in Texas, dismantled, shipped up the Pacific Coast, and rebuilt. Fifty-three thousand soldiers and contract civilians constructed barracks, pumping stations, roads, and bridges. Forest fires, flash floods, landslides, bogs, and plagues of insects hindered progress. It was not until three years later that the last weld was completed and Norman Wells's crude finally began to flow.

Just six months later the CANOL became the target of a United States Senate committee chaired by Harry Truman. Facts regarding pipeline inefficiencies and leakages were damning, and when the Senate threatened to go public with an inquiry, the controversial project was scrapped. In a rush to wash its hands of the entire affair, the U.S. War Department sold salvage rights for a paltry seventy thousand dollars. Within months the pipeline was pulled, and the sixty thousand residual barrels of oil sitting inside were dumped across the land. While machinery was picked over, and engines were stripped from vehicles, the vast majority of what the American Army had struggled so hard to transport and construct was left behind to rust.

Cutting across a rugged stretch of the Northwest Territories' Mackenzie Mountains, landslides and mud rendered the road impassable within a few years. Spring floods and ice quickly tore out all sixty-five bridges. Today the remnants of this massive project, languishing in the remote wilderness of the Canadian northwest, are all but forgotten. All that remains on Canadian topographical maps is a winding dotted line marked "Abandoned."

Ten days is generally accepted as the reasonable limit for self-supported travel. Beyond this, loads grow prohibitively heavy, causing an exponential increase in physical strain and suffering. On longer expeditions, animals, food caches, helicopter drops, or some other form of resupply are normally employed. To test the feasibility of my plans in Tibet, we have chosen to push our limits, and are carrying eighteen days of supplies, just enough to get us across the 375 kilometres (233 miles) of wilderness. These calorie-rich, weight-reduced, dehydrated rations weigh upward of thirty kilograms (66 pounds), and even though we've packed only ultra-light gear and left everything extraneous behind, the packs are oppressive.

The weather remains wet and cool, but we wear only nylon shorts and thin synthetic tops, for the strain of carrying the loads keeps us warm. River and creek crossings are a regular occurrence, and while the water is usually no more than knee-deep, it is fast and frigid. We can't afford to stumble. Hanging our hiking boots around our necks and donning rubber sandals, we shuffle gingerly across the creeks, using our hiking poles for support. At deeper crossings we unclip the waist belts on our packs and bury our cameras in garbage bags, just in case we go for an unplanned swim.

Down into the valley of the Intga River Ferg and I march, up and over Caribou Pass, and on toward the Ekwi River. The high land is barren, apart from two parallel thickets of alder, which enclose the road, springing from the ditches where army diggers disturbed the permafrost half a century earlier. This growth is so dense that we cannot see through it. Branches join overhead, blocking the sun, and we travel down a tunnel of shrubbery.

As the days flow by, we fall into a natural rhythm of travel. At the first sound of our morning alarm – a beeping watch strapped to a loop on the tent ceiling – one of us rises to start a fire, boil water, and prepare coffee. The other packs the sleeping bags, pads, and tent. Retrieving our food from the previous night's cache, one person cooks the oatmeal while the other prepares energy drinks and snacks for the day. Less than an hour after waking we are headed down the trail.

Forests of pine and poplar clog valley bottoms. Birdsong echoes in the still air, waxwings and juncos dart amidst trailside branches as we pass. Families of ptarmigan regularly burst onto the trail before us, running silently until we catch up. Then the parents squawk and beat their wings in a frantic attempt to distract us, occasionally dashing back to peck young fledglings on the head and hurry them in another direction.

We are travelling through prime grizzly habitat, and the path is laden with recent signs of bear; tufts of downy, blond hair snagged on low branches, trailside poplars scarred with claw marks, and overturned plots of hedysarum (a purple wildflower whose roots are a rich store of protein and carbohydrates). Most impressive of all are the scats. The summer has been a good one for berries, and with almost every step we have to avoid bright piles of red soapberry shit that dot the trail. Researchers estimate that an adult bear can consume upward of one hundred thousand soapberries in a single day, and it appears that the berries come out the far end as fast as they go in the mouth.

The constant awareness that a bear could be around the next corner heightens our senses. Our eyes scan the brush. Our ears remain alert for snapping twigs. "HI BEAR! HERE BEAR! HUP, HUP!" we regularly yell at the top of our lungs, hoping to warn any nearby *Ursus* of our presence. We carry a canister of bear spray (pressurized pepper spray) and "bear-bangers" (hand-launched explosive charges), but these are meant as a last resort.

There are a few close encounters. One huge male griz ambles our way, and then sits down smack in the middle of the trail to dine on berries, forcing us to detour through a nearby swamp. Another inquisitive young juvenile will not be deterred by our yelling and clattering ski poles, and approaches frighteningly close. I fumble nervously trying to load the banger, but finally launch a charge, and the explosion sends the youngster scampering back into the bush. The encounter spooks us, and we are cautious by the campfire that night, ears alert for any unusual sounds.

With a long distance ahead and limited supplies, we press on at an unforgiving pace, averaging nearly thirty kilometres (18 miles) a day. The packs have rubbed our shoulders raw. Purple and yellow bruises – the size of dinner plates – spread across our hips where the waist bands tighten. Ankles, knees, and backs grow sore from the strain of uneven terrain. Blisters grow, burst, and harden into callouses. Ferg covers one of his feet in duct tape, convinced it holds a stress fracture. Although he pops a handful of anti-inflammatories at every break and never complains, I can tell he is suffering. My Achilles tendons grow alarmingly sore, grating whenever I move and occasionally bunching up grotesquely within their sheath. At the end of each day I linger knee-deep in icy streams, hoping to reduce the swelling, but there is no noticeable improvement.

This physical suffering pales beside the never-ending hunger that has overtaken us. We carefully maximized the calories in our menu, but it is impossible to carry enough to replace what we burn each day. I focus on chewing everything fastidiously, hoping to eke out every last calorie. If even a single sunflower seed or peanut husk slips from our hands during a snack break, both of us are on our knees, searching the ground in hopes of retrieving the morsel. Dinner, our biggest meal of the day, does nothing to ease these cravings, and my stomach rumbles even as I lower my fork.

We search every building we pass for abandoned scraps of food. At one hut we find a tube of honey, which we squeeze straight into our mouths. At another we discover a sealed bucket marked "Left Over Food." Tearing it open, all that awaits is a German dehydrated meal-in-a-bag, *Karrot Stew mit Tofu*, which we prepare and eat immediately. Despite near ravenous hunger by day fourteen, we cannot bring ourselves to consume a pound of lard unearthed in a hunter's cabin. A few heaping tablespoons mixed with our morning oatmeal is all we can stomach, and the rest is left behind.

It is impossible to forget we are alone, two specks in the middle of a vast expanse of wilderness. The isolation is thrilling, and at times mildly frightening, and our utter dependence on each other helps form a powerful bond. As we trudge onward, one day melting into the next, layer after layer of personality is peeled away. For years Ferg has been the strong, silent type, but now he chatters endlessly; reliving childhood hockey memories, reminiscing about student rituals at military college, and even singing Gordon Lightfoot. "The Wreck of the Edmund Fitzgerald" must have been sung fifty times. I describe my father – a unique man who in many ways was like Ferg – and in turn Ferg relives an earlier marriage. I can't remember ever having understood him so well before, or having felt so close.

Autumn is in the air as we set out across the final Mackenzie swamplands. Yellow rushes sway in dark trailside ponds. Swaths of horsetail flame orange, and thick mats of birch leaves cover the boggy ground. The cacophony of summer frogs, crickets, and cicadas has faded, a brief respite as the land catches its breath and it waits for the harsh northern winter.

After a night of pelting rain, we pull on wet clothes, wring out wet socks, and cram swollen feet back into squelching boots one last time.

The trail before us cuts a perfectly straight line through indistinguishable flats, making it impossible to know exactly where we are. Time crawls by. "It's-the-last-day-and-I-can't-take-another-minute" syndrome has set in. Every step hurts. Waist-deep bogs obliterate long sections of road. Holding our packs overhead, we trudge straight through.

And then the tunnel of bush that has held us captive for so long suddenly opens. The sandy beaches of the Mackenzie River stretch ahead. Red-and-white oil rigs sprout from mid-river islands, orange plumes erupting from their pinnacles, trails of soot stretching across the sky. Bearded, grubby, and happy, we drop our packs by an enormous cottonwood log and take one final photo.

❧

December 23, 2000. 3:10 p.m. Departures Lounge, Calgary airport. Two days before my self-imposed deadline for securing the final piece of Chang Tang expedition's sponsorship.

I frantically plug quarters into a pay phone. Just two months ago I thought I had found the final piece of funding. A major computer manufacturer appeared poised to sign on as a primary sponsor. The senior vice-president was keen; our children's education program offered a perfect opportunity to showcase their new image-hosting software. We were sorting out details in the contract when my phone calls abruptly went unreturned. Two weeks passed. What was happening?

It took weeks to discover that the deal had been scrapped for political reasons. One of my other sponsors had cancelled a contract with the computing firm, and the pullout was retribution. Despite feeling like a helpless pawn, there was no time for dejection. Time was running out and I immediately swung into high gear. Everything else was put on a backburner; every day was spent on the phone. I ate and slept in my small office. Opportunities and leads kept pouring in, and I followed every one up.

As the first snows of December arrived I had thirty-nine active files, and remained in daily contact with each. There were pharmaceutical firms, banks, oil-and-gas companies, utilities, communications companies, along with software providers and hardware manufacturers. It seemed everyone was lukewarm; interested but noncommittal.

Less than a week before Christmas I was shopping at a local mall with my mother when we crossed paths with an old acquaintance. I mentioned the Chang Tang expedition and my dwindling hope of raising the money.

"What? That's all you need?" the man asked, although the sum I needed was astronomical. "I can get that for you with a couple of calls. Give me your business card. I'll get back to you by the end of the day."

And with that he wandered off, melting into the crowds, leaving my mother and me standing in stunned silence. For some reason my heart did not race. I had been here before, down the road of enthusiastic words and disappointing leads. I doubted anything would come of it. It was just too much money, too fast. Hours later, as I prepared a customized package which I ran to the printers and couriered overnight to my friend's contact in Southern California, I realized that I was just going through the motions.

Now I hurriedly check my voice mails from the airport departure lounge. Nothing. I call my primary contact at the Calgary Board of Education. Has there been any interest in the package we sent out? Nope. I call a project manager from a local communications firm who is my most promising lead, and get his answering machine. "*Away for Christmas. Will return January 6. Leave a message.*" Shit.

The final boarding call is announced.

For three years all I have thought about is the Chang Tang. For eighteen months I have worked on nothing else. My very identity seems tied to the plateau. As I begin the walk down the ramp toward my airplane, I know it is done. There will be no more "last tries," the well has run dry. It is time to let it go, at least for now. I feel wretched and hollow.

A year later, after a long summer in the Canadian wilderness has restored my vigour, I am beginning to prepare for a new round of Chang Tang fundraising when devastating news comes across my desk: a group of Americans has just completed the journey, by foot.

Twelve months earlier I pitched National Geographic Television, suggesting a film of the Chang Tang journey. The vice-president of story development, whom I had previously worked with on our Arabian documentary, appeared interested, so I sent in a detailed plan. Three weeks later a curt reply arrived in the mail. "Your proposed journey lacks an interesting storyline, and has no compelling characters." There was no further correspondence.

Now an elite team, sent by National Geographic, including my greatest photographic mentor, Galen Rowell, had just completed an identical journey to the one I pitched. I could still follow in their footsteps, but with the magic of the unknown shattered, my Chang Tang ambitions evaporate.

新疆且末县吐拉牧场公用笺

中国新疆且末县吐拉牧场

且末县吐拉牧场位于昆仑山与阿尔金山之间，临近无人区，人口864人，全新疆面积最大，与阿尔金山脉相连并有飞播草场，人口74万公顷，可利用35万公顷，气候、水位非常适宜，是阿尔金山脉与且末之间7万公顷，可利用的高质性气候，空气、水牧场草场海拔3200米，原子世外桃园，欢迎大朋友来作客！信无污染，是二十世纪的世外桃园，虽海交通便，但可摄像作所处的信无污染。

牧场基地是今年下到经济项目开发：

一、特种野养殖业，……野生动物不……真数量正在全面减少，询国家要请出这些动物进行人工繁殖无法可行，……此类野生动物人工养殖落后不得要求，此行此类野生人工养殖无法可行，……此类野生动物人工养殖落后不得要求，此行此类野生……这……无法可行，询问国家申请准，根据此地牧养殖条件，不但条件了必须动植，询问国家申请……项目，根据此地牧养殖条件。里上方功能作合作开发。询问国家要请出资金和养殖技术，真……种植和国内及合，……资金和养殖技术，里上方功能作合作开发。外朋友也作合作开发。

二、无人区打探险旅游游业：吐拉牧场临近无人区私人区，完全可国内外朋友也作探险力量，……地无熟悉此地方……此地无话寻导的风光，牧场……探险旅游专员，使更多的朋友能探……此里的探险游无人区的大以教给我的无话寻导……此地方……此地无话寻导的风光，牧场……探险旅游专员，使更多的朋友能探……此里的探险游无人区的大了提供有力支援，同年，各种……和步骤的救护设备，2000年10月随着工业也发达的发达，牧场给外界合……旅游无人区的大本意，欢迎国内外朋友合作开发！

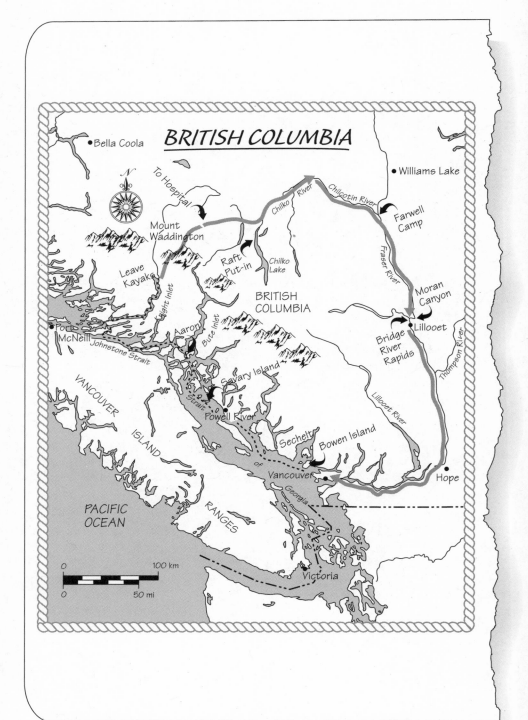

twelve

The Grand Cirque

REDEMPTION IN THE SOUTHERN COAST RANGE

The cure for anything is salt water; sweat, tears, or the sea.

Isak Dinesen

British Columbia, 2001

PART I: THE OCEAN

FOLLOWING THE collapse of the Tibetan expedition, the money I'd raised was returned to sponsors and the student website mothballed. My phone, which rang incessantly for a year, fell silent. There were no more pitches to deliver, no more e-mails to answer, no brainstorming sessions with excited partners. The buoyant enthusiasm that comes with pursuing grand schemes vanished. Facing nothing but an empty calendar and yearning for a distraction, I began poring over maps.

Maps have always enticed me, whispering of adventures waiting to happen and of secret nooks begging to be explored. It may seem strange, even mildly pathetic, to get excited about a flat piece of paper, but with even just a cursory glance at a map, the land springs to life in my mind; ranges rising up steeply, clear blue lakes sprinkled across grassy steppes or tucked in alpine amphitheatres, winding canyons, braiding rivers, tundra marshes. Maps speak of opportunity, of possibility, and as I pass my eyes over the surface of a chart, I am always seeking natural routes of travel buried within the landscape, not yet imagined.

Sitting in my dark office, floating away to remote corners of Patagonian ice caps and Mongolian steppes, I abruptly realized I was falling into a trap, fixated on making each successive endeavour grander than the last: longer, tougher, and more publicized. The cumbersome and ultimately thwarted Tibetan project had shattered the illusion that bigger is always better, and for the time being, I wanted nothing to do with the cumbersome *business* of adventure. Instead it was simplicity I sought; a raw adventure with no updates to file or sponsors to think of; a return to the elements that first attracted me to wilderness travel. With time my mind drifted back to a rainy day in Vancouver, when

Johan Kruss had traced a grand loop on a tattered road map of British Columbia, and I dug out the old notes.

The concept had been straightforward. Jump into sea kayaks in Vancouver, paddle up the coast for several hundred kilometres, drag the boats over the Coast Range ice caps, and run the rivers of the Interior all the way back to the start. It was an aesthetic route, almost poetic, starting and finishing right in the heart of Canada's third-largest city. There would be no funds to raise, no website to design, no permits to secure, no bribes to pay, no international flights to book. I could find no reference of anyone doing anything similar, and most of those I initially approached for information brushed it off as a hare-brained idea. I grew more interested every day.

I was especially drawn to the fact that the journey was at home, in my own backyard. It is easy for Canadians to dismiss the spectacular wilderness areas of their homeland as second-rate, somehow a league below more exotic foreign locales, yet as I researched the "Grand Cirque" journey, it was clear that the route would pass through terrain as rugged and challenging as any I had seen.

I called Johan to see if he was interested in joining me for an attempt, but with a young daughter at home, he could not spend the summer away. Although Ferg's experience was primarily in the mountains, he was a strong, competent partner and a fast learner. Our friendship had flourished since the CANOL trip, making him the next natural choice for the venture. He didn't hesitate when I mentioned the idea, immediately agreeing to give it a shot, eager for his first exposure to the world of sea kayaking and river running.

It did not take us long to realize the original plan – using the same craft for the entire journey – was horrendously impractical. Instead, Ferg and I decided to travel up the coast by sea kayak, traverse the Coast Range by foot, and then use a raft (stashed before the trip somewhere in the forests of the Interior) to return to Vancouver. Additionally, on the way over the mountains, we hoped to make an attempt on Mount

Waddington's northwest summit. (Waddington's main summit, not easily accessible from our route, is the highest peak in the southern Coast Range.)

After a month of planning I suggested to Ferg that my girlfriend, Christine, and my younger brother, Douglas, join us for the sea-kayaking segment. It would not be a challenging part of the journey, and seemed a perfect opportunity to share a bit of my world with two people who were so important to me.

Christine and I had met three years earlier, at a gym in Calgary, where she was a personal trainer and I was preparing for the Everest expedition. Living within blocks of each other, we began running and rollerblading together whenever I was in the city. Although we didn't date for two years, it always seemed inevitable. An extraordinarily talented athlete, Christine regularly followed me up mountains and down rivers near Calgary, making up for her lack of experience with raw strength and enthusiasm.

Doug, an oil-and-gas engineer, was growing increasingly frustrated with the long hours and sedentary nature of his job. Although he never said so, I suspected he felt envious of Jamie's brother, Leigh, who had had the chance to accompany us to Arabia. I knew Doug would treasure an invitation to join this journey.

Ferg, however, objected, maintaining that Doug and Christine's presence would spoil the essence of the expedition. "It dilutes what we are trying to do. The trip will no longer be a go-hard, two-person journey from start to finish."

I knew what he meant, but years of guiding had formed my vision of the coast as a place to enjoy, not to race along. Somewhat selfishly, I viewed the expedition as my creation and stood firm, arguing that partners on an adventure were as important as the journey itself. I had also misguidedly mentioned the expedition to both Christine and Doug without anticipating this pickle. They were both keen and Ferg didn't want to budge, making it an uncomfortable position for everyone.

Before the impasse could be resolved, a second, thornier issue arose.

The whitewater portion of the journey, a series of rivers leading all the way back to Vancouver, would not be easy. Cold waters, steep gradients, and the huge volumes of flow would present serious challenges. With no river-running background, Ferg would be relying heavily on my experience. It is always safer to travel on a river with more than one craft, and as I researched the difficulties facing us, I suggested it would be prudent for an additional raft or kayak to join us on the trip home.

"Why not just run the rapids we feel capable of?" Ferg countered. "And portage the rest."

It made sense on paper, but river trips rarely unfold as planned. "What if we capsize, and end up on opposite sides of the river?" I asked. "Or worse yet, lose our craft? Another boat could help ferry us across, or go for help." It would also help me to have another experienced river runner along, someone to keep a second eye on things in the rapids, and weigh in on difficult decisions.

But Ferg was adamant. "The trip keeps getting watered down. Your plans for the coast sound more like a vacation than an expedition. And with extra boaters along on the river, I'm concerned I'll become more of a passenger than a partner."

We had reached a standoff, and eventually Ferg set an ultimatum: he would accept Christine and Doug joining the sea-kayaking leg, and would continue on over the mountains with me, but if I wanted extra boats on the river, he would leave the trip at that point and hitchhike home. Mindful that Ferg had compromised by allowing Christine and Doug on the coast, I reluctantly agreed to travel the river with him alone.

But my mind could not rest. Endless scenarios of mishap on the river kept me awake at night. After two weeks of silent turmoil, I knew I had to tell Ferg I wanted another boater. Hesitantly, I broached the subject. We yelled, cried, argued, and talked, but in the end felt no better for it. Ferg stuck to his guns – he would not be coming on the river.

Preparations ground on, but both of us were now bitter, and even tiny decisions, like menu choices and equipment lists, led to unbearable arguments and tensions.

"Ferg! Stop the car!"

We are racing down a two-lane highway west of Williams Lake, British Columbia, with the Tragically Hip cranked up on the stereo and the windows down. In just two days we will begin the odyssey. Seventy days of food has been dehydrated, our gear is packed, and the sea kayaks are ready to go. All we need to do is stash a raft on the shores of Tatla Lake and return to Vancouver.

Absently staring out the window, I suddenly realize that the Tatla River – an essential link on the rafting route back to Vancouver – is supposed to be running beside the road. Instead there is a parched creek bed and a scattering of fire-scarred stumps. I feel the first twinges of panic. Taking a GPS reading, I double-check the maps and confirm the shattering news. The Tatla River is bone-dry.

Months earlier I wondered how much water would be in the river, the starting point for the third leg of our journey, but brushed the concerns from my mind, preoccupied with the huge whitewater we would face farther downstream. Even if the Tatla River were only ankle-deep, I reasoned, we could still drag the raft, never once considering there would be no water at all.

Ferg and I drive on in silence. Seventy-five kilometres (46 miles) of dry riverbed separates Tatla Lake from the waters of the Chilcotin River. *Have I once again taken an outlandish idea too far?* I dejectedly flip through a pile of topographical maps trying to clear my mind and weigh the options, but none makes sense. Everything turns the journey into a lark or a penance. Suddenly, I notice a thin blue line, forty-five kilometres (27 miles) to the south: the Chilko River. I know it by reputation. Ten years ago its violent rapids and cold waters killed seven rafters, but it is still commercially run, so it can't be too hard. Hiking to its headwaters will add several days to the mountain traverse, but the Chilko can carry us down to the Chilcotin, and onward to Vancouver. I breathe a sigh of relief. The loop can be completed; the journey sewn together.

The day of departure dawns grey and cool. With three kayaks stacked on their roof racks, my aunt and uncle drive us to Jericho Beach, in Vancouver's trendy Kitsilano district. A stiff breeze ripples the waters of English Bay and thick clouds sweep in from the west, piling against Vancouver's North Shore mountains. Shafts of sunlight struggle to break through, lighting distant shores as the boats are unloaded and an intimidating heap of gear and food piled up beside them.

Half an hour later we push off, two single kayaks and one double, bobbing past the immense container ships moored in the harbour, heading toward a distant lighthouse marking White Rock. Despite sunny skies, it is cool on the water. Motorboats race by, and our unfamiliar kayaks feel tippy in their wake.

After two hours we reach Bowen Island, a commuter settlement sitting in the throat of Howe Sound, just north of Vancouver, and seek shelter along its southern shore. As the kayaks glide into a secluded bay, a group of Canada geese raises a trumpeting protest, swimming rapidly away with heads held high. The scent of salt, cedar, and decaying kelp instantly takes me back to earlier days on the coast. I drag my hands in the water beside my cockpit, watching shafts of sunlight disappear into the green depths below, musing on how far I have come since last paddling these waters.

Sanderlings dance along the beach where we land, nimbly darting out between swells to peck at floating morsels. After fixing a lunch of bagels and hummus, we stretch out across enormous driftwood logs, enjoying the warmth of the sun. In the weeks before a major expedition, organizational pressures build exponentially – last-minute things to buy, calls to place, repairs to make – until they feel crushing. And then in one fell swoop, with departure, all the stress disappears. Nothing can be done about things forgotten now. A weight has lifted from our shoulders, and within minutes I am asleep, Christine's head resting on my shoulder. When I awake, I notice Ferg has already packed his gear and is bobbing in his boat, waiting.

We continue winding northward on the second day, through the Pasley Islets and across Balfour Channel. Stiff breezes push us up the Sunshine Coast, and before long whitecaps are breaking across the decks. Doug and Christine are tentative, their big double kayak being tossed about unnervingly. Also new to kayaking, Ferg struggles to hold a straight line through the confused waves.

"Just keep paddling," I shout over the wind. "Especially if you see a big swell coming. A blade in the water makes you more stable." All three gain confidence quickly, and soon we are sprinting along, trying to catch rides on passing waves. Sandy beaches and cottages rush by. Soaked by spray, we yell and laugh.

All afternoon the winds blow and the swells continue to build. Soon the kayaks around me are disappearing from sight in deep troughs, reappearing moments later, perched on foaming crests. It is with relief that we finally reach the town of Sechelt and nip into the protected waters beyond its point.

The development and urban sprawl that surrounds southern British Columbia's burgeoning population means that much of the coastline we pass is privately owned. "*No Trespassing*" and "*Private Property*" signs make it challenging to find camping spots. Although Canadian law declares everything below the highest high-tide mark to be Crown land, it is hard to tell that to a protective homeowner. Many appear on their decks as we pass, but very few return our waves. One man drives down to the beach on an all-terrain vehicle and sits with arms crossed, motor idling, within shouting distance when we pause to stretch our cramped legs. While I understand their concerns that garbage, fire scars, and human waste might get left behind, the frigid welcome is in stark contrast to my experiences on the Blue Nile.

Luckily, even in stretches jammed with vacation homes, we are able to find small deserted coves where our kayaks and tents go unnoticed. Up at dawn, we are quickly on our way, making sure that no trace of our passing is left.

⁓

The Inside Passage is a protected waterway that traverses Canada's West Coast, affording mariners shelter from the rugged waters of the Pacific. Connecting Seattle to Skagway, the fifteen-hundred-kilometre route winds through a maze of islets, inlets, peaks, and fjords where ocean-moderated temperatures and staggering rainfall have created a mystical blanket of temperate rain forest.

Not until 1791, when Captain George Vancouver arrived on the coast, were these convoluted channels first surveyed in detail. Vancouver came with orders to reclaim the Port of Nootka (on the west coast of what is now known as Vancouver Island) from insurgent Spanish (who had audaciously seized British ships and insulted the Admiralty's flag). During his four-year mission, Vancouver also managed to meticulously chart twenty-eight thousand kilometres of meandering shoreline, all of it packed into a short, one-thousand-kilometre section of coast. Without this monumental effort, it is conceivable that modern Canada would have no Pacific border, for at the time Oregon was intent on spreading its territory northward (and without the survey might not have stopped until reaching 54/40, the southern tip of the Alaskan panhandle).

While spared the raw brunt of coastal storms, the Inside Passage is not benign, and its cold, dark waters have claimed many lives. Howling southeasterlies herald the arrival of bad weather to these parts, and after four days of easy travel, we see a telltale sign: wispy mare's-tail clouds starting to stretch across the sky. Within hours a storm front passes, and the sea turns angry. Whitecaps slam our boats, making travel exhausting and nerves tense. Barely able to communicate over the winds, we decide to wait out the weather, landing on a sweeping pebble beach north of Cape Cockburn.

For the first time in days there is no pressing job to attend to; no rush to pack, paddle, cook, eat, or clean. I wander down toward the breaking waves, and my brother follows. Rolling over a small boulder, we watch hundreds of penny-sized crabs scurry for cover. Doug kneels and timidly picks up one of the crustaceans, but it turns and nips him. I show him how to press down gently on a crab's carapace, pinning it to the ground. "Then it is easy to grasp it behind the back legs, out of reach of the pincers."

Doug gives this a try. The crab breaks free, and scurries in circles around his palm. "It's tickling me!" he laughs and squirms, eventually tossing it to the beach.

We prod a cluster of green anemones that hang from the boulder, letting their jelly-like arms gently close on our fingers. When Doug shifts his position, a jet of water erupts from near his feet, hitting him squarely in the chest.

"What was that?" he screams in mock horror, dropping to his hands and knees and digging in a frenzied search for "piss clams."

The world of engineering that I left ten years earlier now weighs on Doug's shoulders; his oil-and-gas job in northern Alaska demands long hours. I know he has been questioning whether the attractive salary is worth the toll on his health, fitness, and mood. To see those worries drop away on the windswept beach, to experience again the comradeship we shared as kids, make all the stresses of organizing the trip worthwhile.

A light drizzle sets in. Christine and Doug collapse into their sleeping bags early, exhausted from these first days in the fresh air. Ferg lights a fire while I silently prepare dinner. Friction has been constant between us since setting off.

I want to suggest taking a day's rest. Our group has been moving up the coast faster than either of us anticipated, and at the current pace we will reach the head of Knight Inlet in fifteen days. We have budgeted a month, and with the time available it seems a pity to rush, but I suspect Ferg will be keen to press on as quickly as possible.

"What would you think about taking a day off?" I finally break the silence. "It might do those two some good. Doug is pretty tired. I've seen him stumble and fall over a couple of times just on the flat beach."

Ferg holds a match to a pile of red cedar shavings. "Whatever. It's up to you."

"Just wondering what you thought." A long, uncomfortable silence follows.

"If you want the honest truth," he continues, "This whole trip is turning into a writeoff for me. It is certainly not what I would call an expedition. I don't need a day off, but you do whatever you want."

We finish making dinner in silence. A cold wind blows in, and grey clouds race across the sky. I trudge up to the tents with Christine and Doug's dinner, returning to pack the food away just as the first telltale drops of a hard downpour hit.

Powell River, a mill town of fifty thousand, lying 130 kilometres (80 miles) north of Vancouver, offers the last chance to top up our supplies before heading into more remote waters. In 1909, two Minnesotan brothers began the construction of a pulp-and-paper mill here, drawn by the deep anchorage and abundance of hydro-electric potential. The mill they built was the largest in Western Canada, and by 1960 had become the highest producer of newsprint in the world. Despite changing hands twice in the last decade, the enormous mill remains the anchor of the local economy, and as our kayaks round the final headland, it looms unmistakably ahead. Thousands of boomed logs jostle offshore, contained behind a rusting breakwater of permanently tethered, cement-filled ocean liners.

After landing beside the harbour master's house, Christine and I hike uphill to the local supermarket. After five days of living outdoors, the air-conditioned cavern feels foreign and confining. Tourists in khaki pants and golf shirts glance warily at our salt-encrusted clothes.

"Let's get out of here," Christine whispers, and I nod. Racing up and down the aisles, we pile our cart with supplies, happy to re-emerge to the familiarity of the hot sun. Slipping off sandals, we walk barefoot back to the boats with bursting bags. Christine is crushing the new supplies into our hatches when Doug and Ferg arrive with a greasy package of fish and chips. In a moment of kinship, we all sit in a circle on the wharf, devouring its contents.

Doldrums descend, and the waters of the Strait of Georgia fall to glass. Hour after hour we paddle, our progress almost indiscernable. Somewhere ahead on the shimmering horizon, a buoy clangs eerily, marking a shallow reef. It is hours before we finally reach it, and as we do, a lone gull squawks and takes flight, strafing our bows with shit.

Eventually the cliffs of Savary Island grow near. Reflecting the sun and warming the shallow waters, they turn the crescent-shaped sliver of white sand into a quasi-tropical paradise, earning it the moniker "Hawaii of the North Pacific." A few cottages poke from the trees above, but otherwise we have the entire southern beach to ourselves. The waters are exceptionally clear. Schools of minnows dart and weave before our bows. A spiny dogfish shark rushes toward my paddle blade, veering off at the last second. Seals, hauled out on nearby rocks, grunt loudly, their pungent scent unmistakable. We set camp as the sky fades to purple and a full moon floats up in the east.

That night we sleep in the open, tucked between giant driftwood logs. A steady patter of sand hoppers lands on my sleeping bag. Waves lap nearby. Long after the others have drifted off, I remain awake, watching the tide inch upward in the moonlight. Perhaps it is the smell of our dying fire, or maybe sleeping on the sand without a tent or shelter, but suddenly Arabia returns to me. I can remember everything: the rustle of the camels at night, the silence of the dunes, the heat, the smell of frankincense, the smiles of the Bedouin.

That journey cost me one of my closest friendships. At the time I swore never to let it happen again, never to let an expedition ruin a friendship, but history seems to be repeating itself. I look at my three companions, asleep around me, and feel deep affection for them all. Why is this trip laden with such tension?

Ferg and I seem to be at loggerheads over everything: when to start in the morning, what beach to eat lunch on, how far to paddle in the afternoon, what to eat for dinner. The others say little, content to leave the planning to us. Just living outdoors is new for them, providing challenge and reward enough. I know it must be difficult for Ferg, because clearly my girlfriend and brother have allegiance to me, making him the odd man out in a way. But he doesn't make it any easier on himself; he is often withdrawn and rarely enthusiastic.

Not used to such tensions, and sensitive to a fault, Christine is suffering. Just a cold glance or silent response is enough to throw her off. I often catch her fighting silent tears as we paddle the kayak, or lie curled together in the tent at night. When Doug and I fall into a brotherly dispute, he and Ferg become closer, and the group fractures further. Although I consciously try to focus on the good things – the glorious land we are travelling through, the tranquil moments, the presence of friends and family – at times, when I am tired, hungry, and frustrated, the whole undertaking seems like a bloody bamboozle.

———

A week and a half after leaving Vancouver we enter the Discovery Islands, a labyrinth of forested islets that crowd the northern reaches of Georgia Strait. With each rise and fall of the tide, enormous volumes of water are pumped through this sieve. In places the ocean flows like a river, first in one direction, then six hours later in the other, forming violent rapids. We plan our arrival at these constrictions to coincide with periods of slack flow.

Arron Tidal Rapids, near the mouth of Bute Inlet, marks the first obstacle, and as we approach, I notice a weak current pulling our boats along. The tide has turned, but the current is not yet hazardous. Stopping paddling, we sit back and let the kayaks drift noiselessly into the narrows.

Far ahead an eagle takes flight from its perch and soars out over the water. With wings held wide it settles on a barren snag, farther down the shore. I notice two other eagles perched on the same branch. As we drift silently onward, I realize there are eagles everywhere, hopping amongst shoreline rocks, coasting from tree to tree, swooping down and snatching fish from the water's surface. Seals have joined the frenzy too, splashing in the water around us, feeding voraciously.

Seconds later I spot what has brought them: mats of dead and dying fish cover the water's surface, flowing through the narrow passage with us. Thousands more swirl in shoreline eddies. Many are scarred with talon marks, others are mutilated, heads torn off, but most appear uninjured, just dead. Later I learn that as the ocean is drawn through this shallow passage, powerful upwellings often drag schools of Pacific hake to the surface. Brought up from great depths in seconds, the fish die from rapid decompression.

More than twenty eagles are perched on the bare branches of an enormous dead fir. Taking turns, they launch one by one, swoop downward, and snatch the dead fish from the ocean's surface. The late-afternoon sun is setting behind them, and as their talons slam into the water, an explosion of golden spray erupts. The scene is so breathtaking, so staggering, so unexpected, that we decide to stop in the wide bay ahead, set camp, and enjoy the spectacle.

My eyes drift across the thickly forested shores, looking for a spot to pull out. An asphalt path tucked amidst the trees? Moments later a golf cart zooms by. Looking farther up the hillside, a golf course comes into view, built on an abandoned clear-cut. The current carries us past a clubhouse, vehicle garage, gazebo, and several totem poles.

Drifting around the corner we find a sprawling modern resort. An old stern wheeler, now a floating restaurant, is docked by the shore, and lit by thousands of glittering white Christmas lights. Chalets, cottages, and resort buildings fill every cove of the bay. Squadrons of speedboats zip past us, carrying sport fishermen in bright-orange survival suits back to the lodge for dinner.

We paddle around for over an hour, searching for any little place to camp, growing tired and cranky. By the time we realize there is not a single stretch of open shoreline, we are trapped. The tidal rapids guarding the entrance and exit to the bay have strengthened, and there is no way for us to move on. The only place we can possibly find to put the tents is the unsightly terminus of a dirt road, but an overflowing garbage dumpster and recent bear sign convince us it would not be a good choice.

It is hard not to feel bitter. We have paddled more than two hundred kilometres (120 miles) in ten days, a self-contained expedition, and here, in the "wilderness," there is not even a place for four kayakers to pitch a tent. I know we have no more right to this area than anyone else, but the disappointment at finding so much development is hard to shake. We had all imagined a quiet night on our own, watching the eagles and seals.

It is almost dark now, and we pass around hard candies to boost our blood-sugar levels before making one last search. At last, behind a rocky point, we find an abandoned section of dock floating offshore. Gingerly climbing out of our tipsy kayaks onto the high wooden deck, we drag the boats up behind us. Christine and Doug spread out gear to dry while Ferg lights the camp stove. Soon pasta is boiling.

There is merriness in the air, the kind of drunken unity that arises from hunger, exhaustion, and solving a seemingly impossible predicament. Our group dynamics yo-yo daily; sharp divisions appear from nowhere, and disappear just as quickly. Right now we are as close a team as we have been.

"Brucer," Christine approaches me quietly with a personal concern. "How are we going to go to the toilet here?"

"Gather round for a demonstration," I raise my voice. Doug and Ferg look up, Christine shakes her head. There is a decaying yellow rope on the edge of the dock, and after securing it to a stanchion, I tie a big loop around my waist, drop my pants, and lean far over the edge. "Voilà, a comfortable position to do your business."

As I scrunch my face in effort, looks of mild disgust on my partners' faces suddenly turn to wide-eyed horror. There is a sound behind, and I struggle to regain my footing and cover up, but it is too late. A power-boat has zoomed around the point. Travelling at speed, and passing close, ten well-dressed but obviously shocked fishing tourists have almost driven straight into my bare butt. It is five minutes before the others can stop their laughing and join me for dinner.

As the last vestiges of twilight fade from the western horizon, we lay our sleeping bags across a blue tarpaulin and huddle close. I can feel the warmth of Christine, and hear her slow breathing. The dock sways in the sloshing sea, and every few minutes a fish splashes somewhere in the darkness. The Milky Way slowly spreads overhead.

The afternoon's events have stirred me, leaving me reflective. Reinhold Messner, the world-famous mountaineer, once suggested that tracts of the planet be set aside, never to be developed or even mapped. Travellers to these last outposts would be obliged to return without reports or photographs, allowing future travellers the experience of discovery and exploration. Is it too late for that? My mind drifts back to summers on the Tat, and the threat of the copper mine. The pressures of human expansion seem unceasing. After ten days of travel into the wild and unable to find an undeveloped shore to camp on, I once again find myself worrying about the future of our planet's wild spaces.

We continue to paddle northward, along Cordero and Chancellor channels, past Sonora and Thurlow islands, their steep slopes partially obscured by swirling mist. Apart from logging scars and clear-cuts that occasionally loom above, there is little sign of man's presence here. At night we camp under the rain-forest canopy, where thick mats of sphagnum moss make soft and springy beds. Lilting birdsong echoes through these dim cathedrals, and few rays of sunlight ever reach the fern-covered floor, even on the brightest days.

Thirteen distinct indigenous nations once blanketed the byways of the Canadian coast, where ocean-moderated temperatures and abundant food supplies facilitated the settling of once-nomadic hunter-gatherers. Permanent villages grew, and with time came the evolution of complex hierarchical societies, rich lore, and exceptional artistry. Nearly every beach we stop at murmurs of this past, where *middens*, ancient compost piles of shells and bones, can be seen stretching into the surrounding forests, covered in blankets of decay. Upon closer inspection, we can often find thin seams of urchin spines packed between the endless black mussel shells; these distinctive layers are a sign of a plentiful harvest, or perhaps a *potlatch*.

No ceremony was more central or defining for the coastal nations than the potlatch. These lavish gatherings, featuring dancing and feasting, would conclude with the host (usually a chief) giving away everything he owned (and often more, via borrowing). After distributing blankets, furs, baskets of dried fruits and berries, weapons, and even slaves to invited guests, the host would be left destitute, but with enhanced social standing. He could count on getting even more back in the future, as each successive potlatch ceremony strove to exceed the previous one.

The ceremony became mired in controversy with the arrival of Europeans. Traders felt the extended gatherings were a waste of valuable time, and missionaries struggling to convert coastal natives to Christianity saw the potlatch as reinforcing traditional beliefs. In 1884, a Canadian law was enacted that prohibited the potlatch, and coastal tribes, already reeling from colossal change, lost yet another pillar of their identity.

We are careful not to disturb the *midden* sites we find, for buried within their layers are stories stretching back thousands of years. Their presence sparks the imagination. It is not hard to envision the old tapestry and majesty filling these coves: cedar long houses lining the shores, majestic totem poles, carved masks, dances, and great dugout canoes. Surely some remnants lie in the surrounding forests, long buried by moss and decay, slowly returning to the earth.

The land grows wilder and more austere as we leave the misty waters of Sunderland Channel and paddle into Johnstone Strait. Rocky headlands and craggy islets rise from the dark waters, and sun-bleached logs lie jumbled like matchsticks along the beaches. Many of these are wrapped in rusty chains and cables, escapees from the booms towed down the coast, once destined for paper mills in the south. We pause to watch two black bears effortlessly push aside television-sized boulders, licking at the swarms of crabs hidden underneath. Only a few hundred metres further along, a deer swims back and forth in front of our kayaks, scared and confused.

We stop for a pee break on a beach littered with abandoned machinery and old car frames. Just as we conclude that the site is abandoned, a rangy mutt bursts from the trees, barking furiously and leaping in the air. A giant of a man, with a tattered blond-grey beard and dirty red suspenders holding up even dirtier pants follows. I expect to get yelled at.

"Do you have an extra boat for me?" the man beams instead, holding out a thick, calloused hand.

Tapio, a Finn, settled here twenty years earlier to escape his disillusionment with society; now he is clearly keen for some conversation. "A lot of folks came in the seventies. Mostly hippies, seduced by the romantic vision of living off the land. They carved out homesteads, tried to make ends meet, but not many lasted. I'm the only one for miles. It is a pretty lonely existence, here in the middle of nowhere."

Doug spent a summer working in Finland on an engineering exchange, and to Tapio's delight the two of them spend a few minutes testing out his limited vocabulary.

"You're going into Knight Inlet?" Tapio frowns when we tell him our plans. "Well, all I can say is be careful. That is a dangerous place. Big winds, waves and all."

When he learns that Ferg and I intend to continue on over the mountains by foot, Tapio rolls his eyes. "In that case, enjoy the rest of your trip, because I doubt I, or anyone else, will see you again." Then he laughs so hard that he has to throw his arms out for balance.

Ferg is already back in his boat and floating offshore when Tapio offers us a meal. I decline, knowing it will probably be a long-drawn-out affair that will only cause more friction. "How about a sauna then? It will only take a few hours to warm up if we light the fire now."

Besides the unspoken rush to move on, the tide will soon turn and flow against us. Reluctantly declining, we pull on damp life jackets and push off.

A cold and brooding wind blows as we enter the rough waters of Knight Inlet. Low clouds stream in from the Pacific and surging waves rebound from granite cliffs, turning the water into a confused cauldron of white and grey. Two massive purse-seining boats plow past us, jaw-like bows jutting forward menacingly. In minutes they disappear down the yawning throat of the fjord.

The inhospitable shoreline offers no place to stop, so we speed on, tossed by breaking waves. I am trolling for salmon when I notice the red hull of Doug's boat bobbing unnaturally in the dark waters ahead. Grabbing my binoculars, I see he has capsized. Christine and I race to catch up, but Doug has righted his boat long before we get there, and with the help of Ferg, pumped the cockpit clear of water.

"You OK?" I ask worriedly as we arrive. With a kick, Doug flips himself up into his boat. Ferg holds the kayak steady while Doug attaches his spray skirt.

"Totally fine," he turns and smiles broadly. "Just got a little cocky. Tried to surf a big wave."

With a dry fleece and a toque on his head, Doug seems all right. We press on, and hours later, beyond the stark, windblown cliffs of Protection Point, we find an abandoned log-booming yard by the water's edge.

Christine cooks dinner while Ferg and I build an improvised sauna, a chance to make up for what we missed at Tapio's. It feels good to work side by side with Ferg, reminding me of easier times.

Using discarded sheets of plywood, we construct a small lean-to and cover it with a tarpaulin. Then we build a raging bonfire around a pile of rocks. An hour later the crackling, super-heated rocks are carried to the sauna between green saplings and dropped in a pit inside. After packing ourselves in and pulling the tarp closed, Doug splashes water over the stones. Steam erupts, searing our skin and our throats when we breathe. Finally, we can take no more and the door is thrown open. Running madly out, we dive into the cold, salty waters of Knight Inlet, and then dash back toward the sauna again.

A pleasure yacht moors in the waters offshore, and two seniors – a well-dressed couple with identical poodles – land in a small dinghy. As they stretch their legs on the nearby logging road, the husband looks at us with obvious concern. "Be careful," he warns as we run by, half-naked. "There are lots of bears around here. For god's sake, you aren't camping outside are you?"

For five days we follow Knight Inlet deeper and deeper into the Coast Range Mountains. Snow-capped peaks soar around us, and waterfalls cascade down steep walls of black granite. The fine glacial silt they carry turns the inlet's waters turquoise, just like a high alpine lake. Clouds play along ridgelines, and craggy trees cast haunting shadows in the mist. There are few places to land, and we often eat lunch with the boats rafted together, drifting in the wind and gazing up.

Twenty-one days after leaving Vancouver, we linger longer than normal around the fire, clutching steaming coffee mugs to our chests, savouring the surrounding views. It has been our practice to pack quickly, but the end of Knight Inlet lies only twenty kilometres (12 miles) away, and this will be our last day on the water.

Doug makes pancakes, and upon finding both our sugar and syrup supplies finished, sweetens the batter with grape Kool-Aid. The resulting purple cakes look funny but taste pretty good. It is almost noon before we begin tossing empty stuff sacks into open hatches.

A weak sun struggles to break through the clouds, but the mood of the inlet remains grey. We pass cliffs of granite and dark, tangled forests. Pockets of late-season snow mark gullies on the slopes above. A brisk tailwind pushes us onward. The turquoise colour of the water intensifies.

After four hours of paddling the final beach looms ahead. Three boats abreast, we surge toward it. No one speaks. We land in unison, the soft squelch of silt sounding against our bows. Then we hug and wrestle and take photos.

Another massive lumber-booming operation dominates the terminus of Knight Inlet. Thick sections of cedar logs lay in sorted piles and processed logs float in offshore booming yards. Rusting bulldozers, caterpillars, cranes, and oil barrels dot the compound. Everything is covered in scrapings of orange cedar bark, piled up like drifting snow. We are carrying the kayaks up to the abandoned yard when a blue half-ton jolts up and two men jump out. The driver hustles over.

"Hello," I smile enthusiastically, trying to be extra-friendly as I'm worried we might be trespassing.

"I'm Don, the manager of Wahkash Contracting," he barks without offering his hand. "Who are you, and what are you doing here?"

A patch on his orange overalls reads "Albert" but I don't bother mentioning that he is wearing someone else's clothes. Instead I stumble into a hasty account of our trip up the coast, explaining that Ferg and I will be heading over the mountains and that a boat is coming to pick up Christine and Douglas.

Don interrupts me, his tone gentler. "Sorry, I have to be careful. You never know what folk's intentions are. We are very proud of the operation we run here, but there are some who don't take so kindly to what we do."

"No, no. We're not . . ." my voice trails off. I realize with our braided hair and scruffy beards it would be easy to mistake us for hostile environmentalists. I am about to ask if protest groups have ever reached this remote outpost, but before I can Don changes the subject.

"So, this is what you guys call a vacation?" Grinning widely, he points at his tanned sidekick in the pickup. "John here just got back from seven days in Cabo San Lucas. Now that sounds more like a vacation to me!"

"You'll need to be careful up the Franklin," he adds. "That's dangerous land. A young fella died up there a few years back. Mountaineer, from Quebec, I think. He was walking beside the river and fell in. Couldn't get his pack off. The water is freezing, and he didn't last long. His body washed up on a midstream island, and his buddy almost drowned trying to get him. I was in the chopper that went to get him, but it was a body recovery, not a rescue. Nothing we could do. Tragic. Nice kid too, met him when he came through camp." We all fall silent.

"You got a gun?" Don asks, and we shake our heads. "What are you going to do about bears then?"

"Have you seen many bears up the Franklin this year?" I ask, feeling silly as soon as I say it.

"Buddy," Don peers at me over his glasses, "Up here, there are bears everywhere."

Before leaving, Don spends some time detailing the steps his company takes to reduce their impact on the land. His pride is obvious. "There is no garbage in camp. None whatsoever. Everything is incinerated. We haven't had to destroy a problem bear for years. People complain that we are cutting too much, but you've got to understand, these forests grow like weeds. We can't cut them fast enough. Firs grow six feet a year here. I admit, in the old days, things were pretty bad. We bulldozed straight through streams and thrashed hillsides. Now we have to be really careful. Spawning beds are protected. Our cutting plans are drawn up by a certified forester I keep on staff."

It is heartening to realize Don is aware of conservation issues, and seems to truly care about them. It shows the heated debates, taking place on city streets and in Internet blogs a thousand kilometres removed from the trenches, are having an effect. Twenty years ago I doubt front-line logging managers had the same sensitivities.

"Make yourself at home," Don winks as he swings back into the pickup. "And when you get back to Calgary, don't forget to tell the folks there that logging ain't so bad."

We stash our gear in an abandoned shed, and after lighting a bonfire, prepare a celebratory feast. Our last sachet of taco spice is used to flavour a heaping pot of pasta. After devouring it all, we stretch beside the embers, sipping a sweet combination of hot chocolate and berry herbal tea. The final remnants of our crushed cookie bag are sprinkled over freshly picked raspberries. It is long past midnight when we crawl into our tents, perched on the edge of the industrial lot.

The water taxi is expected at noon the following day, but by four o'clock, when it is still nowhere in sight, I begin to harbour a faint hope that Christine and Doug will stay for one more day. A part of me dreads being alone with Ferg. We reached an unspoken truce during the second half of the kayak trip, retreating and simply avoiding each other whenever tensions started to flare. I knew that was going to change soon.

Christine and I wander off to explore a settler's cabin, and are wading through thick brush when a deep growl gives us a start. In a flash Christine dives past me, pushing me toward the threatening sound. As our hearts slow, we realize it is just the distant drone of the engines. The water taxi is on its way.

"I can't believe you shoved me at the bear," I laugh.

"Well . . . I thought it would be better if you dealt with it," she grins back. "Honestly!"

Back in camp the fishing charter has moored on the breakwater. The captain huffs up the gangplank with the two heavy duffels of moun-taineering gear that Ferg and I shipped to him before the trip.

"Lionel Hole," he says holding out a thick hand. "One of many Holes from Coal Harbour. We better hurry. It is getting lumpy out there, and the forecast is for worse."

Ferg and I rip open the duffels, jump into fresh long underwear, and stuff our stinky kayaking gear into outgoing bags. We shuffle cameras and lenses to chest harnesses, sending our waterproof "pelican" cases home. Meanwhile Christine and Douglas carry the kayaks down to Lionel's boat. The two single boats are strapped to the cabin roof and padded with foam mattresses. The double is jammed through the open cockpit door, its bow lashed to the captain's seat, the rudder hanging out over the rear engines.

I hug Doug, overcome with an upwelling of fraternal love. The wilderness has brought out a strength and pride in him I have not sensed for years, and I feel lucky for the chance to travel together. Pangs of loneliness are already seeping in as I kiss Christine. I will miss her support, the whispered sleeping-bag discussions, our bond. She slides her favourite silver bracelet into my pocket. Three years earlier, when we first met, I took it with me to Denali for good luck. Now I wind it around a loop of leather and add it to the strings of necklaces I wear.

The boat slips from its mooring logs. For fifteen minutes I stand by the shore, watching it through binoculars, occasionally waving, just in case anyone is watching. Somewhere on the open water the little speck simply disappears.

Then there were two.

PART II: THE "SUFFERFEST"

A silence hangs over us. Ferg toys with his pack. I rummage through the bags of fresh food that arrived with our mountaineering gear. There are a dozen eggs, fifteen bagels, two tubs of cream cheese, a block of cheddar cheese, sliced meat, apples, oranges, bananas, a tin of Pringles, a jar of pickles, and a jumbo bag of chocolate-chip cookies. We begin to gorge, and by ten o'clock the next morning, everything perishable is gone.

After one last nostalgic look down Knight Inlet, we hoist our packs and stagger from the logging camp, heading inland along a rutted dirt road. On our backs are fifteen days of dehydrated food and all the mountaineering gear we will require to cross the ice caps and climb

Mount Waddington. Water bottles and snack bags are strapped to our waist belts. Cameras are slung in chest harnesses. The loads weigh forty-five kilograms (100 pounds) each. We make no attempt at conversation. Neither of us has the energy; instead we simply focus on putting one foot ahead of the next.

The suffering takes me right back to the CANOL. It seems ironic that my memories from that trip are of glorious canyon lands and remote tundra, not the incessant hunger, sore feet, and aching shoulders. *How could I have forgotten all of that?* Within minutes our feet feel crushed flat, the bones splaying under the load. I am sure enormous blisters are forming on my soles, running from toe to heel. Each step drives our shoulders toward the ground, and the tight waist-straps cut into our hips, leaving bruises and raw, worn flesh. As the cumbersome packs pull us to and fro, stomach and back muscles scream in protest as they fight to maintain balance. Soon my knee cap is clicking ominously.

"I was just thinking back to my bike trip," Ferg breaks the silence. Six years earlier he biked ten thousand kilometres (6,000 miles), travelling from Inuvik on the Arctic Ocean, to Prince Rupert on the Pacific Coast, and finally across Canada to St. John's, Newfoundland, on the Atlantic. "I am pretty sure that doing lighter work for longer periods of time is a far more reasonable demand on the body. I bet if we carried 50 per cent less weight but went 50 per cent further, it would be markedly easier."

I nod weakly in agreement. Ferg groans and wipes the sweat from his brow. "I think we've turned the pain dial up to maximum on this one." Without discussion we fall into the routine we developed on the CANOL: walking for an hour, dropping the packs in exhaustion, taking a ten-minute rest, devouring a small snack, lapping back some water, then setting off again.

Two hours later we arrive at a bridge spanning the Franklin River. Our destination, the Franklin Glacier, is the river's source, and the map provides no clues as to which side of the valley will be easier to follow. After some deliberation, we gamble and cross to the southern side, continuing inland on winding roads. Occasional crashing sounds in the forest keep us alert, and every few minutes one of us shouts "HEY BEAR!" at the top of his lungs. We meet several black bears along the road, but clanging ski poles and loud screams are enough to send them back into the woods.

As we trudge along I find my mind wandering to the ocean. I miss the grace of kayaking; the wide open sea, the call of the gulls. In comparison, backpacking seems nothing more than ugly, brute effort. I once heard that there are two types of souls on the planet, ones that yearn for the ocean and others that yearn for the mountains. I always believed I was a mountain soul. Now I begin to wonder if the opposite is true.

We reach an enormous mess of fallen logs blocking the road, slung down from high mountainsides by helicopter and dropped like matchsticks. The pile is more than six metres (18 feet) high, and stretches for a kilometre. It takes one excruciating hour to stoop, crawl, shuffle, and climb past the obstacle. Ferg lets out a whoop as we clamber over the last log, but our celebration is short-lived. Minutes later the road ends. Overgrown coastal rain forest lies ahead. Like children tentatively poking their toes in cold water, we pace back and forth along the edge, looking for an easy way in. Eventually, we just have to dive.

Branches scratch our face and neck, vines tear at our shins, ankles twist on undergrowth and loose rock. We can see only a few feet ahead of us, and for hours we thrash blindly onward, arriving on the banks of a rushing creek as the sun begins to set. There appears to be no way across; the water is too deep, fast, and cold. We set camp, hoping the creek will drop overnight.

But the creek does not drop overnight. In the morning we walk up and down its banks, occasionally wading out into the silty water, probing blindly ahead with trekking poles. The bottom drops away precipitously, and within steps the waist-deep torrent threatens to tear us away. Downstream are the powerful rapids of the Franklin River. It is not worth the risk. There is nothing to do but shoulder our packs and turn around.

Trudging back through the bush, we crawl past the agonizing pile of logs again and along twelve kilometres (7 miles) of logging road,

(Main) *A pilgrim at Lhasa's Jokhang Temple lights yak-butter candles in memory of a recently deceased relation.*

(Below Left) *Near Tura, in remote western China, where the Tibet plateau descends to the Taklamakan Desert; during a reconnaissance for crossing the Chang Tang.*

(Below Right) *The Chang Tang, a land I long dreamed of crossing. Empty, bleak, and barren, it is an area of uplift encompassing some two and a half million square kilometres.*

Tibet

(Above) *Ferg explores Echo Canyon as we descend from the high mountains toward the Mackenzie River flats.*

(Left) *Stream crossings on the 360-kilometre (225-mile) hike were common, and our packs, loaded with eighteen days of food, were oppressively heavy.*

Northwest
Territories,
Canada

(Above) *Unable to find a suitable landing spot, we "camp" on an abandoned section of dock near Aaron Tidal Rapids.*

(Right) *My brother, Doug, inspects a red sea urchin during a break from paddling.*

Canadian

West Coast

(Main) *Ferg carefully ascends Mt. Waddington's northwest ridge.*

(Below Left) *We follow logging roads into the Coast Range. After they end, we face hellacious bushwhacking, progressing as little as three kilometres (2 miles) a day.*

(Below Right) *Rowing back into Vancouver after completing a sixty-five-day, 1,500-km loop around the southern Coast Range.*

Grand Cirque Expedition

Canadian
West Coast

(Opposite) *Shaun Boughen paddles Bridge River Rapids on the Fraser River.*

(Main) *Christine awaits the arrival of the hornbills. Base camp lies just below the setting sun, and our boat is anchored in the bay below.*

(Below Left) *Paddling through a narrow sea cave, just moments before an exodus of bats sweeps over us.*

(Below Right) *Cedric "Coyote" Gourmelen holds an injured, but highly poisonous, banded sea snake.*

Mergui Archipelago,

(Main) *A procession of monks collecting alms on the streets of Myeik.*

(Below Left) *The glorious blue waters and jungle-tufted islets of the Mergui.*

(Below Right) *Captured by Crescent; Christine and Cedric discuss our options while the pleasure yacht (white light) lies anchored offshore.*

Myanmar

(Main) *Harbour boys, who work tethering the jostling fleets of longtail boats in Kawthaung, take a mid-afternoon break.*

(Below Left) *Decrepit fishing boats fill the Kawthaung harbour.*

(Below Right) *After six weeks of effort, after being chased by the Myanmar authorities and getting kicked out of the country, we finally reached Myeik.*

arriving at the bridge by noon. Crossing the Franklin, we forge our way upstream on the other side, crashing through more thick forest. As the sun fades we find ourselves directly opposite the creek where we camped the night before. An entire day's effort, and we have not made any progress.

There is an overwhelming sense of green in the temperate rain forest, hundreds of different hues, all damp and glistening. Growth in the valley Ferg and I trudge through rivals the tropics for its luxuriance. Our feet sink into thick, spongy moss; fir trees soar up to a canopy far overhead; the distinctive scent of cedar mingles with that of decay. Although the land has been logged once, if not twice, we wind our way through giants, their trunks averaging one metre (3 feet) in diameter or more. Occasionally we spot remnants of the original old growth, decaying stumps more than two metres across, still showing notches where lumberjacks lodged cutting planks a hundred years ago. It is a silent, still world we have entered, disturbed only by the whisperings of unseen songbirds and the occasional caw of a raven.

As beautiful as it is, the bush is our enemy. It slows us, cuts us, slaps us, trips us, and infuriates us. The coastal growth is so dense that we often cannot see our own feet. We try to follow the river's banks, where plains of gravel make travel easy, but rocky headlands and impassable canyons block the shores, sending us scrambling into the forest time and again.

Twigs pull at our hair and poke our eyes. Branches grasp at our packs. Hemlock and balsam needles scratch the backs of our hands till they bleed. Devil's club, a thorny, broad-leafed plant, rips open one leg of my pants. Mosquitoes and no-see-ums surround us in clouds, landing on our shoulders, biting with impunity through the thin polypropylene shirts we wear. The bulky packs make it impossible to slap them away. Worse yet, we inhale them, and perpetually cough up the little sodden black remains.

But nothing is as horrific as the alder. The trunks of this bushy, colonizing tree run along the ground before turning skyward, creating mats of slippery and unstable limbs that trap hiking boots and crush shins. The soft and springy branches are useless for balance, but sling us backward, making us fall like overturned turtles. The heavy packs make it impossible to stand up, and each time we must awkwardly extricate ourselves from the shoulder straps, stand up, and then heave the packs onto our backs before continuing on. Lost in thick groves, we plunge blindly over hidden ledges, occasionally falling two metres (6 feet) or more before landing in yet more alder, and crashing on.

Soon we are able to smell the thickets of alder before actually reaching them, a scent that sends a wave of resignation through us both. After one particularly bad bout of bushwhacking we stop in a clearing for a rest. As I rub my sore feet, I notice blotches of red and purple staining the shins of Ferg's khaki pants.

"Is that from berries?" I point, wondering if a snack is nearby.

"Nope. That's blood," Ferg grunts, lifting his pant leg to reveal the damage inflicted by alder. "This just never lets up. Every time we beat our way through a patch of bush or over a steep cliff, I find myself thinking that it can't possibly get any worse. And then it does. For three days we haven't had a single break."

Finally, only a towering granite buttress blocks our way onto the glacier. We scramble up gullies and over mossy slabs, traversing narrow ledges and loose boulders. Higher and higher we go. The toe of the Franklin Glacier now lies three hundred metres (1000 feet) below us. Have we worked our way into a dead end? What will we do if the descent on the other side is sheer and impassable? Give up and turn back to the coast?

At a snack break Ferg drops his pack and dashes ahead to investigate, returning sweaty and smiling. "I think we can do it. There is only one short exposed section."

"How bad?" I ask, far more cautious than Ferg.

"Let me put it this way: You can't fall."

Minutes later I shuffle hesitantly across the cliff, my fingers shaking as they search for holds. Halfway across I make the cardinal sin of looking down. Fir trees, hundreds of metres below, look like miniature models on a train set. Falling is definitely not an option. But now I am frozen. I can't seem to move my hands or feet for fear of losing purchase. The longer I linger, the more exhausted I become. One of my calves begins to jitter up and down like a sewing machine.

"Trust your feet," Ferg yells back. "There is a ledge just above your right knee. Can you step up to it?"

I take a deep breath and blindly feel with my toes. Finally my boot sticks. "Good, you got it. Now put all your weight on it."

Moments later I am over, quickly scrambling after Ferg. A gulley beyond leads downward, and proves to be an easy descent. Half an hour later we are standing on the Franklin Glacier.

The peaks rising in this isolated stretch of the Coast Range remained almost completely unexplored by mountaineers until 1925. That year, while hiking on Vancouver Island, more than 250 kilometres (155 miles) away, Don and Phyllis Munday spotted a silver tooth of ice on the horizon. Named Mystery Mountain by the Mundays (and later renamed Mount Waddington in honour of a Caribou gold-rush pioneer), the spire proved to be a "far off finger of destiny beckoning," as Don wrote, and it would draw them back to these rugged, inhospitable valleys for a decade.

Every summer the fearless pair returned, slashing their way through thick brush, facing down bears, and fording flooding rivers with steel cables and improvised log bridges. They clambered up steep cliffs and broke trail through deep snow for days on end. Although persistent, the Mundays were ultimately denied their goal of reaching the mountain's main summit, for it is guarded from every angle of approach by extraordinary difficulties. They did, however, manage to climb the peak's slightly lower, northwest twin summit. It was exactly seventy-four years before Ferg and I arrived that Don and Phyllis first strode out across the little-known Franklin Glacier, heading just as we were now, toward Fury Gap.

After the dark, cramped forest, the open space of the glacier is uplifting. Our crampons bite confidently into the ice, and we walk side by side, travelling fast for the first time since leaving the coast. Dark peaks rise around us, their faces plastered with fresh snow. For the first few kilometres the route is relatively flat. Streams of meltwater criss-cross the glacier's surface, some as big as bobsled runs. We jump these with care, for a ride down any of the icy slides would be your last. They inevitably lead to deep crevasses, where they drain into echoing depths.

As we ascend the glacier, its surface grows more convoluted, and before long we are traversing a confused ocean of ice, winding through waves and swells. Crevasses often block the way, some narrow, blue slits which we easily stride over after peering down. Others are as wide as city streets, and force us into lengthy detours. Occasionally, we traverse narrow bridges of ice, but we don't bother roping up, for a fall down their glistening slopes would be unstoppable.

Despite the constant weaving we manage to cover more distance in one hour than we did during the entire previous two days. As the sun dips behind the peaks, and shallow puddles dotting the glacier's surface begin to grow feathers of ice, we set camp on a gentle but slippery slope, where every piece of gear has to be placed in the tent or meticulously attached to an anchor to prevent it from sliding away.

"Do you remember what it feels like to not be hungry?" Ferg laughs at a snack break the next day, rubbing a thick growth of whiskers. "I just ate a Snickers but it didn't make a dent."

"Look!" I pull out my loose pants like balloons. "The waistband on my pack can't grip my hips any more."

We purposefully increased the number of calories in our menu from the CANOL trip, but the food is nowhere near enough to replace what we are using.

Ferg lies back and counts on his fingers. "I figure we are eating about two thousand calories a day, but I bet we are burning six or eight thousand."

We have relied heavily on each other since leaving the coast. The mental and physical efforts have demanded all our energy, relegating everything else, including anger, to relative inconsequence. In a sick kind of way, Ferg and I both savour the struggle. This is the arena in which we excel together, and the tensions of the past month have evaporated, at least for now.

Before getting up Ferg unwraps a Werther's, a small butterscotch candy, and pops it into his mouth.

We have rationed one Werther's per day, and I often notice Ferg still sucking his a half hour or more after our break. How can he make those damn things last so long? For days I have been trying to cultivate the same self-control, but no matter how often I remind myself, I inevitably crunch down on it within minutes. Small things can grow into obsessions on expeditions and as I unwrap my candy and place it gently on my tongue, I command myself to be more prudent, to go slow and take pleasure in the flavour.

With a grunt Ferg and I hoist our packs, cinch the waist bands, check our watches, and set off. Ten steps later I bite down on the small candy. *Dammit, dammit! Tomorrow. For sure, tomorrow!*

We climb on, into a silent, sombre world, almost completely devoid of life. There is no green to be seen anywhere, just rock, ice, and snow. The only signs of life we encounter are the hairlike worms that clog the puddles at our feet. Only a few centimetres long, these tiny creatures live at or near freezing their entire lives, sustaining themselves by consuming spores and pollen blown across the glacier. Averse to bright light, they disappear on sunny days, burrowing into the ice, yet emerge by the millions whenever it is overcast.

Hummingbirds occasionally appear out of nowhere, whirring around our red hats and making us duck before flitting off and disappearing. They have begun their migration south, toward Central America. In the middle of such a barren expanse, each surprise visit uplifts us, and we consider their presence a lucky omen.

At fifteen hundred metres (4,900 feet above sea level) we reach fresh snow. The crevasses are now hidden, and we put on harnesses, stringing a twenty-metre (60-foot) section of rope between us. Pressing onward, across uniform flats, we often plunge into hidden crevasses, falling up to our waists before the rope catches us. The really big cracks remain uncovered, guarded by overhanging lips of snow. We edge forward carefully, searching for snow bridges that will lead us across, but sometimes there are none, and we just have to run and jump.

Seven days after leaving the kayaks we awake to clear skies. It is a surprise, as grey, drizzly weather has followed us from the coast. For the first time we see the steep granite peaks surrounding us, bathed in gentle pink. To the south soar the twin summits of Mount Waddington, impressive walls of sheer rock that dwarf everything else. Above, wispy cirrus clouds indicate a high-pressure system is arriving. Good weather is rare in the Coast Range, and these high peaks are regularly socked in for weeks.

Although racked with exhaustion and longing for rest, we must take advantage of the opportunity and race on at an exhausting pace. Fury Gap lies twenty kilometres (12 miles) away. This pass, which leads to the interior of the Coast Range, is also the starting point for a climb of Mount Waddington's northwest ridge. If we can reach it by day's end, and if the weather holds, we will make an attempt on Mt. Waddington in the morning.

Beep . . . beep . . . beep . . . The 3:00 a.m. alarm wakes me from a fitful sleep. Within minutes, our little stove is hissing, casting a blue glow through the tent and filling it with clouds of steam. We suit up in the dark, apply sunscreen, tighten gaiters, squeezing feet into frozen leather boots. After sharing a pot of oatmeal and forcing down two litres of warm Gatorade, we crawl out into the black night. By 3:37 a.m. we are climbing.

Leading up from Fury Gap, the ridge we are climbing stretches for five kilometres (3 miles) to the northwest summit of Mount Waddington, rising fifteen hundred vertical metres on the way. We will need to travel fast, and have packed lightly, carrying just two litres of water each, and a small ration of snacks. In case of an emergency, we have brought a tiny tarpaulin, a small first-aid kit, and our puffy, insulated jackets.

We scramble up steep scree in darkness, following the beams of our headlights. Soon the eastern sky begins to flush purple, and blood-red streaks shoot across the underside of thin clouds. Ahead the route narrows to an icy crest, just half a metre (20 inches) wide. Both sides drop away precipitously. We rope up and I lead on, placing each foot with care. Gusts of wind test our balance. After several hundred metres a steep drop in the ridgeline appears, forcing us to descend a slope where any slip would be disastrous. Punching fists deep into the soft snow and kicking steps below us, we slither down and continue.

Soon a second, more intimidating drop blocks the way. I peer over the mushroomed edge and see the narrow ridge continuing on, fifty metres (166 feet) below. Getting down to it will not be easy. I force fear from my mind and consider the situation. We will have to retrace the route later in the day, when we are tired and dehydrated. *Will I be able to navigate this safely then?* I'm not sure. Ferg stares at me impatiently from the other end of the rope. *Should I tell him I'm scared?* It would be heartbreaking to turn back here, but it would be stupid to die because I don't voice my concerns.

"What's going on up there?" Ferg yells over the wind.

"Just a sec. It's a tough one. Keep the rope tight."

I decide to give it a try. Turning backward, I place my belly on the lip, and kick blindly below, feeling for a foothold. *Thumph.* The snow is soft, and my boot sinks reassuringly in past the ankle. Slowly, I work my way down the drop. Eventually, Ferg appears above, and follows, sending showers of snow sliding past that whistle off a lip below and launch into thin air with a sickening silence.

Normally the rope between us is taut, but as I near the bottom, it begins to wind around my feet. I pause, and moments later Ferg catches up.

"Boy, this is tenuous," I grimace.

"Yeah, it is, but . . ." Ferg's voice trails off. He looks impatient.

"But what?" I ask, pissed off. Fear is fraying my nerves. "I'm going too slowly?"

"Yup," Ferg nods.

"Shit, I am doing the best I can," I bark back. "Why don't I follow you then?"

Ferg shrugs and passes me, heading down the tiny ridge, standing tall and moving with confidence. I follow his footsteps, stabbing with my ice axe for balance, tugged along by the rope. We move much faster with Ferg out front, and two hours later we have finished traversing the ridge and begun climbing up the gentler glaciated slopes guarding the summit. Breaking trail through the heavy snow is a struggle, and every half-hour we switch the lead. Our lungs heave in the thin air. Snacks no longer provide the surge of energy they once did. I resort to counting my footsteps, a mind-numbing trick. Upon reaching five hundred I start over again.

The snow grows firmer as we climb higher. We wind through crevasses and under seracs. Ferg climbs a sketchy six-metre (20-foot) pitch of vertical ice using both of our clumsy mountaineering axes, and I follow on a tight rope, jamming my fingers into the tiny holes left by the picks. We emerge onto a small, sheltered plateau. The final summit pyramid rises before us, fluted with windblown rime. I focus only on each crunching footstep as I follow Ferg up the steep slope.

Suddenly, there is nothing more above. Ferg stands before me on a tiny summit that sees only a handful of visitors each year. At our feet, the Coast Range stretches out in every direction. Glaciers weave between the jagged peaks like strands of treacle, and in the distance the green forests and blue waters of the coast mingle with low cloud. There is not a single sign of human presence anywhere; not a town, road, clear-cut, or smokestack. We are less than three hundred kilometres (180 miles) from Vancouver, Canada's third-most populous city, but haven't even seen another footprint for seven days. We fall into each others arms, laughing.

After only fifteen minutes we start down again. The snow is already growing sloppy in the sun and balls underfoot, threatening to twist our ankles. We use ice axes to knock our boots clear with every step, breaking away the clumps of slush. An hour passes. Exertion and sunshine turn Ferg's face puffy and red. My mouth is pasty, and I feel dizzy. Our water ran out hours ago.

By the time we reach the narrow ridge, avalanches are rumbling ominously down adjacent peaks. Ferg leads. I let the rope go tight and follow. The void draws my eyes. I tell myself to stop looking at the fall and concentrate on my feet. One step, then another. A crampon point catches the inside of a gaiter, and I hop twice before freeing the gimped leg. Dammit. I know better. The rope pulls me along.

Finally, we arrive at the steep sections we down-climbed in the faint glow of dawn. They are the last serious obstacles, and the snow is now in horrible shape, loose and rotten. There is no way to anchor ourselves. If one of us slips, the other will have to throw himself off the opposite side of the ridge – not an appealing thought.

Ferg starts up, and each step loosens an avalanche of slush which hisses as it rushes down, and then vanishes over the lip. Our rope is short, and Ferg has not yet reached the top when it starts yanking on my harness. I follow, driving my arms straight in a slushy slope which offers little assurance. Finally Ferg disappears over the top, and the rope continues to yank me upward. After an eternity I reach the lip and haul myself over, panting. Ferg is already trotting away down the final section of ridge.

Everything below us is now easy. Safe at last, we collapse on the slope, shoving handfuls of snow into our parched mouths. Too tired to talk, we silently survey the blindingly white wilderness that stretches in every direction.

Thirteen hours after leaving the tent, we crawl back in, falling asleep in our climbing suits.

A steep slope drops from Fury Gap toward the Interior of British Columbia, and the next morning we inch toward the edge, trying to discern a route to the valley below. As we weave downward, through splintered ice and granite buttresses, a cold rain overtakes us. Falling rocks start to whistle past and a serac collapses nearby. This is no place to linger. We begin to rush, plunging down steep snow at the edge of control. Arriving at a cliff, we set an anchor and rappel. Sprinting down snowy slopes below, wet snow balls under our feet with every step. The rope tugs me. I fall, catch myself with my axe, fall again, accelerate downward, launch off the lip of a crevasse, and tumble a few metres before landing in soft snow.

"You OK?" Ferg peers over the top.

"Fine," I give the thumbs-up sign, knowing I am lucky. Clambering out, we race onward, slipping and slithering, until at last we reach the bottom, soaked in sweat.

Ahead lies the flat Scimitar Glacier, a narrow highway of ice bordered by steep granite spires, reminiscent of Pakistan. The weather has turned pleasant and travel is fast. Soon we are peeling off layers of clothing. My mind has drifted elsewhere when Ferg breaks the silence.

"I don't know if this is the time to get into it, but it is sunny and the walking is easy," he starts off. "Now seems as good a time as any to set the record straight on my thoughts regarding the sea-kayaking trip, and some of our differences in general over the last few months."

It is unexpected, and I appreciate Ferg's initiative. Since leaving Knight Inlet, neither of us has mentioned the earlier quarrels and disputes, and while the struggles of the climb have been a distraction, some emotional separation still lingers.

"I think it was wrong for Christine and Doug to come on the trip," Ferg begins. "It defeated the concept of a fast, self-contained team. Plus, I hardly even knew them."

"Well, you got to know them," I counter. "I wouldn't have asked them if I didn't think they were up to it, or good people to travel with."

"They sure didn't pull their weight."

"God Ferg, they were just learning."

"Well, all I can say is you had a lot of patience. Anyways, my point is they weren't *my* friends, or *our* friends. They were *your* friends. I didn't know them, and I don't think a long trip was the place to get to know them. For me, their inclusion was just the first in a series of compromises. The sea kayaking ended up being something totally different from what I originally envisaged: slow starts, a cruising pace, fat menu, unnecessary rest days. It's not the way I'd choose."

In retrospect I can understand. There was a time when I just wanted to go wide open, all the time, every time. But guiding and other wilderness experiences have changed my expectations. "Come on, Ferg, what's wrong with enjoying the travel? It seems a shame to simply race along for speed's sake and not savour the beauty."

"That's your idea of the expedition, not mine. Under the circumstances, I found the whole sea-kayaking experience anything but a knee-slapping good time."

I'm silent. I'd found the twenty-two days of paddling magnificent. Already the discussion is driving us further apart, the subject still raw.

Soon the discussion devolves from issues surrounding the trip to our individual personalities. Ferg finds me flippant and irresponsible. I accuse him of being stern and inflexible. He questions my writing and speaking. "You exaggerate things," he complains. "Make them sound grandiose when they aren't."

"Ferg, you are like an old-school British mountaineer. You could have a gaping flesh wound and still describe it as a minor inconvenience! Is that being honest?"

"I guess I'm just a stickler."

We keep walking, but Ferg has hit a sore spot. I was astounded when I first joined the Everest team to realize how poorly many in the local climbing community regarded the expedition organizers, Jamie and Alan, finding their brash self-promotion and motivational talks distasteful. *Do I dilute the integrity of my activities by sharing them with others?* Ferg, a far better climber than I, and more stoic, seems closer to the "hard-core" element of the lifestyle. Should I just shut up and not talk or write about these things? I know some think so, and I am sensitive to their unspoken criticism.

"We are a strong team in the mountains, that's for sure," Ferg sums up, "but I am starting to think that our friendship can never go further. We just don't have that much in common. You're outgoing. I'm reserved. You like to socialize, and go to bars. You hang out with people that drive me nuts. We never call each other in the city. And for a smart guy, you can be so bloody immature. Your goofing around can be too much. Planning this trip let me see lots of new sides to you, and most I didn't appreciate. The truth is if I was to meet you at a party and didn't already know you, I doubt I would like you. I know that sounds harsh, and it certainly would be a shame to stop doing trips together . . . but it's the truth. I don't know where that leaves us?"

It leaves an ocean between us, and we retreat inward, plodding on in silence. I have spent more time with Ferg in the mountains than anyone else. We trust each other. We are strong together. It seems tragic that this journey, which I'd meant to be fun and light-hearted, might destroy our partnership. I know he is only being pragmatic with his observations, but the rift between us feels unbridgeable. For now, there is nothing more to say. Ferg and I walk on in a violet dusk, each alone with our thoughts.

We have travelled for eight days without taking a rest, humping heavy loads over difficult terrain and hardly eating anything. Despite a long sleep, we awake still feeling devastated.

Our map shows a tiny alpine lake on the route, not far ahead. We decide to make a quick dash, confident we can reach it in a few hours. The plan is to enjoy a day of rest there; bathing, reading, and sleeping on the shores.

The descent brings us back to the world of the living. A single purple flower reaches up from the gravel, *epilobium latifolium*, an old friend from the banks of the Tat. Black spiders scurry underfoot. The smells of sap and damp earth waft toward us on a warm wind.

"Look!" Ferg laughs, pointing to a small tangle of alder shooting up from the boulders. "The enemy. Quick, kill them while we still outnumber them!"

His words prove sadly prophetic. Over the very next rise lies a bog, chock-solid with alder, blocking the entire valley. It appears impenetrable. When we try pushing forward into it, the bush pushes back. Taking a run, summoning every reserve of strength, we crash in a few feet. Continued forward progress requires brute force. Branches are snapped, trees are bent. Hands bleed. Pants are ripped and torn by branches. We trip and fall often, pinned to the swampy ground by our heavy packs. A pair of sunglasses is lost. Foul language punctuates our progress. Drinking water runs out, and although we stand knee-deep in a stagnant, brown swamp, neither of us dares to take a sip. After an hour I suspect we have not gone more than one hundred metres. The lake is still a kilometre (0.6 mile) away on the map, and I have lost all sense of direction in the dense brush.

There is nothing fun about this. I want to call time out. Give up. Be done with it. I dream of a helicopter swooping down and carrying us away. But there are no time outs. We cannot even sit down, the bush is just too thick. All we can do is try to crash onward.

Somewhere along the way my strength ebbs. Out of desperation I switch to a more Zen-like style, where stealth and delicacy become my only objectives. Placing each foot and hand with care, I angle my body between the tight trunks and contort like a yogi to weave through branches, reaching back and gently releasing any twigs that snag my pack. The strategy works amazingly well, and I find myself able to follow Ferg's swath of crashes and curses while expending far less energy than before. Still, nothing about the ordeal is pleasant. It requires constant mental effort not to simply collapse and scream in frustration.

Eight miserable hours later we reach the lake, arriving just as the sun begins to set. The tiny tarn is surrounded by golden peaks. A glacier carving down from above licks the turquoise waters, and meadows of paintbrush spill across the sandy shores. As we fall to the beach, we realize we are not alone.

Grizzly prints litter the sand. A mother and small cubs have wandered back and forth, very recently. Too exhausted to think coherently, let alone to consider moving onward, we bury our precious food under a pile of rocks. It is a token gesture, for a single swipe of a grizzly's paw would decimate the monument. After peeing in circles around the stash, we crawl to the far end of the beach and collapse into a deep, unbroken sleep.

A precarious log-jam spans the torrent of upper Twist Creek. With pack straps undone, we straddle a barkless log and inch across. Twenty kilometres (12 miles) away lie the logging roads of the interior. With the summit of Waddington behind us, it is difficult to gather enthusiasm for crashing through more tangled bush.

We follow intermittent game trails, but they dissolve, leading us into a maze of toppled pines. The trees have been blown over by ferocious katabatic winds that howl off the ice caps during winter, creating a mystical jungle-gym, draped in feathery strands of Old-Man's-Beard. We climb over some obstacles, and crawl on hands and knees under others. A few we precariously traverse like balance beams. Drizzle adds to the suffering.

After two days of this I grow dizzy, and soon realize a fever has set in. When darkness falls we carve out a tiny clearing in the underbrush and set up our tent in the rain. Ferg gathers wood while I huddle by a smoky fire, unable to eat even a bite of pasta. Finally I rise and limp into the darkness, taking the toilet paper with me. Five minutes later I have to go again. Three minutes later, again.

My stomach is in turmoil. We suspect giardia, an intestinal parasite common across North America. Both of us have fought the persistent bug before, but are surprised it could have gotten us now, for we have filtered all our drinking water.

The night proves interminable. Every muscle in my body aches. It hurts to move, yet it hurts more to lie still. One minute I am sweating, the next shivering. Every hour I have to drag myself out into the rain, squat with long johns around my ankles, and wipe using moss, twigs, and gravel. I pray for the night to end, but when morning finally arrives I wish it away. I am exhausted, and cannot imagine taking a single step. After forcing down a few bites of oatmeal, I struggle into soaking clothes and boots.

Ferg packs everything in camp; bless him, I think weakly, there is no way I could have done it myself. We can't call for a helicopter; there is nowhere it could land, and no way to know precisely where we are in the thick bush, so our only option is to keep going. Waiting makes no sense, I will only get worse. Ferg hoists my pack onto me, and then leads the way as we slowly crash on through the forest. Diarrhea attacks me every fifteen minutes, or less. There is little warning, and Ferg displays supreme patience as I am never able to step far from the trail before dropping my pants.

"If I didn't know you so well . . ." he laughs and shakes his head. "Nothing is sacred with us any more." I can tell he is concerned.

When we do get our bearings, the map shows seven kilometres (4 miles) remaining between us and the logging road, and as we stumble through the hodge-podge of fallen trees, I distract myself with mental arithmetic, trying to calculate our average speed. Picking a mark about one hundred metres (330 feet) ahead, I measure how long it takes us to reach it. Ten minutes. *We are travelling at the rate of half a kilometre per hour!* It looks like another night in the bush.

Sometime during the afternoon we pick up a trapper's trail, and begin following a string of decades-old slashes on tree trunks. When the trail disappears into a flooding stream, we follow it, too tired to care about dry feet. We can't find the route on the far side, and wade back and forth in frustration, unable to make any decision. A faint glimmering through a thicket of saplings catches my attention, and pushing ahead, the branches part, revealing idyllic ranchland. Sunlight streams down on fields of golden hay. Chestnut horses whinny and prance toward us. I turn and hug Ferg. We've made it.

That night we stay at the nearby ranch of Laurie and Dave King. Despite a ravenous hunger, I only pick at dinner, and Ferg is troubled. Crow's feet have grown around my eyes. My shoulder blades and hip bones jut out. I weigh myself, and have to double-check the result. One hundred and sixty-eight pounds (76 kilograms). I have lost thirty pounds (14 kilos) since the start of the trip. Although I desperately want to hike directly to the raft, which is stashed nearby, I know I need medical treatment. The next morning we hitchhike to Williams Lake.

"Son, you are drier than a biscuit!" the doctor in the Emergency Room exclaims after taking one look at me. Moments later a nurse slides an intravenous needle into my forearm and attaches a bag of glucose to the drip. I can feel the cool liquid pouring into my arm, an astounding sensation, as if I was drinking through a straw in my wrist.

"Wow," I smile weakly. "I can sure feel that."

"Do you want me to turn it down?" The nurse reaches for the bag.

"Oh no!" I sit bolt upright. "Turn it up."

PART III – THE RIVER

I strain against the oars of my sluggish raft. The shoreline of Lake Chilko slides slowly by. Shaun, an old university buddy, and Derrick, who I've just met, dart around me, paddling whitewater kayaks. The snow-capped peaks of the Coast Range (which Ferg and I stumbled out of just a week ago) rise beyond.

Not until late afternoon do we find the river, its mouth clogged by a maze of wooded islands and gravel bars. Current catches our boats and drags them along, the shallow water so clear that it feels as if we are floating on a cushion of air, soaring like a bird over the stony riverbed. Shadowy trout dart beneath my hull, flashing occasionally in the afternoon sun.

A week of warm temperatures has brought the glacier-fed river to flood. Frigid water is over the banks, flowing through trees and bushes. We remain alert for floating debris, and camp in a dusty clearing just upstream of Lava Canyon.

Shaun wanders to the shoreline, with a cigar and wineglass in one hand, and fishing rod in the other. "Goddamn Kirkby, it is good to be here!"

Our friendship stretches back fifteen years. Always energetic and full of outlandish ideas, Shaun Boughen keeps everyone around him on their toes. As roommates at university, he once convinced me to stuff a freshly roasted chicken with firecrackers. We were hosting a formal dinner party, and the experiment turned into a fiasco when the greasy chicken exploded all over our dates, ending the evening prematurely.

I called Shaun only weeks before leaving on the expedition, asking him to join me for the river section. He didn't even pause to think. "Sure Kirkby, where? And when?"

"On the shores of Tatla Lake, August 6."

I called Shaun again, two weeks later, from a phone booth, leaving a message on his answering machine. "Forget Tatla Lake, make it Chilko. C.H.I.L.K.O. Chilko Lake. It is just a little farther south. You'll find me there on August 6." I knew he would be there.

Shaun visited me in Whitehorse during my first season as a Tat guide, and on the Yukon river, under the midnight sun, I taught him to kayak. For a week he dutifully followed me through easy rapids, but by the time I had returned from my next trip his skills had already rocketed far past mine. In the years since he has travelled around the world, paddling ever more difficult rivers, attaining an exceptional level of expertise.

Shaun had arrived with a friend, Derrick Law, an experienced paddler from the Yukon. Although Derrick and I had never met before, Shaun's recommendation was enough. Quiet, clearly responsible, and quick to smile, I could tell Derrick would be a great companion on the river.

After I was released from hospital, and it was clear that I was going to be all right, Ferg left on a Greyhound bus, true to his word. The parting was awkward, difficult, and confusing. Part of me felt blue as the bus pulled away, painfully aware of the gulf still between us, while another part wanted to scream "Good fucking riddance" at the top of my lungs and be done with the unending conflict.

Tough, shared journeys can bond partners in a way that goes beyond most experiences in the "civilized" world, and the ordeal in the mountains had undeniably brought me closer to Ferg. Without question, I trusted him with my life, admiring his strength and clarity of thought.

But the same journeys can also scar relationships, grinding in simmering animosities, irritating emotional wounds until they can never be forgotten. After two months, Ferg's regular grumblings and unenthused outlook had become too much. I was so pissed off that I doubted our rift could ever completely dissipate.

Shaun and Derrick's light, joking company was a sharp contrast, and just the salve I needed. That night we linger late by the fire, passing a bottle of Jack Daniels and catching up. Before heading to my tent I suggest an early start. "It's gonna be a huge day tomorrow. Lava Canyon and the White Mile. How about we get up at six, and try to be on the water by eight?"

"Haaaa! Kirkby, are you out of your mind?" Shaun bursts out laughing. "Dude, I've been selling trucks in a busy city for six months. I need to relax."

"OK, how about eight o'clock?" I concede. Eight feels shamefully lazy. Shaun and Derrick agree begrudgingly.

The sun hits my tent at 6:45, turning it into a sauna. I try to fall asleep again, but can't. Instead I get up and pack. By eight o'clock the raft is loaded, breakfast is cooked, and coffee is on the fire, but no one is stirring in Shaun's tent. An hour later I begin banging pots and dishes in the hope of rousing someone. Eventually I shake the tent. Groans. It is ten-thirty before Shaun and Derrick stumble into the daylight.

Despite sweltering heat, we squeeze into wetsuits and dry tops, faces quickly turning bright red. Knots are double-checked, throw bags coiled, and maps consulted. Our thoughts are focused on the whitewater ahead, and we shake hands before pushing away from shore.

"Be careful, Kirkby," Shaun looks me in the eye. "I love you lots. It would be stupid to get hurt today."

After an hour the river narrows and picks up speed. The blue water dances over small drops and ledges. Anticipation grows. We stop to scout several blind corners, but each is a false alarm. My mind has wandered when a shrill whistle focuses my attention. Shaun is flashing me the "you-better-start-paying-attention" signal, his index and middle fingers pointed in a "V" at his eyes.

A throaty roar echoes from downstream, and the river disappears. We waste no time getting to shore, and scramble up a pine-covered slope to a sweeping lookout. Below us the river plunges into an S-shaped bend. Churned into froth, it piles into the walls, washes through a sluice of boulders, and then sweeps out of sight. We have reached "Bidwell," the first rapid of Lava Canyon. The White Mile lies beyond.

I stare at the rapid for half an hour, finally deciding upon a route and then memorizing it, trying to visualize how it will appear from the water. The kayakers go first, their plastic boats dwarfed by the huge waves. I follow. Water pummels the heavy raft, and staying on course requires every bit of strength I have. Unable to slow my momentum at the bottom, I take my hands from the oars for just a second to wave at Shaun and Derrick who wait in an eddy, and then crash onward down the river.

Quickly, the kayakers catch up and we enter the White Mile together. There are no more eddies, no more time outs. From here on, it is "read-n-run." Waves are lined up across the river, one after another, ten to fifteen feet high. The shores race by, the sound is deafening. Foam and spray cover me, but I hardly notice. As my raft rises to the crest of each swell, there is just a fraction of a second to scan the waters ahead. Then I drop into the next trough. Although Shaun and Derrick bob nearby, I am only passingly aware of their presence, my focus remaining locked on the oncoming waves. *Control the raft. Stay in the centre of the flow. Watch out for a big hole that is supposed to be hidden somewhere on the left.*

I don't know how long it keeps going, maybe five minutes, maybe twenty. Eventually there is a brief lull, and we quickly confirm that everyone is okay before sliding into Magic Canyon, a darkened slot of rock so narrow that I have to ship the raft's oars to fit through. Brilliant green moss and vines hang from the walls, and the sky is just a strip of blue above. More powerful rapids follow. It is not until dusk that the river flattens. We stop to camp at the ruins of an old ranch house as pink blushes across darkening clouds.

On the third day the turquoise Chilko River carries us into the emerald-green Taseko, which in turn dumps us into the Chilcotin. We have entered arid lands, the interior rain shadow. Big-horned sheep scamper along parched slopes, and the smell of sage fills the air. A landslide has recently crashed into the river, constricting its flow and forming a powerful rapid. As the river tears through the obstacle, the water turns a muddy chocolate-brown, and assumes a more sinister feel. At noon on the sixth day we pass through Farwell Canyon, the final rapids on the Chilcotin. Rafting the boats together, we eat lunch while drifting lazily downstream, awaiting the confluence with the Fraser River.

An hour later Shaun looks up. "Hey, HEY! Wake up boys! Look at what's coming."

Downstream the river walls rear up and close in, the water accelerating around a blind corner. Throwing on our life jackets, we pack food away and slam camera cases shut. The kayakers jump back into their boats. Soon the sun is blocked from sight. We have read the map incorrectly; this is Farwell.

The river plunges into a narrow canyon, thundering over a staircase of drops and pools. The kayaks go first, hopping from eddy to eddy, using their paddles to relay messages back to me on the sluggish raft, pointing to the safest route. Faster and faster it comes, tighter and tighter the walls grow, each drop bigger than the last, until with a massive exhale, the river spits us out. We have passed through a portal, and now drift silently into the grand, barren expanse of the Fraser River valley.

The Fraser is a moving ocean. Just crossing to the opposite shore proves an exhausting exercise. Billowing cushions of water boil up from below, twirling the boats like twigs. Rocky points create whirlpools that threaten to suck the kayaks down. I remind myself that this is the calm section.

Sheer cliffs of golden sandstone press up against the river. Above these spread the parched slopes of the massive valley, a tangle of bunchgrass, tumbleweed, prickly pear cacti, and occasional ponderosa pines. We have entered one of the hottest, driest regions in Canada, and for seven days don't see a single cloud. The sun is unrelenting. Strong winds blast upriver, but rather than bringing relief, they feel like a hair dryer held to our faces. Shaun and Derrick constantly roll their kayaks upside down to stay cool. I stay hidden under a damp bandana, but often that is not enough, and I must dive from the raft and then scramble back aboard.

There are very few trails leading down into the depths, and after passing a single-lane suspension bridge at Gang Ranch (a 1-million acre cattle operation founded in the 1880s), we see no further signs of civilization. Apart from rusting relics dating back to the 1860s gold rush, the land is deserted.

———

"There's a cougar in camp," Derrick whispers, a hint of panic in his voice.

Shaun and I, sitting by the fire's dying embers, swing around in unison. Two green eyes glow in the beam of Derrick's headlamp. A full-grown cougar is crouched behind a nearby boulder, perfectly frozen apart from its whiskers, which quiver with each breath. It stares at us. We stare at it. No one flinches.

I have never seen a cougar before, and the big animal inspires awe, as well as a twinge of fright, for I do not know if it will attack or run away. As my mind reels, struggling to assess the situation, a second cougar appears from the darkness, slinking up and lowering itself behind the first.

In the pit of my stomach I know we are being hunted. The cats have approached from behind, creeping over open, rocky ground to within seven metres (23 feet). From where they crouch, the cats could easily pounce on us with a single leap. All three of our flashlights remain on them, and they remain frozen.

"*HEY, GET OUT OF HERE!*" Derrick suddenly screams, waving his arms overhead.

The cougars don't budge. The longer the bold cats stay, the more concerned I become. They shouldn't be comfortable in our presence. Derrick is crouched behind a large, smooth boulder, and carefully Shaun and I creep to his side.

"I am going to throw a rock at them," Derrick whispers, pulling his arm back.

"Hold on, hold on," Shaun hisses. "Wait till we are ready."

Shaun gathers a handful of stones. I silently pull the bear spray from my river bag, and then gather my own rocks. "OK, on three," Shaun readies himself. "One, two . . ."

Derrick's rock is already whistling through the air. Shaun and I leap up and unleash a fusillade of stones, screaming at the top of our lungs. The cougars explode forward like coiled springs, angling away from us, their lithe bodies stretching out, paws tearing at the ground as they sprint into the darkness.

They do not go far. Our flashlights pick up four unmoving green eyes in the darkness uphill. Shaun yells. Derrick runs toward them, throwing rocks, but when they don't budge he quickly returns to the ring of light cast by the dying fire. I load a bear banger and launch it into the sky. A smoky streak of white light hurtles upward, and the ensuing explosion shakes the canyon. There is a clattering of rocks. Both sets of eyes disappear.

As Shaun tosses a large log across the fire, I pull our tents close. Although we see no further sign of the cougars, I cannot shake the eerie feeling of being watched. Hours later I drift to sleep with the bear spray, a bear banger, and a large steak knife carefully arranged by my tent door.

The Fraser is one of the world's great rivers, draining one-quarter of British Columbia. Carrying half a million cubic feet (15,000 m³) of water per second during spring flood, it pushes a delta of silt out into the Strait of Georgia at a rate of twenty-eight feet (8.5 m) per year. For five days we drift lazily along the gash it carves through the arid Cariboo Plateau, but on the sixth morning the river's character changes.

Just upstream of Lillooet, the Wild-West town that once marked the start of a wagon road leading to the gold fields, the Fraser funnels into Moran Canyon, a tortuous S-bend hemmed in by three-hundred-metre foot cliffs. Borne along by an accelerating current, our boats pass into shadow and the river begins to boil and churn. We feel our way carefully downstream, stopping frequently in eddies to study the map.

Near the exit of Moran Canyon lies Bridge River Rapids, a section of whitewater so dangerous that the government forbids commercial rafts to run it. There are plenty of rapids to navigate before, but there is no margin for error. A flip would be catastrophic, for I doubt we could pull ourselves out before the big drop.

It is difficult to judge where we are in the massive rock labyrinth. Everything looks the same. The water grows more powerful. A boil opens beside my raft, and sucks down the entire front end. The seventeen-foot boat stands on end, almost flipping before suddenly being released. One hour passes, then another. Anticipation frays our nerves, and we swelter in our tight wetsuits.

There is no mistaking Bridge River Rapids when we finally approach, for the thunderous noise is deafening. The river picks up speed, squeezes between two granite buttresses, and disappears. We stroke for all we are worth for the shore, catching the first eddy we find, lashing the boats to a thick stump, and scrambling along a rocky trail for a better view. Cresting a rise, the sight of the rapids stops us in our tracks.

As the river plows over a submerged ledge, it creates a single mammoth wave that stretches almost from bank to bank. Every few seconds it rears up, reaching seven metres (23 feet) in height before crashing down and shaking the earth around us. Behind it lies a confused tumult of froth and foam.

"I've never seen anything so awesome," Shaun whispers. "Not in South America, not in Nepal, not anywhere. This is huge."

As we stare at the rapid, I suddenly realize the water around us is teeming with salmon. They burst from exploding waves, leaping against the current. Thousands swirl in shoreline eddies. A confusion of black fins breaks the surface. Peering further downstream, we see drying racks covering both banks of the river. As they have for centuries, St'at'imc First Nation families have gathered, the men dipping nets into the swirling waters and pulling out heavy loads of salmon with every swing. Rocks run red with blood as fish are slaughtered, gutted, and hung to dry. The air is thick with swarming flies and wasps. Ravens and eagles wait cautiously close by, occasionally hopping nearer to nab a piece of gut and escape. The sky above is full of circling hawks.

A native fisherman strides by. "This is the Horsethief (River) run hittin' now," he nods. "About ten thousand sockeye arrivin' every hour. They don't swim up the rapids at night, so in the mornin' there'll be near a quarter-million fish in that pool below."

Picking our way downstream, we stop to watch a dip netter. Leaning far out over the whitewater, only a frayed piece of yellow nylon rope prevents the man from falling in. Each scoop brings up a net full of salmon. With a flick of the wrist they are dumped into a hollow in the rocks, where another man skilfully snatches the flipping fish, reaches in through the gills and rips their heads back, breaking the spine with a single snap.

"Best to do this while the heart is still beating," he says without looking up. "Pumps the blood out. Makes the flesh firmer."

I wander to the river's edge. Great pillows of water rise up and break over the nearby shore. Salmon trying to avoid the main current are battered along the wall and slammed into crevasses. Many show raw wounds from their battle, but none cease to fight. As the water surges and recedes, stranded fish flip and flap violently, attempting to swim right up the bare rocks. A handful of Native children are playing in their midst, rescuing salmon lodged in cracks, carrying them past the obstacle and tossing them upstream. The powerful slap of a large sockeye's tail sends one boy reeling to the ground. Undeterred, he jumps to his feet and leaps on the fish, wrestling it up and over the rocky barrier, seeing it on its way with a wave.

There are only a handful of spots on the planet I have felt raw, primal spirit exposed. My first experience with such a place came while lying on sun-warmed rocks at the confluence of the Tatshenshini and Alsek rivers. I felt it again at Tissisat Falls, where the Blue Nile thunders off an ancient volcanic ledge. A few years later I recognized the feeling while standing in Tibet's Potala Palace, while nomadic pilgrims with wild eyes and sun-blackened skin rushed by, prostrating themselves before golden stupas. As Shaun, Derrick, and I silently stood, watching the rapids, the fish, the children, and the fishermen, I felt that same familiar sense of peace. Reverence perhaps. We had unwittingly wandered upon a place of power.

But we cannot linger. It is late afternoon and we need to scout the rapids before they are obscured by shadow. The wave in the centre is lethal and must be avoided at all costs. There is not enough room to sneak past on the left, so the only possible route lies along the right-hand bank, which is a difficult and risky line. The water crashes along a wall of sharp rocks, where large recirculating waves threaten to pummel anyone, or anything, they catch, shredding them against its face.

Making it through safely isn't impossible, but it isn't a sure thing either. A broken oar or a sudden surge of the river could spell disaster. As I weigh the risks, I am distracted by thoughts of family and friends. I want to run Bridge River badly, but I realize my instincts are telling me otherwise. I decide to portage. Shaun and Derrick, after much deliberation, decide to run.

We have tied the boats half a kilometre (1/4 mile) upstream, and rather than carry the heavy raft up and over the precipices guarding the entrance to the rapid, we decide to float to the last possible eddy. It does not look like a difficult manoeuvre, but just to be safe the kayakers will go first and give me a hand landing.

Pushing off, we drift out into current and are slowly drawn toward the downstream roar, every sense alert. Shaun is paddling ahead of my bow when a wave unexpectedly rears up and hits him with such force that I can hear the air expelled from his lungs as he flips. Shaun's paddle breaks the surface and he attempts to roll, but the turbulent waters knock him down again. Upside down, he drifts onward. A second time he comes up, only to be pushed back under again. The banks are now racing past. On the third attempt he pops up and immediately sprints to shore where Derrick is already waiting.

Unable to fight the strong upstream currents along the banks, the raft must instead linger in the main flow, waiting to pop into the eddy at just the last instant. I watch the shoreline intently, judging my position, hands on the oars, waiting to go. Suddenly a powerful boil erupts underneath the raft, dragging me far out toward the centre of the river. In a heartbeat I am way out of position, far from the shores, far from safety. The water around me is already beginning to accelerate toward the lip of the Bridge River Rapids.

"*NOW!*" I hear Derrick scream above the roar, his eyes wide, but I am already straining at the oars, bending them with every stroke. I only just manage to claw my way into the last few feet of the eddy. Shaun grabs the raft's bowline as I stumble ashore.

"Forget it, I am not running," Derrick says as we sit together, catching our breath. "It is just too crazy. Too dangerous. What about you, Shaun?"

"Gimme a sec, I gotta look at it again."

As Derrick and I take the raft apart and carry gear downstream, Shaun stands by the edge of the rapids. Half an hour later we are done, but Shaun has not moved. I wander over.

"Buddy, it's not worth it. If you are not sure, too many people love you . . ."

"I'm ready," Shaun interrupts, his eyes never leaving the water. "I'm going."

Derrick and I sprint downstream with safety ropes, although I wonder what good they will actually do if Shaun flips. I watch his small kayak drift from shore, a silhouette on the sparkling water. With a few gentle strokes, Shaun aligns himself, waits a second, and then turns the power on. His paddle flashes. The kayak accelerates down a glassy tongue and slams into the froth. Shaun disappears from sight. A moment later he is balanced atop a wave, then he disappears again. Seconds later he pops out the bottom. Turning as he passes, Shaun simply smiles and nods, but I feel his elation as if it were my own.

Quickly we begin reassembling the raft, on a black pebble beach where surging waves constantly wash salmon ashore. The big fish slap about our feet. An hour later we are ready to launch. The water downstream of the rapids is unbelievable, absolutely clogged with salmon, and my oars thud into bodies with every stroke. Shaun bobs in the river near me, trailing his hands in the water.

"Kirkby, you are not going to believe this, but I have a fish in each hand!" he laughs. "Start the barbeque!"

Soon the sun disappears behind the peaks of the Coast Range. Darkness is falling as we arrive at Lillooet, setting camp under the sheltered ramparts of a highway bridge. The next morning Shaun wanders into town for supplies while I call a local rafting company from a roadside pay phone. I want to verify that the water level at

Hell's Gate, our last major challenge, has dropped to normal, late summer levels.

"Nope, it's higher than usual," the company owner reports. "Too much for your little raft. And the kayaks?! Forget it. We run enormous pontoon boats through there, with two forty-horsepower engines on the back."

As I mull over this off-putting news, Shaun returns with a box of cigars, a case of beer, two bottles of wine, a men's magazine, and three pairs of control-top pantyhose. Derrick and I look at him questioningly.

"The wetsuit has given me a rash on my groin. It's getting pretty bad."

"And . . .?"

"I stopped at the pharmacy, hoping to get some cream or something, but the pharmacist just laughed at me. Told me what I needed to put on my rash was a bus ticket home. That or a pair of pantyhose! I had no idea what he was talking about. Then this old cowboy standing at the counter beside me pipes up. You should have seen this guy, he was wearing leather boots and an old hat and a buckle and all. 'That's right,' he says. 'Pantyhose. I wear 'em under my jeans and chaps whenever I'm ridin'.' Why not give it a try I figured."

As Shaun struggles to pull on the sheer black stockings, ripping two pairs in the process, we chat briefly about Hell's Gate. We all agree there is nothing to do but keep going downriver and take a look.

⸻

Headwinds roar up the Fraser for the next two days, stalling our progress, and we spend the wind-bound hours chatting with Native fishermen camped along the river's edge. Usually reserved when we first approach, they are always accommodating, and warm up quickly, sharing stories and offering their freshly dried salmon leather. Many have been filleting and drying fish for more than a month without a single break, and seem pleased to have visitors.

"We can't leave this camp, not even for twenty minutes," a young man named Dean explains. "Otherwise some damn Indian will come around the corner and steal our fish." We'd heard the same story at Bridge River, and now look at Dean with surprise. "Yeah, it's the money fishers. They ain't feeding their families, they sell the fish for cash. You probably seen their nets in the river. They leave 'em for days."

We have spotted unattended nets, choked with dead and dying sockeye, along the banks. As they struggle fruitlessly to escape, the fish are slowly shredded by the strong filament of the nets.

"That's illegal, right?" Derrick asks.

"Oh yeah. If the DFO (Department of Fisheries and Oceans) catch them, they pull their license. Last year they pulled fifty on this section of the river alone. Then they have to stand up."

"Before a judge?"

"No. Before the tribal council, and believe me, that is a fuck of a lot worse." We stand in silence, watching Dean fillet his fish. He slices the orange flesh, still attached to the skin, into a geometric pattern of thin strips.

"Say, is that your boat?" Dean looks up and points.

Sure enough, my raft is gently floating downstream, quickly leaving us behind. When we landed, I simply pulled the nose up onto the beach, and did not bother tying it. Now a surge in the river has stolen it. Jim Allan's words race through my mind. *There is no excuse, EVER, for losing your boat.*

Shaun's kayak is aboard the raft, balanced over the rear pontoons, but Derrick's is still on shore. Sprinting, he jumps in and begins madly floundering with his spray skirt. Then he stops, and looks up sheepishly. "My paddle is on the raft!"

The raft is quickly disappearing. Without another word Derrick and I race to a promontory of rocks and dive. The current is strong, and we are whisked along, our strokes ineffective. Spitting and coughing, we swim after the raft with all our might. After several minutes we are starting to gain on it, but just as we near, a shoreline eddy spins the raft toward the bank, and unable to follow, we shoot straight past.

"Jesus! Now what?" Derrick yells.

"Get to shore if you can," I holler back.

Spinning in circles and flailing, we struggle toward the banks but make no progress. The river just keeps pulling us back toward the centre. My arms feel like lead and only my life jacket holds me above the surface. Looking upstream, we see the raft has escaped the eddy and is now drifting our way, catching up quickly. With a final burst of effort, Derrick is able to catch the boat, grasping a pontoon and feebly dragging himself aboard.

"Should I paddle to shore?" Derrick calls as I drift away. It is his first time rowing the raft, and he is unsure how to handle the oars.

"*NO!*" I yell back, mouth half-full of water. "Come and get me."

Minutes later we lie on a sandy beach, chests heaving. Shaun appears shortly, paddling Derrick's kayak with a two-by-four plank. A section of dried salmon hangs around his neck.

"Dean was real nervous after you two took off," he smiles. "He told me that no one swims down this river and comes out alive. I told him you were both strong."

Derrick and I shrug and roll our eyes. Next time I'll make sure to pull the raft up a few centimetres further.

～

Swirling, low clouds and cool breezes greet us on the thirteenth morning of the river journey. We linger longer than usual by the smouldering fire, each lost in thought. "Be safe," is all we say before hugging, shaking hands, and launching the boats.

Just downstream of our camp, dark cliffs mark the beginning of the Fraser's Black Canyon, where the great flow squeezes between a crack separating two major mountain ranges, the Coast to the north, and the Cascades to the south. Simon Fraser, the first European traveller to explore the river (in 1808), mistakenly believed he was on the Columbia River and headed toward Oregon, until he reached this abrupt turn where the great flow breaks through the peaks and makes a beeline for the coast.

Travelling in four large bark canoes with French-Canadian voyageurs, Fraser was warned by local Native guides of the extraordinary dangers waiting downstream, but remained adamant his party continue. Only minutes after entering the narrowing canyon, the power of the river grew overwhelming. Canoes quickly were swamped and sank. Men swam for kilometres in the tumult, but astoundingly no one was lost. Fraser eventually managed to portage around the canyon, following narrow footpaths and traversing rope bridges. Looking down from above, he described this section of river as "a dreadful chain of difficulties, apparently insurmountable," a place "where no human should venture." At the heart of the canyon lies the river's most famous rapid: Hell's Gate.

We pass between two great buttresses of rock, and the world seems to darken. The river, long a creamy brown colour, is now steel grey and foreboding. China Bar Rapids come first. Waves and cliffs rush by. My oars feel powerless when matched against the strength of the current, and I struggle to keep the raft straight. A whirlpool opens nearby, pulling in Shaun and Derrick, and they must fight fiercely to break its grasp.

There is no time to catch our breath after being spat free. Not far ahead are the Airtram cables, a gondola carrying tourists down to view Hell's Gate. I hug the right-hand shore. Cliffs block my view downstream, and I drift as far as I dare before ducking into an eddy. The shoreline is sheer rock, offering no place to land. I drift in circles, trying to jam the nose of the raft against a partially submerged boulder, but it won't stick.

Shaun and Derrick have continued downstream, their kayaks able to stop in much smaller pockets of still water. I debate what to do. Hell's Gate appears to be a fair way downstream. *There has to be another eddy where I can stop.* I let my raft float toward the main current, and it is almost out of the eddy when I row back in. *What are you doing? If you can't see what is coming up, DON'T GO.*

Shipping the oars, I unravel the bowline, clench one end between my teeth, and lunge at the canyon wall as it drifts by. Able to find purchase, I shimmy up the rock, tie the boat off, and scramble to railway tracks above. Several minutes later I find Shaun and Derrick, waiting for me on the footbridge that spans Hell's Gate.

"We barely made it to shore, Kirkby!" Shaun yells above the roar. "There was nowhere to stop at all. We pulled in at the very last minute. Good thing you stopped upstream."

We wander through a sea of photo-snapping tourists, conspicuous in our helmets and wetsuits. A security guard arrives to investigate.

"You guys aren't going to run this are you?" He eyes us suspiciously.

"Naw, just taking a look," Derrick smiles.

"I better call my boss on this one. Wait here if you don't mind." The man wanders off, talking into his radio.

We scout the rapid quickly, staring down from the bridge. A crashing wave blocks the left side of the river, a violent eddy rakes the right-hand cliffs. There is a narrow gap in the centre for the boats, but if they are even a metre (3 feet) out of line, either way, they will be flipped and tossed against the walls.

I visually trace the path I want my raft to take, and memorize the rolls and dips leading into the rapid, envisioning what the rapid will look like from the water as I approach, setting landmarks in my mind. There is no doubt I can do it. "I'm goin'," I announce.

"Me too," Shaun agrees. "Let's get out of here before someone tries to stop us."

"Right on," Derrick nods, and we take off in a sprint.

Back at the raft, alone, I find myself facing a moment of commitment. Once I jump down into the boat and leave the eddy, there will be no turning back. Even though the rapid is a kilometre downstream, no matter what I do from then on, one thing is sure: I will be swept through Hell's Gate.

For a brief moment I consider balking, but then confidence returns. I know I can do it. I can see the entire line in my head. Years of practice and experience have prepared me.

Coiling the bowline, I leap down to the floating raft, and am quickly swept from the eddy. The raft bobs down the centre of the gorge. Only a few weathered conifers cling to sheer walls above, otherwise there is just rock, and exploding whitewater on the horizon.

A sense of peace descends. Tourists crowding on the footbridge have spotted us, and are screaming and waving, but my world is silent. I am aware of everything but distracted by nothing. The river begins to accelerate. Waves break off the bow and the raft shudders, but I barely notice, my eyes glued ahead.

Stay left, I tell myself, lining up directly above the huge wave. All the current in the river is pushing toward it and I know I cannot fight the flow. Instead I must wait until the last moment to move aside.

The shores begin to hurtle by. The cement bulwarks of the fish ladder pass in a blur. The water smoothes and begins its final drop toward the great wave. *Now!* I dig in my oars. The yellow shafts bend. Slowly the heavy boat starts to move sideways. The wave is beside me, crashing and loud, but I don't see it. I am looking ahead, straightening the boat as it rockets through the constriction. Spray explodes from every direction. The raft shudders, and a whirlpool opens below the left pontoon. I dig the oars to pull away, but spot Derrick, who has followed closely behind, in the whirlpool below. My oar blade just misses smashing into his helmet. Our eyes meet, we nod, and then angle our craft apart. Seconds later the boats are spat free. Suddenly, noise and sound come rushing back. Tourists whoop from the bridge. Shaun pumps his fist in the air.

⁓

Derrick leaves two days later, catching a bus at the town of Hope and flying home to Whitehorse. Christine arrives in his place, riding on the raft, wearing wildflowers in her hair I have collected. The final one hundred kilometres (60 miles) of river are wide and languorous, and Shaun soon joins us, lashing his whitewater kayak across the raft's rear pontoons. We all take turns rowing, and despite the exhausting, hour-long shifts, the days pass in a carefree blur of laughter and reminiscence.

The river's current is now meagre, and we must make every use of it, launching at first light, using our small stove to brew coffee on the raft.

Meals are prepared aboard and pee stops are quick. Twelve hours are spent oaring. Not until dusk do we pull over.

After three days on the flats we begin passing barges laden with wood-chips, and unending log booms moored along the banks. Steam rises from pulp mills, and equipment lumbers through muddy yards. Soon towns begin springing up. We float past a busy pub, the tempting sounds of its crowded patio drifting across the water, but we do not pause.

On the afternoon of the fifth day, the orange framework of the Port Mann Bridge appears. Carrying five lanes of highway traffic, this steel span heralded my first arrival in Vancouver, ten years earlier, when I began work with Ecosummer. Passing underneath it now, we sense the end is near. Suburban houses crawl up the slopes of New Westminster, and on we push, under the fanning cables of the Skytrain and the C.N. Rail swing bridge. Then the river splits and we stay north, cutting toward the airport.

Grey clouds blanket the sky, and the channel we are following slowly widens. There is no sharp transition, no moment of sudden change or closure, but somewhere in that fading twilight we realize we have reached the ocean. Wearily oaring around a long breakwater, we stop at Wreck Beach, a nudist encampment on the western tip of Vancouver. Bonfires dot the sands. An impressive display of driftwood poles has been erected. Flags and plywood signs adorn their peaks. Crowds of drunk and stoned youth press around the flames, dancing, shouting, and singing. It feels like we have arrived on a South Pacific Island for the meeting of the tribal council. Unnoticed, we haul our gear to a secluded corner, set up a tent, and fall asleep.

The sun has been up for hours when two policemen knock on the tent door, reminding us that camping is prohibited on Wreck Beach. Luckily we have a good story, and in lieu of a ticket we promise to move along quickly. As we load the raft for the last time, crowds of nudists stream down trails from parking lots above. Topless samosa salesgirls wander the beach. Men set up coolers of beer and ice under wide umbrellas. A dreadlocked youth dashes out into the waves, offering us a discount on hash cookies as we paddle away.

The morning is sunny, yet brisk. As we row around bluffs guarding the University of British Columbia campus, the skyline of downtown Vancouver slowly inches into view. An onshore breeze pushes up past Spanish Banks. Children laugh and play on the shore, kites whistle in the breeze.

A dragonboat team passes, the paddlers waving in unison. "You guys look like you have been on a journey! Did you camp overnight?"

Shaun yells back, but they are already gone. Moments later, the raft crunches into the sand of Jericho Beach, at exactly the same spot I launched my kayak from, sixty-five days earlier.

It took a long time to appreciate fully what we had done during that "Grand Cirque" summer. The trip had been one of my most deeply satisfying wilderness experiences. Physically, I had travelled farther than on any trip before; farther than the camel crossing of Arabia, farther than the voyage down the Nile. It took longer to complete than any previous expedition, and the travel had not been easy. I had tested my skills more severely in the mountains and on the river than ever before.

So why did I view the loop, the Grand Cirque, in a diminished light? Was it simply because the adventure had taken place at home? Audiences I spoke to and editors of magazines I wrote for remained far more interested in adventures through exotic locales. Most brushed off the loop, and as a result I think I did too, but today it remains one of my most treasured memories and proud accomplishments.

The Grand Cirque returned to me an appreciation for the simple purity of adventure – a group of friends, planning something on the back of an envelope, packing food in the supermarket parking lot, and heading off from their front door. We had no idea what we were going to find – hake swept up by ocean currents, impenetrable bush, cougars in camp – which was precisely the way it should have been.

Unfortunately, relations between Ferg and I remained tense for sometime afterward. I had sworn not to let another expedition ruin a friendship, yet the wounds created by our journey went deep, and neither of us knew how to start the healing. The entire conflict sprang from our differing vision of the journey, but it took years for me to see that. At the time it felt like there was nothing left to say.

But good partners are as rare as gold. And we were good partners. Of similar physical capacity, bearing similar willingness to suffer, both pragmatic and analytically minded, Ferg and I could do things together that we couldn't with others, or alone. Equally significantly, when our hearts were not cluttered with tensions, we truly enjoyed the minute-to-minute existence of life together on the trail.

So despite the unresolved clash, we continued to go climbing and hiking, a sort of bizarre ritual where anger simmered below the surface, and we guarded our thoughts. Bit by bit, the immediacy of our anger faded, and levity returned. Eventually we came to the realization that some trips worked for us as a team, while others were better done alone; and with that acceptance a new friendship emerged, strengthened yet changed. Soon maps were sprouting up again, and plans for new journeys took seed.

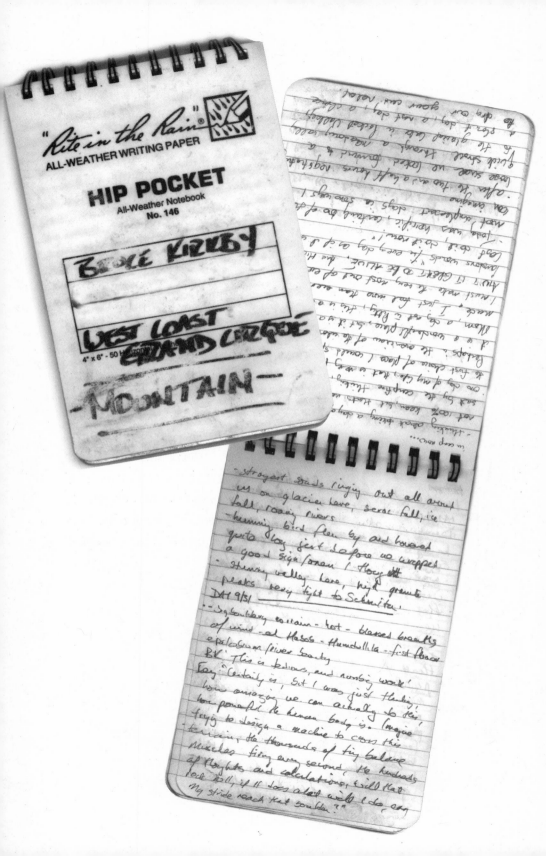

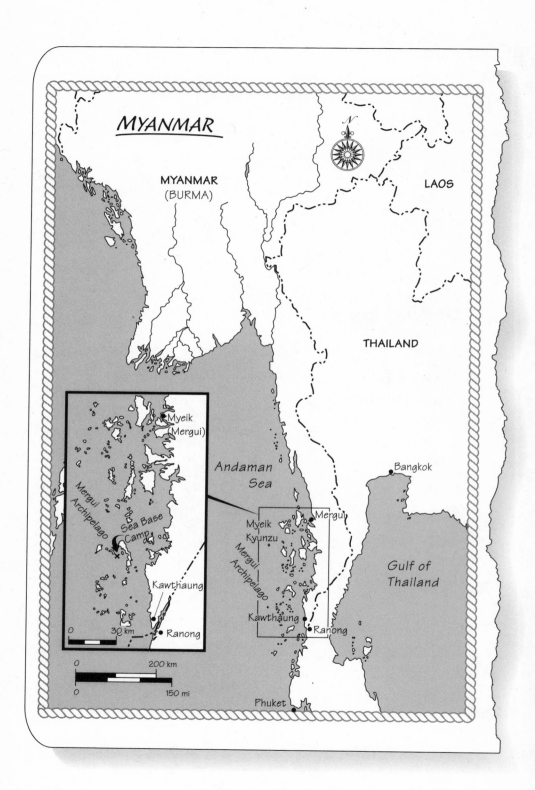

thirteen

Chasing Myeik

HIDE AND SEEK IN THE FORBIDDEN MERGUI ARCHIPELAGO

Then, a golden mystery upheaved itself on the horizon – a beautiful, winking wonder that blazed in the sun, of a shape that was neither Muslim dome nor Hindu temple spire. "There's the old Shway Dagon," said my companion. The golden dome said, "This is Burma, and it will be quite unlike any land you know about."

Rudyard Kipling, LETTERS FROM THE EAST (1898)

Myanmar,
2003

SEVERAL MONTHS after I returned from the Grand Cirque expedition, *Outpost* magazine called, offering me the title of Editor-at-Large. While the position was largely symbolic, more a tip of the hat than involving any actual responsibilities, it provided an enviable opportunity to travel. Plenty of foreign tourism associations were willing to trade airfare, and sometimes accommodation, in return for the promise of an article. A flurry of quick jaunts followed – Bhutan, Bali, the Galapagos, Ecuador – but I found the rushed nature of these visits mildly disappointing, providing only a superficial view of the land and people. At home there was plenty of writing and speaking. A year passed almost without notice.

Somewhere along the way, I realized I was never going back to engineering. You'd have thought it would have been clear earlier, but it wasn't. The epiphany came as I edited eighty-five rolls of slides in a single afternoon, rushing to meet a fast-approaching deadline. Glancing at twenty nearly identical images of a scene and quickly picking the best, I suddenly came to appreciate the myriad small, almost unnoticeable skills I had developed over the years. Competences honed in the fields of expedition travel, photography, and writing had long since surpassed those bestowed by a decade-old engineering degree. For the first time I appreciated that my future, whatever it held, would surely involve some medley of these new skills. The realization did not bring any stability – which was fine, for I was used to an uncertain path – but there was a definite sense of completion; of the lines being cast, the dock pushed away, and a once-familiar land lost forever.

Travel, adventure, photography, words, culture, and landscape: these once nascent interests had grown into core interests and passions. To actually be carving my own path amidst these realms, and making a living, seemed astonishing. I remained constantly grateful; simultaneously aware of the balance such work required. The more successful my endeavours were, the more forces arose pulling me back toward the existence I was trying to escape: month after sedentary month behind a desk, tight deadlines, choking down fast food between conference calls, heavy eyelids, weeks spent living in airports and hotels. Although draped in exotic linen, it was just a different rat running the same race, and the magic could evaporate quickly.

As Christine wrote the final exams for a Master's degree in Psychology, I sensed the time was right for escape. Before she could begin searching for a job, I strategically suggested we take a year off together and travel with a folding kayak. The rough plan was to head to tropical waters for the winter, and then haul the boat to the High Arctic for the summer. It didn't take much convincing. Soon we were poring over maps. For years I had been eyeing a remote group of islands in the Indian Ocean, but initial research revealed a major problem: an abundance of saltwater crocodiles.

"Salties are nothin' like Nile crocs, mate," a rangy Australian barked at me over the phone when I called to learn more. "They make grizzly bears look more like teddy bears. And you're thinkin' of goin' in the breeding season? G'night!"

Just then *Outpost* rang with good news. Air Malaysia had offered to fly us to any destination they serviced, and I needed to make a decision in five minutes. Phone pinned under one ear, websites flashing across my computer screen, the word *Borneo* suddenly appeared and drew me like a magnet. I knew nothing about the world's third largest island, but why not attempt a traverse of its northern coast? After confirming the flights I went back to the crocodile website and looked up Borneo; luckily the saltie population was reported to be significantly less prolific.

Concurrently we were arranging summer transport to the fjords of eastern Greenland. The flights took us through Iceland, and it seemed like the perfect time to attempt another journey, one that had lingered in my imagination for years; a coast-to-coast traverse of the volcanic isle by foot. A fantastic year of travel was quickly coming together.

Preparations raced ahead, and we were just weeks away from our Borneo departure when an unexpected e-mail arrived. SEAL-Asia – a company we had approached weeks earlier with questions about salt-water crocodiles – had invited Christine and me to spend a week at their base camp, tucked in the pristine islands of Myanmar's Mergui Archipelago.

It was a tempting offer, seeing as we had more than a month to spare between Borneo and our arctic trips. "Sounds great," I wrote back. "Out of interest, is there any chance we could take off on our own after the trip, and do some poking around? We'll have our own folding kayak and gear with us."

"Sure," came the reply. "No one has really kayaked in the area, so whatever you do will be a first, an exploratory. One of our guides, Cedric, is interested in paddling to the town of Myeik, which lies about two hundred kilometres (120 miles) to the north of our base camp. Getting permission will be no problem. Leave it to us."

Cedric "Coyote" Gourmelen awaits us on the government jetty in Kawthaung, Myanmar's newly opened but highly restricted southern port of entry. The short Frenchman, wearing a torn T-shirt and hand-woven rope sandals, is tanned and noticeably muscular after a season of guiding in the tropics.

"*Welly* pleased to meet you," he smiles. "*Welly*" is Cedric's trademark adjective. Before long he has pointed out a *welly* beautiful bird, described a *welly* tough hike, and noted that it is *welly, welly* hot. The endearing colloquialism appears to be a union of "really" and "very," pronounced with a French accent.

Christine and I have arrived on a leaky longtail, ferried across the Pakchan River from Thailand. After battling winds and heavy seas for twenty-six days along Borneo's north coast, we are in tune with the tropics; the humidity, the burning sun, the smell of growth and decay. The new surroundings are familiar and comforting, but we still harbour lingering misgivings about our visit. Travel to the region is contentious.

Burma (now Myanmar) achieved independence from Britain in 1948, and after a decade of turmoil, a ruthless military regime grabbed power. Insurgency, civil war, human-rights abuses, and brutal repression have marked the country's history ever since, but few of these horrors have been widely reported (largely due to the regime's long-standing policy of keeping all foreigners out). In 1990, facing increasing international pressure, the ruling junta allowed free democratic elections. To the surprise of many, Aung San Suu Kyi's National League for Democracy won by a landslide, but instead of relinquishing power, the military placed Suu Kyi under house arrest and further tightened its grasp on the country.

Recently, in an effort to grab a share of Southeast Asia's booming tourism revenues, Myanmar has reopened its doors to travellers. Despite the government's somewhat lazy involvement in a UN-brokered program of national reconciliation, Suu Kyi advocates that foreigners not visit Myanmar. By boycotting the country, she believes travellers can exert significant economic pressure. But many members of her pro-democracy cabinet disagree fervently. Comparable to the Dalai Lama's approach in Tibet, they urge foreigners to visit Myanmar, bringing with them news of the outside world, and taking home reports of what they see inside. Whatever your perspective, travel to the country cannot be taken lightly, and demands a moral choice.

Despite these reservations, my first impression of the country is one of great lightness. A warm wind rushes across the choppy waters, and golden pagodas twinkle atop forested hills. The harbour is filled with jostling wooden boats. Fishermen stand and wave as we pass, the tangy smell of their catch filling the air. Fishing and cross-border trade are the business of the southern Myanmar. Only a provisional dirt road connects Kawthaung with the fast-modernizing cities of the north, and that route is almost permanently closed – either for repairs or due to rebel threats. The glittering hotels, cellular networks, and the pro-democracy struggles of Yangôn and Mandalay seem a world away.

As we wait for our bags, an aging ferry steams in from the north and docks beside us. Soldiers on the roof toss their rifles down to companions on the jetty. Streams of disembarking passengers snatch tattered cardboard boxes from the deck and hurry off. A crowd of moped drivers awaits them, held behind a barbed-wire fence, holler-ing for fares. The drivers wear flimsy plastic helmets, the kind you would buy in a toy store, adorned with swastikas. Most faces are smeared with gobs of white *thanakha* paste (made from ground bark and used for both ceremonial adornment and sun protection). Pas-sengers clamber onto the mopeds, as many as four at a time; infants tucked under arms, children standing on gas tanks, and women sitting sidesaddle. Then a stream of high-pitched motorcycles begins to buzz away, weaving through crowded, narrow streets and disappearing into the bowels of town.

Standing on the jetty, beside Cedric and the five other guests destined for SEAL's base camp, is Mojo, an unsmiling official from Myanmar Tours and Travel. MTT is the government agency that controls all foreign travel in the country. Mojo has come to collect our visitor fees and check the group through immigration.

"Everyone leave passport with me," he demands. "For safekeeping."

"For safekeeping?" I repeat, unused to ever letting my passport out of my hands.

"We want to make sure you come back," Mojo flashes a thin smile.

As we begin loading gear into a speedboat destined for base camp, I notice Mojo lean close to Cedric. "No permission," he whispers. "Journey no possible." Instantly I know he is referring to our planned journey toward Myeik, and my stomach tightens. I expect Cedric to cave in, the almost universal response to bureaucratic stonewalling, but he doesn't blink.

"Just keep trying," the Frenchman smiles. "Someone at the SEAL office talked to the Minister in Yangôn. I'm sure he said it would be fine."

"It's no fine, Cedric." Mojo shakes his head. "Too much organizing. Complicated permission. Big headache. My boss say no way."

"Too big a headache?" Cedric scoffs. "All we want to do is paddle our kayaks. What are you worried about?"

"You no understand, Cedric," Mojo snaps, staring away. "Journey no possible. Too dangerous. Maybe you meet pirates, maybe storm. With a support boat, maybe, but now no time to organize. Not possible."

Cedric won't give up. "Give it another try, Mojo," he smiles, getting in the last word as the moorings are cast. Moments later the speedboat accelerates away, climbing over its wake and racing toward the heart of the remote archipelago.

Two hours later we set anchor in complete darkness, a gentle swell rocking the boat. Off the bow lies the barely discernable outline of a tropical isle. The sound of surf crashing on beaches carries through the night. We jump overboard, clothes tied in garbage bags, and swim toward shoreline torches and bonfires marking camp. After a snack of fresh mango, Christine and I climb into a small tent, night masking all surroundings.

Screaming monkeys wake us. The eastern sky is slowly lightening, and a troop of long-tailed macaques races past our mesh tent. We watch on raised elbows as forty or more pass. Timid babies cling to mother's bellies. Youngsters approach the mesh and peer inquisitively in, until a tiny movement sends them racing off in shrieks. At the end of the parade come the large males, swaggering by on their knuckles, never changing pace or looking at us. Upon reaching the beach, the group spreads along the water's edge, chasing crabs in circles, scratching themselves, slowly moving on. Above, a pair of white-breasted sea eagles soars effortlessly, hunting the shallows for schools of fish that ripple the surface.

A loud snort, directly behind our heads, causes us to panic. Frantically wrestling inside our zipped-together sleeping bags, Christine and

I manage to flip around, and come face to face with a wild boar. It is no more than a metre away. It must have been absently rooting through forest undergrowth when it stumbled into our tent. Looking as surprised as I feel, it waddles off quickly.

"Amazing," Christine whispers.

"That's normal," Cedric reports at breakfast. "There are plenty of boars on the island. And the monkeys visit every morning. We have to be careful or they steal our fruit. One day a baby found my shaving mirror. At first he was scared of his reflection. Then he started trying to kiss it. It was *welly* funny to watch."

This is in stark contrast with Borneo's coast, where during a month of camping and travel we saw not a single mammal, apart from domestic cows grazing in swaths of clear-cut rain forest. Rivers that historically ran clear were staining the sea blood-red, carrying topsoil away from the ravaged interior. The orangutan, once rumoured to be able to swing from one end of the great island to the other without touching the ground, was relegated to tiny preserves and fed fruit by the bushel before intrigued tourists. Here we are seeing what Borneo once was.

A maze of trails has been left on the white sand beach during the night; freshly excavated crab dens, prints of civet cat and mouse deer (small, hoofed ruminants with a tapered snout, standing about one foot tall). A winding groove bordered by talon-like claw marks shows where a sizable monitor lizard passed. On a nearby headland Cedric shows us the trails of sea turtles, leading from the ocean to freshly excavated nests. Later, in a bamboo grove, Christine spots the thick coils of a reticulated python. An unidentifiable lump, the size of a hen, protrudes from its belly.

We jump in our kayaks, paddling toward nearby islets. The clear water beneath our bows is thick with glittering schools of fish, and a pod of dolphins greets us, leaping skyward, eyes swivelling to inspect the strange interlopers. Diving in after them, our snorkels and masks reveal staggering coral arches. Christine and I exchange a knowing glance, reminded once again of Borneo, where dynamite and cyanide are regularly used to catch reef fish, and in a month of travel, we saw nothing even remotely similar.

Cautiously we paddle into a narrow, craggy sea cave, no more than two metres (6 feet) wide yet taller than a house. Each swell pushes us deeper into darkness. Something rushes by my head. I duck as the beating of a thousand wings echoes above us. Cedric laughs knowingly. Although at first my eyes can see nothing, as receding waves draw us back into sunlight, I see we have disturbed a bat colony. The cave is belching out an unending stream of grey bodies, forming a great swirling ball in the sky overhead. Two sea eagles appear, feathers whistling as they dive, and slam into the airborne congregation. They fly off slowly, twitching black bodies clutched to their chests.

"There are still wild elephants living in the Mergui," Cedric notes as we sip papaya juice back at camp, pointing to a nearby island on the chart, "but they are *welly* dangerous. Last month a pair charged into the ocean and chased our kayaks. The Mokken (sea gypsies) claim to have even seen tiger prints, but I'm not sure."

We have entered a lost Eden, and as the days pass, I find myself constantly reminded of Jacques Cousteau's words upon diving in the waters of Sipadan, off eastern Borneo, in 1988. "I have seen other places like Sipadan," he noted at the time. "That was forty-five years ago – but now, no more. Here we have found again an untouched piece of art."

⁓

Only a handful of pristine natural environments remain on the planet today, and most of these have been spared the deleterious effects of human advancement because either nature or government has barricaded them behind layers of protection. The Mergui Archipelago is a prime example of both.

For six months of every year these remote islands are pounded by the southwest monsoon. During the past millennia, as the neighbouring Kra Isthmus saw the rise, fall, and subjugation of several civilizations, the Mergui Archipelago remained almost completely uninhabited.

Bereft of freshwater sources, clogged with malarial jungles, and a well-known haven for pirates, it was never an attractive place to settle. Only sporadic bands of Mokken, nomadic sea gypsies, inhabited the region.

After the Second World War, as South East Asia's population exploded and the region became increasingly modernized, the iron-fisted junta took control, forbidding foreign travellers and investors from entering the country. It is no small irony that civil war and strife have kept the delicate environment of the Mergui Archipelago inviolate, for democracy and tourism, no matter how well-meaning, could not have done the same.

Less than three hundred kilometres (180 miles) to the south lies the Thai resort town of Phuket. Five million visitors descend on its beaches each year. Parasail boats and Jet Skis race around the crowded bay, and extravagant yachts anchor offshore. Condominiums press against the waterfront, mazes of hotels and guest houses spreading behind. Hawkers selling fake watches and pirated CDs jam the narrow alleys. Noisy louts and sex-trade workers harangue passersby. Taxis and tuk-tuks race through the confusion, and diesel fumes choke the air. Bars remain open around the clock, catering to sunburned Western backpackers hoping to get laid, and throngs of pasty middle-aged Western men seeking young Asian girlfriends and boyfriends. It is a town that never sleeps.

You will find no wild boars or long-tailed macaques running along the beaches in Phuket. There are no turtle prints in the sand, no monitor lizards resting in the sun, no sea eagles soaring above the shallows.

As our week in camp nears its end, we spend the final afternoon hiking to the crest of a nearby island. The sun is turning crimson and dropping into the Indian Ocean as we reach the summit. Soaked in sweat, we sit gently in the tall grass, trying not to make a sound. Cedric points to a fruiting fig tree that protrudes from the forest canopy below us.

"That is where the hornbills roost," he whispers.

We have caught brief glimpses of plain-pouched hornbills during our stay, enormous birds with long, curved beaks. They always fly by in pairs, foraging the rainforest canopy for nuts and fruits, quickly moving on. However, hornbills are gregarious birds, and return to a communal roost each evening, no matter how far afield they have foraged. We wait patiently.

Hornbills have a unique nesting habit, Cedric softly explains. When the female is ready to lay her eggs, she searches for a large open cavity in a tree trunk, and clambers in. Using chewed fruit and mud, she and her mate will barricade the opening, sealing the female inside. Only a slit remains, with her long beak sticking out. For the next three months the male scavenges for food, returning frequently to feed his mate and their young. During her stay in the nest, the female moults all her feathers, and is completely helpless. Should the male die or be killed during this time, the female and her young family will perish without help. Astoundingly, native hunters have observed that other males in the community will share the responsibility for feeding a widow and her chicks.

Something large flies past, hidden in the canopy below, interrupting our conversation.

"It's a hornbill," Cedric whispers. "They are *welly* noisy flyers. They have no secondary feathers, just primary."

I can hear each wing-beat as the hornbill returns, passing again, a slow and steady sound like an old steam engine. Now a trio has arrived. They circle below us and approach the fig, squawking loudly, dancing from branch to branch. Then they abruptly fly off, their distinctive wing-beats fading in the distance.

"Patience," Cedric nods, pointing out to sea.

Far offshore are more shadows, steadily flying toward the island over golden water. Another set of wings beat behind us. I spin around but see nothing. Soon the hornbills are arriving in droves. Returning from surrounding islands, the enormous birds hoot and swoop over the canopy, their curved beaks silhouetted against a violet sky. One by one they land on the fig and jump about its branches. There are twenty on the tree, thirty, forty. We watch them for half an hour, until the last rays of light fade from the sky.

"*Welly, welly* few people will ever see anything like this," Cedric notes as we stumble down the hill, crashing through the dark forest. Hornbills require vast swaths of forest to feed and find appropriate nests, and are key indicators of tropical ecosystem health. In recent decades their numbers have plummeted. The Mergui is one of their last strongholds.

Swimming out to the waiting powerboat, I notice smoke pouring from the crest of a nearby island. "Flying fox colony," Cedric explains, holding his arms out wide. "They are huge fruit bats, with wings a metre across. They scavenge at night."

It is pitch-black when the captain pushes the twin throttles forward, and the powerboat begins racing back toward base. A glowing green trail, the colour of a lime-green Popsicle, stretches out across the inky waters behind us. A massive bloom of phosphorescent algae is in progress (these algae release a tiny flash of green light when they are disturbed, a defence mechanism). As we speed along, fish resting just below the ocean's surface streak away like green missiles.

The air is warm on my face. I lean back, watching fishing boats bobbing on the horizon, armed with massive arrays of lights that shine down into the depths, luring schools into their nets. Suddenly, something whooshes by, only just missing my head.

"It's the flying foxes," Cedric yells over the wind. "We have caught up to them."

The bats are flying low across the water, skimming by so closely that I can almost reach out and touch them. We pass thousands. I feel like I am in a dream. After a decade of travels, I have never seen an ecosystem so untouched, so pristine. I wonder how long it can last.

As our week at base camp ends, a supply ship stops by. It carries no message from SEAL's office, but Mojo, the steel-faced MTT official is aboard.

"No permission, Cedric," he announces flatly. "You go back."

"We'll call the office on the satellite phone," Cedric promises, side-stepping the issue. Mojo scowls. Returning to his vessel, the engines rumble and minutes later the ship is steaming south. "They will be back soon," Cedric mutters.

Cedric dispatches the other guests back to Kawthaung on the speed-boat. Disregarding Mojo's orders, Tenai (a cheery, thin Burmese porter), Christine and I stay behind. We try the satellite phone, but as I suspect Cedric already knew, it does not work.

"We have no permission, no passports, no MTT guide, and no support boat," Cedric sums up his thoughts, "but we do have kayaks, food and water. We don't know what Yangôn will say, and I don't think it matters. My view is that there is no point in stopping ourselves."

I agree completely, and feel fortunate we are with Cedric, for his defiance is rare. Christine is also keen to go. Tenai smiles and nods, but it is hard to know what he really feels, and I worry we are putting him in a dangerous position. "He'll be fine," Cedric assures me. "If anyone is going to take the hit for this, it's me."

In searing midday sun we hurriedly pack two weeks of rations into dry bags and fill four twenty-litre (5 gallon) water jugs to the brim. Billowing cumulus clouds are already boiling up from inland mountains as we drag the heavily laden boats out through crashing surf and hop in. A sea eagle swoops by as we paddle away, whistling just metres above our heads.

"A lucky omen," Christine points and smiles.

Weeks later we learn that the MTT boat returned to camp less than an hour after we left, with an order from the mainland to halt our journey, but by that time it was too late. We were already long gone, having vanished into a maze of tropical islands.

Myeik, a trading post arbitrarily chosen as our destination, lies 160 kilometres (100 miles) to the north. We head into unknown waters, skipping

338 ~ The Dolphin's Tooth

from island to island, traversing clear blue seas, coral reefs slipping beneath our hulls. Tall, thick forests crowd the shores, pressing up to white sand beaches. Every cove we pass is deserted, apart from the universal prints of macaque and boar.

Our routine is to rise early, before the sun, and paddle in the cool of daybreak. By noon the heat has grown unbearable, and we stop to seek shade, cooking lunch and napping until the crushing temperatures pass. Then our small group presses on again, often travelling until sunset.

The largest crossing between islands is eighteen kilometres (11 miles), and despite leaving at sunrise, the heat quickly catches us, sapping our energy. It is impossible to gauge our progress on the mirror-flat waters, and hour after hour passes without the distant shoreline seeming any closer. We frequently slip from our boats, soak in the cool, blue sea, and then start paddling again. Headaches and grumpiness prevail.

"Hey, what's that?" Christine whispers, pointing to starboard.

Squinting into shimmering reflections, I hear a puff of breath but see nothing. Suddenly, a group of short, stubby fins rises from the water, racing toward our kayaks.

"Dolphins!" Cedric shouts in joy.

The pod of bottlenoses is large, twenty or more, and we instantly take up chase, paddling after them. The dolphins streak back and forth before our bows, leaping into the air, teasing us, and soon I have forgotten about the suffering and heat. The group seems to play with us, dashing ahead, waiting till we catch up, occasionally swimming close. Eventually the fins disappear toward the horizon, but in the process of chasing them, we have finished the crossing.

"Come back," Cedric yells, leaping from his kayak and splashing about in the water. "What was I thinking? I should have jumped in earlier and swum with them."

⟋⟋⟋

During the late eighties, as Burma's economy stagnated, a pro-democracy movement swept through the country, rapidly gaining momentum.

Demonstrators filled the streets, spurred on by the prophecy that Burma would become a free country on the auspicious date of 8-8-88. Unwilling to cede power, the military government moved swiftly and brutally to crush these uprisings. More than ten thousand are rumoured to have been massacred in four days, but with foreigners strictly banned from the country at the time, details remain sketchy. Martial law was imposed, and as part of a concerted effort to purge the nation of its colonial past, the country's official name was changed to the Union of Myanmar. Simultaneously, hundreds of cities, towns, streets, and rivers across the country were also renamed. Rangoon became Yangôn, and hidden in the bowels of the southern archipelago, the fishing village of Mergui became Myeik.

The port of Mergui first rose to prominence during the eighteenth century, when trade ship captains began docking in its protected harbour. Rather than sailing their goods south through the dangerous Strait of Malacca, past Singapore, and then north again, merchandise could be transported overland from Mergui. Bamboo rafts laden with trade goods were floated up the Tanintharyi River, dragged over the centre of the Isthmus of Kra by elephant, and then shipped downriver to the cities of central Siam (Thailand), saving six months of sailing and avoiding the ever-present threat of piracy.

The port's most well-known citizen, Samuel White, was a colourful "interloper" (English trader not associated with the East India Company) before King Nari of Siam appointed him harbourmaster in 1676. Exceedingly brash, White began plundering passing ships in the Bay of Bengal, and before long had amassed a small fortune. His actions invoked the ire of the East India Company, which dispatched two warships under order to apprehend White and enforce British law. Unfortunately, their arrival in Mergui sparked a royal bungle. Convinced that Britain intended to capture the port as a prize, local leaders ordered the immediate slaughter of all the town's British residents. Angry Mandarins repelled both the ships and White. Shortly after, Siam declared war on the East India Company (not Britain), and the two never traded again.

But Cedric, Christine, and I know none of this. We have chosen Myeik as our destination simply because it was a convenient dot on the map, a point to aim for. What draws us onward is the desire to see everything that lies on the way; around the next corner, in the next bay, and over the blue waters of the distant horizon.

We pass almost no signs of human presence or activity as we paddle; no settlements, homes, villages, or camps. Occasional muddy tracks lead back into the jungle, used by small crews of impoverished men to haul huge hardwood logs to the beach. Logging in the Mergui is illegal but it is still done, the wood exported to Thailand under the cover of night. Towering trees are felled and squared by hand, but without the aid of heavy equipment, only those growing close to the water's edge can be taken, and the biggest impact of this activity appears to be on native animal life. Monitor lizards, macaques, squirrels, and large birds all end up in the workers' stew pots.

We see plenty of fishing boats on distant horizons, and pass close to a few. The decrepit, wooden ships are manned by youth who use hand-woven nets weighted with rocks to scour the waters. The exhausted crews appear shocked to see us, and rarely return our waves, instead staring in silence. It must be their way, for as soon as Tenai shouts out a greeting, the tough and hardened men rush to the railings, welcoming and curious. Wrapped in rags, skin darkened by the sun, they laugh when Tenai explains our journey.

"They think we are crazy to travel in such small boats," Tenai smiles embarrassedly. I shudder at the thought of weathering a tropical storm in their creaking, tar-stained craft. Cedric has brought cigarettes to trade in exchange for their catch, and each night we roast the flesh of sweetlips and silver jacks over driftwood fires.

A dim warehouse comes into view, hidden in the recesses of Ka Mar Island. Raising my binoculars, I make out a warren of aluminum-roofed shanties, cut into the dark forest. Silhouettes slip back and forth along a wooden jetty, unloading crates from a weathered ship. The scene feels eerily reminiscent of the opening of a James Bond film. I can imagine the 007 theme music welling up and a subtitle appearing across the bottom of the screen: "Nikko Pearl Farm, Restricted Zone, The Union of Myanmar."

"These farms are strictly off-limits," Cedric whispers as our kayaks jostle together. "Keep your eyes open. There may be armed guards posted on the perimeter."

I exchange a glance with Christine, who is sitting in the bow of our double kayak. We have no choice but to approach the compound. Only a trickle of drinking water remains in our jugs and it is now the height of the hot season. Streams on the islands are dry, and because it hasn't rained for days, we have not been able to capture water in our tarp.

Cedric motions for Tenai to catch up. "If anyone asks, it is very important you tell them we have permission for this journey. Do you understand?"

Tenai nods enthusiastically, despite being visibly exhausted from days of hard paddling. I hope he can pull it off; his answers will be critical.

We start to paddle forward once again, eyes glued to the jetty. The lonesome hooting of an imperial pigeon drifts from the jungle. I steel myself for an alarm, or worse yet, gunfire. Suddenly shouts echo across the water. Men dash along the dock. An outboard motor roars to life, spewing a plume of blue smoke, its throttle pinned wide open. The engine continues to shriek, but the skiff doesn't leave its moorings. We paddle faster and faster, arriving breathless, finding the dock workers hunched over a rack of oysters, still unaware of our presence.

"Hello," Cedric shouts when we are almost upon them. Seven faces look up in shock. The screaming motor, which is being used to pump water over the oysters, is quickly silenced. The workers wear ragged clothes, their cheeks smeared with *thanakha*. Tenai launches into a hasty introduction, pointing to the empty water jugs in our hatches. A rapid exchange in Burmese follows.

Soon a manager appears, running down the jetty from the main compound. As he barks orders, we are escorted from the kayaks and brusquely motioned to line up. I prepare for an interrogation. Instead, the manager joins us, draping his arms across our shoulders and handing a point-and-shoot camera to a co-worker for a souvenir photograph. Our visit is undoubtedly the first of its kind, as this region has been off-limits for over fifty years.

Accepting an invitation for coffee, we stumble through a tour of the facilities, mildly ashamed of our salty, sweaty clothes. As we pass a long wooden dormitory, a shaven head pops out a window before me. I jump back in surprise. Were it not for the olive-green fatigues, I would imagine myself eye to eye with a monk. Instead this man is a soldier, here to guard the harvest. There is an unnerving silence, and then in English so halting that it seems a parody, the blank face demands, "What . . . are . . . you . . . searching . . . for?"

The question jolts me, and touches something deeper than the obvious.

"Myeik," I blurt out, which seems to satisfy the shaven head, for it disappears again.

Not wanting to linger, we scribble the particulars of our passports into the manager's faded log book, fill our water jugs from a cistern, load our kayaks, and hurriedly paddle off. Soon we have melted back into the maze of islands and channels.

***

The day after our visit to the pearl farm, Cedric spots a sailboat on the horizon. We are sitting beside a smoky fire, tucked in the shadows of a sweeping beach, sipping coffee sweetened with condensed milk.

"It's *Crescent*," he mutters, squinting through binoculars at the twenty-metre (60-foot) ketch, "A diving boat belonging to SEAL. She shouldn't be up here. These waters are out of bounds. They must be searching for us. Either they have orders to bring us back, or to act as a support boat." Our tents are hidden in forest, invisible to the pleasure yacht, and they don't see our fire. Soon the white dot has moved past, heading north.

"I am certainly not chasing after her," Cedric announces, putting any thoughts of turning ourselves in to rest. "We'll keep heading north. Maybe we'll meet her, maybe we won't."

A support boat? The words make my stomach knot. Certainly *Crescent* could make our journey easier, carrying all our food and gear, making our kayaks lighter. We would arrive each evening to find camp arranged, chairs set out, a fire burning, and tents erected. There would be freshwater showers, fancy meals by candlelight, weather reports, even movies at night powered by a noisy generator, but with that comfort would come the end of the trip as we knew it.

Crescent represents everything we are trying to leave behind on this journey, and while I want the ship to disappear, I also feel conflicted. Why does it feel so important to carry on alone? By denying help, are we turning the journey into a lark? Are we simply a bunch of well-off Westerners pretending to have an adventure? Are we bitter because our illusion of an adventure is being shattered?

"Cedric," I look up from the embers. "Deep inside I know a support boat would ruin everything important about this journey. I know you feel the same way. But how can you explain that to someone else? Someone who hasn't stood in our shoes?"

He stares at me as if I have lost my mind. "It's the freedom, man! The fucking freedom. What other reason do you need?"

Cedric is defiant by nature. Rules are meant to be challenged. As a child in Paris he excelled at school, and was accepted to a top university. But when his parents pressured him to get good grades, he simply gave up. After his three fruitless attempts at completing a baccalaureate, Cedric travelled to South Africa on a business-school exchange. That was fifteen years ago, and apart from a short shift of mandatory military service, he has never been home since.

He dealt with the French Army in classic style. "On the first day, someone in the barracks told me if I wanted to get out, I had to do it quickly. Otherwise I would be stuck with the idiots for two years. So I froze, completely. I just sat in my room and held my head. I ceased moving or communicating. I refused to talk or look at anyone. They carried me to the mess hall, but I wouldn't eat. They carried me to the washroom, but I refused to go. In the end they had no idea what to do, so they discharged me. It only took two weeks."

Immediately, Cedric returned to South Africa, and found work as a commercial diver collecting shells. Within days the ocean had become his passion, a passion that would shape the course of his life. "One afternoon I was working alone on the sea floor, when I sensed something big, directly above me. I looked up and all I can see is a huge eye. *Welly* close!" he motions. "It was a right whale. Not moving, just staring at me."

Cedric's connection with whales and dolphins verges on the spiritual. For more than a decade he has travelled the world – Baja, Israel, Venezuela, Australia – working as a dive master, always looking for these marine mammals.

"Fish see you; but whales look at you. There is a *welly* big difference. And when you dive with them, the relationship can get *welly* tight."

We wait for an hour to pass after seeing *Crescent*, and then continue north, dodging behind small islands, always trying to stay hidden. By early afternoon we stumble upon a second pearl farm, not shown on our map. A network of buoys fills the wide bay. Boats mill about the smooth waters, inspecting oysters hanging in cages below. A prominent red sign marks the headland before us. Tenai paddles closer and translates the Burmese script. "*No boats. No trespassing.*"

He looks back at me, unsure of what to do. I'm not sure either. Cedric catches up, and paddles straight past without slowing.

"Maybe we should hug the shoreline, try to stay hidden in the shade," I suggest. "There is a chance they won't see us there."

"What for?" Cedric shrugs. "We have no reason to hide."

Within minutes a ship is speeding our way. Cedric paddles away from it, but it catches us quickly, men waving frantically from the upper deck.

"We can talk to them," Cedric pronounces as their motors slow, "but our freedom is not open for negotiation."

The men on the boat are furious. They scream and point at our boats. Tenai hastily explains the goal of our journey. Tensions ease. Satisfied that we are not spies or thieves, the men offer us a bag of waxy, deep-fried minnows, and then wave goodbye to us. Tenai translates their parting instructions; "Avoid the pearl-farm waters. Paddle away from the island."

Cedric ignores them, paddling directly for the main complex. His rebelliousness seems instinctual and deep-rooted, and makes me mildly uncomfortable. As an inherent mediator, I always try to minimize conflict and Cedric's actions confuse me. They are undertaken with a smile, and there is never a hint of anger or maliciousness. Strangers are left to wonder if his defiance is unintentional. Friends know better.

Crescent catches us on the seventh day. We see her mast bobbing on the horizon as black squalls race past, but it is too late. We have been spotted. Soon, an inflatable launch is racing toward us. Mojo stands in the bow, glaring.

"Why you do this, Cedric? You have no permission. Yangôn very angry. You stop now."

"Look, stopping here is impossible," Cedric yells back over the wind. The shoreline is rocky and the swell is building. The chart shows a sandy beach and good anchorage five kilometres (3 miles) away. "We'll meet you up the coast, at the next big bay."

"No, Cedric. You stop now," Mojo barks.

"How can we?"

Short of physically dragging us from our kayaks, the MTT official is powerless. "You hurry, Cedric." After one last scowl, the boat motors off.

We are still headed north, in the direction of Myeik. Cedric has won again. "Things are not looking good," he admits when we reach the bay. "If we get aboard *Crescent*, we'll be at their mercy, and I don't think we should give in yet. You guys go and wait on the beach."

Christine, Tenai, and I head to shore, cooking rice over a small fire and lingering in the shade. The white pleasure boat sits offshore, and feels oddly menacing. Through my binoculars I can see crew members staring at us through their binoculars. As soon as Christine and I drift to sleep, Tenai leaps up and paddles to *Crescent*. I can't blame him. Life in Myanmar has conditioned him to follow orders. Consequences are severe for those who don't. We have already asked too much of him. I suspect things are going to get ugly.

Time seems to pass slowly, and it is three long hours before Cedric returns. He looks exhausted.

"Fucking assholes. Bunch of stupid Aussie surfers who think they can drag us back to base camp. They said we can paddle around there for a few days if we want. Idiots. They don't have the first clue what a journey is about. I told them that was unacceptable, and refused to even talk about it. So, now there are two options. Plan one is simple. We turn around and paddle southward. We rendezvous with *Crescent* three days from now, when their diving trip is over. They return us to Kawthaung. We never get to Myeik. That's what they think we are going to do.

"Plan two involves giving them the finger. And it is a *welly* big finger. You could choose to miss the rendezvous, keep heading north, and try to reach Myeik. I don't know what the authorities will do with you when you get there. You'll be taking your chances. It is your decision though. If you decide to carry on, I will have to decide if I am going to come along, or return to *Crescent*."

We have the night to think about it. The ship is not departing until the following morning. As darkness falls Christine and I crawl into our tent to discuss our choices.

"I think we should keep going," she blurts out immediately. "Well, I mean, I want to but . . . I don't know. How much trouble do you think we'll get into?"

It is not inconceivable that we could be thrown in jail for a few days, but I seriously doubt we'd come to any harm, although I cannot be sure. While I'm not bothered by the possibility of sitting in a cell, I worry for

Christine. The thought of her facing rough treatment is too much to bear, and reluctantly I suggest we call it quits.

"No way! It'd be awful to stop now," she flops back onto her sleeping pad, holding her temples. "I mean, we've come so far. Deep down inside, you want to keep going, don't you?"

Of course I want to keep going. The voyage has sunk roots into us, become a part of us. It has a soul, and to leave it unfinished would feel like dishonouring a close friend. But why?

"It isn't getting to Myeik that's important," I muse. "In fact Myeik doesn't matter at all. It is continuing the journey that matters."

The smells of the rain forest, the grit in our food, the sun burning the backs of our hands; I can picture no other way. We have spent seven days living barefoot, sleeping on beaches, paddling through these jungle-tufted islets, swimming in sparkling waters, watching afternoon thunderheads build. For the moment, this is the only life we know.

To think that some bureaucratic red-tape inflexibility might halt the trip feels unbearable. I curse the universal resistance to anything new or unusual. Cedric has inspired me, and despite the obvious perils of flaunting rules in Myanmar, my instinct is to keep going. I am only passingly aware of the situation's irony. Myanmar is ruled by fear. Our disobedience is a privilege the local population has not known for half a century.

We are caught up in the moment. Our plans spiral into mutiny. *Shit, yeah. Of course we'll keep going.* The possibility of a stay in a Burmese jail seems a small price to pay for such freedom. That night, oblivious to the stifling humidity, we sleep entwined, dreaming of defiance.

In the morning, rather than sneak away, we visit *Crescent* and inform the captain of our plans. No point wasting his time, waiting in vain for us at a rendezvous point we'll never reach.

"What?" Mojo leans over the rail, ashen. I realize that we are putting him in danger of discipline, and suggest we sign a letter confirming our decision to wilfully disobey his clear orders. Mojo's relief is immediate and immense. "Have a good trip," he smiles and shakes our hands.

Cedric scrabbles aboard. As an employee of SEAL, he is unsure what to do. Yells erupt from the cabin. The door slams. Ten minutes later, Cedric emerges, shaking his head. He is staying.

We race away, paddling hard. The bay is several kilometres wide, and it will feel good to put *Crescent* out of sight, re-establish our independence. There is not a twinge of doubt in either of us; we are both utterly sure we are doing the right thing. The far side of the bay nears. The umbilical cord is almost cut.

Suddenly, an outboard motor roars to life behind us. *For shit's sake!* Rather than turning to look, we paddle even faster, rounding the headland just as *Crescent*'s small motor launch catches us. Cedric sits glumly at the bow. It is a good thing he is with them, because at this point I doubt I would listen to anyone else. I know he is being forced to stop us. I also know it is breaking his heart.

"It seems this is becoming a *welly, welly* big problem," Cedric mumbles.

Events are flying out of control. There are unaccounted-for foreigners in the Mergui. Yangôn is furious. The phone hasn't stopped ringing at the SEAL office. "Stop them, or else," the company owner has ordered. If Cedric can't turn us back, the others have been told to use force. Christine and I sit in the kayak, staring blankly ahead. Threats of jail float about. It doesn't matter. It is over.

Crescent turns and steams south. The yacht's diving clients return to their deck chairs and hardcover editions of *Bush at War*. I sit despondently with my feet over the railing, watching familiar shorelines slip by, dark rain forest and sandy beaches. As we pass Ka Mar Island, I stare out to sea. Somewhere on the horizon, where turquoise waters melt into a blue sky, the dolphins are still swimming.

Dragged to the coastal fishing village of Kawthaung, Christine, Cedric, and I await our fate in a dark, humid basement. Sweat soaks our clothes. We toy nervously with the soggy passports that have been returned to us, staring at stamps from past journeys. Eventually two grim-faced Army officers arrive, chests covered with medals and ribbons.

"Are you crazy?" they scream. Fists are slammed on tables. Cigarettes are smoked at a vicious rate, often two or three simultaneously, grasped between shaking fingers. Voices grow hoarse, the fury passes, and the men calm. After smoking a final cigarette, they kick us out of the country.

We part from Cedric at a dusty bus station in Ranong, Thailand. Racked with fevers and chills, he needs to seek treatment for malaria. Christine and I will stay at the border, claiming we want to rest and put the failed attempt out of our minds. The truth is neither of us can bring ourselves to give up on the expedition. I suspect we'll give it another shot.

"Before I go, there is something I want you guys to have," Cedric smiles weakly, pulling a sun-bleached bag from his backpack. Digging through a collection of shells, feathers, and small pieces of driftwood, he finds what he is looking for and holds out two clenched fists.

"Pick one," he nods to Christine.

She touches his right hand and Cedric's fingers slowly open. A small, twisted piece of bone rests inside. Delicate and fluted, it is no bigger than a matchbox. Confused, we stare in silence. Christine turns it in her hands.

"A dolphin's eardrum," Cedric finally explains. He opens his other hand and passes me a tooth. "These came from a bottlenose dolphin. Years ago I found its body washed ashore on the island where the hornbills roost."

Hoisting his pack, Cedric climbs the stairs into the waiting bus. At the top he pauses and turns. "I hope you never forget the dolphin. It still dreams of freedom."

As Cedric turns away, his parting words play over in my mind. They seem important. Something I should understand. Has he distilled everything I have seen, learned, and felt during a decade of wilderness travels into a few words?

The dolphin still dreams of freedom?

Hang on! . . . That isn't profound. It's trite, something you'd hear on Oprah. The words are corny . . . Or are they? I don't know . . . What did Cedric mean?

The bus lurches away, showering us in a cloud of dust.

After spending four restless days at Khoa Lak, a Thai beach resort, trying to forget about Myeik, we go back. We have to. Jumping on a northbound bus, Christine and I board a leaky longtail in Ranong, and begin crossing the Pakchan River toward Myanmar with knots in our stomachs.

"There is no way the guards at the border will know we've been kicked out. Right?" Christine asks anxiously.

"How can they? I didn't see a single computer in the country. I bet those guys just booted us and forgot about it. If we don't hang around Kawthaung, and jump the first ferry to Myeik, I think we'll be fine. I think."

The opposite shore looms nearer, and our driver docks alongside several other jostling longtails at the Immigration office, an offshore house built on stilts. I join a line of locals, nervously climbing a wobbly gangplank with both passports in hand. Christine waits for me in the longtail, as is custom. A crowd of army officers laze about inside, some in uniform, others in sweaty white undershirts. None smile, but none look at me either. A giant framed picture of some unnamed general, his chest covered in medals, glares down at me as I stumble into a hasty explanation of why we already have visa stamps in our passports. The clerk is not interested, he just wants money for another visa. I pay, and the stamp slams down.

We wander through the familiar streets of Kawthaung, feeling uncomfortable. After hurriedly buying ferry tickets to Myeik, we sign into the only hotel permitted to house foreign guests, and hibernate in our room, taking no risks.

The ferry is scheduled to leave the government docks at 6 a.m. the next morning, and we arrive at five. An army officer directs us to the foreigner's queue, where we wait alone, under a tin roof, out of the pouring rain. Before us five hundred locals stand motionless, getting soaked to the bone. Finally the ferry engines roar to life, a great plume of black soot rising in the air. We join the stampede toward the open hatches when an army captain suddenly reaches from the shadows and stops us.

"Passports," he demands, and we hand over our documents. After a brief glance he hands them back. "Visa no good. You no go Myeik."

"But the ferry manager said it was fine! He checked before selling us our tickets."

"Visa no good," the captain shakes his head, but then smiles. "If you want, I can help. Get you good visa. Meet me here, nine o'clock. OK?"

There is no other option. Christine and I drag ourselves back to the hotel. "He said he could get us the right visa," Christine remains optimistic.

"I know, but I hate these ever-changing rules. There is always a problem. What's it gonna be next time?"

Nonetheless, we return to the dock at nine, and find the captain waiting for us. He flags down two mopeds and we jump on the back, the captain on one, Christine and I on the other. After some hurried instructions the whining bikes whiz off. Through town we speed, past the pagoda, past the roundabout where a lazy policeman sleeps, past the market where we saw a monkey for sale. Then a wave of worry passes over me. I realize where we are going. Just then Christine gives me a hard squeeze from behind, but it is too late. The mopeds pull into the MTT compound, and stop in front of the same building where, just a week earlier, Cedric, Christine, and I awaited our fate in the dark, humid basement.

The well-intentioned captain eagerly leads us to the door. "Good visa here," he smiles, taking us down shallow stairs toward the exact room we sat in. The door swings open. The same two men who kicked us out of Myanmar are sitting in the same two chairs, still smoking, probably from the same carton. They look up at us, faces blank. We look back in exactly the same state of confusion. There is a prolonged moment of silence, and then all four of us proceed as if we have never met before.

"You'd like a visa for Myeik?" the plump boss asks. "Possible. But area is restricted by Army, very sensitive. You will need a chaperone, and you must pay his passage, and his hotel, and give him a good tip, because he will be my cousin. And I will need a bribe too."

The next morning we steam toward Myeik, fresh visas stamped in our passports, timid university-student-cum-chaperone in tow.

Myeik – long out-of-bounds to foreigners, and unreachable by road – remains as mysterious today as it was in the time of Samuel White. The picturesque coastal settlement is visited by just a handful of Western travellers each year. Only eleven travellers have registered to visit the city over the past twelve months our chaperone tells us.

Our ferry, which looks like a dirty jumbo jet without wings, slows and grinds up against tires protecting the busy government wharf. Crowding the cement bulwarks are hardened fishermen, their thin, sculpted bodies covered only by rags. A group works together, weaving a net the size of a city block from white string. Others are gathering stones from the beach and lashing the rudimentary weights along one edge of the growing net.

Hundreds of aging longtails jostle in the waters below. Some are laden with heaping piles of fish, and noisy buyers hop from boat to boat, bartering loudly. Blocks of ice rush past us, down a network of mahogany ramps leading from a factory above. Hand-crushed in giant hoppers, the resulting slurry pours into the holds of waiting boats, which one by one join the steady stream of vessels departing the harbour. It feels as if we have gone back in time, to a city existing almost as it did a century ago.

Everyone's face is covered in thick globs of *thanakha*, and as Christine and I step off, the entire dock turns to stare. An instant later, as if a wave passes over them, faces break into smiles. Men drop their work to wave enthusiastically, children play hide-and-seek behind their parents' legs, elders nod. Even the army officer who carefully checks our paper-work beams when I take his photo. Within minutes I am playing hacky-sack (using a wicker ball instead of a bean bag) with a group of laughing moped drivers. A crowd gathers, entertained by my ineptitude, yelling encouragement.

Our chaperone quickly breaks up the interaction, announcing we are heading to a brand-new cement hotel far outside town, used only by visiting businessmen, where no one will bother us. I suspect he thinks this will be great news. We refuse point-blank, suggesting instead a seedy guest house near the harbour. The poor young man's face sinks. He has never dealt with insubordination before, and clearly was looking forward to a comfortable night.

"You no go anywhere without me," he makes clear as we check-in.

I'd like to comply, but the chaperone is such a wet blanket, shooing away beggars and inquisitive children. His dress shirt and slacks clearly identify him as an outsider, which I suspect intimidates the colourful locals. He has to go. Christine is thinking the same thing.

"Why don't we lie down and have a nap before dinner?" she suggests, winking when only I am looking. The chaperone nods his approval, and we make plans to meet him again in the lobby at eight. Two minutes later, after dropping our bags in our room and scanning the hallway for watching eyes, we are gone, racing out the back door.

The hours pass in a blur. We are like children in a wonderland, pausing to watch a bright Hindu parade, dancing with street musicians, sitting silently with Buddhist monks before a golden shrine. I carry heavy rocks on my head while laughing construction workers, all of them children, use my camera to photograph the effort. Christine and I join a soccer game in a dusty alley, and afterward, an Indian woman drags us to her house for tea. Soon more than fifty neighbourhood children have gathered on the porch. Each corner seems to lead to a more fantastic sight: ponds filled with flowering lilies, gregarious rubber workers, towering pagodas. Every interaction flows into the next. Faster and faster it goes. I shoot eighteen rolls of film without knowing it. In fifteen years of travel I have never felt such a sense of place. Perhaps it is simply the result of having tried so hard to reach Myeik, but it doesn't matter. We have found magic, and we greedily lap up as much as we can.

Then we make a critical mistake. In the spirit of complete immersion, we eat sticky rice, wrapped in banana leaves and served at a grimy stand in the busy night market. This breaks one of our long-standing rules of travel: Never eat cold food from the street. Ever.

Sometime after midnight, I wake and limp to the washroom, clutching my stomach. Memories of Mr. Beg and Pakistan flash before me as I weakly struggle to maintain an upside-down spider position over a tiny, stinky hole in the bathroom floor. Minutes later Christine arrives, pressing me aside, claiming the hole as her own. We spend the next three days hobbling between the stinky room and bed, devastated by gut-bombs.

Our visa for Myeik expires on the fourth day, and it takes everything we have, including the use of Imodium and barf bags, to stagger to the departing ferry.

For six weeks we chased Myeik. We paddled hundreds of kilometres, were burned by the tropical sun and stung by jellyfish, pursued by a pleasure yacht, and screamed at by Army generals. We even got kicked out of the country. And in the end it all came down to six short hours. Was it worth it? Of course. Those six hours were magic, and that's what the journey was all about. It just took me a long time to realize.

Epilogue

The Gofrillers of the Wild

Toronto/Arctic National Wildlife Refuge, 2003

SEVERAL MONTHS after returning from Myanmar, I attended Idea City, a conference where fifty artists, scientists, authors, business leaders, and other original thinkers were each given twenty minutes to speak about any topic on their mind.

When Ofra Harnoy's turn came, the renowned cellist walked onto the stage and sat in a lone chair. An assistant followed her, carrying two identical cellos.

"Today I have brought two instruments that I would like to demonstrate," she began. "One was made three hundred years ago in Venice, by Matteo Gofriller, and is valued at $2.7 million. (Gofrillers are considered to be the Holy Grail of cellos, comparable to Stradivarius violins.) The other was made just a few years ago in Germany and is a good example of present-day instrument making. It is worth twenty thousand dollars.

"People often ask me if *they* will be able to tell the difference between two such instruments. Is it something only the *expert* ear can hear? Well, today I am going to ask you to be the judge. I will play a little on each instrument, without telling you which is which, and see if you can discern a difference, and what that difference is."

For the demonstration, one instrument is denoted "Instrument A," the other "Instrument B." From where I sit in the fifteenth row, they both look identical. Ofra begins with a selection from Brahms, played on Instrument A. The music is so lovely that I forget to concentrate on the actual sound of the instrument. It is not until the cellos are exchanged, and the same excerpt is played again, that I remember our task, and the answer seems perfectly clear. The first cello, Instrument A, was miles better.

Why? I ask myself. It's hard to pinpoint. All I know is that the two instruments, although appearing identical, are not comparable. The difference in the sound they produce is vast and undeniable. Ofra continues, playing two more pieces, one by Bach, one by Wagner. Both confirm my gut instinct. Instrument A is in a league of its own.

"Now it is time to vote," Ofra looks up as the last notes fade. Nearly everyone in the audience raises a hand as she holds forward Instrument A. "Good, you have superb taste. Now, who enjoyed Instrument B?" A few hands straggle up.

"Get out!" Ofra points in jest to the door, creating an outburst of applause.

"The Gofriller has a more refined sound, a more noble sound," she goes on to explain. "There is more complexity in its tones. Playing it is like painting with a full palette of colours, while playing the modern instrument is like painting with only one or two. Sadly, more and more of these extremely rare instruments are being bought up by museums, private collectors, and institutional collections, never to see the inside of a concert hall again. Not only are musicians losing out, audiences are losing out too, as you can tell from this demonstration."

Before hearing Ofra's demonstration, one cello was as good as another as far as I was concerned. If I had not heard both instruments side by side, I wonder if I could have appreciated what the modern cello was missing? I doubt it. No words, no argument, no rationalization, could have given me a clear understanding of the value of the Gofriller. I had to hear it myself.

I believe the same is true of wilderness.

Jacob Pokiak sits atop the *Engigstciak* (pronounced En-geese-T-ak), patiently peering through his binoculars. Although it is long past midnight, a soft luminescence lights the land. Screeching terns and gulls wheel overhead. In the distance a pair of musk oxen wanders across swaths of arctic cotton grass.

The forlorn bedrock dome where the young Inuvialuit is perched offers a commanding view. Rising one hundred metres (330 feet) above northern Yukon's coastal plains, it is the sole perturbation in an otherwise unmarred strip of tundra. Jacob looks out over a northern Serengeti, home to polar bear, grizzly, wolverine, and wolf. Millions of migratory birds nest in the grasslands below. For more than ten thousand years, Inuit hunters have gathered on this natural lookout to track the great caribou migrations. Fifty kilometres (30 miles) away, across a man-made border that means nothing to the caribou or anyone else travelling the open tundra, sits the Arctic National Wildlife Refuge. Powerful groups are interested in the oil that lies beneath.

Scampering up a steep ridge littered with purple lupine, I almost bump into Jacob as I crest the Engigstciak. I had not expected to find anyone else at this late hour. All of our rafting clients have retired, and after cleaning camp, I had stolen away, climbing the outcrop to say goodbye to the land. Another summer is ending. A Twin Otter is scheduled to fly us back to Inuvik in the morning. Until next spring these northern realms must live in my memory, but before I go, I want to drink from the chalice one last time.

Jacob and I have guided together for three summers, and it seems appropriate that we meet, albeit unintentionally, atop the outcrop. I silently sit on the ground beside him. Although he does not turn to look, he knows I am there. Like most of his native brethren, Jacob does not talk unnecessarily. He only speaks when he has something to say. Silently, we stare over the expanse.

The caribou have passed recently. Thick mats of floating hair lie in clumps along the river's shores. Muddy paths have been carved up the banks. From this vantage we can see lines of freshly trampled vegetation weaving across the plains before us. It is a flowing pattern, branching out and then rejoining, always pressing onward, beaten by thousands of hooves. Although the land is still, it is not hard to imagine the clatter of hooves, the rustling of bodies, and the bleating of fawns. These coastal plains are the birthing grounds for the great Porcupine herd. Each summer 130,000 caribou return from boreal forests in the south, part of the largest land migration on earth.

"There has to be a bear down there," Jacob whispers without turning or taking his eyes from the binoculars. "If I search long enough, I'll find one."

Jacob has uncanny vision. He can spot wildlife, or signs of its presence, more quickly and consistently than anyone I know. Often while I am preoccupied with navigating through difficult whitewater, a whistle and Jacob's extended arm will lead my eyes to a group of caribou milling along a distant ridge. On hikes he will kneel to inspect paw prints no one else has noticed. Pointing to snapped twigs and overturned rocks, he explains what the land is telling him. Standing on mountain peaks, I can scan the valley with my binoculars and see nothing. With his own eyes, Jacob will point out bear, sheep, muskox, moose, and anything else I miss. I wonder if his superb sight can be attributed to genetics or upbringing. I suspect it is both.

Born in the remote community of Tuktoyaktuk, Jacob comes from a fiercely traditional Inuvialuit family. His father, a renowned hunter, and his mother, a schoolteacher of European descent, raised their children upon the land, teaching them the traditions of sustenance, educating them with the stories of old. Before he was able to walk, Jacob accompanied his father on goose hunts, slung over his back in a skin papoose. As a youth Jacob learned to net whitefish and hunt whale. He would help his mother gather snow-goose eggs in the spring and harvest berries every summer. Fish meat was smoked in the fall. At ten Jacob shot his first caribou. As Inuvialuit tradition demands, he shared the kill with an elder in the community, his grandmother. "It is our way of saying thank you, I respect you, I have learned from you, and now I give back to you," he told me. At fourteen he took his first beluga, and again shipped half the meat to an uncle in a distant community. By sixteen he was hunting alone, able to shoot, skin, and dress the thirty caribou his family required to survive the winter.

Despite his strong ties to the land, and the grounding of Inuvialuit culture, Jacob is caught between two worlds. Jobs and schooling often take him to the larger community of Inuvik, where he fights a constant battle not to succumb to alcohol, fights, disillusionment, and apathy. Such are the ills of a people torn from a meaningful relationship with the land.

Three years earlier, when I arrived in Inuvik for the very first time, Jacob was scheduled to meet me at nine in the morning; we were going to spend the day shopping for supplies. Instead he stumbled into my motel room sometime after midnight, vomited in the bathtub, and passed out on the tile floor. The next day he wore sunglasses to conceal eyes that were swollen shut. I worried about our trip together. Within minutes of arriving on the remote tundra, twenty-four-year-old Jacob was a different person. He stood tall; as strong and proud and free as a man ever could.

"Look, I knew it! A bear. On the edge of that small creek," Jacob points. I raise my binoculars. "Hang on, he has gone behind some bush. Wait. Wait. OK, there he is again, moving fast."

I search and search, finally spotting the bear, a glorious grizzly with light blond hair tufting its muscular humped shoulders. It wanders the creek's banks, sniffing boulders, occasionally pawing or digging at roots. The movements are purposeful yet random. A primordial response, an evaluation of our position as hunter or hunted, flickers inside me. *Does it know we are here? Will it attack?* The bear represents both beauty and danger.

Slowly the bear wanders away from us. Jacob watches its movements intently. Exhaustion creeps over me and I lay back. Soft hummocks support me and grass prickles my neck. I can smell the damp earth below. An unfettered sky spreads above.

For ten consecutive summers I have travelled these northlands, the last three spent on the banks of the Firth River. The land around me whispers of memories. From the corner of a squinted eye I can see the spot on the Buckland Hills where a grizzly sow charged Jacob and me. Later on the same trip I took a wrong turn in the braids downstream and was forced to haul my raft through chest-deep water and over jams of ice, until five hours later, we finally broke free. I remember the wolverine that swam beside our rafts, and the bear cubs we watched playing on a spring snowfield in the high mountains. Another year the river flooded after a freak July snowstorm, drowning fifty bull caribou in the canyons. Within a day twenty-one grizzlies had arrived to feast. I think of the arctic terns that attack our rafts whenever we drift too close to nesting grounds, one persistent bird drawing blood from a passenger's head with a well-timed peck.

As my eyes flutter and sleep beckons, I can see the arctic poppies that decorate the tundra, their pale yellow heads revolving to follow the low summer sun that circles the sky. I can feel the beds of soft moss that grow outside my tent door. I can hear the cry of the peregrine in empty canyons, and can taste the river's clear water.

Aware that my connection to these wilds has formed over just three short seasons, I glance at Jacob, who is still monitoring the bear's movements, and try to imagine the place of the barrens in his heart.

We are all products of our landscape. Whether we realize it or not, the places we inhabit are continually winding their fingers through us, influencing our actions, our thoughts, our beliefs, and even our dreams.

As I return to Toronto, the city of my childhood, thick smog makes it impossible to see across the harbour. Crackling reports on the radio issue the twenty-fifth pollution alert of the summer, warning joggers and cyclists to stay inside. Standing on the lakeshore, I watch traffic crawl along one of the city's major arteries, stop-and-go congestion stretching for as far as the eye can see. Cars creep under signs flashing the obvious: "*Pollution Warning in Effect.*" A thick blue haze rises above them. I left Toronto fifteen years ago. To be forced to live in such an environment now seems more than just unthinkable. It seems outrageous. But none of the high-school friends I meet during my visit show any concern. No one even blinks. "It'll clear in a few days," they tell me. "We can go for a jog then."

I am constantly astounded by how quickly we can grow accustomed to new norms, and accept them; by how desensitized we can become to severities in our existence. Wade Davis refers to this phenomenon as the "fluidity of memory, the capacity to forget." Perhaps no other way can be imagined.

Rushing down crowded streets, navigating a maze of glittering office towers, I know this is an important part of my world, my landscape. I value my visits – the sights, sounds, and endless stimulation. I never question those who have chosen a path here. I only worry that fewer and fewer ever get a chance to hear the Gofrillers of the wild.

Like Jacob's culture, ours too has been torn from a meaningful relationship with the land. Unlike Jacob's, we've forgotten what it's like to have one.

It has been only a couple of days, but the north already seems a lifetime away. Waiting at a red light, I reach up and toy with the tooth Cedric gave me. It hangs on a leather cord around my neck. Once again his parting words play over in my mind. I still don't really know what he meant, but more and more that mystery helps me understand my own path. The search that I once fretted was in vain seems to keep leading me back to the same things, to freedom, magic, and the land.

Jacob rouses me. The bear is just a speck on the horizon.

"Bugs are bad this year," he mumbles, swatting at his ears while lighting a cigarette. We climb down the steep slopes of the Engigstciak together and wander back toward camp. A cool wind is blowing in from the pack ice on the Beaufort, and I pick a clump of *quiviat* (the soft undercoat of musk oxen, warmer than cashmere and three times more insulating than goose down) that hangs from a willow shrub, stuffing it in my pocket to help warm chilly hands, a trick Jacob's father taught me years ago. It is two in the morning when we crawl into our tents, but the sun still shines.

Acknowledgements

Countless souls have guided, taught, supported, and encouraged me on these journeys, and words of thanks pale shamefully beside the enormity of the experiences we have shared. The list is long and I am bound to miss a few, so please forgive my oversights; they are not intended. In particular I would like to recognize:

Chris "Ferg" Ferguson
A powerful partner and close friend who joined me on the CANOL and the Grand Cirque journeys, along with myriad other journeys not mentioned in this book. His willingness to wade into memories of our conflicts, and review my work with an eye toward balancing the portrayal, has helped us both learn and move on.

Neil Hartling
The owner and operator of Nahanni River Adventures, and a good friend, Neil first introduced me to the wonders of the Canadian north in 1995. I have returned north to guide for him every summer since. These wilderness experiences have changed and shaped my view of the natural world more than any other; for this, my gratitude is deep.

George Reid
My instructor at Yamnuska, whose patience and skills gave me the ability to travel with confidence through the mountains, a gift I treasure often.

Jim Allan
For hiring me as a novice sea-kayak guide, when discretion might have dictated otherwise, and for first opening my eyes to the world of natural history.

I have had the great fortune to share many glorious days in the wilderness with a multitude of guides who have offered friendship, mentorship, and teaching. These include Martha Hobbs, Bob Hanley, Craig Ferguson, Ed the Head, Ilya Storm, Bob Sutherland, Jacqui Goldsby, George Gabara, Scott Francis, Tim Boys, Pappy (Hugh

Buller), Marvin Alverez, Kaya (Carroll Palonio), Dick Bauer, Chris Clarkson, Denver Wilson-Rymer, Alex Sabal, Jonesy (Albert Jones), Sean Collins, Kevin Tessier, Diane Gribben, Karen Baxter, Hector Mackenzie, James Pokiak, Jacob Pokiak, Rebecca Pokiak, Griz (Neil Hudson), Nels Niemi, Joe Willy and his crew (Beth, Dan, and Pat), Cindy Adams, Jules (Julia Stevenson), Becky, Chris Hudson, Michelle Harvey, Stew Herd, Kathy Elliot, Morten Asfeldt, Trent Abott, Ian Stibbe, Kolin Powick, Jeff Taylor, Shawn Sparling, and Chris Melmoth. I would like to extend special thanks to all the guides of Nahanni River Adventures, who in the past decade have grown to be a close and valued group of friends.

There is the entire Everest team, including Alan Hobson, Jason Edwards, Jeff Rhoades, Steve Matous, Doug Rovira, Dave Rodney, Ang Temba, Mingma, Gyalbo, Nurbu, Pema Temba, Kami, Lhakpa, Tashi, Pemba, and Ang Dawa. Extra special thanks to Jamie Clarke, a treasured companion both at Everest and in Arabia. It was Jamie, who after meeting me for only ten minutes, fought doggedly to have me join the Everest team. He easily could have given up at that hectic time, and his belief and perseverance changed the direction of my life.

On the Blue Nile: Nevada Weir (who fought for my inclusion as a guide on the expedition), Ginny (Virginia) Morrell, Kelly Shannon, Kate Denoucher, Ephrim, Zelalem, Melessa, and Cassa were all valued companions. Experienced raft guides Mike Speaks and Mike Borcik took me under their wing and treated me as an equal when I clearly wasn't. Most of all, there is the irrepressible Mick Davie, who was a pleasure to travel with, and who has become a great friend in the years since.

While attempting to organize a crossing of Tibet's Chang Tang Plateau, the following individuals and organizations offered support and encouragement for which I am deeply grateful: ePals.com, Calgary Board of Education, Lindsey Park Sports Centre, Kelly Forbes, Sue Chambers, Derald Fretts, Pierre Killeen, and Butterfield & Robinson. Very, very heartfelt thanks to Hugh McMillan, whose immense generosity afforded the reconnaissance, and whose companionship eased its rigours.

The Grand Cirque journey was a glorious experience because of those who joined me: my brother, Douglas, my girlfriend, Christine Pitkanen, the indefatigable Ferg, along with kayakers Shaun Boughen and Derrick Law.

Berg Heil to the "All-Boys Choir" of Yamnuska: Ken, Chris, Rory, Brad, Greg, Craig, Aiden, Dylan, Jeremie, Jason, and Robby; and guides Grant Statham, Bernie Wiatzka, Randy Clement, Jim Keevit, Mark Stanley, and Brian Spears.

Over the years, many outfitters have entrusted me to guide their trips, providing invaluable opportunities to travel and explore this planet's wild places, and these include Wilderness Tours, Ecosummer Expeditions, Nahanni River Adventures, Alaska Discover Expeditions, MountainTravel*Sobek, Butterfield & Robinson, Island Expeditions, and Great Escapes USA.

Organizations that have supported these travels, and to whom I extend my deepest gratitude include *Outpost* magazine, Bankers Hall Club, Iron Fuel, Smith Optics, NEC, Bausch & Lomb, *National Geographic*, Colliers International, Lotus Notes, Boundary Water Paddle Sports, Seaward Kayaks, Mountain Equipment Co-op, The North Face, Lululemon Athletica, Air Malaysia, Blend's Travel Café, Klepper folding kayaks, SEAL Asia, and Kokatat.

As a fledgling writer, struggling with an unruly manuscript, the comments and support of my many proofreaders were invaluable. Thanks to David Finch, Morten Asfeldt, Mick Davie, Kisha Ferguson, Heather Pantry, Mom, Douglas Kirkby, Heather Kirkby, Chris Ferguson, and Christine Pitkanen. In particular, local Calgary authors Chris Koenches and Anik See, who provided wonderful support and mentorship as I took my first tentative steps exploring the craft of words.

A book is always a team effort. I was lucky to have the fantastic support and encouragement of John Pearce (agent) and the editorial/design crew of Susan Renouf, Jenny Bradshaw, and Terri Nimmo, who all caringly shepherded this project onward when I deserted to Mongolia.

My aunt, uncle, and cousins in Vancouver have always opened their doors and hearts to me. Their house has been the staging ground for many of these adventures. I am lucky to have a home and family away from home. Deep thanks to Jonnet, Andy, Cam, Nick, and Beth Garner. Thanks also to the clan of Toronto relatives, the Yeallands and the McEvoys, who often rearrange their schedules when I drop unannounced into town.

Finally, there is Mom, Heather, and Douglas, all great adventurers themselves, who have inspired and encouraged me through these journeys, and beyond. And Christine, a superbly strong partner in the field and at home, who has patiently supported the long process of writing this book, bringing me tea as I scribbled endless notes, and feeding me when I forgot to do so myself.

Thanks to you all.

Selected Bibliography

Bangs, Richard, and Christian Kallen. *Rivergods*. Vancouver: Douglas & McIntyre, 1985.

Barry, Patricia S. *The Canol Project: An Adventure of the U.S. War Department in Canada's Northwest*. Edmonton: P.S. Barry, 1985.

Bruntland, G., ed. *Our Common Future: The World Commission on Environment and Development*. Oxford: Oxford University Press, 1987.

Budd, Ken (Executive Producer). *Tatshenshini: River Wild*, Westcliffe, Englewood, 1993.

Careless, Rick. *To Save the Wild Earth*. Vancouver: Raincoast Books, 1997.

Chester, Jonathan. *Trekking and Climbing in the Himalaya*. Seattle: Cloudcap, 1989.

Clark, L. *The Marching Wind*. New York: Funk and Wagnall, 1954.

Davis, Wade. *Light at the Edge of the World*. Vancouver: Douglas & McIntyre, 2001.

———. *The Clouded Leopard: Travels to Landscapes of Spirit and Desire*. Vancouver: Douglas & McIntyre, 1998.

Fraser, Simon. *Letters and Journals, 1806–1808*. Ed. W. Kaye Lamb. Toronto: Macmillan, 1960.

Gadd, Ben. *Handbook of the Canadian Rockies*. Jasper: Corax Press, 1995.

Garrick, Neville. *A Rasta's Pilgrimage, Ethiopian Faces and Places*. San Francisco: Pomegranate, 1998.

Gauge, S.R. *A Walk on the Canol Road*. Oakville, ON: Mosaic Press, 1990.

Giorgis, Dawit W. *Red Tears: War, Famine, and Revolution in Ethiopia*. Trenton, NJ: Red Sea Press, 1989.

Gore, Al. *The Earth in the Balance*. New York: Plume, 1993.

Haig-Brown, Alan. *The Fraser River*. Madeira Park, BC: Harbour Publishing, 1996.

Harding, Mike. *Footloose in the Himalaya*. London: Michael Joseph, 1989.

Herrero, Stephen. *Bear Attacks: Their Causes and Avoidance*. Toronto: Hurtig, 1985.

Heuer, Karsten. *Walking the Big Wild*. Toronto: McClelland & Stewart, 2002.

Kauper, Frank. *Alpine Style in the Tschang-Tang*. American Alpine Journal, 1998.

King, John. *Karakoram Highway: The High Road to China*. Victoria: Lonely Planet Publications, 1989.

Lomborg, Bjorm. *The Skeptical Environmentalist: Measuring the Real State of the World*. Cambridge: Cambridge University Press, 2001.

Lopez, Barry. *Arctic Dreams*. New York: Charles Scribner's Sons, 1986.

Lyman R., J. Ordonez, and M. Speaks. *The Complete Guide to the Tatshenshini River*. Haines, Alaska: Cloudburst Productions, 2000.

Mackinnon, A., J. Polar, and R. Coupé. *Plants of Northern British Columbia*. Vancouver: Lone Pine, 1992.

Madsen, Ken. *Paddling in the Yukon*. Whitehorse: Primrose Publishing, 1996.

Matthiessen, Peter. *The Snow Leopard*. New York: Viking Penguin, 1978.

McNeill, J.R. *Something New Under the Sun: An Environmental History of the Twentieth Century World*. New York: W.W. Norton & Co, 2000.

Moorehead, Alan. *The Blue Nile*. London: Hamish Hamilton, 1962.

Morrel, Virginia. *Blue Nile: Ethiopia's River of Magic and Mystery*. Washington, DC: Adventure Press, 2001.

Morrow, Patrick. *Beyond Everest*. Camden House Publishing, Camden East, 1986.

Ortner, Sherry B. *Life and Death on Mt. Everest: Sherpas and Himalayan Mountaineering*. Princeton: Princeton University Press, 1999.

Pariser, Harry S. *Explore Belize*. Hunter Publishing, Edison, 1998.

Peedle, Ian. *Belize: A Guide to the People, Politics, and Culture*. New York: Interlink, 1999.

Pielou, E.C. *A Naturalist's Guide to the Arctic*. London: University of Chicago Press, 1994.

Schaller, George B. *Wildlife of the Tibetan Steppe*. London: University of Chicago Press, 1998.

Scott, Chic. *Pushing the Limits: The Story of Canadian Mountaineering*. Calgary: Rocky Mountain Books, 2000.

Snailham, Richard. *The Blue Nile Revealed*. London: Chatto and Windus, 1971.

Rawling, C. *The Great Plateau*. London: Edward Arnold, 1905.

Robbins, Chandler, Bertel Bruun, and Herbert Zim. *Birds of North America*. New York: Golden Press, 1983.

Rowell, Galen. *Many People Come, Looking, Looking*. Seattle: The Mountaineers, 1980.

Worldwatch Institute. *Vital Signs 2002*. New York: W.W. Norton & Co., 2002.